British Gardens

Britain's climate is rarely suited to idleness, so we make gardens (*Zantedeschia aethiopica*, photographed in the rain in the author's garden, is a South African plant).

British Gardens

History, philosophy and design

Tom Turner

Routledge
Taylor & Francis Group

LONDON AND NEW YORK

First published 2013
by Routledge
2 Park Square, Milton Park, Abingdon, Oxon OX14 4RN

Simultaneously published in the USA and Canada
by Routledge
711 Third Avenue, New York, NY 10017

Routledge is an imprint of the Taylor & Francis Group, an informa business

British Library Cataloguing in Publication Data
A catalogue record for this book is available from the British Library

Library of Congress Cataloging in Publication Data
Turner, Tom (Thomas Henry Duke), 1946-
    British gardens : history, philosophy and design / Tom Turner.
       p. cm.
Includes bibliographical references and index.
1. Gardens--Great Britain--History. 2. Gardens, British--History. 3. Gardens--Great Britain--Design. 4.
Gardens, British--Design. I. Title.
SB451.36.G7T87 2013
635.0941--dc23
2012010621

ISBN: 978-0-415-51878-9 (hbk)

Designed and typeset by Sutchinda Rangsi-Thompson

Printed and bound in India by Replika Press Pvt. Ltd.

Contents

THE BRITISH
ISLES

THE STEPPE ROUTE

THE MEDITERRANEAN ROUTE

THE SILK ROUTE

THE
MOTHER
CONTINENT

THE OCEAN ROUTE

P.0 The history of garden design in the British Isles is best understood in the wider context of
human migration and the transition from nomadic pastoralism to settled agriculture on the fringes
of Asia. The key zones of garden development are represented by ovals and the design styles are
illustrated on pp. 416–17.

Preface

The arts which we now call garden and landscape design have three separate origins: sacred space, horticultural space and domestic space. Like *Homo sapiens* (see Figure P.0, on which the important zones of garden development are represented by ovals), the arts of garden and landscape design probably spread to Europe from West Asia. British garden history is best understood as a small incident in the histories of ideas, design and technology. Our ancestors began to design the land when they became settlers.

The design of *sacred space* began in West Asia, some 11,000 years ago and 7,000 years before the invention of writing. The aim, it appears, was to explain ideas about the nature of the world and the nature of human communities. These ideas influenced the design of sacred space, of palaces for god-kings and of fortified dwellings for mortal kings. The most important sacred space in Britain, at Stonehenge, was begun *c.*5,000 years ago, at a time when formerly nomadic tribes were taking up ideas from West Asia and making the first agricultural settlements in the British Isles.

The making of *horticultural space* began in West Asia, over 10,000 years ago and reached the British Isles *c.*3500 BCE, probably by cultural diffusion through Europe. The ideas and the technology came as part of a 'Neolithic package' which included sheep, cattle, stone axes, timber dwellings, pottery, digging sticks and agricultural plants. The food supply was improved by growing carbohydrates which could be stored for winter use and by keeping domestic animals. Formerly nomadic tribes therefore laid claim to land and, it appears, made circular earthworks to symbolise the nature of their world, the nature of human society and the relationship between man and nature. Archaeologists assume that circular enclosures had roles in predicting the seasons and commemorating human events.

The design of private *domestic space* probably began with courtyard dwellings in West Asia. As small outdoor rooms, for cooking, working and living, they are unlikely to have contained plants. The design of larger courts, which became palace gardens with plants, probably began in the same region, about 5,500 years ago. Garden-making had spread to Greece by 1700 BCE, to Rome by 700 BCE and came to the British Isles with the Roman conquest of 43 CE. Yet these islands became home to

P.1 Woad (*Isatis tinctoria*) is native to Central and West Asia. It was cultivated by the Celts (see p. 26) and used to make a body paint which may have given the British Isles the name Britannia (Pretanike, 'the Painted Isles').

the world's most enthusiastic gardeners – and London became the capital city of world gardening. Why? Geography provides the best explanation. A steady stream of immigrants and invaders brought culture and horticulture from Eurasia. Later, an Empire of the Seas brought ideas and plants from everywhere to a group of islands with a climate that is peculiarly suited to gardening: it is rarely too hot, rarely too cold, rarely too wet and rarely too dry. Furthermore, the weather is scarcely ever good enough for idleness. So we make gardens. 'Wooden walls', provided by the navy, made city walls obsolete at a comparatively early date, leading to an urban form in which a house with a garden could be the norm for all social classes. Rasmussen saw London as the *unique city* because of the dominance of this dwelling type.[1]

'British' comes from the earliest recorded name for a group of windswept islands off the north-west fringe of Asia. Pytheas of Marseilles, a Greek, is reported to have used the name Pretanike (Britannia). He called the largest island Nesos Albionon (Albion) and the second largest Ierne (Ériu or Eire).[2] Etymologists link Pretanike with the Welsh and the Celtic words for 'painted' which is associated with the islanders' well-known habit of painting their bodies with an indigo-blue dye: woad.[3] Davies calls them 'the Painted Isles'. Ptolemy used the names 'Albion' and 'Hibernia' for the two largest islands. Pliny the Elder wrote: 'Albion was its name, when all the islands were called Britanniae.'[4] The name 'Britanniae' fell out of use after the Romans left. Germanic immigrants were described as 'Saxons' by the Celts and, in 796, 'Offa (d. 796) was the very first ruler of the former Britannia to call himself Rex Anglorum, 'King of the English'.[5] 'Britannia' was revived in the seventeenth century to name an empire. This continues to make the name unpopular in Ireland, and elsewhere, but 'British Isles' remains the oldest known name for these islands.

The context in which British gardens developed is shown in Figure P.0 and examined in my previous books on *Asian Gardens* and *European Gardens*. As in the earlier books, the text concentrates on the narrative and is extensively illustrated – because garden design and history are 'word and image' subjects. Photographs and plans are used to explain the design character of gardens; style diagrams are used to summarise their characteristic features and the design concepts on which they were based. The three books might have formed a single work, except for my having completed each of them thinking, 'Well, thank goodness. That's it.' This was not because my enthusiasm for the subject was waning. I was working on the Gardenvisit.com website and thinking that electronic publishing offers more scope than print publishing, despite my publisher's generosity in allowing me so many illustrations. I am attracted by the hypertext facility of electronic documents, allowing internal links from 'garden to designer to explanation', and external links to other websites, audio and video. But the linearity of a book is also attractive. In theory, it can proceed from start to finish without hesitation, deviation or repetition. Books and web content should support each other, marrying linearity to circularity, as the next generation of eBooks will do. For the present, links have been provided through companion pages on the Gardenvisit website. They link to maps, aerial photography, bibliography and additional information on the gardens and designers mentioned in the text:

- *Asian Gardens*: http://www.gardenvisit.com/history_theory/asian_gardens_companion;
- *European Gardens*: http://www.gardenvisit.com/history_theory/european_gardens_companion;
- *British Gardens*: http://www.gardenvisit.com/history_theory/british_gardens_companion.

The book has three appendices:

- Appendix I summarises the relationship between the theory of garden and landscape design in Asia, continental Europe and the British Isles.
- Appendix II considers alternative names for styles of garden design in the British Isles, with explanations of how the names used in this book were chosen.
- Appendix III, Michael Simonsen's study of Wollaton Hall, illustrates the way in which an appreciation of garden history can, and should, inform the management of historic gardens.

This completes what has been a long project and I would like to thank my wife Margaret for her help, advice and patience over many years.

CHAPTER 1

Prehistoric landscapes and gardening, 3500 BCE–43 CE

1.0 The Goodwin Sands accumulated on once-dry land which allowed migrants to cross from continental Europe to what became the British Isles.

1.1 The Indo-European Homeland may have been between the Black Sea and the Caspian Sea.

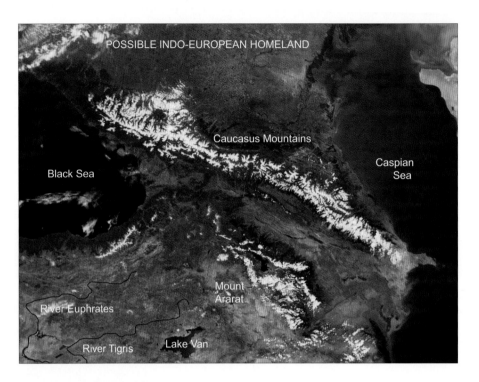

POSSIBLE INDO-EUROPEAN HOMELAND

Caucasus Mountains

Black Sea

Caspian Sea

Mount Ararat

River Euphrates

River Tigris   Lake Van

1.2 The Younger Dryas was a cold period from 10800–9500 BCE. It takes its name from the plant which is used as an indicator of tundra conditions *Dryas octopetala*, seen here on Spitzbergen. After 9500 BCE, the climate grew warmer, the sea level rose, the forests returned, the woolly mammoth became extinct and Britain's human population began to grow in number.

Introduction

Britain is thought to have been without human residents at the Last Glacial Maximum (*c.*20000 BCE).[1] However:

Following the end of the last Ice Age, some time between 12500 and 8000 BC, the animals and plants upon which Man subsisted re-established themselves, and Man himself rapidly appeared in their wake. The environment in which he lived was a harsh and treeless steppe, inhabited by mammoth, woolly rhino, wild horse and giant deer. Human groups survived by the specialized hunting of these migratory fauna as they moved to and from the brief summer grazings revealed by the seasonal release of the tracts of land from the grip of the ice.[2]

In 10000 BCE, the sea level was 120 metres lower than today and hunter–gatherers crossed a tundra landscape from North Europe to Britain. The sea was just as far below its present level as the White Cliffs of Dover are above the present sea level (Figure 2.0). By *c.*6500 BCE the once-inhabited Doggerland had become the bed of the North Sea and the British Peninsula had become the British Isles. Little is known of the language and beliefs of the early Britons, except that their ancestors were Africans and the land they colonised was tundra.

Farming in the British Isles began *c.*4000 BCE and, if Colin Renfrew is right, cultivation techniques arrived with the Proto Indo-European (PIE) language (see p. 20). The

1.3 Skara Brae, occupied *c.*3180 BCE–2500 BCE, is the best preserved Neolithic village in North Europe. The houses are unusual for being built in stone, and for having survived, but their plan form is similar to that of other Neolithic settlements. Land was cultivated on what must have been a horticultural scale.

1.4 A wooden plough, at the experimental Butser Ancient Farm in Hampshire. Ploughs may have been drawn by men or animals.

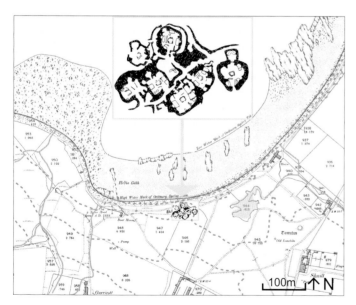

1.5 The floor plans at Skara Brae, ranging from circular to rectangular, have central hearths. Stone shelves and beds are beside the walls. The settlement forms a single community with no space for horticulture between dwellings.

crops, animals and techniques definitely came from West Asia. The old view was that mounted warrior Celts 'invaded' Britain. Modern DNA analysis indicates that technology transfer was more significant than migration. The M17 marker (Y-DNA,

1.6 The Celtic Shield, found in the River Thames during the construction of Chelsea Bridge, is thought to have been thrown into the river as a gift to a river god. Decorated with lotus buds, red glass medallions and 27 swastikas (a symbol first found in the Indus Valley), its role must have been ceremonial.

1.7 Boadicea is famed, and romanticised, as a warrior queen who led resistance to the Romans. Tacitus reports that the Celts had horse-drawn chariots.

Haplogroup R1a1a) shows 'a massive genetic influx into India from the steppes within the past 10,000 years'[3] but it is not common in Iran or Europe. This indicates that the Indo-European influence on these regions was more cultural than genetic.[4]

Ox-drawn ploughs were being used in Britain by *c.*2500 BCE and the development of agriculture led to permanent settlements within which horticulture may have taken place. Carbonised barley found at Skara Brae indicates the inhabitants were cultivators as well as hunters.[5] Neolithic settlers made both circular and rectangular huts with posts supporting thatched roofs. Walls made of sticks and mud ('wattle and daub') filled the gap between the roof and the ground. Tribes had chiefs but no palaces and no god-kings. What little is known of religious beliefs in Neolithic Europe implies a similarity with the animist beliefs of Central Asia. 'Ancient Celtic religion … had more in common with the Indo-European belief system of the ancient Hindus than with that of the contemporary Greeks and Romans.'[6] Forces of nature were associated with the sun, rivers, mountains and other natural features believed to have power over human affairs. Writing 50 years after the Roman conquest, Tacitus compared the culture of Britain to that of Gaul (France):

But a general survey inclines me to believe that the Gauls established themselves in an island so near to them. Their religious belief may be traced in the strongly-marked British superstition. The language differs but little; there is the same boldness in challenging danger, and, when it is near, the same timidity in shrinking from it. The Britons, however, exhibit more spirit, as being a people whom a long peace has not yet enervated.

...

Some tribes fight also with the chariot. The higher in rank is the charioteer; the dependants fight. They were once ruled by kings, but are now divided under chieftains into factions and parties. Our greatest advantage in coping with tribes so powerful is that they do not act in concert. Seldom is it that two or three states meet together to ward off a common danger. Thus, while they fight singly, all are conquered.[7]

Tacitus does not mention gardens but must have known the three types of enclosed outdoor space made in Italy and West Asia. This chapter will review what is known of garden space in the British Isles prior to the Roman invasion of 43 CE:

- *horticultural space*, for growing fruit and vegetables;
- *domestic space,* private yards for cooking, working and living;
- *sacred space,* sanctuaries associated with gods, kings and god-kings

Garden space

Early Neolithic farmers cleared woodland to grow cereals, including emmer wheat and six-row barley. But 'So far, no trace has been found of any vegetables and it may

1.8 The Céide Fields, in Ireland, date from *c.*3500 BCE and are one of the oldest-known field systems in the world. They were probably cultivated with digging sticks and used for cereals.

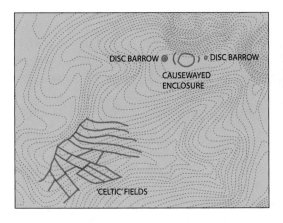

1.9 a, b There are three circular barrows and a causewayed enclosure on the high point of Coombe Hill. The ancient fields on the slope below, now surrounded by trees, were cultivated on a horticultural scale. The date of the field system is not known but they are described as 'Celtic'.

be that this area of the diet was filled by gathered food such as blackberries, barberries, sloes, crab apples, haws and hazel nuts.'[8] The extent to which land cultivated for cereals by early farmers was walled, fenced or otherwise enclosed is unknown but small 'Celtic fields' survive from a later date. They appear to belong to the history of agriculture but could just as well be called 'Celtic gardens', because of their small size and the use of hand cultivation. The earliest account of growing conditions in the islands comes from Tacitus, who says they were used for 'all ordinary produce':

> Their sky is obscured by continual rain and cloud. Severity of cold is unknown.
> ...
> With the exception of the olive and vine, and plants which usually grow in warmer climates, the soil will yield, and even abundantly, all ordinary produce. It ripens indeed slowly, but is of rapid growth, the cause in each case being the same, namely, the excessive moisture of the soil and of the atmosphere.[9]

Since flat and low land in the British Isles was thickly wooded and often waterlogged, settlements tended to be on hills and fields were often on the slopes below, as at Danebury, Coombe Hill and Dyrham. One can imagine how they looked when in use and one can speculate that humans always like their handiwork to look well. But there

1.10 Dyrham Camp (also known as Hinton Hillfort) is on the right of the photograph and has ancient fields, to the left, on land which was probably cultivated in prehistoric times.

1.11 a–d Danebury was occupied c.600–100 BCE and is one of the most fully excavated hillforts in the British Isles. There were circular huts and rectangular grain stores within the enclosure and small 'Celtic' fields on the slopes of the hill. The photographs show external and internal views of the hillfort. The plans show the ancient field pattern and the woodland pattern as it is today.

is no evidence of aesthetic considerations having influenced the construction or plant-ing of the garden-like 'fields'.

Domestic outdoor space

In pre-Roman Britain the most common dwelling type was a circular hut with a pitched roof and a central fire (see Figures 1.12 and 1.30). Some huts stood alone, in woods and fields, some were in groups and some stood within embanked enclosures described as hillforts. Little information is available about how the open space within enclosures was used, but it has been supplemented by guesswork and a number of hypotheses can be seen in reconstructions of Iron Age settlements. Post holes for elevated grain stores have been found, confirming that the land within hillforts was used for storage. Evidence of craft activities has also been found. Fire pits have been found inside huts and firewood must have been stored in dry places. Space under

1.12 Firewood may have been stored under the eaves of Iron Age huts. Animals would have caused damage if allowed to walk near buildings.

1.13 Reconstructed Iron Age hut, at Michelham Priory.

1.14 The experimental Iron Age village at Butser Ancient Farm has circular huts and a similar plan arrangement to Skara Brae (see Figure 1.3).

the eaves of thatched roofs is an obvious place for this to have been done but might have been a fire risk. Farm animals were tended by herders. During the day, sheep, goats and cattle were grazed on land outside hillforts. At night, animals were probably brought into enclosures for protection. Since animals would have damaged the roofs and walls of huts, they must have been tethered or corralled.

There can have been no privacy in Iron Age settlements and the existence of private gardens is improbable. Surviving hillforts in upland areas, often with thin soils and inhospitable climates, make one doubt that the land beside huts could have been used for horticulture. But the possibility exists, especially if the climate was warmer and the surrounding land was wooded when the settlements were established. Or they may have been in open land so that potential attackers could be seen. In Scotland, 'it seems incredible that places so far above sea level could have been occupied during the winter'.[10]

When considering the possible existence of private gardens in Celtic Britain, the absence of palaces is significant. Palaces and palace gardens were part of the Mycenaean-Graeco-Roman culture of South Europe and the Eastern Mediterranean. They were not part of the Celtic culture of North Europe. Ancient Britain had Celtic warrior chieftains whose role is likely to have been similar to Tacitus's account of tribal leaders in *Germania*. Celtic society was governed by warrior chiefs who did not have religious authority, did not live in temple-palaces and did not have palace gardens. Clearly, these were barriers to the development of a garden culture as it existed in the ancient civilisations of West Asia and the Eastern Mediterranean. The safest assumption is that there were no individual domestic gardens in the British Isles before the Roman conquest.

Sacred outdoor space

Though prehistoric megaliths and earthworks in the British Isles have been intensively studied, they remain subject to diverse interpretations. There is no evidence for their having been gardens but the activity of designing earthworks relates to the activity of designing gardens:

- Earthworks were located and designed with regard to existing landscapes.
- Earthworks were symbolic arrangements of landform, structures, pathways and, perhaps, vegetation.

Even when enclosures had defensive and residential roles, as implied by the term 'hillfort', this was probably combined with a sacred role. But little textual information about religious beliefs in the British Isles is available. Tacitus, writing in 98 BCE,

1.15 Megaliths at the entrance to West Kennet Long Barrow with the man-made Silbury Hill beyond. Prehistoric earthworks are widely agreed to have had a sacred role but there is little evidence for this.

1.16 a, b (a) Windmill Hill causewayed enclosure. Pottery has been found, indicating its use for seasonal rituals before the construction of Avebury. (b) Avebury Henge, seen from Windmill Hill.

remarks only that they were characterised by 'superstition'. Gildas, writing several centuries later, knew more than he was willing to tell. He declared:

> I shall, therefore, omit those ancient errors common to all the nations of the earth, in which, before Christ came in the flesh, all mankind were bound; nor shall I enumerate those diabolical idols of my country, which almost surpassed in number those of Egypt, and of which we still see some mouldering away within or without the deserted temples, with stiff and deformed features as was customary. Nor will I call out upon the mountains, fountains, or hills, or upon the rivers, which now are subservient to the use of men, but once were an abomination and destruction to them, and to which the blind people paid divine honour.[11]

Gildas's knowledge of Egyptian gods may have come from the Bible.[12] When he wrote of the 'diabolical idols of my country', he was probably referring both to images placed in sacred groves by the British and to Roman statues which he regarded as idolatrous. Gildas's reference to 'divine honour' being paid to mountains, hills and rivers is typically Indo-European and provides a clue to the interpretation of the archaeological evidence. Indo-European history was recorded in songs, known as the *Vedas* in India, myths in Ireland and sagas in Iceland, which are reminders of a shared cultural heritage in Eurasia (see p. 20). It was a region in which the skies, mountains, rivers and forests were believed to be 'animated' by special powers and honoured in special places. Assisted by music, dance, rituals and drugs (*entheogens*), shamans made contact with spirits. In Mesopotamia, a sacred marriage (*hieros gamos*), between divinities or between a king and a temple prostitute was a 'wedding of matter and psyche'.[13] At Tara, in Ireland, the High King had sex, in public, with a maiden who was regarded as an incarnation of a river goddess.[14] Taking a broad overview of prehistoric cultures, Mircias Eliade commented on the sacredness of enclosures:

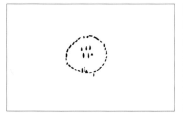 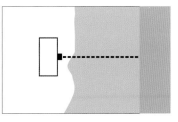 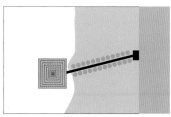 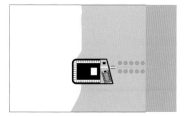

1.17 a–d Egyptian temple types: (a) stone circle; (b) pre-dynastic enclosure (before 3100 BCE); (c) Old Kingdom pyramid (*c*.2630–2181 BCE); (d) New Kingdom mortuary temple (*c*.1550 BCE–1069 BCE);

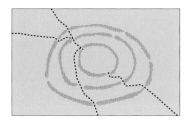 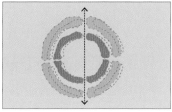 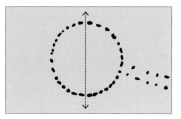 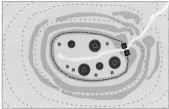

1.17 e–h British enclosure types: (e) causewayed enclosure (*c*.3000–2500 BCE); (f) henge (*c*.2800–2400 BCE); (g) stone circle (*c*.2500–1800 BCE); (h) hillfort (*c*.600 BCE–43 CE).

The enclosure, wall, or circle of stones surrounding a sacred place – these are among the most ancient of known forms of man-made sanctuary ... The same is the case with city walls: long before they were military erections, they were a magic defence, for they marked out from the midst of a 'chaotic' space ... a place that was organized, made cosmic, in other words, provided with a 'centre'.[15]

Monumental earthworks were made by digging circular ditches. In some places, such as hilltops, the ditches follow the contours. In other places they are in concentric circles. Standing stones were sometimes added to existing earthworks and sometimes placed on separate sites, alone, in groups or in circles. Several categories of roughly circular enclosure can be identified. Collectively described as prehistoric earthworks, they are listed below in the order in which they are believed to have been made:

- *Causewayed enclosures* are often on hilltops and have between one and four rings of ditches with internal banks. Causeways pass through the mounds and cross the ditches. They are regarded as territorial markers for tribes with a common descent. A religious/ceremonial/symbolic role is assumed because they are unsuited to military, agricultural or residential use. They could have been places for feasts, ceremonies and trade.[16]
- *Henges* are circular or oval enclosures formed by casting excavated material outward, so that a ditch was formed within the enclosure. Some henges had portals and rings of posts. Stonehenge, from which the term 'henge' derives,

1.18 Dun Carloway was built *c.*100 BCE and occupied for over 1,000 years. Brochs used to be regarded as fortresses and are now thought to have had a symbolic role, like country houses, in agricultural landscapes.

is not a true 'henge' because the ditch is outside the bank. The locational difference between henges and causewayed enclosures is that henges tend to be on lower ground. This suggests they were made by communities for whom farming was more important than hunting.[17] Henges are now regarded as the successors to causewayed enclosures: meeting places for members of a chiefdom and, conceivably, a permanent home for the chief.

- *Stone circles*, well described by their name, were made with large undressed stones, known as megaliths. The sites display no evidence of human dwelling and rarely contain graves. This suggests that stone circles were used only on ceremonial occasions. The type of ceremony is unknown. They may have been religious and may have included weddings, funerals and tribal councils. Some stone circles are within henge monuments (as at Stonehenge).

1.19 a, b Edin's Hall Broch in Southern Scotland was built (*c*.100 BCE) within an existing hillfort. There are round houses inside the enclosure and there is a second hillfort on the peak above (Cockburn Law). The photographs show Edin's Hall from both sides of the valley.

- *Hillforts* usually follow the contours of the elevated land on which they are built and have internal banks. Many contain settlements and appear to have been built for the defence of people, herds, grain and tools. As their name implies, most are on hills. There are Roman reports of them being used for defence, and they had external ditches. Internal ditches facilitate attack. 'No archaeologist is satisfied with the term "hillfort", but all the alternatives which have been suggested are open to even more objections.'[18] 'Fort' suggests a purely military use, rather than a settlement or a cattle kraal. Scotland has many hillforts on inhospitable sites, leading to the reasonable assumption that 'these high-level hillforts could have been used for protection when the herds were moved up to the summer pastures'.[19]

- *Brochs* are circular towers found only in Scotland and made in the first century BCE. They resemble fortifications and, though formerly interpreted as 'castles', have come to be seen as 'the "stately homes" of their time, objects of prestige and very visible demonstrations of superiority for important families'.[20] Examination of the siting of brochs shows that few have good defensive positions but many have significant locations in the landscape.

Few artefacts have been found in or near prehistoric enclosures, leading to a multiplicity of theories about their functions. As well as having a sacred role, they may have been: settlements, fortifications, animal pounds, trading places, cremation sites or community spaces for feasts, weddings and other tribal gatherings. Individual enclosures could have had single uses, multiple uses or changing uses. Richard Bradley, in his book, *The Significance of Monuments*,[21] argues that farmers have a different

1.20 The stone circle at Loanhead of Daviot is in a woodland enclosure with an outward view of farmland. The prehistoric use of this land, and the vegetation pattern, is unknown.

sense of time from hunters and that the seasons are of greater importance. Aubrey Burl, after a lifetime's study, concluded that:

> *Neolithic and Bronze Age ritual enclosures had a multiplicity of purposes: as family shrines, for seasonal gatherings or as trading-places. Widespread across western Europe in space and time, stone circles are unlikely to have been colleges for dispassionate musings on the nature of the universe. Dancing, drums and drugs may have been the ingredients for the rites.*[22]

The British Isles were thickly wooded in Neolithic times, making it likely that pre-historic enclosures were considered in relation to the woodland pattern. They could have been in woodland clearings or on the fringes of woods. Whatever other roles they may have had, they are agreed to have been sacred. This makes them a type of space with similarities to the Neolithic and Bronze Age sanctuaries, groves and gardens made in West Asia and South-East Europe (see Figure 1.17). The first prehistoric earthworks and megaliths in North Europe were built by settlers, native or immigrant, in areas where the lifestyle of nomadic hunter–gatherers was dominant, making life difficult for the first settlers.

Conflict between nomads and settlers has occurred in many parts of the world and at many points in history. Settlers need to protect their dwellings, tools and crops. Nomads lose their traditional hunting grounds, often their best land, to the settlers. Many commentators have interpreted monumental earthworks as symbolic territorial

1.21 Avebury is a Neolithic henge. The embankment prevents outward views from the enclosure and it may have been surrounded by trees in Neolithic times.

1.22 Mayburgh Henge near Penrith. Unusually, the embankment was made with stones brought from a nearby river. There can have been few outward views from within the enclosure and it might well have been set within woodland, as the present vegetation suggests.

markers, used for ceremonial meetings relating to the identity of a tribe and its 'ownership' of a territory. Solstices proclaimed meeting days and had a significance in the farming year. Henges are uncommon outside the British Isles but a comment from Tacitus's *Germania* is illuminating. The language of Transalpine Europe had split into Germanic and Celtic *c.*500 BCE but the cultural affinities continued. Tacitus described the use of solstice dates to set dates for tribal gatherings in *Germania*:

1.23 a, b Callanish Stones. The henge is thought to have been constructed in *c.*2750 BCE. It probably began with a single standing stone, followed by a stone circle, and then an 83 m avenue of standing stones pointing to a southern moonset.

In their ancient songs, their only way of remembering or recording the past, they celebrate an earth-born god ... as the origin of their race, as their founders ... Their country, though somewhat various in appearance, yet generally either bristles with forests or reeks with swamps; it is more rainy on the side of Gaul, bleaker on that of Noricum and Pannonia [Roman provinces with Celtic populations, now parts of Austria, Hungary and Slovenia]. It is productive of grain, but unfavourable to fruit-bearing trees; it is rich in flocks and herds, but these are for the most part undersized ... They assemble, except in the case of a sudden emergency, on certain fixed days, either at new or at full moon; for this they consider the most auspicious season for the transaction of business. Instead of reckoning by days as we do, they reckon by nights, and in this manner fix both their ordinary and their legal appointments.[23]

1.24 a, b (a) The original use of Newgrange, in Ireland, is unknown but, on the winter solstice only, sun shines along the passage to the chamber within the mound. (b) Model of Newgrange as it might have been.

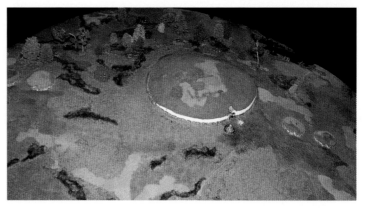

Tacitus's comments are supported by other evidence, including the placement of standing stones in the landscape. Often they were on shoulder sites, overlooking farmland (see Figure 1.40).

Large stones (megaliths) were also used to make and mark tombs which frequently 'stand just above and overlook a patch of fertile arable land. Even though commanding hillside and hilltop sites were often chosen for the monuments, they marked the upper margins of the farming territory, the wilderness edge.'[24]

It appears that megaliths, tombs and other works of art were sited to inform neighbouring tribes that: 'our ancestors farmed this land and it is ours'. The Uffington White Horse, high on the Wiltshire Downs and near a hillfort, is interpreted as a landmark of this type. It is believed to have 'crept up the hill' and to have been more visible when it was originally carved.[25]

Britain also had sacred groves. No archaeological evidence has been found but they were common in Indo-European societies and Roman texts confirm their presence in North Europe.[26] In the British Isles, the priests who managed sacred groves were known as druids. 'Druid' is thought to derive from *dru-* ('tree' – especially an oak tree) and *wid-* ('to know'):

> *The druids, both male and female, formed a hierarchical caste, commanding the greatest authority in Celtic society. The etymology of their name is variously derived from 'oak' and 'knowledge'. Guardians of the tribal lore, in which they were systematically trained for decades, they were priests, judges, magicians, shamans and healers, bards, seers, and diplomats – all rolled into one. Their decisions were paramount, and were enforced by spells*

1.25 A standing stone outside East Linton, in Scotland, with North Berwick Law beyond.

1.26 a, b The Uffington White Horse was made between 1400 and 600 BCE. It is near a hillfort and is interpreted as a territorial marker for a tribe which farmed the area. The white chalk would have become overgrown if it had not been maintained for *c*.3,000 years.

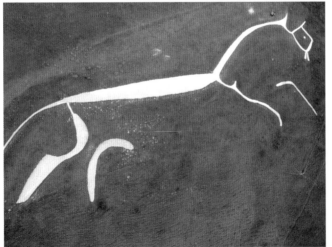

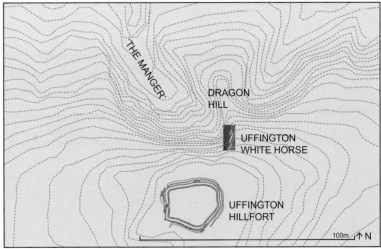

THE MANGER

DRAGON HILL

UFFINGTON WHITE HORSE

UFFINGTON HILLFORT

100m   ↑ N

1.27 An oak wood beside Loch Trool. No British sacred grove sites have been identified but they are believed to have been clearings in woods and there are Neolithic sites in Galloway (which means 'Land of the Foreign Gaels').

and curses. They ruled the groves, gave orders to kings and warriors, and left the strongest of all romanticized legacies. The Isles were said by Caesar to be the greatest centre of their learning. And within the Isles, their most sacred groves were to be found on the island of Mon.[27]

The Celtic word *nemeton* was used for a natural space dedicated to religious activity[28] and it is possible that *nemeton* is related to the Greek word *tenemos*, used for a sanctuary 'cut out' from the landscape.[29] *Nemeton* is sometimes translated as 'sacred grove' but Dowden believes it is better interpreted as 'sanctuary'.[30]

Lucan (*c*.60 CE) wrote an account of a savage yet sacred grove in Gaul, which Caesar had felled:

A grove there was, untouched by men's hands from ancient times, whose interlacing boughs enclosed a space of darkness and cold shade, and banished the sunlight far above. No rural Pan dwelt there, no Silvanus, ruler of the woods, no Nymphs; but gods were worshipped there with savage rites, the altars were heaped with hideous offerings, and every tree was sprinkled with human gore. On those boughs – if antiquity, reverential of the gods, deserves any credit – birds feared to perch; in those coverts wild beasts would not lie down; no wind ever bore down upon that wood, nor thunderbolt hurled from black clouds; the trees, even when they spread their leaves to no breeze, rustled of themselves. Water, also, fell there in abundance from dark springs. The images of the gods, grim and rude, were uncouth blocks formed of felled tree-trunks. Their mere antiquity and the ghastly hue of their rotten timber struck terror; men feel less awe of deities worshipped under familiar forms; so much does it increase their sense of fear, not to know the gods whom they dread. Legend also told that often the subterranean hollows quaked and bellowed, that yew-trees fell down and rose again, that the glare of conflagration came from trees that were not on fire, and that serpents twined and glided round the stems. The people never resorted thither to worship at close quarters, but left the place to the gods. For, when the sun is in mid-heaven or dark night fills the sky, the priest himself dreads their approach and fears to surprise the lord of the grove. This grove was sentenced by Caesar to fall before the stroke of the axe; for it grew near his works.[31]

An Asian hypothesis

The Shakespearean tendency to view England as a 'precious stone set in a silver sea',[32] combined with a Churchillian determination 'to defend our island', should not blind us to the fact that people, ideas, plants and animals from the neighbouring continent influenced these Isles at all periods in history. Britain's Neolithic revolution was one incident in an evolving man–landscape relationship on the west fringe of a great continent. In *Asian Gardens*, I put forward a hypothesis about the relationship between nomads, settlers and the making of gardens in Eurasia:

My hypothesis is that the art of making gardens originated in the zone of interchange between the lifestyles of nomads and settlers. The gods of the nomads, known only from linguistic analysis, were associated with natural phenomena. They included the sky, the dawn, the rivers, the mountains and the earth. When nomads became settlers, they retained a love of wild landscapes. In Iran, for example, Aryan settlers made a type of space which they called a paradise. It is likely to have been a walled enclosure used for hunting and stocked with exotic plants and animals. Similar enclosures were made in other parts of Eurasia's 'Garden Fringe'. We call them hunting parks but they also had ceremonial, didactic and religious roles. This is recorded in connection with the great landscape parks of China and survives in Islamic and Christian use of the word 'paradise'. Ancient parks reminded kings of the wild landscapes in which their ancestors had

1.28 The 'Neolithic package' (of crops, animals and technology), which made cultivation and settlement possible, spread from West Asia to North Europe.

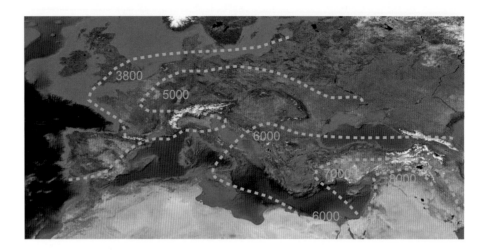

lived and roamed, as in the story that the 'Hanging Gardens of Babylon' were made for a beautiful concubine who, on the plains of Mesopotamia, yearned for a garden to remind her of 'meadows on mountain tops' in Persia. Settlers' gardens could reflect the nature of the wilds and the nature of civilization. These two natures remain the most astonishing things on earth.[33]

This hypothesis relates to the British Isles with regard to the symbolism of:

- settlements (the change from nomadism to sedentism);
- beliefs;
- ceremonies;
- hunting (and the use of enclosures in organised hunts);
- horticulture (as an aspect of civilisation);
- landscape design.

Indo-European culture

Linguistic analysis has shown that the relationship between Europe and Asia was cultural as well as technical (see p. 22). The shared heritage is called Indo-European but the name is misleading: the culture did not originate in India or Europe. It spread either from the North Caucuses (the Kurgan Hypothesis) or from Anatolia (the Renfrew Hypothesis). The technology of the farmers, who became users of Indo-European terminology, included 'permanent villages of rectangular houses, religious objects and structures, and domesticated plants and animals, as well as pottery and ground stone tools'.[34] Whether or not the Indo-European languages arrived with the new technology, as Renfrew argues, there is no doubting the diffusion of Neolithic

1.29 Yeavering Bell Hillfort is a Votadini site with evidence of over a hundred roundhouses. Cultivation may have taken place on the plateau below the hill, where an Anglo-Saxon palace was built in the seventh century CE (see Figure 2.26). Sheep were brought to the British Isles as part of the Neolithic package.

technology and culture in prehistoric Europe. Woodard examined the links between Indo-European and Graeco-Roman culture.[35]

'Celtic' was the word used by the ancient Greeks to describe the peoples of North Europe, though it is not known whether it was used by the people themselves. 'Celtic' now describes a language which belongs to the Centum group of Indo-European languages (which includes Italic, Germanic and Greek). These languages are related to each other and to a language spoken in the assumed Indo-European Homeland. Studies of Proto Indo-European (PIE) have yielded information about the farming techniques, beliefs and family structure of Indo-European societies. The following information is from Barber's *The English Language: A Historical Introduction*.

PIE agriculture

They herded cattle and sheep and there are common words for these animals in several languages: for example, ox is ych *in Welsh,* uksan- *in Sanskrit and* okso *in Tocharian. Ewe is related to the Latin* ovis *and the Sanskrit* avi- *... The Indo-Europeans had horses, for which a rich vocabulary has survived, and they also had vehicles of some kind, for there are words for wheel, axle, nave, and yoke.*[36]

PIE family structure

There is a large Indo-European vocabulary for family relationships, and it seems that the family played an important role in their social organization ... For

1.30 Interior of a reconstructed Neolithic hut at Butser Ancient Farm.

example there is a widespread Indo-European word for daughter-in-law (seen in Latin nurus, Greek nuous, Sanskrit snusa), but no such widespread word for son-in-law.[37]

1.31 a, b The Celts associated gods with mountains, skies and other natural features. (a) Traprain Law, the largest Votadini settlement in Scotland (*c.*1000 BCE–400 CE) cannot have been a comfortable place to live, or a site for cultivation, but a hoard of Roman silver found on top of the hill suggests that defence was a major consideration in choosing this site. (b) Nor can comfort have led to the construction of this Votadini hillfort at Earnsheugh. Symbolism may have influenced the choice of both sites.

PIE beliefs

There are some common gods to the European and Asiatic languages, and they seem to be personifications of natural forces; they do not, however, include a Great Mother Goddess or an Earth Goddess. Prominent among them, however, is a Sky God: the Greek Zeus, the Sanskrit Dyaus, the Old English Tiw (whose name

survives in our word Tuesday). He was a Father God, as we can see from his Latin name, Jupiter, which means 'Sky Father'.[38]

Dagda, a Celtic god, is equivalent to Zeus and Dyaus,[39] indicating the shared cultural heritage of North Europe, South Europe and South Central Asia.

Ceremonies

The fact that processions took place in the ancient world is known from both linguistic and archaeological evidence. The Indo-European word **h2eg'-mn* is the ancestor of the Sanskrit *ajman* and the Latin *agmen* ('procession, military column'). Religious and military processions were represented on works of art, as at Persepolis and Yazılıkaya, Egyptian paintings and Roman sculptures. Physical remains of ancient avenues have been found in Babylonia, Egypt and Rome. In Egypt, for example, the Beautiful Festival of the Valley was an occasion when the sacred barge of Amun-Re was taken from the land of the living on the East Bank of the Nile to the land of the dead and the mortuary temples on the West Bank.

There is some archaeological evidence for ceremonies in ancient Britain. The stone circle at Callanish is 'approached by a number of stone avenues or rows, with

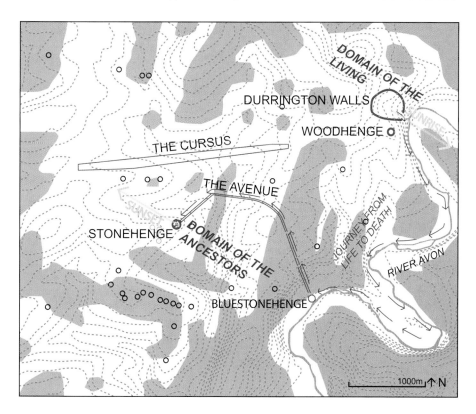

1.32 Plan of Stonehenge *c.*2900 BCE. The cursus is older than the henge and was probably used, like a stadium, for competitions. The avenue is thought to have been part of a processional route from Durrington Walls to Stonehenge. The vegetation pattern is based on Allen's studies of mollusc shells.[40]

1.33 A tree-lined Indo-European processional route (at Persepolis, Iran).

1.34 The cursus at Stonehenge, looking west, with the mounds of long barrows on the left horizon. It was enclosed by banks and is thought to have been made in a grazed open landscape. A GIS study of the views and viewsheds led to the conclusion that 'it was designed in order that people should walk from west to east' so that they left the old world of the long barrows and arrived in a new world with 'extensive vistas to the south (which were not visible from the western terminal) and a fine view of Stonehenge'.[41]

1.35 A study of mollusc shells has led to the conclusion that Stonehenge was in open grazing land but that, as today, there were nearby woods. The Stonehenge Riverside Project concluded that the stone circle was a place to gather at the winter solstice and see the sunset.

a chambered cairn situated in the centre'[42] (see Figure 1.23). Marija Gimbutas associated standing stones with 'the sea, rivers, brooks, and wells'.[43] She saw this as evidence of Celtic animism and linked it to the Kurgan culture of the steppes, which she saw as Indo-European culture. There is a cursus and an avenue at Stonehenge. The Latin word *cursus* means 'course'. It is defined by banks and may have been used for athletic competitions. Since the alignment of the 'avenue' is not straight, 'processional route' is a better description. Avenues and allées are now associated with Baroque gardens, hunting and visual axes (see Chapter 5).

The Stonehenge Riverside Project investigated the region as a landscape designed for the commemoration of tribal ancestors.[44] The great circles of Durrington Walls and Stonehenge are seen as poles for the 'Land of the Living' and the 'Land of the Dead'.

1.36 The dwellings within the circular embankment at Durrington Walls were similar in plan to those at Skara Brae (see Figure 1.3). Large numbers of pig bones and arrowheads indicate that hunting took place in the vicinity. An avenue, aligned with the sunrise, led from the circle to the River Avon.

A processional route (see Figure 1.32) links the two Lands, branching north-west from the River Avon at Bluestonehenge. This echoes the use of processional routes in Bronze Age Egypt, where they inter-connected sanctuaries. Crossing the Nile was a progression from the Land of the Living to the Land of the Dead. Egyptian temples were aligned on the axis of sunrise and sunset.[45] Durrington Walls, it is postulated, was a place to view the sunrise. Stonehenge was a place to view the sunset and, perhaps, for male cremations. The great bluestones (Preseli Spotted Dolerite, an igneous rock) were transported 240 km from Wales, which may have been the homeland of the settlers' ancestors. Each stone weighs between 2,000 and 4,000 kg and they may have been pulled, by men or oxen, on wooden rails.

Before the advent of maps and nations, enclosures appear to have been a way of symbolising tribal territories. In West Asia, royal and sacred enclosures symbolised wild landscapes and connections between the forces of men and the forces of nature. In the Aegean, sacred landscapes outside royal cities were places to make offerings at shrines and then to build temples for gods or goddesses. In the British Isles, sacred enclosures were formed in territorially significant locations and, it is assumed, used for ceremonies which linked communities to their ancestors. The chosen sites related to rivers, hills, farmland and woods.

Hunting

Durrington Walls was a large circular enclosure containing dwellings, which have a similar plan form to those at Skara Brae (see Figure 1.3). It was also a ceremonial site and large numbers of pigs' bones and flint arrowheads, some embedded in the bones, have been found. This implies that hunting and feasting formed part of the ceremonial activity. It is an interesting fact that ceremonial hunts and royal enclosures were made throughout the settlement zones on the fringes of Asia[46] and in Europe:

Judging from cave paintings, hunting was the principal activity in Paleolithic societies. It had both economic and sacred characteristics. Axes, bows and spears were used to kill the animals upon which families lived. There are no written records from the period but studies of contemporary hunter–gather societies confirm the intuitive point that success in hunting would give an individual high status and power over food supplies, tribesmen and women.[47]

1.37 Woad growing in an enclosure at Butser Ancient Farm (with a four-posted grain store beyond).

1.38 Archaeolink Prehistory Park puts forward the hypothesis that cereals were grown in horticultural-scale 'gardens' near Iron Age dwellings.

Horticulture

Vegetables may have been grown within hillfort enclosures, perhaps in separate fenced compartments where crops would have benefitted from animal manure. Some reconstructions suggest rectangular gardens and others suggest vegetables were grown beside huts. Both are possible.

Julius Caesar recorded that, during the first century BCE, the Celts were little interested in cultivation but painted themselves with woad:

> The most civiliz'd people among them are the Kentish men, whose country lies altogether upon the sea-coasts; and their customs are much the same with those of the Gauls: the inland people seldom trouble themselves with agriculture, living on milk and flesh-meat, and are clad with skins; but all of them paint themselves blue with woad (vitrum), that they may look the more dreadful to their enemies in battle.[48]

The word *vitrum* is a Latin translation of the Celtic *glas*. It can mean 'glass' or 'blue' but is generally taken to mean 'woad'. Woad (*Isatis tinctoria*) is a plant of Middle Eastern origin that yields indigo, a blue dye which was also used to dye fabric. Woad probably came to Britain with the Neolithic package. It belongs to the *Brassica* family and flourishes in alkaline soil. Today it is grown, like cabbages, by sowing, thinning and transplanting. In the Iron Age, it could have been grown within hillforts or in small fields. The hypothesis on view at Butser Iron Age farm is that it was grown near circular huts. Pytheas was a Greek from Massilia (Marseilles) who sailed north in c.325 BCE and wrote of the 'Pretanike' group of islands. This word is believed to come from the Celtic term for 'painted' and to be the origin of the word 'Britain'.[49] If correct, it is appropriate that the name for a nation of gardeners derives from the cultivation of an imported plant (see p. viii).

Conclusion

In early Neolithic times, England was heavily wooded and had a population of perhaps 20,000 people. The first settlements were on woodland margins with access to land for cultivation, grazing, hunting, fishing and firewood. This range of habitats was found on the flanks of hills, near coasts and beside rivers. The ancient Britons did not make 'gardens' in the modern sense but they enclosed outdoor space for symbolic, horti-cultural and security reasons. This parallels the gardening activity of the Egyptians, Mesopotamians and Romans, who made symbolic enclosures (sanctuaries), horti-cultural enclosures (for growing vegetables) and domestic enclosures (courtyards).

Before moving on to Roman Britain, let us imagine ourselves in a stockaded Celtic settlement (Figure 1.39). It is on the edge of a forest with hills above and a wooded valley below. There are circular huts and grain stores within the stockade. Looking up, a circular earthwork can be seen on the shoulder of the hill, with grazing and scrub beyond. Looking down, there is a clearing in the forest with small fields and a river beyond. Some of the fields are cultivated. Others are used as pounds for sheep, goats and cattle brought in for the night. Felling trees with flint axes, clearing tree roots and

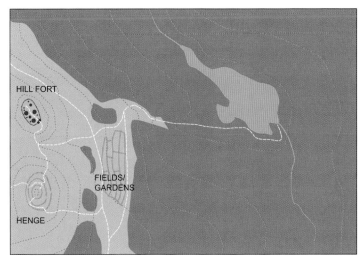

1.39 A hypothetical Neolithic landscape.

1.40 Castlerigg is a classic shoulder site, with the stone circle centre left (in the light-coloured field beside a wood).

making fields had been a great work. The settlers were proud of their achievements and those of their ancestors. Standing stones, communal tombs and circular earthworks symbolised the identity of the tribe and its territorial claim to areas used for hunting, grazing and horticulture. Stone and earth circles commanded territory and symbolised ownership. In the Iron Age, they also had defensive roles.

The design of relationships between symbolic structures and local landscapes, in the British Isles, began *c.*4000 BCE and continued for the following 6,000 years:

- Causewayed enclosures, henges and hillforts were made from the start of the Neolithic revolution until the Roman conquest in 43 CE (see p. 6).
- The Romans re-used Neolithic sites for fortifications, settlements and temples (see p. 45).
- The early Christians were advised to adopt temple sites for churches, influencing the countryside for centuries to come (see p. 46).
- The Normans built castles to command territory, symbolically and physically (see p. 69).
- Renaissance and Baroque country houses had central positions in large country estates (see p. 153).
- Romantic country houses were carefully sited in picturesque scenery to create a transition from the works of man to the works of nature (see p. 275).
- The first users of the term 'landscape architecture' discussed the location of country houses in relation to the surrounding scenery (see p. 319).
- Early town and country planners sought to achieve a transition from compact towns through agricultural hinterlands to scenic backgrounds (see p. 289).

Landscape design ordered the use of land for cultivation, settlement, defence, processions and burials, all within a symbolic framework. It was, as it remains, an essential preliminary to architecture, agriculture and other uses of settled land.

CHAPTER 2

Romano-British gardens and landscapes, 43–1066

2.0 Pliny the Elder wrote that this island 'Albion was its name, when all the Islands were called Britanniae'.[1] 'Albion' may derive from *alba*, meaning 'white'. Tacitus (56–117), whose father-in-law had governed Britain, wrote: 'Their sky is obscured by continual rain and cloud'.[2]

2.1 A scene from Trajan's Column in Rome. The Roman Empire reached its greatest extent under Trajan (98–117 CE), half a century after the conquest of Britain. It was ruled by military force but, after the victories, produced the settled conditions in which garden design can flourish.

Introduction

Legend dates the foundation of Rome to 753 BCE, when the Italian Peninsula was occupied by ethnically and linguistically diverse tribes. The Romans came to dominate the language and culture of the Peninsula, adopting words, ideas and techniques from the regions they conquered. By 265 BCE, this included the whole Peninsula. In 27 BCE, the Republic became an Empire and in 117 CE the Empire reached its maximum extent, under Trajan. Claudius invaded the British Isles in 43 CE and much of the land which later became England remained under Roman occupation until 410 CE. Fortunately for Britain, the period of occupation included Rome's Golden Age (96–180), about which Edward Gibbon wrote:

> *If a man were called to fix the period in the history of the world during which the condition of the human race was most happy and prosperous, he would, without hesitation, name that which elapsed from the death of Domitian to the accession of Commodus. The vast extent of the Roman Empire was governed by absolute power, under the guidance of virtue and wisdom. The armies were restrained by the firm but gentle hand of four successive emperors, whose characters and authority commanded respect. The forms of the civil administration were carefully preserved by Nerva, Trajan, Hadrian and the Antonines, who delighted in the image of liberty, and were pleased with considering themselves as the accountable ministers of the laws.*[3]

2.2 Caractacus, a Celtic chief who was defeated and taken to Rome, encountered the technically advanced civilisation which the Romans brought to Britain.

A Golden Age provided the settled conditions in which garden design can flourish. In the British Isles, the Romans found tribal settlements with circular huts, thatched roofs, canoes, art and music – as did the British themselves when, sixteen centuries later, they colonised North America. The natives had no written literature nor any organisation above the tribal level and the expeditionary forces found that, with professional soldiers and technically superior weapons, it was relatively easy to defeat the local tribes.

Strabo, who lived from *c.*64 BCE–24 CE, wrote of the largest Britannic island that:

> *Most of the island is flat and overgrown with forests, although many of its districts are hilly. It bears grain, cattle, gold, silver, and iron. These things, accordingly, are exported from the island, as also hides, and slaves, and dogs that are by nature suited to the purposes of the chase; the Celti, however, use both these and the native dogs for the purposes of war too. The men of ... although well supplied with milk, make no cheese; and they have no experience in gardening or other agricultural pursuits. And they have powerful chieftains in their country. For the purposes of war they use chariots for the most part, just as some of the Celti do. The forests are their cities; for they fence in a spacious circular enclosure with trees which they have felled, and in that enclosure make huts for themselves and also pen up their cattle – not, however, with the purpose of staying a long time. Their weather is more rainy than snowy; and on the days of clear sky fog prevails so*

long a time that throughout a whole day the sun is to be seen for only three or four hours round about midday.[4]

Agriculture and mining were established in Celtic Britain but benefitted from the Roman introduction of new tools, new techniques, new crops and specialised buildings. Pre-Roman huts were built with timber and mud, often in enclosures. The Romans introduced a Mediterranean approach to residential planning and it was adopted by local chiefs who helped administer the empire. Virgil explained that Roman policy was 'to spare the vanquished and to subdue the arrogant'.[5]

Many villa sites have been discovered but few have been fully excavated with careful regard to their gardens. Since more villa gardens are sure to be excavated in the years to come, we may assume that new information will come to light and that conclusions in this chapter will be challenged. Garden archaeology is a relatively new discipline.

Roman gardens in Italy

Like colonists everywhere, the Romans who came to Britain wanted to live in similar conditions to those enjoyed at home. Courtyard housing was the norm in Italian towns, as it had been in Greek towns, and it is likely that courtyards in the first

2.3 a, b The main types of Roman garden in Italy were: (a) town gardens; and (b) villa gardens.

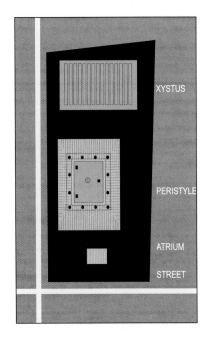
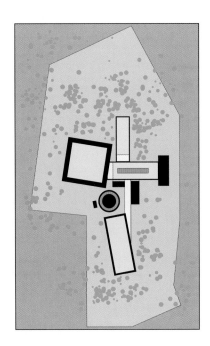

Greek-influenced Roman towns were paved, like rooms, for family use. As Rome became wealthier, houses became larger, towns became more secure and courtyard-type space became available for planting. This was easier in Italy than it had been in Greece, because Italian towns were often on or near agricultural land. By the age of the Five Good Emperors (96–192 CE), Italy was protected by a well-organised standing army. This made it possible for towns to be less dense. With the countryside secure, villa gardens could be made in suburban areas. Roman villas were like villages with farmland, woods, gardens and palatial houses. Pliny the Younger, who left detailed accounts of villa gardens in his letters, is thought to have owned some 500 slaves.[6] A villa included woodland, farmland, labourers' dwellings, a palace and extensive gardens.

Food was produced in three types of space:

1   *ager* (ploughed fields, used for grains which grew in the wet season without irrigation);
2   *saltus* (woodland pasture for sheep, goats and pigs);
3   *hortus* (enclosures, cultivated with hand tools and used for fruit trees, vines, vegetables and flowers).

In town gardens, plants were grown for both use and ornament, sometimes in separate enclosures but more often with overlaps between the two sets of objective. Luxurious Pompeian town houses had the three types of courtyard shown in Figure 2.4:

1   *atrium* (a lightwell, usually at the front of the property and often with a pool to catch rainwater);

2.4 a, b The Villa Oplontis, near Pompeii, is a good example of a villa garden with a peristyle. Archaeology has provided evidence of trees, but not of hedges or grass.

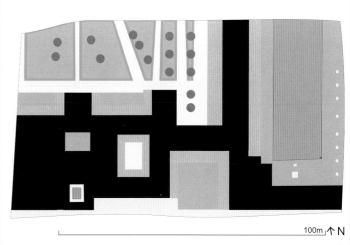

2   *peristyle court* (a pleasure garden, enclosed by a roof corridor – the peristyle); *cortis* (also, *curtis*, *curtus*) was the word used for a court or courtyard;

3   *hortus* (a productive garden, usually at the rear of the property, sometimes called a *xystus*).

The physical form and the uses of an *atrium* and a *hortus* were distinct: the former was paved and the latter was a place to grow plants. Peristyle courts, surrounded by colonnades, tended to be part-paved and part-planted. At Pompeii, many peristyle courts now have mown lawns and paths flanked by box hedges. The evidence for this treatment seems to be the text references, discussed below, to box hedges being clipped to make animal shapes (see p. 40). This is countered by a great many garden paintings which do not show topiary or lawns. They have a type of planting which compares with what is now called 'cottage garden planting': a free mixture of flowers, fruits and herbs, grown for beauty and ornament (see Figure 10.32). Pompeian garden paintings show a profusion of birds, fountain basins and decorative masks. Many of the paintings are on the walls of peristyle corridors and could well have mirrored the garden planting on the garden side of the corridor. Trelliswork is often shown between the columns, which is where it would have been needed to keep children away from the plants and planting out of the corridors. Low walls with niches were also built. There is no reason to doubt the fact that Roman garden paintings were illustrations of Roman gardens and their planting. Andrew Wallace-Hadrill deals with the points as follows:

> The decoration mirrors in detail the conventions of the gardens themselves; the formality with which the plantings are enclosed within latticed trellises of canework, the elaborate setting of marble statuary, including herms, rectangular panels set on stands, and circular oscilla or theatrical masks suspended in the air, and crater fountains, and finally the fondness for Egyptianising themes are all points where decoration (both paintings and mosaics) and gardens run precisely parallel. Sometimes the painting acts as conscious extension of the garden, notably in the many cases where it covers the back wall of a peristyle and supplies a continuation or variation to the colonnades on the other sides of the garden.[7]

Gardens are places for rest and places for exercise. Pliny wrote of his *gestatio* ('a place to be carried') and his *hippodrome* ('a place for horses') as areas for garden exercise – on foot. Robert Castell explained their shape ('*gestatio in modum circi* ') as being like the circuses made in cities for chariot racing. He writes that Pliny's *gestatio* was like a public circus:

> with this Difference only, that as the Ornaments of That were of Stone, those in This consisted of Trees cut in the same Shapes, and this Gestatatio was bounded with Degrees of Box, as the Circus with Seats of Stone for the Spectators: And as the middle Part of That was filled with Obelisks, Altars, Pillars, and Arches, so This was with Box-Trees and other Shrubs, probably cut into the same Forms.[8]

The 'degrees' (tiers) of clipped box represented seating and cones of box represented the turning posts (*metae*) in a public circus.[9] Pliny says nothing about box in courtyards though, as shown on Castell's re-creation of his Tuscan villa, he had his own name and that of his architect cut in box. The *metae* in Pliny's garden could be the origin of box cones in later European gardens. But the Roman villa gardens made in the British Isles were on farming estates and no evidence of *gestatio* or exercise areas has been found.

2.5 Columella's *De Re Rustica* is the fullest Roman agricultural treatise. It was reissued and illustrated during the Renaissance, when this volume appeared.[10]

Roman horticulture in England

Agriculture was well established in the British Isles before the Roman conquest, particularly in southern England. The region had free-draining chalky soils and the people were in trade contact with continental Europe. The emphasis was on producing grains which could be stored for winter use and this pattern of agriculture continued after the conquest. The most significant change after the Romans arrived was in vegetable growing. It is thought that this component of the diet was met in Celtic times by gathering fruits, leaves and berries from the wild.

Archaeology has yielded some information about Roman horticulture in the British Isles and it can be supplemented by the technical information in Roman books. Columella (*c*.4–70 CE) was a Roman author who took up farming after a military career.

2.6 A re-created Roman garden at Fishbourne. Planting in peristyle courts may have been like this. The Romans grew: cherries, medlars, plums, damsons, apples, mulberries, roses, lilies, violets, pansies. rosemary, myrtle, lavender, sweet bay and wormwood.

2.7 Roman gardening tools, displayed in the Museum of London.

The twelve volumes of his *De Re Rustica* provide extensive information about Roman techniques of cultivation and husbandry.

The range of horticultural and agricultural implements used in the British Isles after the conquest included: the coulter, the plough, the sickle, the billhook, the two-hand scythe, the pruning hook, the hoe, the mattock, the spud, the rake, the iron spade, the iron fork, the turf-cutter, the ox-goad, the carding comb and the axe. Ploughs and coulters were used to prepare land for growing cereals. Fields were long and narrow, because ox-drawn ploughs were heavy and unmanoeuvrable. Sickles, billhooks and scythes were used to harvest cereals and could have been used for lawns but there are no records of this. The range of cereals included barley, oats, wheat, rye. Forks, spades, hoes, mattocks and rakes were used for weeding fields and also for the horticultural cultivation of vegetables and flowers. The vegetables grown in Britain before the Roman conquest are thought to have been limited but to have included beans for human consumption and fat hen for animal consumption. The Romans brought a deep knowledge of horticulture and introduced a wide range of plants, including:

- *vegetables*: cabbage, broad bean, parsnip, pea, radish, turnip, celery, carrot, mustard and vetch (as a fodder crop);
- *fruits*: cherry, medlar, plum, damson, bullace (damson), grape, apple and mulberry;
- *flowers*: rose, lily, violet and pansy.

They must have been grown in walled, fenced or hedged enclosures within and near villas.

Roman gardens in England

The Romans made villa gardens in the British Isles, as they did in Italy. Little evidence concerning their character is available, partly because there were no volcanic eruptions of the kind which preserved Pompeii. They also made town gardens but the sites have been re-used down the centuries, so that little survives. A few towns, like Viroconium Cornoviorum (now Wroxeter) were abandoned and have been excavated. The most common building type was a strip house, with a street frontage used as a work area and shop. Larger houses had courtyards and gardens but not *atria* or peristyles.[11] After centuries of farming they yield little or no information about gardens. Roman towns in Britain were planned like legionary camps: 'they have no atrium and peristyle, like the houses of Pompeii, nor are they tenement-houses, like those of Ostia and Rome'.[12] It is, however, clear that Rome's influence on British architecture and gardens was revolutionary. New building materials including bricks, tiles, stone and mosaic tiles were used to make palaces and palace gardens of a kind which had

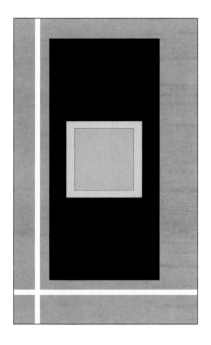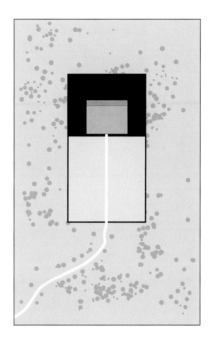

2.8 a, b The Romans made two types of garden in Britain: town gardens and villa gardens (cf. Figure 2.3).

hitherto been unknown in the British Isles. Some information comes from villas in country areas which did have space for gardens.

Initially, the Romans introduced two types of farm building to the British Isles. The first was a large 'basilica' barn, with a nave and aisles; the owners lived in the nave and the animals lived in the aisles. The second was a two-room house. One room was

2.9 Wroxeter, though one of the best-preserved Roman towns in Britain, was farmland for centuries and yields little information about gardens. The site of the bathhouse is now maintained like a golf course.

2.10 Model of a Roman town house, from the Museum of London.

2.11 a–d (a) Roman town house at Verulamium Insula XIV (St Albans), with a metal grill protecting the shrine (b) at the back of a strip house. The bronze statuette, found nearby (c), is believed to represent Venus and to have been made for a household shrine. (d) John William Godward's painting of a Roman garden shrine.

 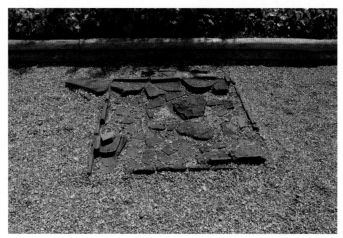

2.12 a, b (a) Fishbourne's Roman villa was excavated under the supervision of Barry Cunliffe. The space now planted with hedges may well have been flower beds. The conical tree (assumed from a 0.76 m diameter planting pit) may have been a topiary animal or a fruit tree. (b) Cunliffe suggests the stone base on the lower right edge of the photograph was a pedestal for a statue.

used for humans and the other was for animals. The Romans introduced the technology for well-digging which allowed a reliable water supply and, with barns and stored grain, facilitated the over-wintering of livestock. When farming estates became prosperous, the two building types were fused to make a 'winged-corridor house'. The corridor gave sheltered access to rooms and barns. On the largest villas, as in Italy, roofed corridors were used to enclose what became courtyards. Separate structures were made for farming and the owners' house became a large dwelling in the middle of a luxurious villa estate. This was the first appearance of a palace-and-wine lifestyle in the British Isles.

The most fully investigated Roman garden in Britain, at Fishbourne, was excavated in the early years of garden archaeology and raises as many questions as it answers.

2.13 Espalier apple trees have been planted at Fishbourne, where alternating planting pits and post holes were found. Acanthus, in the foreground, inspired the decoration on Corinthian columns but there is no reason to think it was planted like this.

2.14 a, b Reconstruction of a *triclinium* at Fishbourne, based on evidence from Pompeii.

Barry Cunliffe supervised the excavations (1961–8) and wrote a book about the project. In a chapter on 'The Gardens and the Environment', he wrote:

> *In size, it is approximately equivalent to Nero's Golden House in Rome or to the Roman villa at Piazza Armerina in Sicily, and in plan it mirrors the basic organisation of the Domus Flavia on the Palatine Hill in Rome. Fishbourne is by far the largest Roman residence known north of the Alps. At about 500 feet (150 m) square, it is comparable in size to Buckingham Palace.*[13]

After digging some trial pits, Cunliffe concluded 'there *was* a formal garden and it *was* discoverable by excavation'. The decision to excavate was commendable but Cunliffe's use of the word 'formal' at such an early stage has the troubling implication that he was expecting to find a Renaissance-style parterre (see p. 116). In connection with gardens, 'formal' is a critical term which took on its current meaning ('rectilinear') in the eighteenth century. It was reasonable to assume that the layout of the paths was rectilinear but the evidence for 'formality' in the planting design remains non-existent. Possibly because the literal meaning of 'renaissance' is 're-birth', many people have, like Robert Castell, let their conception of Roman gardens be influenced by Renaissance and Baroque gardens (see p. 230).

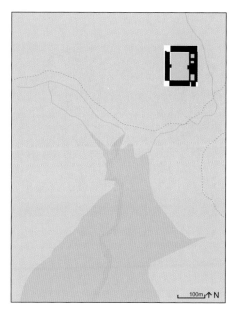

2.15 Fishbourne's Roman villa was a courtyard palace, built on fertile land near Chichester harbour.

Other sources of information about Roman gardens argue against the present arrangement of the courtyard at Fishbourne as a mown lawn enclosed by 'formal'

2.16 *Buxus sempervirens*, growing wild on Box Hill, illustrates the ability of box to thrive in thin soil on dry chalk downland.

2.17 A *lararium* in the *atrium* of the House of Vettii in Pompeii. The triangular *tympanum* has symbols of sacrifice (a knife and an ox-skull). The left and right figures are Lares, who carry a horn and a wine bucket. The central figure is 'the *genius*, dressed in a toga, and with veiled head, holds a *patera* in his right hand an incense box in his left – as if offering sacrifice); the serpent, moving towards offerings of fruit on a small altar (far right), probably symbolises the earth's fertility and the prosperity of the household'.[16]

hedges. First, the courtyard frescos at Pompeii, Herculaneum and elsewhere do not show clipped hedges bounding flower beds. Second, excavation of other Roman sites has provided no evidence of hedged lawns. Third, the famous references to the use of box in Pliny the Younger's letters have too often been read with images of French parterres in mind. Pliny refers to cut box near a *xystus* (roofed walkway) beside a *gestatio* (exercise ground). He says nothing about a parterre-style use of box, in courtyards, with grass and flower beds in the Baroque manner (see p. 159). Here is Pliny's text followed by a translation with the Latin words in square brackets:

Ante porticum xystus in plurimas species distinctus concisusque buxo; demissus inde pronusque pulvinus, cui bestiarum effigies invicem adversas buxus inscripsit; acanthus in plano, mollis et paene dixerim liquidus. Ambit hunc ambulatio pressis varieque tonsis viridibus inclusa; ab his gestatio in modum circi, quae buxum multiformem humilesque et retentas manu arbusculas circumit. Omnia maceria muniuntur: hanc gradata buxus operit et subtrahit.[14]

In front, there is a terrace [porticum xystus] *laid out in different patterns* [in plurimas species distinctus] *and bounded with an edging of box* [concisusque buxo, 'box which was cut']; *then comes a sloping ridge with figures of animals* [bestiarum effigies] *on both sides cut out of the box-trees* [invicem adversas buxus], ... *then comes an exercise ground* [gestatio], *round like a circus* [modum circi], *which surrounds the box-trees that are cut into different forms* [quae buxum multiformem], *and the dwarf shrubs that are kept clipped* [humilesque et retentas]. *Everything is protected by an enclosure* [omnia maceria muniuntur], *which is hidden and withdrawn from sight by the tiers of box-trees* [hanc gradata buxus operit et subtrahit].

The text does not support Cunliffe's interpretation that the trenches discovered at Fishourne were used for box. W.J. Bean describes the growing conditions for box as follows: 'The boxes succeed in almost any soil, and are often found wild on a limestone formation.'[15] There would have been no need for soil improvement to grow box on the fertile coastal plain of Sussex. Common box (*Buxus sempervirens*) is probably indigenous to Britain. It has strong fibrous roots and can flourish on very dry soils of the type found on Box Hill in Surrey. The plants Cunliffe suggests may have been grown at Fishbourne include rose, lily and box. It is difficult to see why he should have assumed that the bedding trenches in the courtyard were used for box. Lilies and roses are much more in need of rich soil. They are low-growing and need the weeding and watering which are easy to provide near a path. Experience of planting both box and flowers leads me to conclude that the trenches were more likely to have been planted with exotic flowering plants than with box.

Excavating one of Cunliffe's box trees (planted at Fishbourne in the 1960s) would provide useful information. My guess is that the roots will be found to have outgrown

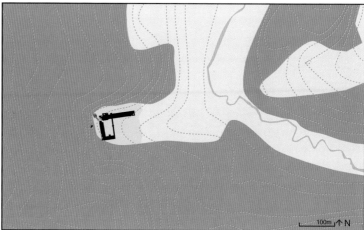

2.18 a, b (a) Chedworth was a wing-corridor villa. The corridor joined the wings and enclosed what is assumed to have been a courtyard garden. If so, my guess is that it was managed like the planting shown in the garden paintings at Pompeii, as suggested by the photomontage. (b) The woodland planting shown on the plan is also hypothetical.

and destroyed the archaeologically attested Roman 'bedding trenches'. The free-standing tree in the photograph looks peculiar in an eccentric position on a lawn. The planting position was archaeologically determined but the tree may have been surrounded by herbaceous vegetation and, if it was clipped box, Pliny's letter suggests it is more likely to have been cut into an animal shape.

Chedworth is a well-excavated villa and is thought to have been one of over 50 large Roman villas in the Cotswolds. Its location might have been determined by a spring which became the site of a water shrine. The octagonal pool survives and is just above the level of a courtyard which is assumed to have been a garden. The garden area was excavated but no evidence of paths or plants was found. It may well have

2.19 a, b A drawing and a model of the Roman villa at Bignor. The lawns, the hedges and the layout are equally improbable: they are Baroque ideas which have been reverse-engineered into a Roman courtyard.

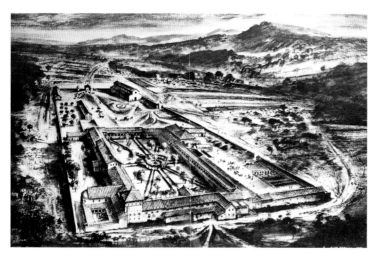

2.20 The summer dining room (*triclinium*) at Bignor has a hexagonal basin (*piscina*). It may have been used for fish or for bathing. The hexagonal mosaics portray dancing girls.

2.21 a, b, c Over 1 million litres of water flow into the pool of the Sacred Spring at Bath each day (at 46°C) and over 12,000 votive coins were found in the pool. (a) The Gorgon's Head on the Temple pediment was a symbol of Minerva. She was the Roman equivalent of the Greek Athena, the goddess of poetry, music, medicine, wisdom and commerce. (b) The Sacred Spring has been venerated since Celtic times. (c) The buildings above water level date from the nineteenth century.

been an area of flowering herbs and fruit of the kind shown on garden frescoes at Pompeii.[17] This type of planting was also found in West Asian gardens.

Bignor Roman villa, 25 km north-east of Fishbourne, began with the construction of a rectangular farmhouse *c*.200 CE. This became the west wing after *c*.400 when three new wings were built and an internal courtyard was created and enclosed by a villa

2.22 a, b The shrine at Chedworth Roman villa is likely to have been dedicated to a water deity. It was probably used both as a family shrine and as a water supply. Mown grass is improbable.

with some 65 rooms and fine mosaic floors in the north wing. Two reconstructions of the courtyard layout are shown in Figure 2.19. Both conceive it as having been more like a Baroque parterre than the type of space depicted on Roman garden frescoes.

The Romans built Aquae Sulis, now called Bath, on a site with a natural hot spring. There had previously been a Celtic shrine dedicated to the goddess Sulis on the site and the Romans identified her with their own goddess, Minerva. Pre-Roman coins were found in the Sacred Spring, with images of a ship, human heads and three-tailed horses. The Roman Temple became known as Sulis Minerva, illustrating the affinity between Celtic and Roman polytheism.

Polytheist landscapes

More is known about sacred space in Italy than in Roman England. The beliefs of the Romans were polytheist, animist and contractual. Edward Gibbon described the place of religious ritual in the daily life of Rome:

> *The innumerable deities and rites of polytheism were closely interwoven with every*
> *circumstance of business or pleasure, of public or of private life; and it seemed impossible*
> *to escape the observance of them, without, at the same time, renouncing the commerce of*

2.23 A niche with a shell-canopy, found at Chedworth, was probably used as a shrine and held a statue (cf. Figure 2.11).

2.24 A Roman relief, carved in limestone, thought to portray three Celtic mother goddesses with an unidentified fourth figure.

mankind, and all the offices and amusements of society. The important transactions of peace and war were prepared or concluded by solemn sacrifices, in which the magistrate, the senator, and the soldier, were obliged to preside or to participate. The public spectacles were an essential part of the cheerful devotion of the pagans; and the gods were supposed to accept, as the most grateful offering, the games that the prince and people celebrated in honour of their peculiar festivals.[18]

The contractual aspect of Roman beliefs lay in the fact that gods were regarded as divine powers which had to be rewarded with sacrificial gifts for past boons and future favours. Emperors had private altars. Cities had public altars. Houses had family shrines, often in gardens. The father of the family (*pater familias*) presided over family ceremonies. Rituals were particularly associated with family events. 'Sacrifice was *the* most important feature of Roman religion'.[19] A domestic animal was killed. The entrails were examined as auguries and offered to the gods. The rest of the animal was then eaten. The *Penates* were household gods. The *Lares*, as protective deities, could be gods of fields, households or cities. The *Larium* was a family shrine:

In the household the Lares were offered sacrifices of grapes, table scraps, garlands, grain, honeycakes and wine. They were worshipped on special feast days and probably were venerated in daily acts of homage. When a Roman boy and girl came of age, they dedicated to their Lares, the small emblem of their childhood, the bulla, *which was worn around their necks before adulthood.*[20]

The polytheist aspect of Roman culture is evident in the earliest records of Roman beliefs but was diversified through contact with the Greeks, the Egyptians, the Celts and other civilisations.

Cicero explains why gods were assumed to be like humans:

Concerning the appearance of the gods we have both the hints offered by nature as well as the teaching of reason. It is clearly due to nature that all people of all races conceive of the gods in none other but human form. For in what other shape do they ever appear to anyone, either awake or asleep? But not to reduce everything to the most basic concepts, reason itself proves the same thing. For it seems logical that what is naturally the highest form of existence, whether because of its supreme happiness or because of its immorality, should also be the most beautiful. And what arrangement of limbs, what cast of features, what shape or form can be more beautiful than the human?[21]

The Latin word *religio*, from which our word 'religion' derives, was used for 'the natural fear or awe which semi-civilised man feels in the presence of what he cannot explain'.[22] This led to the idea of performing obligations to unseen powers. The animist aspect of Roman beliefs was similar to, and probably derived from, the animism of Central Asia:

[T]here are names which express some natural object or thing: e.g. Fons, *fountain;* Terminus, *boundary;* Tellus, *earth;* Ianus, *door;* Vesta, *hearth. Here we clearly have an inheritance from animism; the worship that is to say of the spirits or forces thought to be resident in these objects.*[23]

In the British Isles, as elsewhere, the Romans took a sympathetic interest in the beliefs of the local population:

[W]hereas British art all but perished under romanization, British religion throve on it. Or rather, it hardly underwent romanization at all … The Romans were always willing to come to terms with the genius loci; they could not do it in art, but they could in religion; and consequently the history of Romano-British religion is the history of a blend of cultures in which, by degrees, the Celtic prevails.[24]

Beard comments:

[T]he Latin words for 'god' and 'goddess', as well as the Latin names of at least some of the gods and goddesses, belong to the very earliest stages of the history of the Latin language, and must in fact go back to the Indo-European ancestors of the Romans.[25]

The Romans believed that gods could preside over a place or inhabit an object:

A glance at that dark mysterious grove would bring to your lips the words: 'There is a numen in it' [lucus Avention suberat niger ilicis umbra quo posses viso dicere numen inest].[26]

The Latin word *numen* came to mean 'divine power' and can also be rendered in English as 'spirit'. The phrase 'Genius of the Place', meaning 'the spirit of a place', is a translation of *genius loci* and is now used in garden and landscape design history (see p. 228). To the Romans, *numen* was a broad and important concept. Halliday explains that:

It is etymologically connected with the verb nuere *and connotes the idea of will power. It seems to mean that incalculable force, the intervention of which in any process or action makes the difference between success or failure, safety or disaster. It is this force which arouses the feeling of awe,* religio, *in its primary sense, and it is the object of* religio, *in its secondary sense of the performance of religious duties, to harness it, as it were, in the service of man or to prevent its adverse operation.*[27]

The compatibility of Roman and British conceptions of the sacred is well illustrated by the shrine at Bath. Aquae Sulis was the city's Roman name. Sulis was a British-Celtic goddess who became equated with the Roman goddess Minerva, as a goddess of healing. The name 'Sulis' is thought to go back to the Indo-European word for 'sun', as reflected in the Old Welsh *houl* and the Breton *heol*.[28]

2.25 Relief carving of Mercury and Rosmerta, found in Bath, England. Mercury is a Roman god of abundance and commercial success. Rosmerta is the Celtic goddess of fertility and abundance. Together, they symbolise the affinity of Roman and Celtic beliefs.

2.26 There was an Anglo-Saxon palace (Ad Gefrin) on the plateau between Yeavering Bell Hillfort and the River Glen. A henge and Neolithic tools were also found on the site and there was a large hillfort on top of the hill (see Figure 1.29).

Anglo-Saxon gardening

When they settled in Britain, the Anglo-Saxons took over towns and farms with remnants of a sophisticated Roman civilisation. It is evident from the *Anglo-Saxon Chronicle*, commissioned by King Alfred and kept by monks from 891 to 1154, that the period did not provide the settled conditions in which the art of garden design flourishes. The *Chronicle* has many references to raiders arriving by ship, usually from Scandinavia, and to conflicts in which there was 'much slaughter made on either side':[29]

> *Though barbaric in their origins, much of their thinking, their secular literature and their social structure, the late Saxons consciously endeavoured to emulate their civilized neighbours on the Continent and further east ... The Saxons had adopted the Roman faith, Roman art, Roman thinking: Charlemagne regarded Offa of Mercia as his equal. Yet inside every civilized Saxon was a restless barbarian ... A Saxon king was little more than a tribal war-leader, dressed up in civilized clothing.*[30]

Kings and nobles lived in fortified towns, which were often burned during or after a siege. By the end of the first millennium, kings were living in palaces, as Charlemagne had done. They had orchards and vegetable gardens but did not continue the Roman tradition of luxurious villas with gardens maintained by slaves. Yeavering Palace is associated with a wild lifestyle.

Churches in the landscape

The earliest reference to British Christianity is Tertullian's comment (*c*.200 CE) regarding 'the diverse nations of the Gauls, and the haunts of the Britons (inaccessible to the

Romans, but subjugated to Christ)'.[31] Christian shrines were built in towns and villas but the religion did not become strong. One of the few surviving Roman shrines was made inside a large villa at Lullingstone in Kent.

Gildas (c.500–70) wrote a short vivid book on the *Ruin of Britain* and the decline of Christianity after the Romans' departure. He describes raiding parties of Picts and Scots and the appeals to Rome for protection. When this was unsuccessful, the British population of southern Britain made a request that 'sealed its doom by inviting in among them like wolves into the sheep-fold, the fierce and impious Saxons, a race hateful both to God and men, to repel the invasions of the northern nations'. As a result:

> *all the columns were levelled with the ground by the frequent strokes of the battering-ram, all the husbandmen routed, together with their bishops, priests, and people, whilst the sword gleamed, and the flames crackled around them on every side. Lamentable to behold, in the midst of the streets lay the tops of lofty towers, tumbled to the ground, stones of high walls, holy altars, fragments of human bodies, covered with livid clots of coagulated blood, looking as if they had been squeezed together in a press.*[32]

Gildas's two main concerns were civil disorder and the set-back to Christianity consequent upon the paganism of the invaders. He called them 'Saxons'. Bede and later historians called them 'Angles, Saxons and Jutes'. Modern historians call them Anglo-Saxons for convenience but recognise that they belonged to at least six Germanic tribes. Germany was not part of the Roman Empire and the beliefs of the invaders were related to the pre-Roman paganism of the British Isles. Feasts were held at the solstices and animal sacrifice had an important place in rituals. This was a set-back for the Christian religion in Britain but, after Gildas's time, the Anglo-Saxons

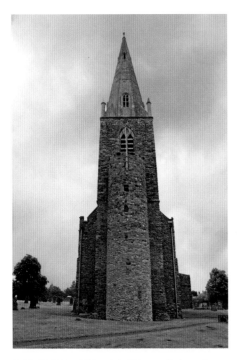

2.28 All Saints' Church in Brixworth dates from the seventh century and is one of the best examples of Anglo-Saxon architecture in Britain.

2.29 Rudston Church, recorded in the *Domesday Book* (1086), stands beside the largest megalith in Britain. The name means 'cross-stone', linking Christian and pagan worship.

2.30 The monastery on Skellig Michael, a small island off the west coast of Ireland, is thought to have been founded in the seventh century and to have survived because of its remoteness (see also Figure 3.39). Its position in the landscape is crucial.

2.31 a, b Glastonbury Tor and Burrow Mump were probably pagan sites before they became Christian sites.

became Romanised and Christianised, as did their fellow countrymen in continental Europe. Sacred groves were common:

> A grove is a wooded cult-site. It is a place amid trees, but not of course obstructed by them. If in a wood or forest, it is therefore a clearing ... Groves are among the most universal features of Indo-European and indeed any pagan religions and they are among the features of paganism most detested by urban Christians.[33]

In the fifth century, Christianity reached Ireland, from Roman Britain. Then, in the sixth and seventh centuries, Irish monks became evangelists in Scotland and England, converting the Anglo-Saxons who had come to Britain as pagans. The only surviving Anglo-Saxon buildings are Romanesque churches. Pope Gregory assisted the conversion of the Anglo-Saxons by sending Augustine to Kent and advising him that:

> I have, upon mature deliberation on the affair of the English, determined upon, viz., that the temples of the idols in that nation ought not to be destroyed; but let the idols that are in them be destroyed; let holy water be made and sprinkled in the said temples, let altars be erected, and relics placed. For if those temples are well built, it is requisite that they be converted from the worship of devils to the service of the true God ... For there is no doubt that it is impossible to efface everything at once from their obdurate minds; because he who endeavours to ascend to the highest place, rises by degrees or steps, and not by leaps.[34]

Churches were therefore built on sites which had been sacred to the pagans and an appreciation of landscape character became fused with English Christianity. This

2.32 Avebury Church was built at the west entrance to Avebury Henge.

2.33 a, b The church of Stanton Drew is on the edge of three stone circles.

point can be observed but not proved. Rural churches are usually focal points in landscapes, in villages and in towns. The word 'pagan' derives from the Latin *pagus* meaning 'rural district'. Christianity became paganised in the sense of becoming a religion of the landscape, as well as an urban religion, and in the sense of making a pagan response to places. Church design responded to landscapes, as castles and manor houses were to do in later centuries. Similarly, the dates chosen for the celebration of Christmas and Easter were based on the dates of the solstice festivals of pagan times.

There is an interesting parallel between the development of beliefs in China and Europe. Daoism, like European paganism, was animist. Forces of nature were thought to be strong at specific points in the landscape (hills, rivers, forests, etc.). Confucianism, like Christianity, was more concerned with relationships between people than with relationships between humans and the natural world. Confucianism subsequently merged with Daoism and Buddhism, as did Christianity with paganism and Classical philosophy. A further similarity is that the influence of Buddhism on Daoism

2.34 Midmar Kirk was the last church to be built on the site of a stone circle, in 1787. This may have been done for one of the old reasons: because the site was holy or to demonstrate the triumph of Christianity over paganism.

was discounted at a later date, just as the influence of paganism on Christianity was discounted by theologians. When disparaging Christianity for its heedless attitude to nature, Ian McHarg forgot its pagan regard for landscape character (see p. 397).

CHAPTER 3

Medieval gardens and landscapes, 1066–1485

3.0 Medieval gardens produced the ingredients for pottage: beans, peas, cabbage, onions, leeks and garlic, which were cooked slowly in animal fat and flavoured with garden herbs.

3.1 a, b (a) Philip de Loutherbourg, *Norman Horseman at Hastings*. (b) An abbey was built on the site and symbolises the Normans' approach to landscapes and architecture.

Introduction

The Norman Conquest of England in 1066 was a watershed. It closed the Early Middle Ages, dated from the departure of the Romans, and began the High Middle Ages. Though modern historians are finding more before-and-after continuity than their predecessors, the conquest remains a fulcrum: politically, socially, linguistically, artistically and for garden design. The *OED* gives Foxe's *Book of Martyrs* (1570)[1] as the first use of 'Middle Ages' as a historical category and the pre-Raphaelites, after 1848, were the first to use the word 'Medieval'. It was a translation of *medium aevum*, as used by Petrarch and others.[2] 'Medieval' is now the accepted name for the gardens of the period but, borrowing from architectural history, they could be classified as 'Romanesque', 'Gothic' or 'Norman'. These alternatives tell us something about the style: 'Gothic' associates it with northern Europe, 'Roman' points to its distant origin and 'Norman' to its immediate origin.

'Norman' derives from 'Norseman' (meaning 'Northman') and the word 'Viking', as found on rune stones, is thought to derive from *vik*, meaning bay or fjord. The Vikings were 'the people from the bays' who travelled in long ships and unsettled much of north Europe. They established a colony in northern France and contributed to the development of a feudal society in which military power and the ownership of land were more local than national. The Normans left Scandinavia as Norse-speaking pagans, but in a treaty agreed with Charles the Simple in 911 they agreed to become Christian. The conversion led to a wholesale adoption of the French culture which they subsequently brought to England. By the eleventh century, the Normans were speaking French, writing Latin and practising a style of art and architecture called

3.2 The White Tower protected London from invaders and the Normans from the people they had conquered. Henry III (1216–72) added a Garden Tower which overlooked a garden and the River Thames. It is behind the Traitors' Gate (in the centre of the photograph).

Romanesque because of its debt to the civilisation of the Italian peninsula. Another group of Normans colonised Sicily.

In the autumn of 1066, England's last Anglo-Saxon king, Harold II, defeated a Viking force at Stamford Bridge and soon after was defeated by a Norman army at the Battle of Hastings. An estimated 8,000 Normans then took control of England and launched a building programme which included cathedrals, monasteries and castles. Castles were new to the British Isles. The Romans had made forts, for soldiers, and fortified towns, for administrators and tradesmen. Norman castles were a new building type, part-palace and part-fortress. Known as *donjons* and *tours*, they developed in the context of fighting between the French and the Normans. Castles supported a high

culture and the making of pleasure gardens. The Tower of London was built to dominate a capital city.

Rome's first emperors lived in palaces on the Palatine Hill, within the city's fortifications. When the army had secured the countryside, palatial country villas could be built outside the city. Charlemagne, crowned *Imperator Romanorum* in 800, had a palace and garden in Aachen. It resembled Roman palaces and did not have its own fortifications. Castles, in the modern sense of fortified palaces occupied by princely families, were a product of the feudal system. The first Norman castles in England were made with timber palisades and earthworks. A motte, in Old French, could mean either a moat or a mound. The word was used for fortifications made by digging ditches, casting the soil inward and fixing wooden stakes at the top of the slope. The result was like a private hillfort. A fortified enclosure at the base of the mound, called a bailey, was a later addition. 'Bailey' comes from the French *baille*, or *basse-cour*, meaning 'lower court' (see p. 130). Motte-and-bailey fortifications did not have pleasure gardens but with the passage of time castles came to be built in stone and evolved into elaborate structures and cultural centres.

In England, the Normans made domestic gardens, castle gardens, hunting parks and monastery gardens. The Latin words used for green space in these estates included the following:

- *hortus* (or *ortus*): a generic word for garden grounds of all kinds (and *ortolanus*, a gardener);[3]

3.3 a, b Warkworth Castle illustrates the motte and bailey pattern, with a stone *donjon* built on a motte. There could have been a herber within the bailey, a pleasance outside the walls and vegetable gardens beyond the battlements. The castle protects the neck of a loop in the River Coquet and overlooks the river and the sea. There are views of the River Coquet and the North Sea from the battlements.

3.4 a, b (a) Diagram of an eleventh-century castle with wooden pallisades enclosing the baileys. (b) Model of Carisbrooke Castle, as re-built in stone, in the fourteenth century.

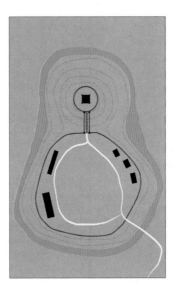 

3.5 A laughing meadow is a good place for listening to minstrels (see pp. 96–7). Turf was cut in meadows and re-laid at regular intervals, probably because the flowers died in courtyard conditions. The Lady's Bedstraw (*Galium verum*) in the foreground contains coumarin, which kills fleas.

- *gardinum*: a kitchen garden (and *gardinarius*, a kitchen gardener);[4]
- *pomarium*: a utilitarian orchard for fruit;[5]
- *vergier*: a pleasure orchard for enjoying the summer, often surrounded by walls, hedges and moats;[6]
- *viridarium*, *virgultum*, *virectum*: a green place for pleasure. Bartholomew de Glanville (also known as Bartholomew the Englishman) wrote an encyclopaedia in 1240 which noted that: 'And sometime an herber is called *virgultum*, (*viridarium*) or *viretum*, and is a green place and merry with green trees and herbs';[7]
- *herbarium* (or *herber*): a small garden for flowers, aromatic herbs and turf;[8]
- *pratum*: a meadow, primarily for grazing animals, but also a place to enjoy grass and herbs.[9]

England's High Middle Ages lasted from 1250 to 1400. Gardens were unaffected by the Italian Renaissance during this time but there were several garden types. Instead of '*the* Medieval garden', it is necessary to consider the similarities and differences between village gardens, castle gardens, castle parks, manor gardens and monastic gardens.

Village gardens

Place names often survive longer than artefacts and this evidence has been used to argue that because the names are old, the villages must be old.[10] It now seems more likely that, before the Norman Conquest, most people lived in simple mud-and-thatch huts near the fields they cultivated. Peasants owned little of value, except animals, and there was more need to protect crops from animals than possessions from raiders. It is possible that craftsmen lived in more village-like clusters. The word 'peasant', like the word 'pagan', derives from the Latin *pagus*, meaning 'country district'. The word 'hamlet', deriving from the Frankish *haim* ('home'), is applied to a small group of buildings without a church.

The Normans created new centres of power. William the Conqueror granted land to vassals in return for military and other services. The *Domesday Book* shows the king holding 17 per cent of the land, the barons had 48.5 per cent and the Church had 26.5 per cent.[11] The lord-to-vassal relationship was replicated down to peasants who cultivated the land and gave a tenth of their produce, a tithe, to their lord. Historians call this the feudal system and are increasingly aware of its pre-Norman roots. As used by the Normans, the system created great concentrations of wealth and reasons for establishing towns and villages: near castles, manor houses, cathedrals and harbours. But rich and poor families continued to grow food on land near their dwellings. Poorer families sent their children to work as servants in better-off households. One could describe the fenced and cultivated land beside dwellings as 'gardens' but in every class of society, the primary use of land near dwellings was to grow food. Flowering plants were a luxury, especially for the poor folk who might have to use any fruit they grew, or chickens they raised, to pay taxes. Any person with a superior position in the feudal hierarchy could have inferiors to help work the land but most people, including priests, were involved with growing their own food.

Sir Thomas More's *Utopia* was published at the end of the Middle Ages (1516) and, though he looked to the future, his ideas about gardens were Medieval. The gardens in Utopia were cultivated

> *with great care, so that they have both vines, fruits, herbs, and flowers in them; and all is so well ordered and so finely kept that I never saw gardens anywhere that were both so fruitful and so beautiful as theirs ... indeed, nothing belonging to the whole town that is both more useful and more pleasant.*[12]

He also wrote of a garden where he and a guest 'sat down on a green bank and entertained one another in discourse'.[13] This was an upper-class activity.

Croft gardens

The layout of post-Conquest Medieval villages is known from excavations and from aerial photographs of abandoned settlements. Dwellings were usually on both sides of a track but were in separate plots and set behind fences and hedgerows, making them unlike the 'Medieval' English villages which have survived. Tracks were unpaved

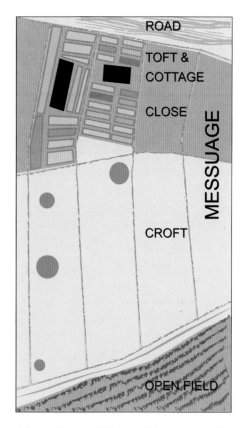

3.6 A 'toft and croft' (also called a 'messuage') was the area of land granted by a feudal lord to a tenant family to use for a homestead, vegetables, grazing and fruit. The 'toft' was the building site. The 'croft' was for growing food. The enclosure in which the cottage stood could be called a 'close' or a 'curtilage'.

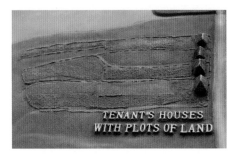

3.7 Model of toft and croft village housing, at Bodiam (see Figure 3.37).

3.8 Laxton is one of the few English villages where a 'champion' open field landscape survives (i.e. 'an expanse of level open country; a plain unbroken by hills, woods', *OED*). One can imagine teams of oxen ploughing long thin strips.

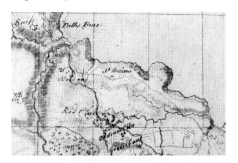

3.9 a, b Only the stone church in a walled cemetery survives in this part of the 1747–55 Roy Map. It shows dwellings in red and crofts bounded by red lines. The grey lines outside the settlement indicate cultivation in run-rig strips.

and wide, because of the cart drivers' need to avoid mud and ruts. Plots were usually long and thin, extending from the track at the front to a footpath at the rear. Beyond were the communal fields, woods and pastures. Open fields were divided into ridge-and-furrow strips, typically ploughed by teams of six or eight oxen. This arrangement was called 'run-rig' in the north of England and in Scotland because of the alternating 'runs' (depressions) and 'rigs' (ridges). Tenants also had grazing rights on meadow land (L. *pratum*, mead, meadow or hay-field). The enclosed land surrounding the dwelling was part cultivated and part grazed.

No garden plans or drawings survive but manorial records describe the use of peasant gardens. The cultivated land was used for vegetables and herbs, grown for the pot. Pottage (also called porray) was the normal meal in Medieval England (see Figure 3.0). The ingredients were beans, peas, cabbage, onions, leeks and garlic. They were cooked in fat, slowly, and flavoured with salt and herbs. Having cooked pulses in many ways, I recommend this recipe – the granularity of the pulses blends with the slipperiness of the vegetables and the aroma of the herbs. Cereals, grown in open fields beyond the garden gate, were added to the pottage and used to make bread and beer. Meat was an occasional luxury, most often from chickens and pigs.

Medieval property terms can be confusing and inconsistent but provide useful information about dwellings and gardens:

- *cottage*: a small dwelling house;
- *close*: an enclosure around or beside a building;
- *toft*: a level surface (literally 'site for building'); a homestead, the site of a house and its outbuildings;

3.10 A scene from *Les Très Riches Heures* shows a cottage and close, in France. The close has a wattle fence, a sheep pen, bee hives, an apple tree and magpies.

3.11 Cottages at Na Geàrrannan on the Isle of Lewis, with small fields beyond. The Anglo-Saxon word 'croft' survives in Scottish and means a smallholding used as arable or pasture land. Cottages with thatched roofs, known as 'black houses', were often stone-built but did not have chimneys or glazed windows. The 'toft and croft' arrangement was common in Europe.

- *croft*: a piece of enclosed ground, used for tillage or pasture; a small agricultural holding worked by a peasant tenant;
- *messuage*: the area of land intended for a dwelling house and its appurtenances;
- *curtilage*: a small court, yard, or piece of ground attached to a dwelling house and forming one enclosure with it.[14]

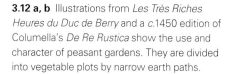

3.12 a, b Illustrations from *Les Très Riches Heures du Duc de Berry* and a *c.*1450 edition of Columella's *De Re Rustica* show the use and character of peasant gardens. They are divided into vegetable plots by narrow earth paths.

The above definitions help make sense of the word pairs found in legal documents: 'croft and toft', 'messuage and curtilage', 'cottage and close'. The key distinctions are between built/unbuilt and enclosed/unenclosed land. They do not say much about the use of land, which varied with the size of a landholding, soil conditions, crops grown, animals kept and the nature of any other trades carried on by members of the family. But some generalisations can be made. Land near the house door was used for outdoor activities, including washing and preparing vegetables. With the door open for much of the year, the close could function as an outdoor work-room. Other fenced land was used for growing food. If the family had sufficient land, a wattle fence, hedge or ditch would be used to create a second enclosure for animals (pigs, cows, ducks, sheep) which would be taken to graze on common land during daytime. Fruit trees could be planted in the second enclosures and prosperous villagers had separate orchards. An illustration from *Les Très Riches Heures du Duc de Berry* shows a messuage and curtilage in winter (Figure 3.10). The magpies in the foreground were welcome because of the noise they made if a fox or a human intruder entered the yard.

3.13 a, b A timber-framed wattle-and-daub Medieval house at the Weald and Downland Open Air Museum.

Re-creations of Medieval gardens often have mown grass paths and decorative wattle fencing round planting beds (see Figure 3.62). There is a lack of textual or archaeological evidence for this arrangement and there are reasons for thinking it would not have been used in village gardens: (a) lawn mowers had not been invented and scything narrow paths would have been awkward; (b) narrower and weed-free paths would have allowed more food to be produced; (c) low wattle fences would not have protected vegetable beds from chickens or other animals but might have been used to form slightly raised beds with horticultural advantages (warmth, drainage, protection, etc.).

Houses were usually set back from roads and built at right angles to tracks. When the thatched roof and mud walls began to decay, a new house was built alongside and the

3.14 Bayleaf is a fourteenth-century farmhouse, originally from Chiddingstone, in Kent, and now at the Weald and Downland Open Air Museum. The Medieval garden, designed by Dr Sylvia Landsberg, has mown grass paths between vegetable beds.

3.15 The lines on the grass in the foreground mark the walls of a manor house at Wharram Percy. The red tiled building is post-Medieval and the land on the skyline was formerly open fields.

3.16 Wharram Percy is one of the most fully excavated Medieval villages in England. The plan shows tofts and crofts on both sides of a wide track with ridge and furrow fields surrounding the village. Gardens were used for vegetables, animals and fruit trees. They are unlikely to have contained non-utilitarian plants.

older structure became a store or byre. In a two-room long-house, one of the rooms was used for the family and the other room for protecting animals in winter. Cottagers kept chickens and one of the reasons for wattle fences round vegetable beds may have been to protect the crops from the chickens. Dorking chickens, which are a breed which survives from the Middle Ages, can only jump about 1 metre.[15]

Manor gardens

Manors, as the administrative units of the feudal system, were extremely varied. The Latin *manerium*, from which the word derives, meant 'a residence' but the term was applied to large swathes of territory. Some manors had several villages. Some villages had several manors. Some manors were fortified. Other manors were run by monasteries. The manor house was an administrative centre. It could control law courts, markets, fisheries, woods, commons, the appointment of priests and the allocation of land to peasants. By 1086, the Archbishop of Canterbury had feued 17 per cent of his land in order to meet his military obligation to supply 60 knights.[16] The manorial system was formalised by the Normans but existed in France and England before 1066. It is thought to be a hybrid of the Celtic tribal system with the Roman villa system. The manorial system reached its peak in 1300 and by 1500 its day had passed.

3.17 Ightham Mote is a fourteenth-century moated manor house with an internal courtyard (see Figure 3.44).

Extensive manorial records were kept, in Latin, and provide limited but conclusive information about the existence of gardens. The manor house (mansion, capital messuage) of Salton, in Yorkshire, can serve as an example:

They hold a manor in the vill of Salton where various houses are built, namely one hall with three chambers and a chapel, a kitchen, bakehouse, brewhouse, great stable, an orchard and a garden called the Pengarth. And on the north part of this manor one hall called the Guesthall with a chamber at the end, and the Gatehouse, and one great grange, woodshed, piggery and one maltkiln newly built; an orchard called Kilngarth and a garden called the Bengarth.[17]

The types of outdoor space around a manor house were similar to those on the peasant holdings discussed above. A nobleman could own several manors and several manor houses. He moved between them during the year, dispensing justice when in residence. Garden produce was used to feed the family when it was in residence and to generate income when production was surplus to needs. Some manor houses had pleasure gardens as well as productive gardens but, since there is no clear line of demarcation between manor houses and castles, discussion of these will be included with that of castle gardens, below. William the Conqueror created a host of feudal lords and it was only in the Late Middle Ages (after *c.*1350) that anyone outside the topmost stratum of society might have had pleasure gardens.

Castle gardens

The building of castles and castle gardens in the British Isles began in 1066 and continued for centuries. Their military effectiveness was diminished by cannon in the fourteenth century but castles still offered security against local disturbances. In the eighteenth century, their popularity returned for aesthetic and Romantic reasons. Castles were strongly built and many survive. Much is known about castle life and, although it is certain that castles had gardens, disappointingly little information about their character is available, for several reasons.

The first reason, itself poorly documented, is that the Christian ethics of the Middle Ages did not encourage luxury. Roman gardens had been places of ease, ostentation and occasional debauchery. Even worse, for devout Christians, they accommodated pagan shrines, family shrines and graven images of idolatrous gods. In 380, Theodosius, who was a Spanish-born emperor and had visited the province of Britannia, issued an edict (the *Cunctos populos*) which declared Catholic Christianity the one true faith:

> *It is decreed that in all places and all cities the* [pagan] *temples should be closed at once, and after a general warning, the opportunity of sinning be taken from the wicked. We decree also that we shall cease from making sacrifices. And if anyone has committed such a crime, let him be stricken with the avenging sword.*[18]

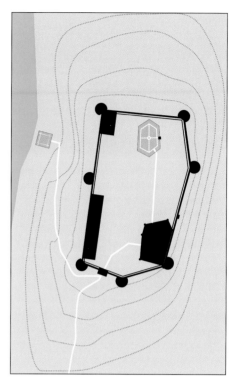

3.18 Diagram of castle, with a herber in the bailey, a pleasance beside the lake and a wall-walk (alure) giving views of the landscape.

3.19 Tintagel Castle has a garden enclosure dated to *c*.1230. Creighton comments that 'Given its incredibly exposed, wind-blasted position on a rocky coastal promontory, there is no chance that the garden was intended as a utilitarian feature.' He sees it as a 'medieval literary landscape made real' and a 'venue for lovers' trysts'.[19] Mowl suggests it was a bowling green.[20]

3.20 There are garden enclosures beneath the walls of Craigmillar Castle, outside Edinburgh. They can be seen from the wall-walks but it is not known how they were planted: they may have been places to walk in which flowers and luxury foods, such as rare fruits, were grown.

3.21 a, b, c The Little Castle at Bolsover was built in a revived Medieval style, in 1621, with the inner bailey as a garden and the outer bailey (base court) as a service yard. The fountain has a Renaissance character but there is a Medieval flavour to the enclosed garden and the way in which it is viewed from the castle windows and the wall-walk. It cannot have been a striped lawn.

Gildas, in Britain, had the same ideological framework and wrote of 'those diabolical idols of my country, which almost surpassed in number those of Egypt, and of which we still see some mouldering away within or without the deserted temples'.[21] Pagan idols were made of wood. They had been burned, or had rotted away, by the eleventh century, but their existence had not been forgotten. Edward English questions how we should understand 'the preoccupation of our early Medieval sources with pagan practices' and concludes that 'the condemnation of pre-Christian patterns of behaviour helped define the identity of the Christian community'.[22]

A second problem with castle gardens is that castle life was busy and there was always a shortage of land within castle precincts. Open land served many purposes. Vegetable patches were rare within castle precincts and 'most castle gardens were accessories to a lady's bower'.[23] In times of siege, land within the bailey had to

3.22 Restormel Castle had a private stair from the lord's apartment to the wall-walk so that 'Access to the most panoramic views of all was thus directly available from the "deepest" and most private space within the entire site.'[24]

3.23 Viollet le Duc's drawing of the Castle of Arques shows a wall-walk and the probable mixture of mud, men, animals, plants and buildings within the bailey of a Medieval castle.

accommodate food, fuel, soldiers and animals. When castles were abandoned, their gardens did not survive. Then, as society advanced, land uses changed. Castles became stately homes and land was used for lawns and flowers. When early archaeologists explored castles, they had no technical skill in garden archaeology.

A third problem is that Medieval art was religious and symbolic. The few illustrations which show castle gardens tend to have been produced at the end of the period.

A fourth problem is that monasteries were the great repositories of books and, when Henry VIII dissolved the monasteries, their libraries were lost. This may be why most of the surviving illustrations of Medieval gardens are from continental Europe.

A fifth problem is that the use of castles changed. Sieges of Stirling Castle and Blair Athol Castle during the 1745–6 Jacobite Rising ended the age of castle warfare in Britain. After that, some castles remained in government ownership as military quarters, some were abandoned as ruins and many became aristocratic residences with grand gardens. In 1882, Sir John Lubbock piloted an Ancient Monuments

3.24 a, b Stirling Castle had a wall-walk, gardens within the fortifications and a pleasure garden in the hunting park below the castle. The castle has a courtyard which may have been used for football – the world's oldest surviving football (*c.*1540) was found here.

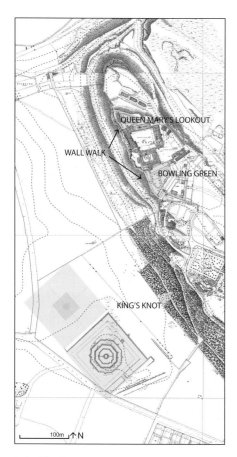

3.25 The Renaissance garden below Stirling Castle is believed to have been made in 1627–8, by a 'skilful and well-experimented' gardener, called William Watts.[25] The King's Park in which its lies was enclosed by William the Lion at the end of the twelfth century, for hunting. The wall-walk (alure), shown in yellow, had views of the King's Knot. There was a bowling green within the fortifications.

Protection Act through parliament. He was the author of *Pre-Historic Times,* the best-known archaeology book on the nineteenth century, and his father-in-law, General Pitt Rivers, became the first inspector of Ancient Monuments.[26] Pitt Rivers is regarded as the originator of scientific archaeology and also made a large eclectic garden, the Larmer Grounds. But his two interests do not seem to have come together and when ancient monuments received statutory protection, in 1947, they came to be managed

3.26 The bailey of Rochester Castle, now maintained like a sports field, is likely to have been more like the drawing (Figure 3.23) of the Castle of Arques. The battlements provided fine views of the Medway Valley. Nesting boxes for doves are built into the north wall, above the roofline of the *donjon*.

like sports fields. This makes it difficult to imagine how the external space around castle buildings might have looked in Medieval times.

As discussed in Chapter 2, Anglo-Saxon kings, unlike their Roman predecessors, did not make sophisticated gardens. Pleasure garden design therefore re-started after the Norman Conquest and the models, as for Norman architecture, came from northern France. An un-Germanic and un-Nordic palace culture was reintroduced to the British Isles. The best evidence for the existence of English castle gardens and fortified palace gardens comes from the royal account books which detail payments to builders and gardeners. They yield little information about the use or the visual character of castle gardens.

3.27 Flowers were often planted beneath windows in Medieval gardens, as perhaps here, at Little Moreton Hall.

3.28 The Palace of Westminster in the fourteenth century (shown in colour). Westminster Hall, the Jewel Tower, two cloister-garths and the Infirmary Garden survive.

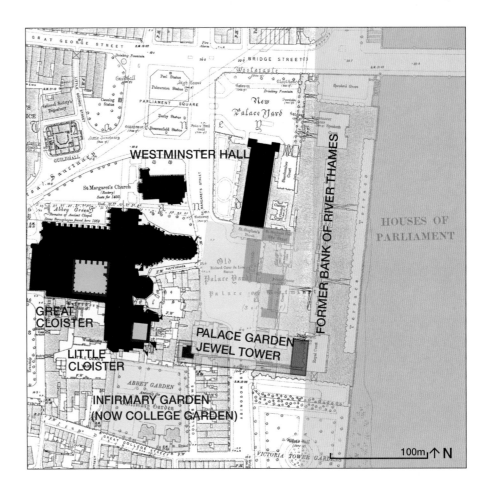

John Harvey spent 40 years trawling building records before publishing a book on Medieval gardens in 1981. He had a keen interest both in the functions of different types of planting and in the Latin words used to describe what we loosely call 'gardens'. Harvey explains that the idea of making pleasure gardens, forgotten since Roman times, was reintroduced to England after the Norman Conquest:

> *Somewhere about 1092 can be placed the famous visit of William Rufus to the garden of Romsey Abbey. Wishing to see Edith of Scotland, the heiress of the Saxon line, then aged twelve and boarding in the convent school, he and his courtiers demanded admission 'as if to look at the roses and other flowering herbs'. Gerard, Archbishop of York, died on 21 May 1108 'in a certain garden* (viridario) *near to his house' where, being somewhat ill, 'he had gone to lie down to enjoy the open air with a healthier breeze, to which the flowers of the plants, breathing sweetly, gave life'.*[27]

3.29 a, b The Jewel Tower and a moat, now dry, bounded the garden of the Palace of Westminster. A case could be made for restoring the water and making a re-created Medieval garden, as illustrated on the notice board.

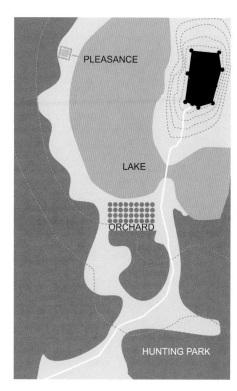

3.30 Diagram of a castle in a designed landscape with an artificial lake, a hunting park, a pleasance and an orchard. Park scenery was viewed from wall-walks and windows.

Bartholomew de Glanville gives a charming description of flowers growing in a mead (Trevisa, 1399, spelling modernised):

> *Meads are high with herbs and grass and flowers of diverse kinds. For their fairness and greenness, it is said that meads laugh. They please the sight, have a sweet odor and feed the taste with the savour of herbs.*[28]

In a chapter on grass, de Glanville stresses the importance of treading or beating turf to prevent it becoming too lush and to make it burst into seed.

Castle landscapes

The English word 'castle', derived from the Latin *castrum* and the French *castel*, took on its present meaning after the eleventh century. The Norman word *donjon* (from the Latin *dominarium* 'power of a lord', cognate with *dominus* and *domain*), explains why the Normans built castles in England: to dominate the land. The Anglo-Saxons fought on foot at the Battle of Hastings, with a shield-wall behind a stockade. The attacking Normans fought as cavalry, using heavy warhorses and armoured knights. After a hail of arrows, they charged and fought from horseback (see p. 53). The tactic

3.31 a, b Dramatic sites gave castles military strength, an imposing character and good views. (a) Norham Castle commanded the border between England and Scotland. (b) Bamburgh Castle commanded the Northumberland coast.

worked at Hastings and enabled the Normans to take control of England. Mobile cavalry was then quartered in hastily built castles (see Figure 3.4). Earth was dug to form a circular ditch with a central mound (the motte) defended with stakes made from prepared timber brought from Normandy. A larger fenced area (the outer bailey) was then added to accommodate men, horses and equipment. If a castle had two baileys, the inner bailey gave access to the hall, kitchen, well and residential chambers, often

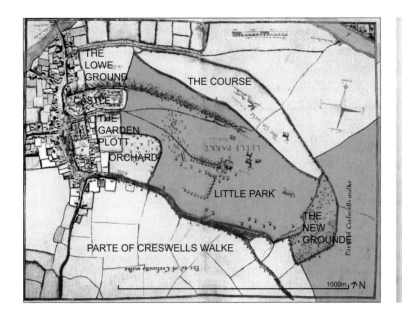
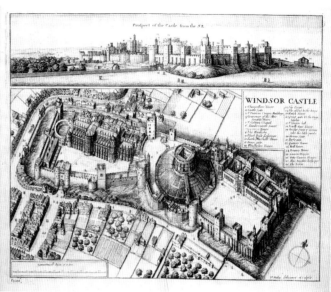

3.32 a, b William the Conqueror built a motte and bailey castle at Windsor. The three baileys, which survive, were wooden stockades in 1200. (a) John Norden's plan of 1607 shows the Little Park, the Course, the Orchard, the Garden Plott, the Lowe Ground and three baileys (now called the Upper, Middle and Lower Wards). The River Thames is north of the castle and Windsor High Street is across the river. (b) Wenceslaus Holler's plan c.1660 shows the Upper Ward (right) with an unkempt Medieval bailey.

built against the castle walls. The outer bailey contained stables, workshops and stores. Tournaments could be held within a bailey, or outside the castle wall, and viewed from the wall-walk.

When the knights' families arrived from France, timber *donjons* were replaced with well-built stone towers. The aim was still to dominate territory and they were placed at carefully chosen points in the landscape: on high ground, beside rivers, overlooking towns and on sites which the Romans or Anglo-Saxons had fortified for similar reasons. The word 'castle' is now used to describe buildings with domestic, military and visual roles. The domestic role was to allow a comfortable and cultured life. The military role was to govern England. The visual role was to symbolise lordship. Intimidating the Anglo-Saxon peasants was cheaper and more pleasant than fighting them. In peacetime, castle residents seeking wide views and fresh air could walk on the battlements. As England became a safer place, parks, orchards and gardens could be made below the battlements. The Normans made herbers for herbaceous plants, as discussed above, and hunting parks beyond the fortifications, as discussed below. The sea made Britain relatively more secure than continental Europe.

John Harvey assembled the evidence for the design of landscape parks in the vicinity of English castles. He wished to correct the orthodox view that English landscape design and woodland planting began with the Renaissance:

> *To sum up, it may be said that there is ample proof that ornamental gardening flourished, in England as well as in north-western Europe, from the late eleventh century if not earlier;*

3.33 The bailey of Warwick Castle is now surrounded by a curtain wall. Once busy with servants, craftsmen, mud, animals, noble visitors and those summoned to manorial courts, the bailey is now thronged with tourists.

that it was based on a keen delight in the appearance of plants and their perfumes, and also in the sight and sound of running water. Trees were planted, not only for timber or for fruit, but as decorative adjuncts to houses; the therapeutic value of their shade was recognized, and walking under trees, or where their beauty could be appreciated, was an accepted recreation and also a factor in convalescence ... For the Middle Ages, like all periods of high and refined culture, was a time when men and women loved gardens and trees.[29]

Harvey's evidence came from building accounts, manorial rolls and other documents. He discovered, for example, that by the time of Edward I (1239–1307) London had 'a nursery trade able to supply trees, flower plants and turf ready for laying'.[30] Since this was written, in 1981, study of the physical remains of castle parks and gardens has become 'one of the fastest growing branches of modern British archaeology'.[31]

Hunting was less important in the culture of Greece and Rome than in West, Central and East Asia.[32] But when the Roman Empire disintegrated 'Europe became dominated by its own kind of equestrian warrior, the Medieval mounted knights. Therefore, 'the royal hunt acquired new significance and elite hunting became commonplace, even mandatory'.[33] Prowess in hunting became a training for war, an exciting sport, a demonstration of power and:

There was also a strong religious element to the pleasures of the chase. It was believed that Man had once had the same level of senses as the animals but that this had been lost at the Fall; thus the appreciation of the quarry's skill and dexterity during the chase represented a way of getting closer to the perfect nature of Mankind that had existed in

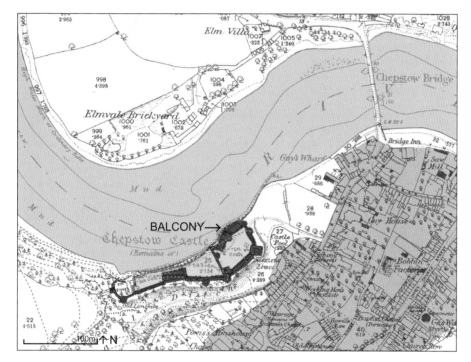

3.34 a, b (a) Chepstow Castle overlooks a gorge on the River Wye. (b) The gloriette, recorded in 1271, is thought to have been part of the Great Hall. It stands on the cliff edge in the Lower Bailey and has spectacular views. The balcony overlooking the river is thought to have been a garden-type space.

Eden. There was also a strong sexual dimension to hunting. Hunts were often elaborately planned and staged activities, involving hundreds of men and women, and the themes of pursuing and capturing the quarry readily lent themselves to the ideas of courtly love and sexual largesse.[34]

Hunting parks were formed on land near castles. The men hunted and the women watched, admiringly, often from a special building known as a 'gloriette'. The

3.35 a, b, c (a) Leeds Castle is advertised as 'the loveliest castle in England'.[36] (b) The gloriette has a view of the lake and former hunting park (now a golf course). (c) the lake was made by Edward I in the 1280s, for Eleanor of Castile. He was a strong king and she was a devoted wife. The gloriette was built as a pleasure palace with views of a designed landscape used for hunting and festivities.

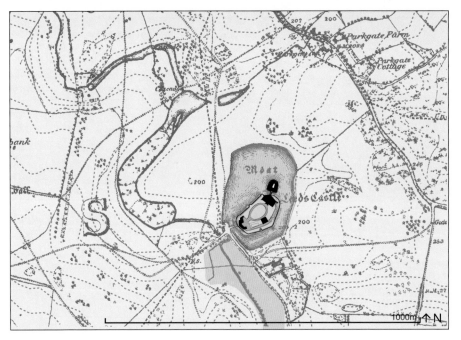

etymology of 'gloriette' is uncertain but in England it is associated with castles rather than fortified manors.[35] Gloriettes have been identified at Chepstow Castle, Leeds Castle, Corfe Castle and Canterbury Cathedral Priory.

Leeds Castle has a famous gloriette surrounded by designed parkland. Its present appearance has been changed by post-Medieval alterations but the structure of the landscape remains Medieval. The Normans built a timber motte-and-bailey fort on a site previously used by the Anglo-Saxons. This was replaced with a stone castle in 1119 and when Edward I married Eleanor of Castile, in 1278, it was re-built as a

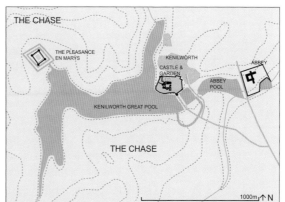

3.36 a–d (a) Kenilworth Castle, looking across the former lake bed. (b) Plan of the castle, the former lake and the pleasance in the fifteenth century (based on John Harvey). (c) Montage to show the Medieval lake. (d) Reeds growing in the dock at the head of a channel which led from the lake to a pleasance on the far shore (indicated by a red arrow). The original pleasance was made by Henry V in 1414–17 and one can imagine it being used like the garden in Chaucer's 'Franklin's Tale' (written in the late fourteenth century):

palatial castle. The River Len was damned to make ponds and between 1278 and after Eleanor's death in 1290, the site became 'a huge water garden',[37] as John Harvey explains:

> *Count Robert II of Artois there enclosed the park in 1295 and also began a 'House in the Marsh' with a Gloriette in a great pool, approached by a bridge, an aviary and a 'chapel of glass', still unfinished at his death in 1302. Count Robert's works included a fantastic series of water-engines based on the Arabic* Book of Mechanical Devices *(AD 1206) of Ibn al-Razzas al-Jazari of Diyarbakir* [in eastern Turkey]. *These produced surprise jets and showers, a talking owl, gadgets which dropped the unwary into a mass of feathers, blew soot and flour in their faces before confronting them with mirrors, and played many other practical jokes ... it is of the highest significance that the tradition of* burladores *in Spanish gardens, to drench the visitor, is not a device of the Renaissance but has a far older Islamic origin.*[39]

When Harvey writes of 'the highest significance', he implies a possible Islamic influence on Renaissance gardens. It could be that the making of square enclosures and knot gardens in Renaissance Italy was influenced by Islamic gardens in

> *Now one fine day, not too long after dawn,*
> *Into a nearby garden they had gone,*
> *In which they had arranged to be provided*
> *With victuals and such else as they'd decided,*
> *And there they frolicked all the livelong day.*
> *This happened on the sixth morning of May,*
> *May having painted with its tender showers*
> *This garden full of many leaves and flowers;*
> *And man's hand with its craft so skillfully*
> *This garden had arranged that truthfully*
> *There'd never grown one like it, such a prize,*
> *Unless you count the one of Paradise;*
> *So fresh the smell of flowers and the sight,*
> *There's not a heart that wouldn't there be light.*[38]

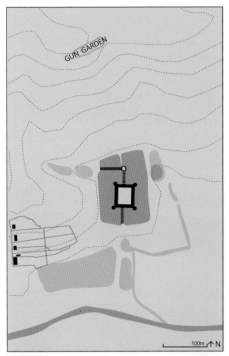

3.37 a, b Bodiam Castle was set in a designed landscape, with shallow artificial lakes, and could be viewed from a terrace now called the Gun Garden (see Figure 3.50).

the Levant, Sicily, North Africa and Southern Spain – just as the design of European castles was influenced by Crusader castles. Another Norman, King William II of Sicily, made a famous palace garden for Zisa Castle in Palermo. Known as the Genoard, or Gennoardo, its name derived from the Arabic *Jannat al-Ard* meaning 'earthly paradise'.

Another lake with aesthetic and defensive roles was made outside Kenilworth Castle. Henry V then added a pleasance on the west side of the lake.[40] Howard Colvin states that 'The quadrangular site [of the pleasance] was moated; there were towers at the four corners. The center was laid out as a garden and there was a dock for boats to bring parties of courtiers on summer outings from the castle.'[41] Castles also had orchards and vineyards outside the fortifications. Their management is detailed in estate records. A large orchard is shown in John Norden's 1607 map.

Monastic gardens

Indian monasticism pre-dates Western monasticism and has similarities.[42] The movement of ideas is hard to tack but the earliest records of asceticism are in Hindu sacred texts. Hymn 136 in Book 10 of the *Rig Veda* (1700–1100 BCE) describes how 'The Munis, girdled with the wind, wear garments soiled of yellow hue. They, following the wind's swift course go where the Gods have gone before.' The *munis* and *rishis* of the *Vedas*, the *Ramayana* and the *Mahabharata* were acestic hermits, some of whom, like the *munis*, took vows of silence. They were succeeded in historic times by *yogis*, *sadhus*, *swamis* and other ascetics. Nearer to Europe, the Essenes were an ascetic Jewish sect who lived on the west shore of the Dead Sea. The encounter between Christianity and Eastern asceticism is thought to have begun in Alexandria during the first century CE. St Anthony (c.251–356) is known as Anthony of Egypt, Anthony of the Desert and the Father of All Monks. Earlier monks had lived on the fringes of towns. Anthony withdrew to the desert. His biography records that after a desert journey of three days and three nights, he came to 'a very lofty mountain, and at the foot of the mountain ran a clear spring, whose waters were sweet and very cold; outside there was a plain and a few uncared-for palm trees'.[43] Friends brought him a spade and St Anthony

having found a small plot of suitable ground, tilled it; and having a plentiful supply of water for watering, he sowed. This doing year by year, he got his bread from thence, rejoicing that thus he would be troublesome to no one, and because he kept himself from being a burden to anybody. But after this, seeing again that people came, he cultivated a few pot-herbs, that he who came to him might have some slight solace after the labour of that hard journey.[44]

St Anthony became an early subject for hagiography. Books spread monastic ideas across Europe. Anthony had lived alone and the word 'monk' derives from the Greek *monos*, meaning 'single' or 'alone'. Later monks were often cenobitic, from the Greek from *koinos*, 'common' and *bios*, 'life'. Archaeological evidence indicates that monastic ideas reached the British Isles from North Africa and the Levant, probably arriving with traders in small boats. The early Celtic monasteries 'were merely settlements where the Christians lived together – priests and laity, men, women, and children alike – as a kind of religious clan'. Single-sex monastic communities of monks and nuns formed at a later date. Two of the best-known examples are Skellig Michael and Monkwearmouth-Jarrow. Skellig Michael has circular clochans, as used for other dwellings in Ireland, and Monkwearmouth-Jarrow, though built in stone and with Roman details, resembles the planning of Anglo-Saxon long houses. Skellig Michael is scenically dramatic but there is insufficient evidence to determine the extent to which scenery determined the location of Celtic monastery sites.

St Benedict (480–547) founded 12 monasteries near Rome and wrote a Rule which became the kernel of European monasticism. Benedict stated:

The monastery should be so situated that all the necessaries, such as water, the mill, the garden, are enclosed, and the various arts may be plied inside of the monastery, so that there may be no need for the monks to go about outside, because it is not good for their souls.[45]

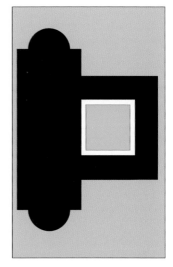

3.38 a, b (a) Diagram of a cloister garth. (b) The Little Cloister at Westminster Abbey was made for the infirmary and is now a semi-Baroque garden.

3.39 The clochans on Skellig Michael (the Great Skellig) symbolise the landscape isolation in which monasticism was established (see also Figure 2.30).

3.40 The St Gall plan shows a cloister-garth, a cemetery orchard, a herb garden and various enclosures for farm animals.

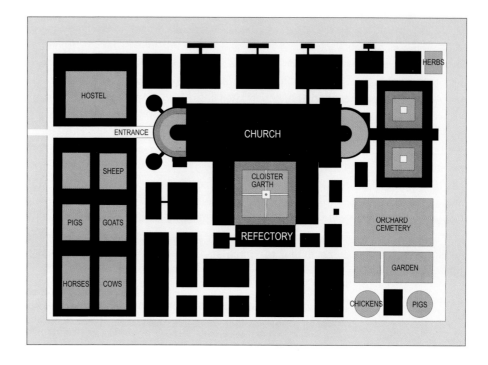

This led to plans for closed and self-contained communities which grew as much of their own food as they could. Benedict saw the 'Work of God' (hymns and prayer) as the most important task for a monk and believed that 'Idleness is the enemy of the soul; and therefore the brethren ought to be employed in manual labour.'[46] From Easter until the first of October monks were enjoined to 'go out in the morning from the first till about the fourth hour, to do the necessary work'.[47] The monks lived as a community and, like Adam and Eve after they left the Garden of Eden, and St Anthony, they grew their own food. The oldest plan of a Benedictine monastery was found in the St Gall library. It shows what became the classical plan for European monasteries, including those in Canterbury.

Pope Gregory, as discussed in Chapter 2, sent St Augustine to England in 595 and his mission resulted in the first cathedral at Canterbury. It was entirely destroyed at a later date but probably had a basilical plan and a cloister (see Figure 3.43). Britain's monasteries were repeatedly sacked during the Viking Age. They became secure after the Norman Conquest and the Benedictine monastic plan, which included cloisters, horticultural plots and orchards, was adopted. Many monastic buildings survive in good condition, though their use and management have changed. There are also ruined monasteries, often in country districts, which were abandoned when the monasteries were dissolved. They tell us much about the settings of monastic buildings but little about the use of the surrounding land. To discover how the land was used, it is necessary to use textual and archaeological evidence.

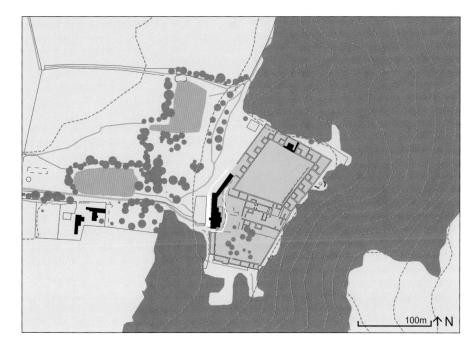

3.41 a, b, c Mount Grace Priory had private cells and gardens which only the resident monk entered. There are no records of what they grew but, given the austerity of the Carthusian order, the plants are more likely to have been functional than decorative.

After the Norman Conquest, British monasteries were laid out in the Benedictine manner. This had similarities with the layout of Roman villas. An abbey church took the place of a nobleman's mansion and was usually built, with a west–east axis, on the north side of a cloister-garth. 'Garth' is cognate with 'garden' but the space was not like a domestic herber. The garth was a peristyle courtyard enclosed by covered walks and gave corridor access to the main buildings of the monastery: a church for

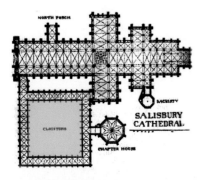

3.42 a, b Salisbury Cathedral cloister has a perfect cloister-garth, now managed in a semi-Gardenesque style.

prayer, a dormitory for sleeping, a refectory for eating and an infirmary for the sick. The infirmary was often built round a second garth, later called the 'little cloister'. As in a Roman villa, the main buildings were surrounded by horticultural plots used for growing the ingredients for pottage and for making drinks, including cider and wine. Monks were vegetarian in the early centuries but most of the orders were eating meat by the sixteenth century.

The Carthusian order remained vegetarian. They are sometimes called the 'gardening monks'. Each monk had a private cell and a private garden enclosed by a high wall. Food was delivered via a revolving compartment, called a 'turn', so that it could be received without the hermit being seen by the servant who brought it. No visitors entered the monks' cells and, consequently, there are no written accounts of how their gardens were used. Given the extreme austerity of Carthusian life, it does not seem likely that these gardens were intended for pleasure. At Mount Grace, Cell 8 had rectangular beds defined by paths of roofslate and Cell 9 had small square beds edged with stones.[48] Extrapolating from this find, the garden of Cell 8 has been 'restored' to a character somewhere between that of a Medieval lady's herber and a Baroque parterre (see Figure 3.41 (c)). Monastic gardens have also been recreated at Haverfordwest Priory.

Many cloister-garths survive in Britain, enclosed by beautiful arcaded walks. All have neat squares of mown grass. Some contain ornamental planting and some have gravestones and other features, like the recently made labyrinth in Norwich Cathedral. The Medieval character of cloister-garths is unknown: John Harvey found no evidence of their being used for ornamental horticulture and the gravestones in cloisters are post-Medieval. Similar spaces made for colleges, known as 'quadrangles' in Oxford and 'courts' in Cambridge, were used for fruit trees.[49] The famous waterworks plan of Christ Church Canterbury (see Figure 3.43) does not show the treatment of the cloister-garth but does show a rectangular garden nearby. It is 'marked on the plan as Herbarium, enclosed between wattled fences. Rows of plants are shown, so that there can be no doubt that the correct translation in this case is "herb-garden", especially as it lies on the way to the Infirmary.'[50] My hunch is that cloister-garths were managed in the same way as other areas of grass in Medieval gardens, now described as 'flowery meads' (see pp. 96–7), the scent of herbs being sweeter than that of unwashed monks.

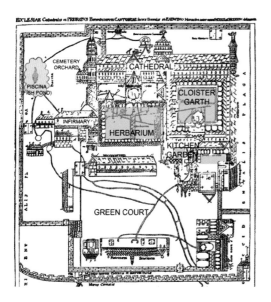 

3.43 a, b (a) Plan of the Benedictine Priory of Christ Church, Canterbury, in 1165 (related to the St Gall plan). (b) The cathedral cloister, rebuilt after 1377, has been used as a burial ground.

Medieval garden features

The following notes make use of word derivations and quotations, mainly from books printed after 1473. They confirm the persistence of ancient garden objectives: food, fruit, flowers, fish, visual delight, scents, places to sit, places to walk and places to play.

Hortus conclusus

The term *hortus conclusus* is often used in connection with Medieval gardens and comes from the Vulgate, a fourth-century translation of the Bible from Greek and Hebrew into Latin. Translated into English, *hortus conclusus* from the Song of Songs became 'well kepte garden' in the Coverdale version of the Bible (1535) and 'a garden inclosed' in the King James version (1604–11):

> *12: A garden inclosed is my sister, my spouse; a spring shut up, a fountain sealed.*
> *12: Hortus conclusus soror mea sponsa hortus conclusus fons signatus.*

The *OED* has two derivative meanings of *hortus conclusus*:

> *An enclosed, inviolate garden; in spiritual and exegetical tradition, the symbol of the soul, the Church, or the virginity of Mary.*

> *In Art, a painting of the Madonna and Child in an enclosed garden.*

Compared to the use of *hortus conclusus* by garden historians, these uses are older and much more significant. Frank Crisp, whose book on Medieval gardens was published in 1924, complained that 'no writer referring to a *Hortus Conclusus* can apparently avoid quoting Solomon'.[51] But they are right to do so. St Jerome (*c*.347–420) linked the enclosed garden to the Virgin Mary with his explanation of Line 12 of the Song of Songs:

> *That which is shut up and sealed reminds us of the mother of our Lord who was a mother and a Virgin. Hence it was that no one before or after our Saviour was laid in his new tomb, hewn in the solid rock. And yet she that was ever a Virgin is the mother of many virgins. For next we read: 'Your shoots are an orchard of pomegranates with precious fruits.' By pomegranates and fruits is signified the blending of all virtues in virginity. Song of Songs 5:10 'My beloved is white and ruddy'; white in virginity, ruddy in martyrdom.*[52]

St Jerome's account led to a host of Medieval paintings showing the Virgin Mary in enclosed gardens. They may have had an undue influence on historians' understanding of Medieval gardens. John Donne was the first writer in English to use *horti conclusi* in an English sentence, in 1624:

> *The University is a Paradise, Rivers of knowledge are there, Arts and Sciences flow from thence. Counsell Tables are Horti conclusi (as it is said in the Canticles) Gardens that are walled in, and they are Fontes signati, Wells that are sealed up; bottomlesse depths of unsearchable Counsels there.*[53]

The term *hortus conclusus*, and its English translation 'enclosed garden', is better suited to descriptions of religious space than of domestic space.

Courts and courtyards

'Medieval courtyard garden' is a cliché which should be used with extreme caution. The outdoor spaces described as courts and courtyards in Medieval literature were not gardens and did not belong to castles. They were domestic service yards (base courts) in Late Medieval manor houses. Before mansions had corridors (see p. 130), access to rooms was from courtyards. They were sometimes areas of grass with muddy paths, as in the drawing of Windsor Castle (see Figure 3.32). They sometimes had paved paths and the whole courtyard was sometimes paved. These courts were not herbers.

Herbers

The word 'herber' derives from the Old French *erbier* (or *herbier*) meaning 'a place covered with grass or herbage, a garden of herbs' (from the French *erba*, 'herb', and the Latin *herba*, 'grass', 'green crops', 'herbage', 'herb'). The primary component of a herber was herbs, in the botanical sense of plants which die back in winter and do not

3.44 Ightham Mote is a fourteenth-century house with an internal court that served as the base court of the house, not as a garden.

3.45 The courtyard in the gloriette at Leeds Castle may have contained sweet-smelling herbs but can never have been a sunny place.

have woody stems. We now group them as annual and perennial 'herbaceous plants'. Most grasses are herbaceous in the botanical sense of dying back each year. Some of the plants in a 'herber' had medical and culinary uses but they were not called herbs for this reason, as they are in modern English. Herbs could be grown in a border or in a sward, where grasses and flowers were natural companions. There was no reason to remove flowers from grass, because flowers were loved. This is revealed

3.46 The Pearl Poet dreamed of his lost daughter in a 'blissful bower'.

by the late fourteenth-century *Pearl Poem*. It tells of a father's sorrow at the loss of his young daughter, his pearl:

> *I entered in that garden green,* ['erber grene' in Middle English]
> *As August's season came around*
> *When corn is cut with sickles keen,*
> *There that pearl rolled into the ground,*
> *Shadowed with plants both bright and clean,*
> *Wallflower, ginger, gromwell abound*
> *Bright peonies scattered in between;*
> *Though they were seemly to be seen*
> *No less in their scent my sense caught;*
> *And there that jewel long has been,*
> *My precious pearl without a spot.*[54]

The Pearl Poet is thought to have lived in the north of England. After his young daughter's death, he falls asleep and dreams of being on the far side of a river. Now in a paradise garden, his daughter tells him not to grieve. He asks to see her 'blissful bower' (*blysful bor*) and is told 'thou may not enter within his tower' (*Þou may not enter wythinne hys tor*). 'Bower' rhymes with 'tower' and associates her with a castle. When herbers were made outside castles, it was easier to find space for trees and the word evolved into 'arbour', linked to the Latin *arbor*, 'tree' and the Italian *arboreta*, 'bower'. 'Herber' and 'arbour' were sometimes distinguished and sometimes conflated. An orchard, with trees growing in grass, could be a herber, a bower or an arbour.

Orchards

The word 'orchard' was probably formed by combining *hortus* with 'yard'. It was originally an enclosed space for growing both herbs and fruit. The *Gesta Romanorum, or, Entertaining Moral Stories* was written in Latin (*c.*1300) and translated into English (*c.*1510) with a vivid description of a Medieval castle. It has a lake, a fountain, a flower garden and an orchard 'with goodliest fruits':

> *A lofty tower and strong, the building stood*
> *Midst a vast plain surrounded by a flood;*
> *And hence one pebble-pavèd channel stray'd,*
> *That compass'd in a clustering orchard's shade:*
> *'Twas a choise charming plat; abundant round*
> *Flowers, roses, odorous spices cloth'd the ground;*
> *Unnumber'd kinds, and all profusely shower'd,*
> *Their fragrance might have stay'd man's parting breath,*
> *And chas'd the hovering agony of death.*
> *The sward one level held, and close above*

3.47 a, b Orchards at: (a) West Dean; and (b) Culross Palace. Medieval orchards were enjoyed as places to walk and pick ripe fruit. 'Flowers, roses, odorous spices cloth'd the ground' (see p. 84).

> *Tall shapely trees their mantles wove,*
> *All equal growth, and low their branches came,*
> *Thick set with goodliest fruits of every name.*
> *In midst, to cheer the ravish'd gazer's view,*
> *A gushing fount its waters upward threw,*
> *Thence slowly on with crystal current pass'd,*
> *And crept into the distant flood at last.*[55]

Fruits were highly valued and more often used to make drinks and desserts than eaten fresh. Cider was the most popular drink, after ale. Cottagers might grow one or two fruit trees in a croft. Manor house gardens might have three or four acres of enclosed orchard for apples, pears, cherries and nuts with vines on the walls. Peach and quince trees were more difficult to grow, and more expensive, but were good for making desserts. *The Pistil of Swete Susan*, written in the late fourteenth century, has a delightful account of a gated and moated garden with fruit trees, nuts and herbs. The planting includes 'the cherry and the chestnut', 'lovely pears', 'fresh walnuts', chives, shallots, peony, lovage, sage, marigold, rue, hyssop and rhubarb. Susan 'removed her clothes unguardedly' to wash in the garden and, following the story of Susanna in the Book of Daniel, was spied upon by lecherous old men.[56]

Bowers

The Anglo-Saxon *Chronicle* records that in 755 'As soon as the king's thanes in the lady's bower heard the tumult, they ran to the spot, whoever was then ready.'[57] The lady's bower was a private room in a palace which was little more than a large hall. Used in connection with gardens, a bower became 'a place closed in or overarched

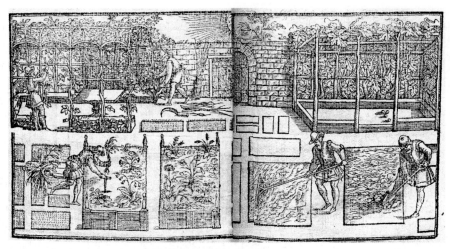

3.48 a, b (a) Thomas Hill's drawing of arbours. (b) A re-created arbour at Southampton Tudor House.

3.49 Sylvia Landsberg's re-creation of a bower, beside the Great Hall of Winchester Castle.

with branches of trees, shrubs, or other plants; a shady recess, leafy covert, arbour'. The *OED* gives an example of this usage from 1325 (*He busked hym a bour* – 'he built him a bower'). The distinction between bowers and arbours was established in the eighteenth century: 'Care must be had that you do not confound the word Bower with Arbour; because the first is always built long and arch'd, whereas the second is either round or square at Bottom, and has a sort of Dome or Ceiling at the Top.'[58]

Arbours

Arbours, in the sense of 'trees or shrubs, such as the vine, trained on framework or trellis-work' (*OED*), were popular in the Middle Ages but were probably given this name, instead of being called herbers, in the sixteenth century. Sir Philip Sidney writes of

> a fine close arbour: it was of trees whose branches so lovingly interlaced one the other, that it could resist the strōgest violence of eye-sight; but she went into it by a doore she opened; which moved him as warely as he could to follow her, and by and by he might heare her sing this song, with a voice no lesse beautifull to his eares, then her goodlinesse was full of harmonie to his eyes.[59]

This type of space came to be called a bower.

Vineyards

The evidence for Anglo-Saxon vineyards in Britain is 'not very substantial'.[60] Wine was drunk but may have been imported from the Continent. The arrival of the Normans, and the warming of the climate between the tenth and thirteenth centuries,

3.50 View of Bodiam Castle from the earthwork known as the Gun Garden (see Figure 3.37). 'It is most likely to have been a garden or a pleasance containing buildings and other features but it surely must have also functioned as a viewing platform for the landscape setting of the castle below.'[61] Grapes were cultivated in Norman England but there is no record of this site having been a vineyard.

encouraged the planting of vines and the making of wine. Vines suffered in the colder conditions of the thirteenth and fourteenth centuries but John Mirk wrote in *c.*1450 of 'a husband-man ... [who] hired men to his vineyard for labour' (*hyryd men to his vyneȝorde for labour*).[62]

Parks

Hunting, as a sport, has long been the favoured explanation for making parks in England but Rackham sees this as a myth.[63] Other explanations are that parks were a way of maintaining a supply of fresh meat, with the deer killed by officials, and a way of managing woods and grassland which created high-status scenery 'carefully arranged, in some sense landscaped, [as a] backdrop to castles and manor houses'.[64] As Sir Gawain approaches Bertilak's castle, he is deeply impressed by the scenery:

> *The hero had not crossed himself more than thrice ere he was aware in the wood of a dwelling on a hill above a clearing, on a mount, hidden under the boughs of many a huge tree about the ditches; a castle the comeliest that ever knight owned, set on a prairie a park all about, with its beautiful palace pinnacled full thick and surrounded with many a tree for more than two miles. The hero gazed at the castle on that one side as it shimmered and shone through the fair oaks.*[65]

Alures

The pleasure of walking on castle battlements was a precursor to the later pleasures of walking in gardens (see p. 140). A castle bailey accommodated outbuildings, servants, firewood, horses, cattle, chickens and, one may assume, deep sticky mud.

3.51 Deer had several roles in estate management. Depending on the size of the park, they provided a way of maintaining the land, a food supply, a sporting activity, a component of the scenery and a symbol of the lord's place in the world. Richmond Park had these roles for Richmond Palace (see Figure 4.16).

Unlike the bailey, wall-walks had paving, fresh air, good views and a degree of seclusion from the hubbub of castles, villages and fields. A wall-walk was called an alure (from the French *aller*, 'to go', which is cognate with 'alley'). The chronicle of Robert of Gloucester (*c*.1260–1300) records that:

> *Upon the alures of the castle the ladies then stood, and beheld this noble game, and which knights were good. All the next three days this noble behaviour, food and games, went on, in halls and in the fields.*[66]

The alure at Carlisle Castle was called the 'Ladies Walk'.[67] An alure could be 'a gallery, a walk by the parapets of a castle, a cloister'.[68] In the fifteenth century, the word

3.52 a, b Bodiam Castle has an alure with fine views. Women enjoyed wall-walks but the only female inhabitants of a castle were members of the lord's family.

3.53 Warwick Castle has fine views of the River Avon.

3.54 a, b Helmsley Castle had a wall-walk (alure) and an outer defensive bank which might also have had a recreational use. The apartments on the far side of the *enceinte* overlook the deer park (see Figure 3.55).

'alure' was occasionally used for garden walks: 'In this garden/ of many diverse hue ... In the allures/walking to and fro' (*In this gardyn / of many dyuerse hwe ... In the Allures / walking to and fro*). Later, it became the garden alley or allée.

Trellis

The word 'trellis' came into Middle English from Old French. It is derived from the Latin *tri* + *licium* ('three threads'). 'Trellis' was used for things made with woven wire. It was applied to a lattice grille and then to a framework made of wood and used for

3.55 Assumed boundaries of Helmsley Castle's hunting parks, overlaid on a mid-nineteenth-century Ordnance Survey map. The de Roos family apartments overlooked the Inner Park, also known as La Haye.

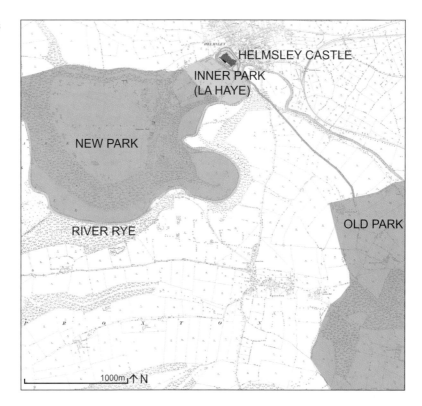

3.56 a, b There are good views from the battlements of Herstmonceux Castle and Bodiam Castle – and they would not have ornamental façades or windows if their primary purpose had been to resist a siege. The internal Green Court at Herstmonceux is overlooked by galleries and arcades.

climbing plants, vines or fruit trees. In Medieval gardens, trellis-work was frequently used to make vine tunnels.

Vegetables

As discussed in the first half of this chapter, the production of food was the primary role of Medieval gardens. Vegetable gardens produced the ingredients for making pottage and little else: beans, peas, cabbage, onions, garlic, leeks and herbs for flavouring. A pleasance with a herber was a luxury which noblemen could provide for their womenfolk or bishops for their distinguished guests. In the later Middle Ages, when rich men were moving from castles to grand houses with adjacent gardens, the compartments used for vegetables were the least likely to be used for pleasure and the most likely to be used for bee-keeping. Honey was the only available sweetner before the Crusades and bee hives were common in vegetable gardens of all types. Hives, made of wicker and straw, were protected from the rain in shelters or with bark, lime and dung.

Wattle fencing

The word 'wattle' was used in Old English, as a noun and a verb, to describe fences, walls and roofs made by interlacing the branches of trees. In Medieval gardens, the normal practice was to drive stakes into the ground and weave twigs between

3.57 A drawing of trellis-work by Thomas Hill. The central bed is likely to have been planted with flowering and sweet-smelling herbs.

3.58 Vegetables growing in beds supported by boards on either side of a narrow footpath.

3.59 Bees were kept in vegetable gardens, usually in a skep (an upside-down basket made of wicker or straw) from which extracting the honey was difficult. The photograph was taken at Kellie Castle, which is an Arts and Crafts re-working of a castle garden. The oldest part of the castle dates from 1360.

3.60 a, b Culross Palace was built 1597–1611 and the character of the original garden, like the restored garden, may have been halfway between Medieval and Renaissance.

3.61 Beds raised by boards, in a re-created Medieval garden at Michelham Priory. There is no evidence for wide gravel paths in Medieval gardens.

them. The resulting woven fence was rhythmically strong and attractive. Used round a lady's herber, the objectives are likely to have been shelter, privacy and elegance. Used round a vegetable plot, the objectives could have been aesthetic but seem more likely to have been functional. If the paths between raised beds were mud, not grass, as seems likely, then the vegetable garden would not have been a pleasant place for recreational walking. The functions of the wattle fence could have been to raise the soil, for warmth and drainage, and to protect plants from trampling by humans and hens.

Fish ponds and moats

The names 'fish pond' and 'moat', used in connection with Medieval dwellings, imply functional roles. They surely had these roles but, as Creighton argues, they also had the roles we associate with lakes and with garden water features at all points in history:

> *Traditional explanations for the phenomenon of moated sites, involving the need for defence and drainage of the homes of lesser lords, can only take us so far ... Moats have significant potential as ornamental sites, and four particular arrangements can be defined: moated platforms that contained gardens as well as a principal residence; small moats that are clearly subsidiary to a major residential site; paired moats; and sites with double (i.e. concentric) moats.*[69]

Future garden archaeology is likely to find more evidence of gardening activity in moated sites. At present, the best example is the pleasance at Kenilworth Castle (see p. 75) which survives as an archaeological site. There is a textual record of its use as

3.62 A symbolic Medieval garden with wattle fencing, bee hives and a fountain.

3.63 Linlithgow has been described as a 'palace' since 1429, at least, and it appears that 'the new approach from the east was deliberately contrived for visual effect, with the palace intended to be seen rising above the waters of Linlithgow Loch'.[70]

a pleasure garden and the moat could not have had a military function. Francis Bacon's Water Garden (see p. 124) has more in common with Medieval moated gardens than with Renaissance water features. The Kip and Knyff drawings, published in 1707, have many vignettes of moated water features. In Medieval gardens they were known as 'stew ponds' (from the French *estui*, a tub for keeping fish in a boat).

Fountains

Continental illustrations of Medieval gardens show fountains in herbers and girls bathing in them, as described in the *The Pistil of Swete Susan* (see p. 85). Fountains were also placed in courtyards to supply residents with fresh water. The oldest working fountain in Britain is in the courtyard of Linlithgow Palace.

Flowery meads and turf seats

'Meadow' and 'mead' are equivalent words. In Old English, 'meadow' was spelt *mædewan*, *mædua*, *mæduen*, *medwa*, etc. In Middle English, 'mead' was spelt *mæd*,

3.64 The cover of Frank Crisp's *Mediæval Gardens* shows a fountain in a *hortus conclusus*.

3.65 a, b Linlithgow has a castle-palace which took its present form in the two centuries after the 1424 fire. Its character is Late Medieval/Early Renaissance. The fountain, first recorded in a repair bill of 1542, is thought to be the oldest surviving fountain in Britain. Its closed crown is a royal symbol.

med, maied, meede, mede, etc. In modern English, 'mead' is a poetic equivalent of 'meadow' and the type of space described, as always, is a permanent sward of mixed grasses and herbs used for hay or pasture. A water-meadow was a special type of sward, carefully irrigated in spring so that the land warmed and then came to life earlier than other pastures.

Grass areas in Medieval gardens were made by laying turfs cut from meadow land and replaced every three to five years. Turf was also used as a fuel and as a building material for houses, garden walls and roofs. The best quality material for these purposes was 'flayed' from 'the uppermost portions of tightly knit sod from established grass-sedge pastures'.[71] Given this method of construction, it is natural that turf should also have been used for making the raised seats so often seen in illustrations of Medieval gardens. In 'The Merchant's Tale' (*c.*1386), Chaucer mentions a bench made of turfs:

> *This kyng of ffairye / thanne adoun hym sette*
> *Vp on a bench of turues / fressh and grene.*[72]

It may have been Milton who initiated the poetic love of flowery meads among English poets and gardeners. He wrote, in *Paradise Lost*, that 'Soft on the flow'ry herb I found me laid.'[73] Stephen Switzer's version of this passage quoted him as 'Soft on the flow'ry mead I laid me down.'[74] The popularity of flowery meads in gardens returned in the late nineteenth century (see p. 332).

3.66 A flowery mead in a (modern) garden.

3.67 After the Middle Ages, it was discovered that short turf from upland sites is better suited to making lawns than lank meadow grass. The foreground grass in the photograph is growing on oolitic limestone. The house in the middleground is Chedworth Roman Villa.

3.68 A re-created flowery mead at Michelham Priory.

3.69 A turf seat could be a place for romance.

3.70 a, b Re-created turf seat in Winchester Palace and Prebendal Manor House. The central areas are more likely to have been meadow grass.

Caespes, translated as 'turf' or 'sod', could also mean a hut or an altar made of sods. 'Level turf' was not made by sowing grass seed. It was made by laying sods and beating them into a level surface. Account books record the operation being repeated at frequent intervals. It could be that when removed from its natural habitat, the beautiful wild flowers which gave meadow turf its sweetness were succeeded by dock, thistles, nettles and other rank weeds.

Crescenzi advised his readers to 'Mow the meadows of the garden twice a year, so that they may remain beautiful' (*Secentur bis in anno prata viridarii, ut pulcra permaneant*) and Trevisa noted the distinction between grass from the hills and grass from valleys which is generally 'more ranke and fatte'.[75]

Turf seats are shown on continental European illustrations of Medieval gardens and their position was described by St Albertus Magnus:

> *Care must be taken that the lawn is of such a size that about it in a square may be planted every sweet-smelling herb such as rue, and sage and basil, and likewise all sorts of flowers, as the violet, columbine, lily, rose, iris and the like. So that between these herbs and the turf, at the edge of the lawn set square, let there be a higher bench of turf flowering and lovely; and somewhere in the middle provide seats so that men may sit down there to take their repose pleasurably when their senses need refreshment.*[76]

St Albertus Magnus's text was adapted by Crescenzi:

Along the edge of the garden should be planted fragrant herbs of all kinds, such as rue, sage, basil, marjoram, mint, and the like, and also flowers of every type, such as violet, lily, rose, gladiola, and the like. Between these plants and the level turf [caespitem planum] *raise and form* [another] *turf* [caespis elevator] *in the fashion of a seat, flowering and pleasant* [et quasi per modum sedilium aptatus, florens et amoenus].[77]

Turf seats are assumed to have been made in English Medieval gardens and feature in re-creations.

Cloister-garths

A cloister was the part of a monastery to which there was no public access. In English, the word is now used for a square greenspace surrounded by an arcade. The greenspace is sometimes called the cloister garden, with has tempted green-fingered church wardens into managing them as gardens. The Old English term was 'garth', normally used with a defining word, such as 'cloister-garth', 'apple-garth', 'willow-garth' and 'garden-garth'. 'Garth' meant 'a small enclosure' and there is no evidence for mown lawns or for ornamental plants having been planted in Medieval cloister-garths. They contained grass but how the grass was managed is unknown. Flowers were loved and grass-garths may well have been managed as level turf (*caespitem planum*) with meadow flowers. The modern name for this is a 'flowery mead'.

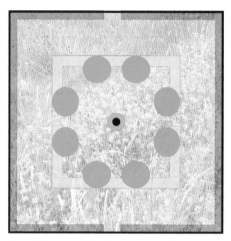

3.71 Diagram of a herber based on St Albertus Magnus's text.

3.72 The cloister-garth at Byland Abbey, in June. Buttercups hint at the flowery character which cloister-garths may once have had.

3.73 Drawing of a raised 'bed' by Hans Weiditz (from Frank Crisp's *Mediæval Gardens*).

Beds

The *OED* gives *c.*1000 as the earliest example of 'bed' used to mean 'a level or smooth piece of ground in a garden, usually somewhat raised, for the better cultivation of the plants with which it is filled; also used to include the plants themselves which grow in it'. This usage derives from the Anglo-Saxon *wyrt-beddum*. 'Wyrt' (wort) means 'plant' and, in connection with gardens, a 'bed' meant a 'cultivated' area. Anglo-Saxon and Medieval garden beds were primarily for utilitarian plants. 'Flower bed', for non-utilitarian plants, was an eighteenth-century name for what probably began as a Renaissance luxury. Early Medieval peasants slept in straw-filled sacks on earthen floors, so that making one's own bed probably required as much levelling as making a bed for vegetables.

Paths between beds were recessed and sometimes used for the European equivalent of Middle Eastern flood irrigation. An illustration in the *Gardener's Labyrinth* shows paths being used for irrigation (see Figure 4.15 (a)) and Thomas Hill explains that:

> The Gardener possessing a Pump in his ground, or fast by, may with long and narrow troughs well direct the water into all bedes of the Garden, by the pathes between, in watering sufficiently the roots of all such hearbes, which require much moisture.[78]

Crescenzi refers to irrigation ditches between garden plots.[79] This may be the source of Thomas Hill's idea and it may have been an Italian rather than a British tradition.

Borders

The *OED* has *c.*1400 as its earliest use of 'border' in connection with gardens: 'With all odour of herbs that on earth springs; /The borders about abashed with life' (*With all odour of herbis Þat on vrthe springes;/ The bourderis about abasshet with leuys*). Edmund Spenser, in 1590, wrote of butterflies in flowery beds and borders:

> There he arriving, round about doth fly,
> From bed to bed, from one to other border;
> And takes survey, with curious busy eye,
> Of every flower and herb there set in order.[80]

The word 'border' derives from the practice, often shown in old garden books, of using boards to make raised beds. Markham and Lawson advised their readers, in 1668, to make 'comely borders with the herbs aforesaid' adding that for these herbs 'you need not here raise your beds, as in the other garden, because summer towards, will not let too much wet annoy you, and these herbs require more moisture'.[81] Their comment explains a primary reason for 'borders': to improve the drainage. With the advent of knot gardens, 'border' came to be used for the strips of flowers behind the boards. This usage survives in the modern 'flower border', generally made without a 'board'

3.75 Thomas Hill (1571) shows a 'border' made with boards and used for choice flowering plants. The gardener is not a peasant.

3.74 A re-created Medieval garden at Southampton's Tudor House.

and around the edge of a space. In Medieval gardens it is likely that rectangular beds were raised and boarded, as a protection from wet trodden mud, and that there were no 'border beds', because vegetables do not flourish when competing with hedge plants.

Re-created Medieval gardens

Knots and mounts are features often linked with Medieval gardens. The reason for their not having been mentioned before is that they do not appear in records of Medieval gardens. Knot patterns were probably a Renaissance innovation (see p. 135) and are discussed in Chapter 5. The use of box to make garden patterns was probably a Baroque innovation and is discussed in Chapter 6.

Frank Crisp's *Mediæval Gardens* of 1924 was richly illustrated and he 'created a series of model mediaeval gardens in his garden at Friar Park, near Henley-on-Thames'.[82] Many more re-creations were made in the second half of the twentieth century. They are important, because no actual Medieval gardens have survived, but they have suffered from the sparcity and diversity of textual, archaeological and visual information. This makes it easier to criticise what has been done than to feel confident about what should have been done. To me, the re-creations do not have the 'look and feel' of Medieval gardens. The central problem may be that garden types have been confused. Peasant gardens, which were the vast majority, must generally have been 'rustic' in the sense of 'characteristic of rural workmanship; of a rough, plain, or simple

3.76 Despite its pattern, the use of box makes this twentieth-century 'knot garden' in Westminster College Garden more like a parterre. It has been replaced with a more appropriate design since the photograph was taken.

form or style' (*OED*). But monastery gardens, castle gardens and large manor house gardens may not have had these characteristics. They are more likely to have been beautifully made by skilled workmen for elite clients. The buildings, books, clothes and paintings they possessed were wonderful. Why should they have wanted rustic gardens? The main problems with British re-creations of Medieval gardens are:

- Herbers, cloister-garths, orchards, herb beds and vegetable gardens have been confused. This is like re-creating a 'Medieval room' without respecting the differences between room-types: great hall, solar, kitchen, brewhouse, chapel.

3.77 The National Trust has made what it called a knot garden at Little Moreton Hall. The building dates from the fifteenth century. The knot pattern, though borrowed from the house, looks ill-at-ease in the garden: knot gardens are associated with the sixteenth century, box hedging and topiary with the seventeenth century, mown lawns with the nineteenth century. It was a mistake.

3.78 Ightham Mote has grass paths between low wattle fencing, which encourages the growth of weeds.

- 'Rustic' garden craftsmanship is often used (in the sense of clumsy, gauche, graceless, inelegant, rough-hewn, awkward).
- Wattle fences are used as symbols of Medievalism, not for well-thought-out functional and aesthetic reasons.
- Box hedging, which is probably post-Medieval, is used in Medieval re-creations. This is like using bricks to edge a fire pit in a re-creation of an Iron Age hut.

- There is no evidence for flower-free, close-mown lawns in Medieval gardens. Their use in re-creations can be compared to plastic armour. It tells you something but not as much as could be told.
- Re-created gardens are made and maintained with modern tools, modern techniques and modern plants. This is like using plastic thread instead of gold braid for a re-created uniform.
- Re-created paths in vegetable gardens tend to be too wide and too often surfaced with gravel, which was a luxury, or mown grass, which could hardly have been scythed in narrow strips between beds. The primary use of vegetable gardens was for growing food. Gravel has to be weeded and is soon lost if weeds are cast onto it. Grass has to be cut or beaten, to stop it seeding, and competes with vegetables for water and nutrients.

The 'Middle Ages' is a chronological term but, unlike the Plantagenet Dynasty or the Hundred Years War, no start or end point can be defined. Britain's sixteenth century was part-Medieval and part-Renaissance. Renaissance garden ideas, which are the subject of Chapter 4, are therefore a necessary perspective for an appreciation of the character of Medieval gardens.

Renaissance gardens, 1485–1660

4.0 Living on Mount Olympus, the Greek gods made 'a golden race of mortal men'. They lived in an age 'without sorrow of heart, remote and free from toil and grief'.[1] Hesiod's *Works and Days*, thought to have Indo-European roots, outlines the deterioration in human life in the ages which he characterised as Golden, Silver, Bronze and Iron. Renaissance artists hoped to re-create the Golden Age, as did generations of garden designers.

4.1 The frontispiece to a 1662 edition of Virgil's *Eclogues* illustrates a vision of the Golden Age.[5]

4.2 Petrarch believed that in ascending Mount Ventoux he was the first man since antiquity to climb a mountain for pure pleasure (painting by Pierre Marcel).

Dreams of a Golden Age

Giorgio Vasari coined the term *rinascita* in the 1550s. It was translated into French as *renaissance*. Then, in the nineteenth century, it was applied to the period of 'art's rebirth' and 'state of perfection' during which Vasari had written his *Lives of the Artists*.[2] This book made Vasari the 'father of art history'.[3] Today, 'Renaissance' is used for several different chronological periods and for a broad cultural movement which affected different arts in different countries at different times. The unifying narrative is of societies shedding the political, social, artistic, scientific and material culture of the Middle Ages and, everyone hoped, advancing to a new Golden Age. It involved two steps backward, to Rome and Greece, and one step forward, to the world of science.

Dreams of a Golden Age are found in many world cultures,[4] and may derive from a pre-agricultural era in which food was gathered from the wild. Hesiod (*c*.700 BCE) is the oldest literary source for the dream. He wrote that the gods of Mount Olympus made 'a golden race of mortal men' who

> lived like gods without sorrow of heart, remote and free from toil and grief: miserable age rested not on them; but with legs and arms never failing they made merry with feasting beyond the reach of all evils. When they died, it was as though they were overcome with sleep, and they had all good things; for the fruitful earth unforced bare them fruit abundantly and without stint. They dwelt in ease and peace upon their lands with many good things, rich in flocks and loved by the blessed gods.[6]

Similar dreams are found in the *Idylls* of Theocritus (*c*.300–260 BCE), in the *Ecologues* of Virgil (70–19 BCE) and in the *Odes* of Horace (65–8 BCE). Theocritus set his Golden Age in Sicily. Arcadia, in Central Greece, was the place chosen by most authors.[7] Sir Philip Sidney, who lived at Penshurst Place, used *Arcadia* as the title of a pastoral tale, written for his sister, *c*.1580. Dreams of a 'pleasant place' (*locus amoenus* or 'pleasance') permeated Medieval literature and the word was also used for a place of resort, such as Henry V's pleasance outside Kenilworth Castle (see p. 75):

> If we now look back at Homer, Theocritus, and Virgil and ask ourselves the question: What types of ideal landscape could late Antiquity and the Middle Ages get from these poets? We cannot but answer: the mixed forest and the locus amoenus (with flowery meadows ad libitum).[8]

> Its minimum ingredients comprise a tree (or several trees), a meadow, and a spring or brook. Birdsong and flowers may be added. The most elaborate examples also add a breeze.[9]

4.3 a, b Petrarch's *Triumphs* were popular in the sixteenth century, encouraging readers, and gardeners, to judge modern life in relation to ancient life.[10] The illustrations show Apollo in a chariot of gold, drawn in triumph by the Nine Muses, the seven Liberal Arts and the four Cardinal Virtues.

Petrarch (1304–74) is now seen as 'the father of humanism'.[11] He was famous in his day for collecting Latin literature. Vaucluse was the *locus amoenus* and where he composed sonnets to Laura.[12] Later, he saw himself as the first man since antiquity to climb a mountain for the pure pleasure of it:

> To-day I made the ascent of the highest mountain in this region, which is not improperly called Ventosum [Mount Ventoux] ... The idea took hold upon me with especial force when, in re-reading Livy's History of Rome, yesterday, I happened upon the place where Philip of Macedon, the same who waged war against the Romans, ascended Mount Haemus in Thessaly, from whose summit he was able, it is said, to see two seas, the Adriatic and the Euxine ...
>
> Happy the man who is skilled to understand
> Nature's hid causes.[13]

Petrarch's account of his day on the mountain reflects humanist themes: a love of antiquity, a desire to understand Nature and a zest for scenery. Petrarch held Medieval scholasticism in contempt and 'astonished his contemporaries by retiring from his work at the papal court in Avignon to a secluded country estate at Vaucluse ... he may be seen as the first in a tradition of country-dwelling humanist authors stretching through Montaigne to the present day'.[14]

By the fifteenth century, Petrarch's humanist concerns had spread. Classical texts were assembled and translated, in part 'to understand Nature's hid causes'. Classical buildings and gardens were studied for inspiration. The best survivals were temples and palaces, like Hadrian's Pantheon in Rome and his Villa outside Tivoli. Renaissance princes lacked the visual information about Roman gardens now available from Pompeii and other archaeological digs. But they had textual information and, in the early fifteenth century, could read about horticulture in Columella (see p. 35 and p. 59) and about the pleasures of villa life in Pliny the Younger's letters (see p. 33). Early Renaissance gardens were made of compartments, often within protective walls. They were unlike Roman villas and the resulting garden type is described below as a 'compartment garden' (see p. 130).

Wealthy landowners in Renaissance Europe began to feel sufficiently rich and secure to plan gardens in which they could re-live the pastoral idyll of antiquity and make their own Edens. New country houses were built and the design of gardens became progressively integrated with the landscapes in which they were set:

- Medieval gardens had been inward-looking rectangles nestling behind protective walls.
- Renaissance gardens became outward-looking palaces with expansive views.
- Baroque gardens became geometrically integrated with the landscapes they dominated.
- Post-Baroque gardens became Classical landscapes, merging into the surrounding country.

Rural retirement in Britain

The first aspect of a Golden Age dream to take root in Britain came from the Book of Genesis. Eden, where Adam and Eve lived before their fall from grace, was a garden and a paradise. The Book of Genesis (3:17) recounts the events as follows:

> *And the Lord God planted a garden eastward in Eden; and there he put the man whom he had formed. And out of the ground made the Lord God to grow every tree that is pleasant to the sight; and good for food; and the tree of life also in the midst of the garden, and the tree of knowledge of good and evil. And the Lord God took the man and put him into the Garden of Eden to dress it and keep it.*
> *But Adam and Eve disobeyed God's command and ate of the tree of knowledge of good and evil.*
> *And unto Adam he said, Because thou hast hearkened unto the voice of thy wife, and hast eaten of the tree, of which I commanded thee, saying, Thou shalt not eat of it: cursed is the ground for thy sake; in sorrow shalt thou eat of it all the days of thy life; Thorns also and thistles shall it bring forth to thee; and thou shalt eat the herb of the field; In the sweat of thy face shalt thou eat bread, till thou return unto the ground: for dust thou art, and unto dust shalt thou return.*

Before the Fall, Adam and Eve were required to 'dress and keep' the Garden of Eden. When expelled from the Garden, they were condemned to cultivate the earth 'in the sweat of thy face' and to eat 'the herb of the field'. The joy of living in paradise was replaced by the onerous task of eking a livelihood among thorns and thistles. Man was involved with gardens before and after his Fall from grace. Christian thinkers saw gardening as one of the purest and most divine activities open to humans – and a way of recreating the paradise once shared with God.

4.4 Adam and Eve being expelled from the Garden of Eden, as drawn by Gustave Doré. They were sent to cultivate the earth and their descendants learned how this skill could be used to make beautiful and productive gardens.

4.5 'THE RETREAT 1745', a doorway in Berwick reflects the spirit of the times.

Pomfret expressed the dream of retreat to a garden in *The Choice* (1700):

> *Near some fair town I'd have a private seat,*
> *Built uniform, not little, nor too great;*
> *...*
> *A little garden, grateful to the eye;*
> *And a cool rivulet run murmuring by:*
> *On whose delicious banks a stately row*
> *Of shady limes, or sycamores, should grow.*
> *At th' end of which a silent study plae'd.*[15]

4.6 'A little garden, grateful to the eye; And a cool rivulet run murmuring by' (see p. 107).

4.7 The frontispiece to London and Wise's *Retir'd Gardener* has a quotation from Virgil's *Georgics: Regum aequabat opes animis* ('He equalled the wealth of kings with his spirit').[16]

English writers on architecture, agriculture and gardening joined their contemporaries in turning to Italy for artistic inspiration and technical knowledge. They looked to Renaissance authors, including Alberti, Palladio and Colonna, and to their Roman predecessors, including Virgil, Vitruvius, Pliny and Columella. For practical advice, the most useful sources were Virgil's *Georgics* and Columella's *De Re Rustica*. Here, they found Classical allusions combined with a wealth of advice on tillage, agricultural tools, raising trees, pruning, caring for animals and the management of bees. Columella loved rural life and took agriculture to be 'without doubt most closely related to and, as it were, own sister to wisdom'.[17] English garden books were strewn with quotations from these authorities. Here is Virgil's advice on ploughing:

> *Who with the hoe breaks up the sluggish clods,*
> *And harrows them with wattles (approvingly*
> *Will golden Ceres watch him from high Olympus);*
> *He too who turns the plough and again crosswise*
> *Breaks through the ridges which he raised when first*
> *He clove the soil. Thus evermore he disciplines*
> *The ground, and gives his orders to the fields.*[18]

Virgil relishes practicalities. 'Georgic' means 'to do with agriculture'. It derives from the Greek *georgikos*, 'of a husbandman'. But the poet's aim was not to write an agricultural treatise. He had political and philosophical aims. Like Horace, his contemporary in first-century Rome BCE, Virgil delighted in the idyll of rural retirement. The two poets contrast the virtues of pastoralism with the civil war, waste and political turmoil which plagued Rome after the assassination of Caesar in 44 BCE. They dreamt of a new Golden Age embodying the virtues of peace, productivity and continuity. In particular, they pointed to the lifestyle of what Maren-Sofie Rostvig has called the Happy Husbandsman.[19] Later than continental Europeans, the English began to dream of rural retirement and peaceful toil, free from the temptations of money, power and political advancement. *The Georgics* often return to this theme:

4.8 The 'Arcadian' site of Horace's farm in the Sabine hills (in Licenza) was found in the early twentieth century.

> *Blest too is he who knows the rural gods,*
>
> *...*
>
> *Meantime the husbandman with crooked plough*
> *Has cleft the earth: hence labour's yearly meed,*
> *Hence feeds he little child and father land.*
> *Hence are milch-cow and honest ox maintained.*
> *Earth never rests: either with fruit she flows,*
> *Or with young lambs, or with the wheaten sheaf*
> *Beloved of Ceres: increase the drills*
> *And barns are overcome.*

The first line of the above quotation characterises the rural retirement theme which enchanted seventeenth-century England, beset as it was by civil war and political strife.

Greek poets originated the rural retirement theme. The peacefulness of rural life was a favourite topic of Homer and Theocritus, upon whom Virgil and Horace modelled their poetry. Horace had studied at the Academy in Athens as a young man and may have been taught philosophy in an olive garden, as had been the custom of Plato and Epicurus. Horace particularly admired Epicurus's doctrine that happiness results from the enjoyments of the mind and the sweets of virtue. Offered the job of private secretary to Augustus, he turned it down, preferring the life of rural retirement on his farm in the Sabine Hills:

4.9 Theocritus and other Greek poets originated the rural retirement theme (seventeenth-century engraving by Johan Heinrich Roos).

> *Happy the man who bounteous Gods allow,*
> *With his own hands Paternal Grounds to plough.*[20]

There he could live among Happy Husbandmen with cheerful faces engaged in pruning vines, shearing lambs, gathering fruit, ploughing and keeping bees. To Virgil, Horace and all those who admired their poetry, the Age of Augustus was a Golden Age. For poets, *Beatus ille* ('Happy is he …') became a popular genre.

4.10 a, b (a) A statue of Charles I in the country (at Glamis Castle). (b) A statue of Oliver Cromwell in the city (outside the House of Commons).

England suffered from civil war, waste and political turmoil in the seventeenth century and comparisons were made with Rome in the first century BCE. The English troubles, which centred on the conflict between the Royalists and the Parliamentarians, led to a greater appreciation of country life. As in Roman times, it appeared safer and more virtuous than living in towns. Political perils were experienced alternately by the opposing parties. During Charles I's reign, many of the Protestants who formed the core of the Parliamentarians, were persecuted. After the outbreak of civil war, in 1642, both parties suffered.

Charles I's execution in 1649 brought the war to an end. Cromwell exiled the defeated Royalists to the country and they made a virtue of necessity, by devoting themselves

4.11 a, b (a) The Garden of Eden, as illustrated in a 1688 edition of Milton's *Paradise Lost*.[21] (b) An illustration of rural husbandry from a 1774 edition of Virgil's *Georgics*.[22]

to agriculture and estate improvement. The Commonwealth period lasted until 1660 and ended with the restoration of the monarchy in the person of Charles II. A new period of religious and political persecution began. The regicides were executed and it became the turn of Protestant landowners to find life safer in their country seats. John Milton, the poet and apologist for the Commonwealth, retired to the country after the restoration and began writing *Paradise Lost*. Book IV contains a description of the Garden of Eden before the Fall. Frequently quoted by eighteenth-century poets and gardening authors, the following lines compare Eden to a rural estate:

> *Thus was this place,*
> *A happy rural seat of various view;*
> *Groves whose rich*
> *Trees wept odorous Gumms and Balme,*
> *Others whose fruit burnisht with Golden Rinde ...*
> *Betwixt them Lawns, or level Downs, and Flocks*
> *Grasing the tender herb, were interpos'd,*
> *Or palmie hilloc, or the flourie lap*
> *Of some irriguous Valley spread her store.*[23]

Persecution of Protestants reached a climax in the short reign of James II (1685–88). This led to the Glorious Revolution of 1688, in which he was overthrown, and to an invitation to the Protestant William of Orange to assume the British throne. Once again, the Catholics found safety in the country.

By the end of the seventeenth century, writers on many topics, including gardening, were praising rural retirement as an ideal. William Temple exemplifies this attitude. He was a Protestant statesman whose diplomatic career, from 1655 to 1688, had been in stormy times. The crowning achievement of his diplomacy was the negotiation, in 1668, of a Triple Alliance of Protestant countries to protect Holland from Catholic aggression. This had been done during the reign of a British king, Charles II, with strong French and Catholic sympathies. The alliance came to nothing, to Temple's regret. Temple was offered a secretaryship of state towards the end of his career but he was weary of political strife and declined the offer. In Horatian style, he retired to his rural seat at Moor Park and devoted himself to estate management, gardening and literature. Temple's essay of 1685 'Upon the gardens of Epicurus' extols

> *The sweetness and satisfaction of this retreat, where since my resolution taken of never entering again into any public employments, I have passed five years without once going to town, though I am almost in sight of it, and have a house there always ready to receive me.*[24]

This remark was buttressed with a quotation from Horace: 'Let me less possess, so I may live, What'er of life remains, unto myself.'[25]

Temple also refers to other Classical authors. He admired the philosopher whose name appears in the title of his essay: 'Epicurus passed his life wholly in his garden: there he studied, there he exercised, there he taught his philosophy', because

> *the sweetness of air, the pleasantness of smell, the verdure of plants, the cleanness and lightness of food, the exercises of working and walking; but above all, the exemption from cares and solicitude, seem equally to favour and improve both contemplation and health.*[26]

Temple's model for his own garden was the estate in Hertfordshire, also called Moor Park, where he had spent his honeymoon in 1655. It was remembered as 'the sweetest place, I think, that I have ever seen in my life, either before or since, at home or abroad'.[27] His description of the garden is one of the fullest accounts of a garden made in the years before the Civil War. It had been granted to Lucy Harrington, Countess of Bedford, by James I and the design of the garden is attributed by Roy Strong to Isaac de Caus. Moor Park stood on a gentle slope and contained three large rectangular enclosures stepping down a hillside (see Figure 4.12 (a)):

● The first enclosure lay at the top of the slope and in front of the house. It was 'a quarter of all greens ... adorned with rough rock work and fountains'.[28]

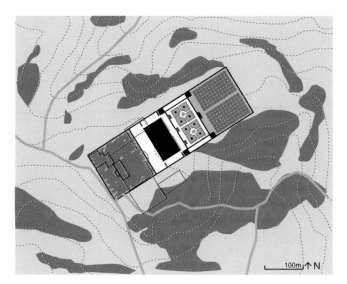

4.12 a, b (a) Moor Park, Hertfordshire, a reconstruction of the plan based on Temple's description, with the lines of the present house and garden in red (the location of Lucy Harrington's house is a guess). (b) The present park was designed by Lancelot Brown and is used as a golf course.

- The second enclosure was lower down the slope and on the other side of the house. It had a terrace adjoining the house and three flights of steps leading down to a space 'divided into quarters by gravel walks and adorned with two fountains and eight statues'. There were summer houses at each end of the terrace and at the far corners. Shady cloisters with stone arches and climbing plants ran along two sides and, from the front, flights of steps led around an Italianate grotto to a lower enclosure.[29]
- The third enclosure was 'all fruit trees ranged about the several quarters of a wilderness which is very shady'.[30]

Temple's idea of a garden was, like his gardening philosophy, in the Italian Renaissance tradition. His own garden had a series of rectangular compartments devoted to lawns, flowers, vegetables and fruit. Temple was especially interested in fruit trees. His essay is by no means a pomological treatise but, following the *Georgics*, contains practical advice culled from the author's experience.

Anthony Ashley Cooper, the Third Earl of Shaftesbury, is another writer who praised the joys of rural life. Two friends conduct a debate in his 'philosophical rhapsody', *The Moralists*. Out for a walk, they 'fell naturally into the praises of country life, and discoursed a while of husbandry, and the nature of the soil'.[31] This led on to a discussion of nature, ethics and aesthetics. Shaftesbury believed that gardens should induce peacefulness and spirituality. He wrote:

Therefore remember ever the garden and the groves within. There build, there erect what statues, what virtues, what ornament or orders of architecture thou thinkest noblest. There walk at leisure and in peace; contemplate, regulate, dispose: and for this, a bare field or common walk will serve full as well, and to say truth, much better.[32]

Stephen Switzer is a third example of a gardening author who was influenced by the Classical idea of rural retirement. His first book was published in 1715 but its philosophy belonged to the previous century. Switzer is careful to acknowledge his sources, beginning with the Garden of Eden. Epicurus was credited with making the first town garden and praised for using it as a place to teach philosophy. Virgil is admired for the way he 'mixes the poet, philosopher and gardener together'.[33] The art of choosing a good site and planning the layout is properly ascribed to Vitruvius. John Evelyn was seen as a second Virgil on account of his grasp of the technical and philosophical aspects of country life, and, among other writers, Switzer mentions Homer, Horace, Columella, Ovid, Milton, Cowley, Temple, Addison and Pope. He gave grateful thanks to his former employers, London and Wise, and to the French designers and authors who provided the model for his work. In the course of a long apprenticeship, Switzer had learnt more about the practicalities of estate work than Temple or Shaftesbury had ever known. He was a nurseryman and designer who sought to combine 'the pleasures of the country with the profits'.[34]

Renaissance gardens in continental Europe

The Renaissance approach to garden design had begun in fifteenth-century Italy. The country was recovering from political disorders and from the Black Death which had ravaged Europe in the preceding century. Life was becoming safer, cities were becoming wealthier, power was flowing to the aristocracy ('from *commune* to *signoria*'[35]) with Italy becoming a land of princes and princely gardens:

> *The princes' domains extended to the realm of culture, for they saw themselves as more than political, military and economic leaders. They felt responsible for the vitality of cultural life in their territories, and art was a major component for developing a cultured populace. Visual imagery also appealed to them as effective propaganda for reinforcing their control. As the wealthiest individuals in their regions, princes possessed the means to commission numerous artworks and buildings. Thus, art functioned in several capacities – as evidence of princely sophistication and culture, as a form of prestige or commemoration, as public education and propaganda, as a demonstration of wealth, and as a source of visual pleasure.*[36]

Renaissance and Baroque gardens took on roles which had previously belonged to castles and cathedrals. The Italian *duomo*, equivalent to the English 'cathedral', derives

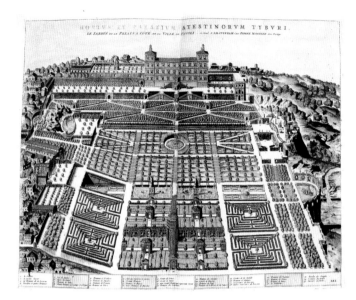 

4.13 a, b (a) The Villa d'Este, drawn by Étienne Dupérac in 1575, is a flower, fruit and pattern garden. (b) The features remain but the Villa d'Este planting is now Gardenesque.

from *domus Dei*, 'house of God'. It was a place of prestige. When princes assumed the intellectual and artistic leadership which had formerly lain with the Church, they encouraged study of the humanities (grammar, rhetoric, history, poetry and moral philosophy) and shifted the emphasis of scholarship from God to men. Humanist gardens became places to display political, economic and cultural power. The princes' land, money and power facilitated the making of gardens which contributed to a design objective of great significance: display. Medieval gardens had been for romance, solace and healing. Renaissance villas became social, intellectual and cultural centres. Palaces and gardens proclaimed their owners' place in society. Ideas from natural philosophy and the arts guided the integration of buildings with plants, water, woods, landform and sculpture. Garden-making evolved from a craft to an art; intellectuals with expertise in painting, sculpture and drawing were given responsibility for their design – with more land and more money than their Medieval predecessors.

The following summaries of the use and form of Renaissance gardens are from *European Gardens* (2011):

Early Renaissance

Use: Renaissance gardens developed by stages from their medieval precursors. Noblewomen continued to use gardens to take the air in safety, but men resumed their involvement with gardens – and more resources became available. The principles of ancient garden design were rediscovered and combined with new artistic and scientific ideas about the 'nature of the world'. As in Roman times, Renaissance gardens were used for social gatherings and great occasions.

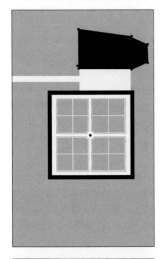

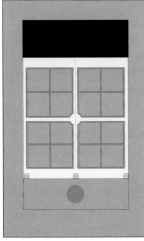

4.14 a, b These diagrams show the styles of Early Renaissance and High Renaissance gardens in continental Europe. In Britain, the phases were less marked but the design progression was comparable (e.g. from Kenilworth to Ham House).

Form: As castles evolved into fortified manor houses, more space became available for gardens. Square and rectangular planting beds were laid out like carpets, so that their unity, order and regularity could be viewed from upper windows. Crusaders may have seen Eastern gardens with geometrical beds of flowers, or traders may have seen them in Muslim Spain. Patterns, taking their name from carpet patterns, were used in the design of what became known in England as 'knot gardens'.[37]

Late Renaissance
Use: Alberti advised

> making open places for walking, swimming, and other diversions, court-yards, grass-plots and porticoes, where old men may chat together in the kindly warmth of the sun in winter, and where the family may divert themselves and enjoy the shade in summer ... and have a view of some city, towns, the sea, an open plain.

Medieval gardens had been inward-looking places, physically and spiritually. High Renaissance gardens began to reach outward, physically and intellectually. Displaying antique statuary became an important garden use – a way of connecting with history, the fine arts and the landscape.

Form: The organising principles of High Renaissance gardens were developed by Bramante, following a suggestion from Alberti. Bramante used a central axis to integrate house and garden. A series of rectangular enclosures with terraces at different levels was thus fused into a single composition. Flights of steps, alcoves, niches and fountains were disposed in relation to the axis and embellished with statues, fountains and terracotta pots containing flowers and fruit trees.[38]

Renaissance garden literature

Gardening was a recognised craft in Medieval England and royal account books detail the employment of gardeners from Norman times onward. The first record of a Worshipful Company of Gardeners is in 1345 and the Company received a Royal Charter in 1605. *The Feate of Gardening*, the oldest known English garden book, is thought to have been written by Mayster Jon Gardener *c.*1390. 'Feate' means 'Action'. Though in verse, it is a practical manual. Harvey comments that

> It is likely to have been the work of a leading master gardener, possibly at the Royal palace of Westminster or at Windsor Castle. There was probably no thought of publication in any form; it will have been simply a memorandum for internal use.[39]

Garden workers might have memorised the poem for guidance.

 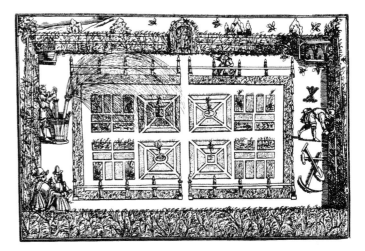

Thomas Hill was the author of the first gardening book printed in English, in 1568. Under the pseudonym Didymus Mountain, he then published *The Gardener's Lab-yrinth* in 1577.[40] Like many subsequent works, they were Renaissance books in which practical advice is interspersed with references to Pliny, Cicero, Columella, Cato, Varro and other Classical authors. References to the Bible were also popular in garden books and Ralph Austen published a book on *The Spiritual Use of an Orchard or Garden of Fruit Trees: Set Forth in Divers Similitudes Betweene Natural and Spir-itual Fruit Trees, According to Scripture and Experience* (1657). Austen explains that:

> *The world is a great library, and fruit trees are some of the books wherein we may*
> *read and see plainely the attributes of God, his power, wisdome, goodnesse &c. and be*
> *instructed and taught our duty towards him in many things.*[42]

'Christian humanism' sought to integrate Christianity with pre-Christian knowledge. Since there was only one God, who must also have created the pre-Christian world, there was no great logical problem to be overcome. Art, science and garden writing were all affected by Renaissance culture.[43] Two translations of François Gentil's *Le jar-dinier solitaire: The Solitary or Carthusian Gard'ner* were published in 1706. The Tooke edition explains that 'The author of *Le Jardinier Solitaire*, or the Dialogues that stand foremost in the Treatise now before us, is Francis Gentil, a Lay-Brother of the Order of Carthusians, who has been above Thirty Years Gard'ner to the Charter-House in Paris', part of which became the Jardin du Luxembourg. The Tonson edition of *Le jardinier solitaire* was by two famous garden designers, George London and Henry Wise, 'with several alterations and additions, which render it proper for our *English* Culture'. As discussed in Chapter 3 (see p. 79), each Carthusian monk lived in seclusion with a small garden plot. It seems likely that the monks used their cell gardens to grow vegetables and herbs and that the Charterhouse also had an orchard which Gentil managed. There is a dialogue between the author and a Gentleman who explains his interest in rural life:

4.15 a, b The garden plans in Thomas Hill's *The Gardener's Labyrinth* (1577) show modest northern counterparts of the Villa d'Este.[41] (a) Hill explains that the level of the earth is raised with dung and a line is used to set out internal paths which are then 'trodden out' so that the path is one foot below the bed if the soil is dry and two feet below if the soil is wet, as when the garden can be irrigated with a pump. (b) The garden irrigated with a sprinkler. A wooden balustrade is used to separate the beds from the ornamental walk. The owners can be seen in the bottom left corner and there are beehives in the top right corner.

You being acquainted with the resolution I have taken of purchasing a seat in the country,
where I propose to pass the rest of my days, and taste the sweets of a country life; it will be
highly obliging in you, if you will take the pains to instruct me in what is necessary to the
raising of a kitchen-garden, and to the cultivating of Fruit-Trees.[44]

Practical Christian humanism became an important strand in the progress of English garden design.

Fifteenth-century gardens: Late Medieval

The Renaissance approach to gardens appears to have reached England during the reign of Henry VII (1485–1509). A timber-built palace caught fire in 1497 and was rebuilt as Richmond Palace, taking its name from his family seat in Yorkshire. A Herald proclaimed the appearance of his Renaissance palace garden, in 1501:

Most fair and pleasant gardens, with royal knots, alleyed and herbed; many marvellous
beasts, as lions, dragons and such other of divers kinds, properly fashioned and carved
in the ground, right well sounded and compassed with lead; with many vines seeds and

4.16 a, b (a) Richmond Palace, seen across the River Thames. (b) Only the gatehouse survives, shown in red, near Richmond Green. Henry VII died here in 1509 and Elizabeth I died here in 1603. Richmond Park, where they hunted, lay to the east. The plan is based on Wyngaerde's drawing (c.1588) and is overlaid on a nineteenth-century OS map which shows the bank of the river pushed outward.

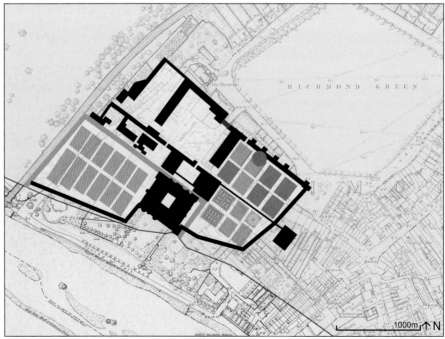

118

strange fruit, right goodly beset, kept and nourished with much labour and diligence. In the lower end of this garden be pleasant galleries and houses of pleasure to disport in, at chess, tables, dice, cards, billiards; bowling alleys, butts for archers, and goodly tennis plays – as well to use the said plays and disports as to behold them so disporting.[45]

Sixteenth-century gardens: Early Renaissance

England's sixteenth-century gardens are often classified as 'Tudor'. This was the family name of Henry VIII, who founded the dynasty, but his name tells us nothing about the character of gardens. Roy Strong used the term 'Renaissance', borrowed from art history, in the title of his book on *The Renaissance Garden in England*. There are three issues with this title. First, it was a period of transition in which many aspects of art and society were more Medieval than Renaissance. Second, the period covered by his book ends *c*.1650 and, as argued below, the period in which the Renaissance had most influence on British gardens was from 1660 to 1714. Third, Strong's main interest was 'the garden of the palace and the great house from its inception in the

4.17 a, b (a) Theobalds House was built 1564–85, visited by Elizabeth I and destroyed *c*.1650. The plan shows a tracing of Lord Burghley's drawing on an OS map. Baron Waldstein wrote: 'There is a fountain in the centre of the garden: the water sprouts out from a number of concealed pipes and sprays unwary passers-by … In the garden you see lilies and other flowers growing among the shrubs. An outstanding feature is a delightful and most beautifully made ornamental pool (at present dry, but previously supplied with water from 2 miles away): it is approached by 24 steps leading up to it.'[46] Some garden walls survive, and a maze has been made, in what is now Cedars Park. (b) The flint arch at Theobalds (with a newly made maze beyond).

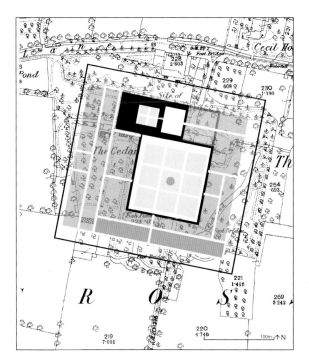

4.18 a, b (a) The painting allows a glimpse of the Privy Garden at Whitehall. (b) A re-creation of the design idea at Hampton Court.

reign of Henry VIII until the outbreak of the Civil War'.[47] His use of the word 'Renaissance' in the title is justified but, given his focus on palace gardens, he might have chosen to call the book *Tudor and Stuart Gardens*.

Strong stated that his book was not concerned with 'the horticultural aspect of gardening'.[48] It was a reasonable limitation but we should not lose sight of the functions of Renaissance gardens. Tudor garden books confirm the fact that growing

4.19 a, b Edzell Castle. Scotland had close connections with continental Europe in the sixteenth century and its gardens may have been influenced by Renaissance ideas at an earlier date than England.

food was the main objective. In Medieval manors, gardening was the work of peasants. Sixteenth-century books were printed for the aristocracy but were not DIY manuals. Only the rich could read and could afford books. Knowledge about growing choice fruits and flowers was a humanist pursuit. Medieval lords had of course enjoyed eating fruit. Renaissance princes turned the selection, production and consumption of fruit into connoisseurship. Fruits were candied and served at banquets in special banqueting houses, often in gardens. The banquet was a dessert course served after the feast and after the walk to a pleasure house, usually with a view (see p. 147). Banqueting houses survive on the roofs of Longleat and Burghley and are set into garden walls at Melford Hall, Edzell Castle, Hales Place, Weston Hall, Montacute and elsewhere.

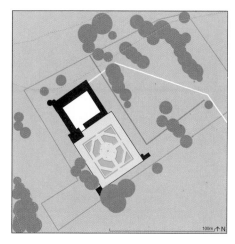

4.20 The relationship of Edzell Castle to its garden corresponds to the Early Renaissance diagram (see Figure 4.14 (a)). The planting designed by Scotland's Inspector of Ancient Monuments in the 1960s is an anomaly.

Seventeenth-century gardens: High Renaissance

Elizabeth I died in 1603, unmarried and the last of the Tudors. She enjoyed the fine estates of her courtiers but, unlike her father and grandfather, did not commission palaces or gardens for her own use. The Stuarts assumed the throne after her death and lacked her self-restraint. They patronised all the arts and, in Inigo Jones, found 'the first Englishman who had a true understanding of Renaissance architecture'.[49] The sixteenth century is sometimes classified as 'Late Medieval' and sometimes as 'Early Renaissance'. But there can be no ambiguity about the seventeenth century: it was as near as English and Scottish gardens came to a High Renaissance phase.

4.21 a, b Longleat. The 1675 painting by Jan Siberechts (1675) shows the Renaissance forecourt, with later fountains. There are small banqueting houses on the roof offering the type of views previously available from alures (see p. 87).

4.22 Bust of Inigo Jones (at Plas Brondanw).

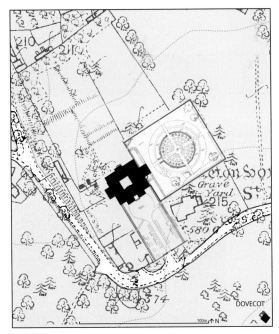

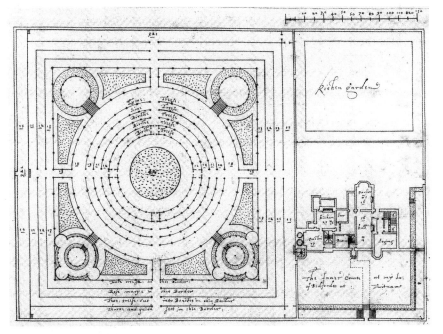

4.23 a, b, c (a) The garden of Chastleton House. (b) Plan of Chastleton House. (c) Plan of Twickenham Park by Robert Smythson – which may show a design by Francis Bacon.

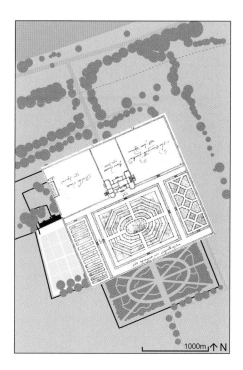

4.24 a, b, c (a) Ham House. (b) Robert Smythson's 1609 design for Ham House, overlaid on the present plan. (c) The garden today, as partly restored to its plan.

During the seventeenth century 'Western Europe attained the fastest rates of economic growth in the world' with England 'the fastest growing economy'.[50] The Civil War and the Commonwealth were disruptions but Cromwell supported manufacturing and agriculture benefited from new tools. Farm output grew rapidly and an agricultural revolution gathered pace. A quarter of England was converted from open country ('champion', see p. 58) to enclosed fields.[51] Feudal manors were broken up and manor houses became country houses owned by families which often had non-agricultural wealth to spend on palatial homes and gardens. Large estate gardens acquired almost as many specialised outdoor 'compartments' as they were acquiring specialised indoor rooms.

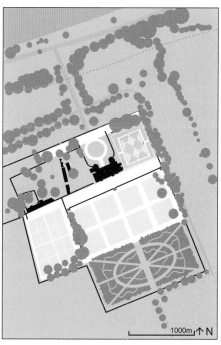

Enough survives from the High Renaissance phase in British garden design to form a picture of the characteristic gardens of the period. Francis Bacon is a central figure. Henderson argues that he probably designed the quincunx garden for Twickenham Park (Figure 4.23 (c)). The house was designed by Robert Smythson and the garden shown on his plan resembles the surviving garden of Chastleton House. Smythson also drew a plan for the garden at Ham House. The site is flat and it was difficult to make the terraces which are so characteristic of Renaissance gardens in Italy.

Bacon included a proposal for a palace garden in his essay 'On gardens' (1625):

> *The Garden is best to be square, encompassed on all the four sides with a stately arched hedge; the arches to be upon pillars of carpenter's work, of some ten foot high, and six foot*

4.25 a, b (a) Old Gorhambury House. (b) The remains of the water garden at Gorhambury.

4.26 a, b John Evelyn was born at Wotton House and designed the garden for his elder brother. It has a colonnaded grotto with a terrace above.

broad, and the spaces between of the same dimension with the breadth of the arch. Over the arches let there be an entire hedge of some four foot high, framed also upon carpenter's work; and upon the upper hedge, over every arch, a little turret, with a belly enough to receive a cage of birds: and over every space between the arches some other little figure, with broad plates of round coloured glass gilt, for the sun to play upon: but this hedge I intend to be raised upon a bank, not steep, but gently slope, of some six foot, set all with flowers.[52]

 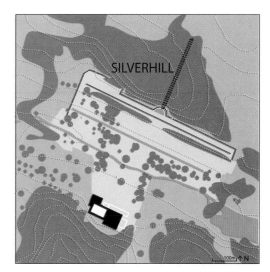

4.27 a, b Albury Park in 2010. The terraces and the tunnel beneath Silverhill survive from John Evelyn's design. The planting has changed and the mansion, though rebuilt by Soane, Pugin and others, is in the same position as Evelyn's mansion.

Bacon owned Gorhambury House and made a water garden in the valley below. Both the site and his drawings survive.

John Evelyn, discussed in Chapter 5 because of his role in bringing Baroque ideas to England, lived from 1620 to 1706. As a royalist, he spent much of the Civil War period (1642–51) abroad and took the opportunity to visit Renaissance gardens in Italy and France. He advised his brother on the garden at Wotton House and designed the garden at Albury Park for Henry Howard between 1655 and 1677. They are Renaissance gardens, more Italian than French, with terracing.

Salomon and Isaac de Caus, whose exact relationship is uncertain, were French engineers and garden designers who both worked in England and had detailed knowledge of Renaissance gardens. Salomon worked in the gardens of Somerset House and Greenwich Palace before moving to Germany, where he designed a great Renaissance garden for the Hortus Palatinus. Isaac, evidently with knowledge of this plan, used the title Hortus Penbrochianus on his drawing of the garden at Wilton House.

The Baroque tendency waxed after the restoration of the monarchy with King Charles II in 1660, as will be discussed in Chapter 5, but the making of fundamentally Renaissance gardens continued. Garden historians are fortunate that many of the men who made the gardens of the late seventeenth century wanted their work to be recorded. Dutch artists and business men followed William III to England. They came from a country in which Protestants objected to religious art but were proud to have paintings of the

4.28 a, b Wilton House. This is the site of Isaac de Caus's Renaissance garden, designed in the mid-1630s. The river crosses the site and now runs beneath a Palladian bridge. Celia Fiennes described the garden, c.1685–96: 'The gardens are very fine, with many gravel walkes with grass squaires set with fine brass and stone statues, with fish ponds and basons with figures in the middle spouting out water, dwarfe trees of all sorts and a fine flower garden, such wall fruite: the river runs through the garden that easeily conveys by pipes water to all parts.'[54]

landscapes they had defended against Catholic aggressors.[53] English patrons commissioned topographic artists to illustrate the great gardens they were making. The Renaissance aspects of these gardens are discussed below. Their Baroque aspects are discussed in Chapter 5 (see p. 164).

Painters Johannes Kip, Leonard Knyff, Jan Siberechts and others produced a brilliant set of drawings and paintings. They show English gardens in greater detail than any earlier illustrations. The bird's eye viewpoint makes them somewhat otherworldly, so that one wonders if England really had, and lost, so many formal gardens. Yet some survive, with changed planting, and evidence from archaeology and estate maps shows the Kip and Knyff's drawings to have been largely accurate. The main exception is that features which the owner intended to build were sometimes put in the drawings and not built.

In succession to the organically planned Medieval manors with toft and cottage villages, yards, orchards, vegetable plots and herbers of Medieval England, Kip and Knyff show geometrically ordered estates with:

- newly built country houses;
- canals and moats;
- rectangular enclosures, used as lawns, knot gardens, parterres, orchards and vegetable gardens;
- lines of trees often pushing into deer parks.

Doddington Hall is a good example of a seventeenth-century estate. The house was completed in 1600 and the garden was drawn by Kip and Knyff c.1700. Since then,

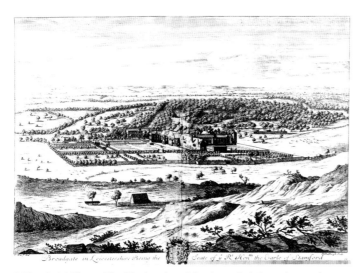 

4.29 a, b (a) Kip and Knyff's drawing of Bradgate Park from the south.
(b) Bradgate House from the east. The house and garden are ruins but the
deer park survives in good condition, managed as a country park.

4.30 a, b The vegetable garden at Doddington Hall in 2010 and as drawn by Kip
and Knyff in 1707.

there have been surprisingly few changes to the layout of the garden though the use
of the compartments has changed. They have become more thickly vegetated, more
ornamental and less productive. Wollaton Hall, as discussed in Appendix III, was also
drawn by Kip and Knyff.

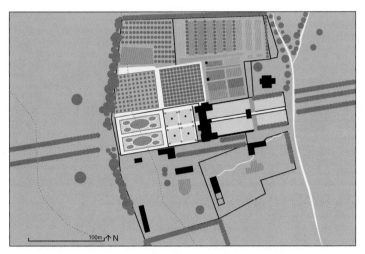
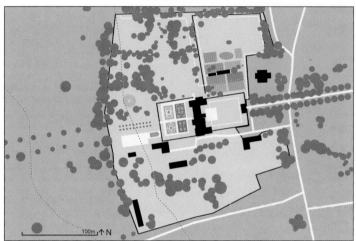

4.31 a, b Comparative plans of Doddington Hall in 1700 and 2010.

Renaissance garden features

Medieval castles, as discussed in Chapter 3, are known to have had herbers, fruit gardens, vegetable gardens, places to walk and places to hunt. These types of compartment continued to be made in Renaissance gardens. But when people became wealthier, and living outside fortifications became safer, there were more opportunities for luxury and ostentation. Howard Colvin observed that, 'Where Tudor gardens were

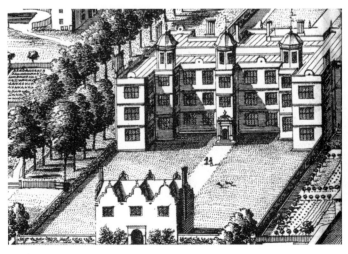

4.32 a, b Doddington Hall was probably designed by Robert Smythson in 1593–1600 and, except for the planting, the entrance court is unchanged.

clearly designed to impress, their Medieval predecessors were designed, one suspects, more for relaxation than display.'[55] The trend continued with Tudor and Stuart princes displaying wealth and power with palaces and the garden features outlined below.

Gatehouse courts

Gatehouses continued to have a role in protecting estates from thieves and malcontents when, because of artillery, they no longer performed the military role of castle gatehouses:[56]

> *Throughout the sixteenth century, the gatehouse continued to function as a protective barrier to the house but it also perpetuated the message of strength, power and position of the builder.*[57]

The space between the main house and the gatehouse compares to the inner bailey of a Medieval castle, as outlined below. It was a green court in which visitors dismounted and were received.

Courtyards

Courtyards were a characteristic feature of residential planning in Renaissance Europe but, as with Renaissance rooms, there are few recorded details of how they were used. English courtyards are related to baileys (see p. 56). The French origin of

4.33 a, b The gatehouse at Charlcote Park gives entry to the base court.

4.34 The moat and base court at Great Chalfield.

the English motte-and-bailey is *motte et basse-cour*. *Basse-cour* came into English as 'base court' (it could have been translated as 'lower court'). The base court of a castle was a fortified enclosure below a motte. It was used as a barnyard, a service yard and a place of refuge during sieges. When Medieval English houses had double court-yards, from the fourteenth century onwards, the base court was a service court and the inner court, also called the green court, was a private space for residents and guests. As can be seen from John Norden's drawing of Windsor Castle (see p. 71), the inner court was a circulation space criss-crossed by paths. The central fountain was used as a water supply. But it was not a pleasure garden. Large houses had lodgings for large numbers of guests, who accessed their rooms from the courtyard. Internal corridors were uncommon before the sixteenth century.

Three-sided base courts became popular in the seventeenth century and four-sided internal courts were given architecturally coordinated façades to make them elegant. They were sometimes used as theatres. Medieval dramatic performances had been enactments of Bible stories in churches. When secular plays became popular, the venues changed to inns, halls, purpose-built theatres and courtyards. In Italy, palace yards were used for tournaments, festivals and even firework displays.

Compartments

'Compartment' is the best term for the square and rectangular spaces which were the compositional units of Renaissance palaces.[58] It derives from *compartimenti*,

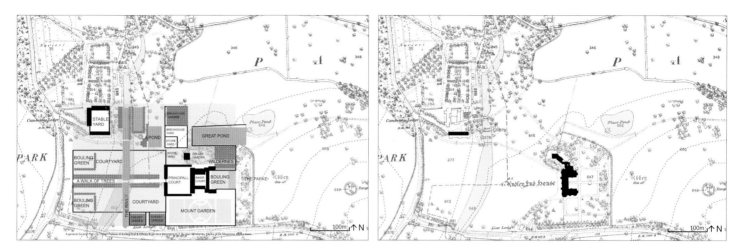

4.35 a, b Henry Winstanley's plan of Audley End, traced and superimposed on a nineteenth-century OS map. The *c*.1676 plan has unusually detailed information on the use of the garden compartments. The Mount Garden could be used for walking in the sun and the Wilderness for walking in the shade.

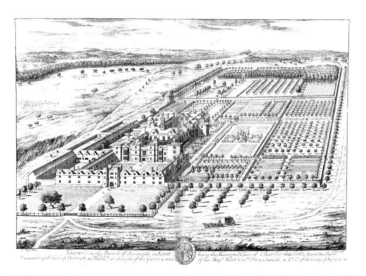

4.36 a, b Garden compartments are shown on Kip and Knyff's drawing of Knole. They survive but are managed as Gardenesque woodland.

which was their Italian name.[59] Specialised compartments were used for knot patterns, flowers, fruits, herbs, vegetables, fish ponds, trees, walking, sculptures, bowls, archery, viewing mounts and many other purposes. The change from fortified manors to spacious country living affected both indoor and outdoor space: house plans evolved from a great hall with an open hearth into assemblies of specialised rooms with separate fireplaces and chimneys; rooms were accessed from internal corridors instead of outdoor courts; houses were surrounded by specialised compartments accessed from gravelled walkways.

Celia Fiennes was much interested in the use of compartments. At Coleshill House in Berkshire, she admired the 'green walke with all sorts of dwarfe trees, fruit trees with standing apricock and flower trees, abundance of garden roome and filled with all sorts of thing for pleasure and use'.[60] At Hillesden Manor in Buckinghamshire, she admired 'the grass and gravel walkes with dwarfs and flower trees and much fruit'.[61]

Walks

The best place to walk in a Medieval castle had been on the battlements (see pp. 88–9). Renaissance gardens, with more space, could have safe, mud-free walks at ground level. The typical arrangement was a grid of walks between compartments. The main walks were surfaced with gravel and sufficiently wide for several ladies and gentlemen in fine clothes to walk abreast and enjoy views of neatly kept grass, statues, fountains, flowers and fruits. Other types of space which might have been used for exercise were less appealing: a *road* was a place to ride a horse or drive a cart; a *street* was a paved road; a *way* was usually a path through fields, forests or open land. In gardens, a walk, alure or alley became a place for elegant exercise. Thomas Hill wrote, in 1577, that 'Thus briefly haue I touched the benefites of walkes and Alleyes in any Garden ground.'[62] Bacon wrote that 'closer alleys must be ever finely gravelled'.[63]

Labyrinths

The earliest designs for ornamental garden compartments are for mazes and labyrinths. A *maze* offers the user a choice between many paths: it is multicursal. A *labyrinth* has a single path from the entrance to the centre: it is unicursal. Labyrinths are religious symbols. Mazes are symbolic games. Though maze and labyrinth are used interchangeably in everyday speech, it is best to keep their meanings separate.

Interest in labyrinths was stimulated by Renaissance philosophy. One of Plato's books (the *Timaeus*) was known to the Medieval world and highly influential. At Cosimo de Medici's request, Marsilio Ficino translated more of Plato's books and the core texts of the Hermetic tradition (the *Corpus Hermeticum*). Ficino wrote a book on *Platonic Theology* which aimed to strengthen Christianity by integrating it with Greek philosophy:

> *It is plain that, on the one hand, the Good that is in all things is God Himself, through whom all things are good, and that Beauty is the ray of God, spreading through those four circles ... the splendour of Ideas in the first circle, that of reasons in the second, that of seeds in the third, and that of forms in the last.*[64]

4.37 A maze (left) offers several paths to the centre and a labyrinth (right) has one true path.

4.38 The unicursal labyrinth at Alkborough is on a hillside overlooking the confluence of two rivers. It was first documented in 1697 but is likely to be older.

The labyrinth symbol imitated the nature of the world. It was arranged in circles and showed the importance of finding the one true path through life's vicissitudes. Early labyrinths were used to decorate buildings but they had obvious potential as decorations for garden compartments.

During the thirteenth and fourteenth centuries, unicursal labyrinths were made in the cathedrals of Sienna, Chartres, Amiens and elsewhere. Church windows and wall paintings typically had illustrations of Hell and colourful scenes of eternal agony to illustrate the necessity of good behaviour. The symbolic meaning of a labyrinth was that, with the Virgin Mary's help, one could avoid Hell and find the true path to Heaven. In the fifteenth century, designs for labyrinths began to appear in Italy. They include a drawing by Giovanni Fontana c.1420[65] and another by Sebastiano Serlio, published in 1537. The date at which labyrinths were first made in gardens is unknown. But by the sixteenth century, two types of labyrinth were being made in Italian gardens: with herbs and flowers, and with trees and shrubs trained on fences. A herbaceous labyrinth was an ornament to be viewed from windows and loggias or in the course of a garden walk. Circular planting patterns and labyrinths appear in drawings of English Renaissance gardens. Unicursal turf labyrinths were also made, and eight survive in England: one is in a garden; three are in the hills; four are on village greens or similar locations.[66] Woody labyrinths may have been a stage in the development of garden mazes.

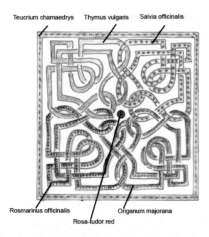

Teucrium chamaedrys   Thymus vulgaris   Salvia officinalis

Rosmarinus officinalis   Origanum majorana

Rosa-tudor red

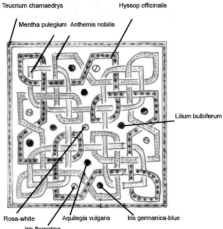

Teucrium chamaedrys   Hyssop officinalis

Mentha pulegium Anthemis nobilis

Lilium bulbiferum

Rosa-white   Aquilegia vulgaris   Iris germanica-blue

Iris florentina

4.39 Proposed re-creation of a knot garden, by Michael Simonsen for Wollaton Hall (see p. 427ff).

Mazes

The word 'maze' meant 'a state of confusion' in the fifteenth century. It was used for 'a delusive fancy or trick' and thus 'a network of winding and interconnecting paths or passages' (*OED*). Trevisa, in 1387, used 'maze' as a translation for *laborintus* and Goodge, in a 1577 translation of Heresbach's *Foure Books of Husbandry*, wrote of 'roses growyng in borders, and made in a maze' (*OED*). Multicursal mazes had secular and spiritual roles. They were games and puzzles; they were decorative; they could bring young people together; they could teach lessons about the nature of divine, romantic and erotic love; they were humanist devices. Homer had written about the use of a labyrinth (which he called 'a green, like that which Daedalus once made') in the *Iliad*:

> *Hereon there danced youths and maidens whom all would woo, with their hands on one another's wrists. The maidens wore robes of light linen, and the youths well woven shirts that were slightly oiled. The girls were crowned with garlands, while the young men had daggers of gold that hung by silver baldrics.*

Ringhieri, perhaps with Homer in mind, published his rules for *The Game of the Labyrinth (Giuoco del labirinto)*, in 1551.[67] The game was played in a multicursal maze:

> *The players form a circle, alternating men and women, and hold hands ... In the center of the labyrinth is the allegorical figure of Amore (Cupid), who directs a 'School of Love' for six attending maidens; outside the labyrinth wait Theseus, Ariadne, and six gentlemen. As the encircling players raise and lower their arms, a gentleman and then a lady in turn try to find their way out of, and into, the labyrinth. Should they meet along the path of the maze, they are encouraged to kiss and exchange affectionate words, for this is Cupid's desire.*

These rules are followed by recommended points for debate:

- Why is the maze called 'blind'?
- Why does the state of love resemble a labyrinth?
- Is it appropriate to believe that human life is an inextricable maze?
- Why is a woman's golden hair, or blonde braids, an intricate yet very sweet maze?
- Should the study of philosophy be called a maze because the inquiring mind could find a way out?

Mazes with tall hedges had even better opportunities for romantic encounters.

Pirro Ligorio designed labyrinths for the Villa d'Este (see p. 115). Salomon de Caus, after leaving Greenwich, designed a maze for the Hortus Palatinus in Heidelberg. The first English drawings showing this type of space appeared in the sixteenth century.

The Wyngaerde drawing of Richmond Palace (1562) provides a glimpse of a circular planting design in the garden. It could be a labyrinth or, just possibly, Ficino circles constituting an imitation of the Platonic forms. Planted circles were popular in French gardens and interest in Plato was stronger in France. Mazes and labyrinths could be romantic, instructive and philosophical.

Knots

In Tudor England, patterns made with decorative plants were often described as 'diverse knots'. Today they are called 'knot gardens' and sometimes considered to be Medieval.[68] This makes sense only if the Tudor period is regarded as Medieval. Some 'knot' gardens used patterns from rope, ribbon or carpet knot. Others used patterns drawn from heraldry, wood carving, stone carving, painting, dress and embroidery. There is a need for further research as to how, when, where and why 'knots' were made and managed. But the reason for making them is clear: they were 'conceits', 'inventions' and 'devices' to amuse and delight viewers.

Etymologically, the words 'knot' and 'knit' derive from the Old Germanic *knutton* meaning: 'An intertwining ... of anything flexible enough, made for the purpose of fastening them together' (*OED*). There is an early use of the word (*c.*1225) in the Legend of St Katherine of Alexandria:

> *He has wedded himself to my virgin state with the ring of true faith, and I have truly devoted myself to him. So are we united and bound into one, and the knot is so knit betwixt us two, that neither craft nor strong force of any living man may loosen or slacken it.*[69]

4.40 a, b, c Henry VII's Nonsuch Palace. (a) and (b) Drawings by John Speed and Joris Hoefnagel, both from the south. (c) The plan shows John Speed's knot gardens in position. Hoefnagel shows trees within the wall but the layout is not shown. There were more knots within the Privy Garden and there was probably a view of the deer park from the Banqueting House.

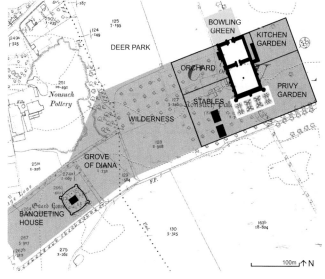

4.41 Illustrations of knot and labyrinth patterns from Thomas Trevilian's *Miscellany* (1608).

4.42 Elizabeth I translated *The Miroir or Glasse of the Synneful Soul*, penned the text and embroidered the cover.[72] It has Katherine Parr's initials at the centre of what is probably a true lover's knot. Heartsease (*Viola tricolor*) at the four corners could symbolise the love between Katherine Parr and Henry VIII.

Katherine's lover was Christ. She was whipped for her devotion and tied to what came to be called a Catherine Wheel. Miraculously, she was rescued before her torture began. Her name was taken by St Catherine's Monastery, in the Sinai Desert, and she became a beloved saint in Medieval England. Her true love was legendary. A Medieval blend of divine love, passionate love and pain contributed to the popularity of the 'true lover's knot' symbol during the Middle Ages and the Renaissance. King Louis of Sicily instituted an Order of the Knot (*Ordre du Nœud*) in 1352. Its badge was a true lover's knot inter-twined with gold. Shakespeare wrote of a swain being seen 'from the west corner of thy curious-knotted garden'.[70]

Physically, knots were made with herbs, flowers, stones, sand, gravel and grass. The French word for this type of pattern is *entrelacs*. It means 'interlaced' and explains the key characteristic of a knot. Words were still being borrowed from French in the fifteenth century and if the idea of making knot gardens had come to England from France, which is possible, then they would probably have been called *entrelacs* instead of knots. It seems more likely that the design idea travelled separately to France and England, from Italy, and that the name 'knot' came from Old English. After the introduction of printing to England in 1476, Latin works became available and Latin became the primary source for additions to English.

Italy was the leading cultural power in Europe when the term 'knot' came to be used in connection with English gardens.[71] There are well-known paths of influence

4.43 A modern knot pattern, in Birmingham Botanical Garden, using box and brick paving, which were not used until the Baroque period.

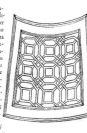

4.44 St Katherine, tied to a column and ready to be scourged. She contributed to the popularity of the 'true lover's knot'.[73]

4.45 a, b, c Drawings from the *Hypnerotomachia Poliphili* (*The Dream of Poliphilus*) which contains some of the oldest illustrations of garden features, including knot gardens and vine arbours.[74]

running north from Italy and a good deal of textual evidence for the use of herbs and flowers in fifteenth-century Italy 'but the visual evidence is confined to the imaginary garden in Francesco Colonna's *Hypnerotomachia Poliphili*'.[75] Colonna writes of 'little square gardens of marvellous work, showing arrangements of various edible plants'. He does not call them knots but does explain their design, construction and planting:

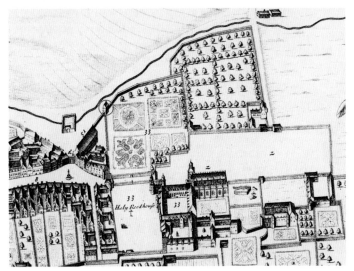 

4.46 a, b John Gordon's 1647 plan of Edinburgh shows the Palace of Holyrood with a set of knot gardens. The building now called Queen Mary's Bath House (marked with a red circle) is the only survivor. It could have been a gazebo from which to view the knots, or a bathing house, or a banqueting house or a pavilion for use with the tennis courts that preceded the knot gardens.

The first quadrangle was defined by the paths on either side, which caused it to be an irregular square. It had a four-sided lineament of knot-work three palms wide, made out of bunches of flowers ... The loops of the first band open out inside the second square to make a circle that filled it ... in the middle of that circle was an eight-petalled rosette. In the centre of this was set a hollow round altar of yellow Numidian stone with three ox-skulls ... the first band was densely planted marjoram, the second with aurotano, the third with ground-pine, and the lozenge with mountain thyme.[76]

This description is of the patterned garden shown in Figure 4.45 (a). The 'bands' which make the pattern are made of 'simples' (medicinal herbs). A second patterned garden, Figure 4.45 (b), shows 'a marvellous distribution of plants and a splendid knot-design picked out by the colours of various simples':

The lines of the pattern were made with bands of white marble fixed in the ground, four and a half inches wide on their surface and bordered on either side with simples. Within the boundaries of this stone enclosure there grew various little herbs, dense and level ... By Jupiter, it was a wonderful exhibition, giving great delight to the senses! ... Every free square was covered with flowering cyclamen, and their bands were of myrtle.[77]

These ways of using plants resemble the use of plants in Utens's paintings of a century later. He shows patterns of flowers and herbs (simples) in geometrical beds and separated by ribbons of gravel. The patterns, it must be noted, were 'never of box as they were in later gardens'.[78] Colonna's book circulated in England and France and English accounts of how to make 'knots' resemble Colonna's. Thomas Hill published designs for knots in 1594. He uses Classical quotes in the Renaissance manner and also wrote books on dreams and astrology. John Marriot published a set of designs for 'Certaine excellent and new invented knots and mazes, for plots for gardens' in 1618. The designs appear to relate to those published by Colonna in 1499 but this does not explain their ultimate origin.

Gothein suggested that the idea of making knots may derive from Islamic carpets, which were made by tying knots and had abstract representations of gardens. John Harvey believed that 'the artistic sense of the word "knot" derived from the carved bosses of stone vaulting or wooden roofs and implies only a circumscribed design of any kind'.[79] Other authors have identified other sources from which knot patterns may have come. Robin Whalley gives examples of knot patterns from Sumerian cylinder seals, Celtic art, the floor of Chartres cathedral, the Lindisfarne Gospels and elsewhere.[80] There is no conclusive evidence of when or how knot patterns were first used in gardens – but there are many possibilities awaiting further research.

Orchards

Orchards were one of the main components of Medieval gardens (see p. 84). They remained important in Renaissance gardens but occupied a lower proportion of the garden space and disappeared from smaller estates. It may be that an expansion of commercial fruit production, markets and road transport made it less necessary for estates to be self-sufficient in fruit. Farming, in the sense of renting land at a firm (or farm) price led to great houses producing less of their own food.

4.47 An orchard at Hardwick Hall.

4.48 a, b (a) Kirby Hall (*c.*1690). Gardens were used for walking when wall-walks were no longer available. The countryside was muddy, unsafe and intensively farmed. (b) The Stoke Edith tapestry (*c.*1710–20) shows how gardens were used: for walking and for viewing flowers, fountains and statues.

Grass plats and lawns

Grass does not seem to have been used as sitting space in Renaissance gardens as it had been in Medieval herbers. Castles had been cramped and offered little or no private sitting space. Renaissance palaces were spacious and gardens became places to walk rather than sit. Grass plats, as shown on plans and drawings, became ornamental and were used to display valuable statues. The *OED* definition of a grass plat is 'A piece of ground covered with turf, sometimes having ornamental flower-beds upon it.' But a plat, or plot, could also be utilitarian, as in 'When your chicks have got strength, you shall feed them abroad in some close walled grass-plat'[81] and 'you shall make a large green court, being either walled, paled; or otherwise very strongly fenced about, in which your hounds may play, sport, scummer, and do other offices of nature fit for their health.'[82]

The word 'lawn' derives from the Old French *launde* and the Latin *saltus*. It formerly meant 'an open space among woods, a glade' (*OED*) and was defined in Philip Miller's *Gardeners Dictionary* (1733) as 'a great plain in a park ... as to the situation of a lawn, it will be best in the Front of the House'.[83] Stephen Switzer, in 1718, advised that made up ground should be allowed to settle but that 'the lower quarters of a parterre, or an open lawn, or bowling-green, that is not so raised, may be immediately turfed'.[84] Switzer's former employers, London and Wise, advised that:

> There's nothing so handsome as a quarter of green turf, because the grass of it grows always very short; and formerly, when the method of making several sorts of green quarters was not known, or not approved of, nothing but green turf was made use of. The great charge [change] that attends it, especially in great quarters, has since brought other methods of making them in vogue.[85]

4.49 The bowling green at Aberdour Castle now has a sundial in the centre.

4.50 The great sundial at Glamis Castle, believed to date from *c.*1670, has 84 component dials.

The 'great change' London and Wise refer to is the use of turf from thin upland soils where 'the grass is fine' and the use of 'the seed of hay from the finest upland pastures'. It then had to be mown (i.e. scythed), Markham and Lawson advising that 'a man may well mow ... of very thin and short grass, or upland meadow, two acres at the least every day'.[86] It may be assumed that London and Wise are referring to *Agrostis* and *Fescue* species and that their use to make lawns dates from this time. Loudon reports Evelyn having seen that in Paris 'all the short grass was cut in the night-time'.[87]

Bowling greens

The game of bowls was popular in the Middle Ages but banned periodically because archery was seen as the important skill and bowling was associated with drinking and gambling.[88] Husbandsmen, journeymen, artisans and seamen could play only during the twelve days of Christmas and, by licence, in their masters' gardens. With the spread of well-kept lawns, bowling greens became a popular feature of Renaissance gardens.

At Woburn Abbey, Celia Fiennes took note of

> *a large bowling-green with 8 arbours kept cut neatly, and setes in each, there is a high tree that ascends from the green 50 steps, that commands the whole parke round to see the Deer hunted, as also a large prospect of the country.*[89]

Fiennes's note is a reminder that watching a hunt retained its popularity.

4.51 The sundial at Pitmedden has 27 faces and the inscription '*Tempus Fugit*'. The garden dates from 1675 but the original plans were lost in a fire. This space may have been like the garden of Holyrood Palace (see p. 138) or it may have been a vegetable garden; there are very old apple trees on the walls. It is unlikely to have been a Baroque parterre.

Sundials

Sundials were made in ancient Egypt, where an example survives from 1500 BCE, and continued to be made in subsequent centuries. Renaissance science led to the invention of sophisticated multi-faceted dials and they became popular garden ornaments. John White commented that:

> *This dial may be made into sundry forms, either four-square, six, or eight square, or round as you please, and it is to be placed on the head of a Post, either in Garden, Yard, or at the out-side of a glass-window where the Sun cometh: behold the form.*[90]

Sundials are often the oldest surviving features from Britain's Renaissance gardens. In addition to their ornamental qualities, they were the most accurate means of knowing the time. The enthusiasm for dials continued into the Baroque period.

Mounts

Garden mounts were a Renaissance innovation with a similar role to Medieval wall-walks (see pp. 88–9). Lazzaro states that in Italy 'mounts, little mountains of *montagnette*, were popular from the mid-fifteenth century at least',[91] and gives Giovanni Rucellai's 1459 account of his garden at Quaracchi, outside Florence, as an example. The mount had a diameter of 59 metres and was planted with firs, juniper, arbutus, laurel, broom and box. Giovanni Battista Falda's drawing of 1683 shows a mount at the Villa Medici in Rome:

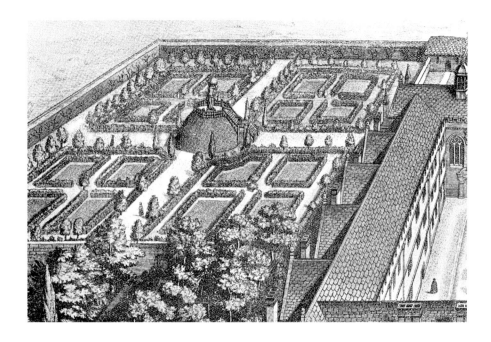

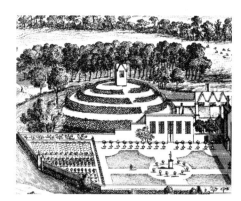

4.52 a, b Mounts at Wadham College, Oxford, and at Dunham Massey.

4.53 Mounts were sometimes provided with spiral paths so that they became, in effect, three-dimensional labyrinths, as at Packwood House. The topiary dates from the nineteenth century.

Visitors who followed the spiral path, or climbed the 60 steps to the summit, were rewarded with a vista of the city, surrounding countryside, and ordered garden below which was yet more spectacular than the view in antiquity because of the still greater height.[92]

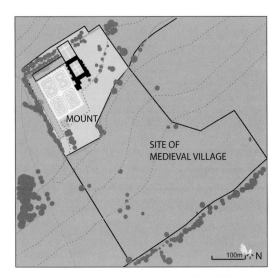

4.54 a, b There is small mount on the edge of the garden at Kirby Hall, which would have allowed outward views.

Similar design objectives appear to have guided the making of mounts in English Renaissance gardens. They gave views of knots and of scenery beyond the enclosed garden. Though often associated with Medieval gardens, it is much more likely that they are Renaissance features. Francis Bacon's 1625 essay 'On gardens' recommends a banqueting house on a mount:

> I wish also, in the very middle, a fair mount, with three ascents and alleys enough for four to walk abreast; which I would have to be perfect circles, without any bulwarks or embossments; and the whole mount to be thirty foot high; and some fine banqueting house with some chimneys neatly cast, and without too much glass.
> ...
> At the end of both the side grounds I would have a mount of some pretty height, leaving the wall of the enclosure breast-high, to look abroad into the fields.[93]

Hampton Court Palace had the earliest recorded mount in an English garden. It was made in 1532 and survived until 1690.[94] William Schellinks described it in 1662:

> One goes through a door up some steps to a very pleasant octagonal summer-house, which stands on a higher level; from which one has a view over the whole garden; in its middle stands a marble table on a pedestal, and its ceiling is painted with a heaven full of cupids. There is nothing but glass windows all round, and under them are nicely carved benches. Below this place is a deep vaulted wine cellar.[95]

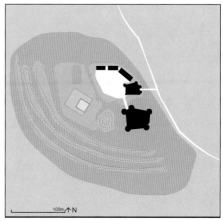

The mount at Warwick Castle, which survives, was painted by Canaletto in 1751 and described by Celia Fiennes, *c*.1697. She wrote that the garden had

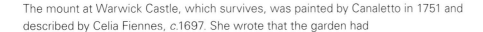

good gravell and grass walks, one walke to another, the whole of which I saw at one view on the top of the Mount, together with the whole town and a vast prospect all about, the Mount being very high and the ascent is round to and again secured by cut hedges on the side of the path.[96]

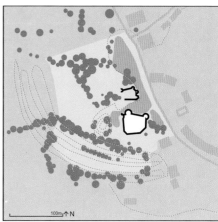

4.55 a, b, c (a) There is a mount at Whittington Castle for which a date of 1413 has been suggested. This would make it the oldest-known garden mount in Europe, which is improbable. (b) Plan of Whittington Castle, showing what is thought to be the position of the Medieval garden. (c) Whittington Castle in 2010.

4.56 Warwick Castle, painted by Canaletto in 1751, shows the mount being used as spiral ramp to take the residents of a stately home from the wall-walk to a landscape park, illustrating the evolution of garden design after the Middle Ages.

4.57 The present banqueting house at Hampton Court was designed by Talman in 1700 and stands near the site of Henry VIII's banqueting house.

4.58 a, b The banqueting house in the north-west corner of the garden at Melford Hall has views over the garden and land beyond the garden. Plan and photo.

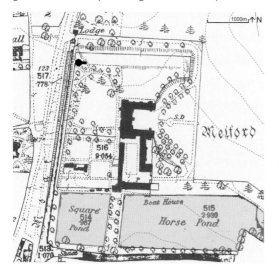

Banqueting houses

Renaissance princes and scholars found Classical precedents for elegant outdoor feasts in the *Song of Solomon*, in Plato's *Symposia*, in Ovid's *Fasti* and elsewhere. Ovid described a 'banquet of the gods' in a garden:

> *Some roamed at haphazard in the vales of shady Ida; some lay and stretched their limbs at ease on the soft grass; some played; some slept; some, arm linked in arm, thrice beat with rapid foot the verdant ground. Vesta lay and careless took her peaceful rest, just as she was, her head low laid and propped upon a sod. But the ruddy guardian of gardens courted nymphs and goddesses, and to and fro he turned his roving steps.[97]*

The dashing Lord Beaufort, in Ben Johnson's *New Inn,* has more liking for Ovid's sensual poetry than Plato's philosophy:

> *I relish not these Philosophical Feasts;*
> *Give me a Banquet o' Sense, like that of Ovid.[98]*

'Banquet' derives from the French *banc*, 'bench', referring to a small table. Tudor banquets were romantic occasions to eat delicate foods in delicious company. The banquets took place in small rooms with good views, often after a feast in a great hall, with the food set on the 'banquet'. The foods were rare and exotic: oranges, cherries, dates and prunes, flavoured with spices and sugar. Small banqueting houses were made on the roofs and in the gardens of great houses (see Figure 4.19 (a)). Henry VII had one on a mount overlooking the River Thames at Hampton Court. Another banqueting house was built overlooking the river at Hampton Court, *c*.1700.

Pleaching

The word 'plashing', with the same root as 'platting', was used for the art of interweaving branches to make a hedge. 'Pleached' is a poetic version of the word and was used by Shakespeare, as in 'a thicke pleached alley in mine orchard'[99] and in 'bid her steale into the pleached bowere'.[100] Pleached walks were made in Italian Renaissance gardens and illustrated in early English garden books. They were used to support grape vines and as sheltered garden walks running between rectangular lawns and knots.

Fountains

Illustrations of Medieval European gardens show fountains being used for bathing but, with the Renaissance, the use and character of fountains began to change. Richmond Palace (*c*.1501) had a fountain in an inner courtyard. It was ornamented with rose branches, reminding visitors of the wounds of Christ.[101] This was a Medieval conception. Henry VIII had two fountains built on the Field of the Cloth of Gold in 1520 and shown on a painting 20 years later.[102] Symbolic Tudor roses are prominent

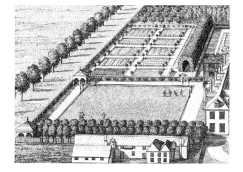

4.59 A pleached walk at Grimsthorpe.

4.60 a, b (a) Two fountains built for Henry VIII on the Field of the Cloth of Gold in 1520. (b) A copy, in wood, at Hampton Court.

but Renaissance-style ornament can also be seen. There are statues, shell niches, swags and pilasters.

Nonsuch Palace (see p. 135), built by Henry VII, 1538–41, had a Renaissance fountain. As described by Paul Hentzner in 1598, there were 'so many casts that rival even the perfection of Roman antiquity' and 'two fountains that spout water one round the other like a pyramid, upon which are perched small birds that stream water out of their bills' and

> *in the grove of Diana is a very agreeable fountain, with Acteon turned into a stag, as he was sprinkled by the goddess and her nymphs, with inscriptions. There is besides another pyramid of marble full of concealed pipes, which spirt upon all who come within their reach.*[103]

The imagery is Classical. Nonsuch was built made to rival Francis I's Renaissance palace, the Château de Chambord.

Bolsover Castle, commissioned by Sir Charles Cavendish, was a Medieval re-creation by Robert Smythson, completed in 1621 (see Figure 3.21). The castle garden, though made after 1608, feels Medieval. The fountain, made after 1628, 'combines the personal and bawdy with the elegant and classical'.[104] Lucy Worsley believes the statue of Venus took its inspiration from a Mannerist original, by Giambologna, in Florence.[105]

Statues

Pre-Christian Roman towns were crowded with statues. Eusebius recounts that the heathens had 'not only filled every city, and village, and district with temples, shrines, and statues in their honour, but have followed their evil example to the ruin of their own souls'.[106] He describes 'a well watered and shady grove, and in it were several marble statues of those whom he accounted to be gods'.[107] Eusebius therefore admired Constantine for making Christianity the official religion of the Roman Empire. He saw Constantine as 'our prince, who enjoyed the favour of the King of kings' and emptied Rome of pagan statues:

> *As soon, then, as his commands were issued, these engines of deceit were cast down from their proud eminence to the very ground, and the dwelling places of error, with the statues and the evil spirits which they represented, were overthrown and utterly destroyed.*[108]

The biographies of saints contained proud records of the pagan statues they had destroyed. The placing of statues in gardens was discontinued.

Christian attitudes to statuary changed with the Renaissance. As antiquity was rediscovered, so was its imagery. Now used to illustrate moral truths, pagan imagery became central to Renaissance art. The idea seems to have been that if one God

4.61 This 1607 map of Windsor shows 'The Fountaine' which supplied water to 'the Lodginges for the Howshold'. Paths criss-cross the Upper Ward, which appears to comprise untidy grass with muddy paths (see also Figure 3.32 (b)).

4.62 Kneeling slave in the Middle Temple Garden. John Dryden asked: 'Shall I, who, to my kneeling slave, could say, Rise up, and be a king; shall I fall down, And cry, Forgive me, Caesar!'.[109]

made the entire world, including its Greek philosophers, then pagan art and philosophy are to be counted among God's works. Roman statues were excavated from ancient gardens and placed in Renaissance gardens.

English visitors admired the statues in Italian gardens. The greatest collection of pagan statues was displayed in the Vatican's Belvedere Courtyard. It became a powerful advertisement for a new Christian attitude to statuary. Noblemen returned from the Grand Tour with collections of both ancient and modern statues. The Earl of Arundel assembled a famous collection. *Peacham's Compleat Gentleman* (1634) observed that the pleasure of statues 'is best knowne to such as have seen them abroad in France, Spaine, and Italy, where the Gardens and Galleries of great men are beautified and set forth to admiration with these kinds of ornaments.'[110] Peacham then praised the Earl of Arundel to whom 'this angle of the world oweth the first sight of Greeke and Romane Statues, with whose admired presence he began to honour the Gardens and Galleries of Arundel-House about twentie yeeres ago'.[111] There is a glimpse of the Arundel Garden in a portrait of Thomas Howard, the Second Earl of Arundel, by Daniel Mytens the Elder. Other paintings and drawings show that a typical arrangement was to place a valuable statue in a square of grass edged with a *plat-band* (a 'flat band' of flowers on the edge of the grass).

4.63 a, b The Arethusa Fountain in Bushy Park (by Francesco Fanelli) was made for Henrietta Maria's garden at Somerset House. As shown on Kip and Knyff's drawing, the Somerset House garden had other statuary.

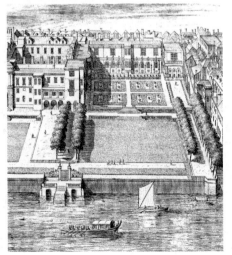

Conclusion

The Renaissance began in Italy and spread north, affecting society, technology and the arts. Literature and music came under its influence at an earlier date than the visual arts, and architecture was affected before gardens. Renaissance garden design did not influence England until the end of the fifteenth century. Plantagenet kings had fought the Hundred Years' War, from 1337 to 1453, to retain their hold on Normandy. Then they fought the Wars of the Roses, from 1455 to 1485, to retain their hold on England. When they lost, the House of Tudor took the throne and led the introduction of Renaissance culture. Henry VII laid the foundations for a confident, rich and independent English nation which sought to surpass the cultural achievements of

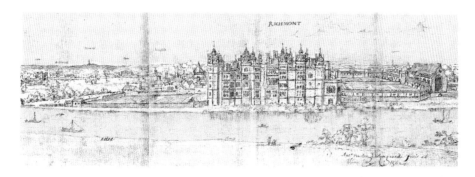

4.64 Antony van den Wyngaerde's drawing of Richmond Palace and garden in 1562.

4.65 The gatehouse is the only fragment of Richmond Palace which survives.

continental Europe. His son, Henry VIII (1491–1547), had the education, the taste and the spending habits of a Renaissance prince. He inherited a well-stocked treasury from his prudent father and spent lavishly on palaces and palace gardens.

Richmond Palace Gardens in 1501 (see p. 118) had the earliest known examples of the Renaissance garden features which became popular in sixteenth-century England: gravel walks, plant collections, knots, mazes, labyrinths, mounts, grass plats and statues. They could not have fitted within the confines of Medieval fortifications but provided for gracious living in palace grounds. Renaissance garden features became geometrically organised towards the end of the sixteenth century and, during the seventeenth century, were furnished with box parterres, axes, canals, avenues and other new ornaments. They can be classified as Baroque but, as discussed in the next chapter, the predominant character of seventeenth-century English gardens was as much Renaissance as Baroque. The Tudor period, from 1485 to 1603, was transitional. Partly Medieval and partly Renaissance, one could make a case for either categorisation. Renaissance influence continued through the seventeenth century and, as discussed in Chapter 5, was joined by a wave of Baroque influence.

Baroque gardens and landscapes, 1660–1750

5.0 Greenwich Park has some of the oldest avenues in Britain and typifies England's attitude to the Baroque – more pragmatic rather than dogmatic, more empiricist rather than rationalist. Regrettably, the northward view of the avenue has been blocked by a bin-store for a café.

The Baroque Age

Autocracy flourished in the seventeenth century, partly because cannon manufactured with Renaissance science made cities and castles insecure. Standing armies under centralised political control became necesssary. The Church was challenged by Renaissance ideas, leading to wars between Protestants and Catholics. The arts were cultivated, in part to proclaim the power of kings and princes. The calm of the Renaissance gave way to dynamic art forms (see p. 421). They could be called Late Renaissance but are normally seen as Baroque. The old simplification that 'the Baroque style expresses the spirit of the Counter-Reformation'[1] has given way to an acceptance that the Baroque Age was multi-dimensional. In addition to their political, religious and territorial ambitions, Baroque princes sought to dominate the worlds of art and ideas:

> *Princely art in the baroque age aimed to offer the court and the people a display of the supernatural powers of the prince, and to create intense emotions that would lead to universal deference to the prince's will.*[2]

One can smile at the over-grown egos but using Baroque prestige to maintain order was kinder than using cannon. The word 'baroque' is thought to derive from a jeweller's term meaning 'rough pearl'. In the seventeenth century it was a little-used term and meant 'bizarre' or 'irregular'.[3, 4, 5] Then, in 1888, Heinrich Wölfflin gave the word a new life as an art-historical term[6] and its use has been expanding ever since.

5.1 The Baroque aspect of Vanbrugh Castle is its dramatic position and its role as a feature in Greenwich Park.

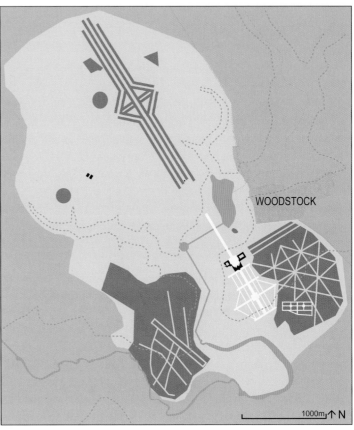

5.2 a, b The design of Blenheim Palace, begun by Vanbrugh in 1705, was unusual but largely Baroque.

5.3 a, b Before the present landscape garden was made, Castle Howard had a Baroque garden (see Figure 6.52).

5.4 Seaton Delaval, by Vanbrugh, is almost a stage set.

The Baroque painting style was known for its use of dramatic effects to arouse the emotions. In large part, though, Baroque art and architecture reflected the search for power that was such a large part of the seventeenth-century ethos. Baroque churches and palaces were magnificent and richly detailed. Kings and princes wanted other kings and princes as well as their subjects to be in awe of their power.[7]

'Baroque' is now used in connection with literature, painting, sculpture, music, drama, architecture, liturgy, politics, philosophy, science, warfare, literature[8] – and gardens. Marco Mincoff, a Shakespearean scholar, explains the links between Baroque painting and drama in a way which relates to the drama of Baroque garden design:

Renaissance pictorial composition depends on strongly stressed horizontal and vertical lines, giving an architectural effect, still further brought out by the strict adherence to symmetry or balance and the strong accent on the central figure ... It is not hard to establish a parallel with Shakespeare [1564–1616], who places the whole of the action within the framework of his drama, representing the first meeting of Romeo and Juliet, Hamlet's discovery of his father's murderer, the marriage of Othello, Coriolanus's rise to fame. Fletcher [1579–1625] on the other hand prefers to begin with a situation whose general lines have been laid down before the opening of the play ... And just as the commencement of the dramas represents an open form, so too the preference for the tragi-comedy in which the characters remain alive at the end, thus pointing forward into the future, may be taken as an open tendency.[9]

Baroque literature projected beyond 'the framework of the drama'. Baroque avenues projected beyond the frame of Renaissance gardens (see Figure 5.8). The sonnet form, as popularised by Petrarch, was typical of the Renaissance.[10] Baroque poetry had equally formal structures but they were used to project lines of argument. Andrew Marvell, in *To His Coy Mistress,* is concerned both with persuading her to yield to his desires and with the impermanence of earthly pleasures.[11]

John Vanbrugh had a Baroque enthusiasm for drama, architecture and gardens. He was a Whig and, at the age of 24, was arrested in France for helping to arrange what is now called the Glorious Revolution (1688). He became a dramatist after returning to England in 1693. This led to him designing a theatre and launched an astonishing career, as a surveyor, which included the design of Castle Howard (1699) and Blenheim Palace (1704). His own house, Vanbrugh Castle (1719), has a dramatic position overlooking Greenwich Park. Vanbrugh worked closely with the leading garden designers of the day and became George I's Surveyor of the Gardens and Waters in 1714. Vanbrugh's stay in France had given him a liking for Baroque architecture and a liberal's hatred of French politics. One could argue, with Mincoff, that:

> *Pure baroque is indeed nowhere remarkably in evidence in England, and the avoidance of the Continental term in favour of such expressions as Stuart or seventeenth century is perhaps better justified than in the usual nomenclature of English art with its substitution of Norman for Romanesque, of Elizabethan for Renaissance.*[12]

Or one could argue, with Peter Davidson, that Baroque is a 'universal' concept which identifies 'the wholeness of the arts of early modern Europe' and 'is not confined to one geographical area or religious confession: most of all, it resists the idea that Baroque is the style of the Catholic south of Europe'.[13] Or one could argue that the 'Baroque' took such different forms in each country that special names are required, much as English critics write of 'Metaphysical poetry' instead of 'Baroque poetry'. I find 'Baroque' a more useful term than 'formal', or 'geometric', or 'Stuart', or 'Williamite', or 'Italian', or 'French', or 'Dutch', or anything else I can think of, to describe the strongest influence on British garden design between *c.*1650 and *c.*1725. It is necessary, however, to acknowledge that the Baroque tendency was less defined in Britain than in other large European countries, largely for political and religious reasons. It would not be wrong to say that English gardens were more 'Baroqued' than 'Baroque'. Scotland retained its strong links with continental Europe in the seventeeth century and imported Baroque ideas through direct contacts, rather than through England.

There is an interesting comparison between Europe's Baroque Age and the near-contemporary 'Manchu ambition to dominate the cultural, physical, and metaphysical geographies of Eastern and Central Asia'.[14] The palace gardens and the layout of Beijing were highly symbolic and Baroque princes, even in Britain, had a comparable ambition to dominate the cultural, physical, religious and political geographies of the lands they aspired to rule.

Baroque gardens in continental Europe

5.5 a–d The Baroque style of garden design originated in Italy, flourished in France and influenced Britain: (a) the Villa Garzoni; (b) the Boboli; (c) Vaux le Vicomte; (d) Versailles.

5.6 a, b Hampton Court and Melbourne Hall are classified as 'formal' in England but, in a European context, they are Baroque.

5.7 a, b (a) Hampton Court's Renaissance garden, overlaid on the subsequent layout. (b) Hampton Court with Baroque avenues and parterres.

Marie-Luise Gothein used the term 'Baroque' in her 1913 *History of Garden Art*.[15] The term remains popular in Germany and is gaining ground with garden historians in other European countries. The eminent French garden historian Marguerite Charageat wrote a chapter on the Baroque gardens of Italy, Austria and France for her 1962 book *L'art des jardins* but she did not use the word in a chapter on the grand style of seventeenth-century French gardens: they are *jardins classique*. France has 'almost completely refused' to adopt the term 'Baroque'.[16] Prévôt, however, has a section on

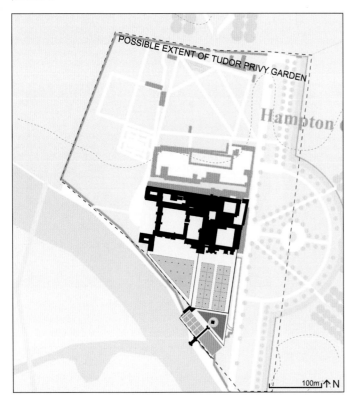

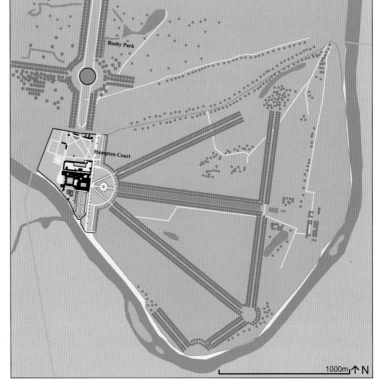

the 'Age baroque: le triomphe de la perspective longue' in his 2006 *Histoire des jardins*.[17] English garden historians also tend to avoid the word 'Baroque'. They use the names of monarchs or dynasties (e.g. 'William and Mary', 'Queen Anne' or 'Stuart') when discussing the Baroque style. Or they call it 'formal', without defining the term (see p. 221). But use of the word 'Baroque' is gaining ground and books on French and English Baroque gardens may yet be written. I found 'Baroque' a useful category when writing a general history of European gardens. Renaissance gardens had outward views of the landscapes in which they were set but did not have axes projecting beyond garden boundaries. Baroque gardens had external axes and internal axes connecting structures, garden features and distant scenery. The visual integration of gardens with landscapes was a key aspect of Baroque garden design.

The term *hortus conclusus* (see p. 81) draws attention to a characteristic of gardens made between the Norman Conquest and the English Civil War: enclosure. After the Renaissance, views were admired and gardens were opened to view. 'The ubiquity of prospect in Italian gardens was always attested by English visitors, and this characteristic ingredient of their variousness was rarely if ever a feature of French gardens.'[18] In Italy, the journey from Medieval to Renaissance to Baroque was one of pushing views outward (from terraces, lines of sight and avenues) and then of increasing inward views. Avenues dramatised the location of palaces. Radiating and intersecting stars of avenues accentuated the Baroque drama.

The 'formal' nature of Baroque gardens

Bertrand Russell reflected that:

> One might say it is the nature of an acorn to grow into an oak, and in that case one would be using the word in an Aristotelian sense ... Nature is in form rather than in matter.[19]

Equally, one might say that 'it is the nature of land beside a house to grow into a garden and in that case one would be using the word "nature" in an Aristotelian sense. Nature is in form rather than in matter.' The title of Aristotle's book on *Physics* comes from the Greek word for 'nature': *physis*.[20] Aristotle used *physis* in two senses: to mean 'general nature' and to mean 'particular nature'. The distinction comes from Plato's Theory of Forms (see p. 222) and both senses were current in English. It is often unclear whether an author is using 'nature' in both senses or in one sense – but one should try to find out.

John Ray is an example of an author who placed great store on the distinction between nature as a forming power and nature as the world formed by the power. He

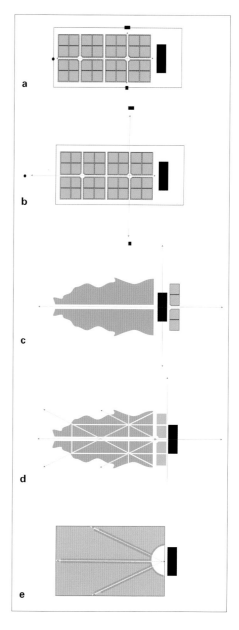

5.8 a–e The use of axial lines in garden design began in Italy, developed in France and spread to England. The evolutionary sequence was: (a) axes focused on points within gardens; (b) axes focused on points outside gardens; (c) axes projecting from centrally positioned dwellings into the landscape; (d) goose-foot stars of avenues pointing everywhere; and (e) radiating lines of trees in parkland.

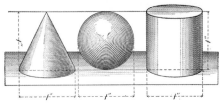

5.9 a, b, c (a) and (b) Circular ('Platonic') pools at Melbourne Hall. (c) The cone, sphere and cylinder were thought to 'gratify the minds of men'.

is considered one of the 100 most important scientists in history, because he prepared the ground for Linnaeus.[21] In *The Wisdom of God Manifested in the Works of the Creation*, Ray uses the existence of species groups (e.g. mammals) to prove the existence of God. Ray begins with a quotation from Psalm 104: 24: 'How manifold are thy works, O Lord! In Wisdom hast thou made them all.' Ray believed that 'after the first Formation of the Universe all Things were brought to pass by the settled Laws of Nature'. God's laws form the world; human ideas form artefacts; hearts distribute blood in mammals; channels distribute water in gardens:

> Is it not admirable, that from this Fountain of Life and Heat, there should be Channels and Conduit-Pipes, to every, even the least and most remote, Part of the Body; just as if ... from one Fountain in a Garden, there should be little Channels or Dykes cut to every Bed, and every Plant growing therein, as we have seen more than once done beyond the Seas.[22]

In the 1660s, John Ray toured the gardens of continental Europe with his patron, Sir Francis Willoughby of Wollaton Hall (see also Appendix III on p. 427). They liked to see evidence of forming powers and Ray believed the most beautiful things were those in which these powers were most evident. Ray appeals 'to any man that is not sunk into so forlorn a pitch of degeneracy' to acknowledge that some forms have 'a settled idea and nature, as a cone, sphere or cylinder'. They will 'gratify the minds of men, and pretend to more elegancy of shape than those rude cuttings or chippings of free-stone that fall from the mason's hands'.[23] Ray was influenced by the Cambridge Platonists[24] and preferred 'formal' shapes to irregular shapes. He conceives 'formal' as in Plato's Theory of Forms. The classic expression of this view is the axiom that 'Art should imitate Nature'. Christians interpreted the axiom to mean that the art of man should imitate the formative principles used by God. Henry Wotton, in *The*

Elements of Architecture (1624), wrote that even when planning the sewer pipes in a house 'Art should imitate Nature', i.e. they should be kept out of sight in the 'lowest and thickest part of the foundation', as in our bodies. Wotton, like Ray, wondered at the plenitude of nature as well as its forming power. He is best known to garden historians for his comment on the difference between gardens and buildings:

> *First, I must note a certain contrariety between building and gardening: for as fabriques should be regular, so gardens should be irregular, or at least cast into a very wild regularity. To exemplify my conceit; I have seen a garden (for the manner perchance incomparable) into which the first access was a high walk like a terrace, from whence might be taken a general view of the whole plot below; but rather in a delightful confusion, then with any plain distinction of the pieces. From this the beholder descending many steps, was afterwards conveyed again, by several mountings and valings, to various entertainments of his scent, and sight: which I shall not need to describe (for that were poetical) let me only note this, that every one of these diversities, was as if he had been magically transported into a Garden.*[25]

Wotton admired both the 'formal' aspects of terraces and the 'delightful confusion' of plants. He was interested in the forming powers and their formal expressions.

Baroque influence on British gardens

Information about Baroque gardens reached England direct from Italy, which was a hazardous journey, and through travel to France and Holland, which was relatively easy. The exodus of royalists from England after 1649 and the arrival of William and Mary, from Holland in 1688, were key events. Holland and England were Protestant countries, sympathetic to the artistic and scientific culture of the Baroque Age but hostile to political absolutism and Roman Catholicism. To describe Dutch Baroque gardens as half-hearted and English Baroque gardens as quarter-hearted would be to make French gardens the standard by which the High Baroque is judged:

> *In England royal expenditure on the baroque priorities of self-glorification and self-indulgence were limited in much the same way as were the powers and prerogatives of the crown. A parliamentary system is by nature incompatible with the baroque, and doubly so in an increasingly middle-class and anti-Catholic country like England ... the 'baroque' art and literature of England bear a similar relationship to their Continental counterparts as the Anglican church did to the church of Rome.*[26]

The first Baroque garden within easy reach of London was the Jardin du Luxembourg in Paris. It was commissioned by Marie de Medici and work began in 1612. She had lived in the Boboli Gardens, one of the first Baroque gardens in Italy, and appreciated

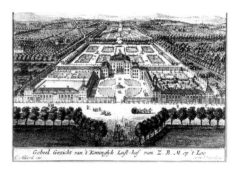

5.10 a, b (a) William and Mary made a Baroque palace garden at Het Loo, in Holland, before taking the English throne. It has parterres, a central axis and avenues projecting into farmland. (b) The garden at Het Loo was fully restored from old drawings.

the aesthetic and political role of the arts in proclaiming the prestige of the Medici family. Marie's daughter, Henrietta Maria, married the king of England (Charles I) and was the mother of Charles II. John Evelyn, a friend of both kings, wrote a description of the Luxembourg Garden:

> *The walks are exactly fair, long, and variously descending, and so justly planted with limes, elms, and other trees, that nothing can be more delicious, especially that of the hornbeam hedge, which being high and stately, buts full on the fountain. Towards the farther end, is an excavation intended for a vast fish-pool, but never finished, and near it is an in-closure for a garden of simples, well-kept; and here the Duke keeps tortoises in great number, who use the pool of water on one side of the garden. Here is also a conservatory for snow. At the upper part, towards the palace, is a grove of tall elms cut into a star, every ray being a walk, whose centre is a large fountain. The rest of the ground is made into several enclosures (all hedge-work or rows of trees) of whole fields, meadows, bocages, some of them containing divers acres.*[27]

Evelyn was a key figure in steering English gardens towards the Baroque and, as noted below, brought many important garden terms into English. John Dixon Hunt believes Evelyn wished to write a treatise which would raise garden designers above the level of 'cabbage-planters'. But he was not a talented theorist and consequently failed to complete the *Elysium Britannicum*. Evelyn wrote about Nature in connection

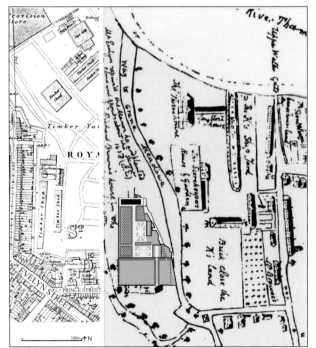

5.11 a, b (a) Drawing of Evelyn's Sayes Court garden, superimposed on his plan of Deptford and a nineteenth-century map of the Royal Dockyard (in which Peter the Great learned ship-building). Butt Lane was renamed Deptford High Street in 1825. The site of Sayes Court lies between the present Czar Street, Prince Street and Sayes Court Street. (b) Model of Evelyn's Sayes Court garden.

5.12 a, b Stanway is unusual, for England, in describing itself as a Baroque garden. The canal and the cascade were made in the 1720s and the fountain jet was added in 2004. One could think of it as a Renaissance garden which was 'Baroqued' and then 'Picturesqued'.

with gardens and stated that 'the Principle of all these Principles is nothing less then Nature herself'.[28] Hunt, opposing the view that 'Evelyn is Capability Brown or Uvedale Price before his time', explains that:

> [I]t was perfectly clear to Evelyn that the garden was always the result of a collaboration between art and nature; between, if you will, the plenitude and random data of the natural world and man's control over it via technology, science, and design. Although recently writers have tried to make Evelyn a spokesman for natural gardening, he provides, when carefully read, no hostages to that position.[29]

Evelyn designed his own garden at Sayes Court and designed gardens at Wotton and Albury (see pp. 124–5). He may also have advised on the design of Greenwich Park

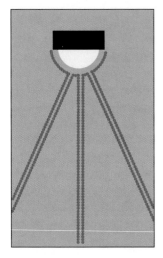

5.13 Diagram showing Phase I of the Baroque in England, as used in London's palace gardens.

5.14 Roy Strong describes Mollet's reconstruction of Wimbledon House as 'the last Renaissance and the first Baroque garden in England'.[30]

(see p. 167). In each case, his work can be interpreted as conferring a general nature (a Form) on a particular nature (a real place). Evelyn's own garden, at Sayes Court in Deptford, had an avenue and parterres but was not an integrated Baroque plan with radiating or projecting axes.

Baroque phases in Britain

Three phases of Baroque influence on British gardens can be identified:

- *Phase I, 1630–88*: Avenues in parkland are associated with the reign of Charles II (1660–85) and with the influence of André Mollet and André Le Nôtre on London's Royal Parks: Greenwich, St James's and Hampton Court. The avenues were not cut through woodland. They were planted with lines of trees in enclosed deer parks.
- *Phase II, 1688–1714*: Parterres, canals and avenues outside the main garden are associated with the reigns of Queen Mary, William III and Queen Anne (1688–1702 and 1702–14). London, Wise and Bridgeman were the leading designers. The avenues were often centred on great houses and projected into farmland beyond garden boundaries.

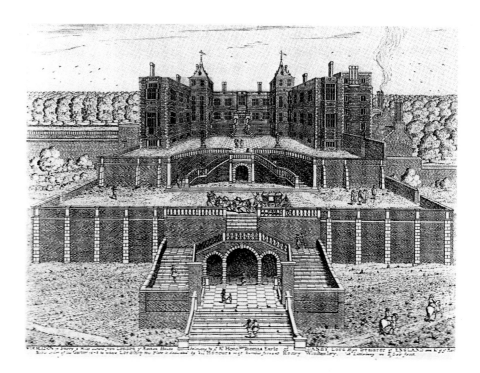

- *Phase III, 1714–27*: Avenues in woodland are associated with the reign of George I (1714–27), the early years of the Whig supremacy and with what Stephen Switzer called 'Extensive, Forest and Rural Gardening'.[31] The avenues often gave access to forest plantations on land which might have been used for parterres.

The dates, which relate to political events, are far from defining watertight compartments: the first phase could be dated from 1640 and the taste for 'formality' lingered well into the eighteenth century.

Phase I, 1630–88

A Baroque approach to garden design came to England with Queen Henrietta Maria and her retainers. Her father was King Henry IV of France and she was born in the Louvre Palace. Her mother, Marie de' Medici, had lived in the Boboli Garden as a girl and had made the first Baroque garden in France (see p. 166). Henrietta Maria, though married to Charles I at the age of 16, in 1625, learned little English and never lost her love of French culture and the Roman Catholic faith. In 1639, Charles purchased Wimbledon House for her. Inigo Jones was employed to modernise the house and, in 1642, André Mollet added Baroque parterres. Strong describes the result as

5.15 a, b, c Boscobel. (a) The Royal Oak is to the left of the summer house, beyond the hedge. (b) The drawing shows the mount and beds as they are today but it is a Renaissance garden and they are unlikely to have been planted with Baroque-style box hedges when Charles I looked down at them from his tree. (c) The planting of the rectangular beds is unclear from the seventeenth-century drawing.

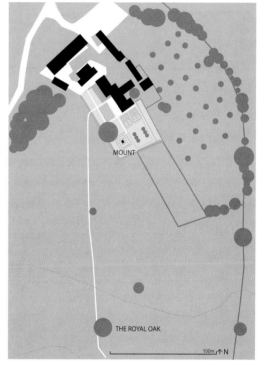

5.16 This plan from Mollet's *Le Jardin de plaisir* (1651) was seen by David Green as 'the gist and pith of the resplendent Le Nôtre's teaching'.[33] It inspired the design of London's Royal Parks: St James's, Greenwich and Hampton Court.

'the last Renaissance and the first Baroque garden in England'[32] but Henrietta Maria did not have an opportunity to enjoy the garden. The Civil War began in 1642 and she left England.

The future Charles II spent the night of 6 September 1651 in an oak tree overlooking a modest Renaissance garden, at Boscobel House (see p. 165). He was 21 years old and, having lost the Battle of Worcester, was hiding from Cromwell's troops before escaping to live with his mother, Henrietta Maria, in Paris. She was back in the Louvre Palace and could watch developments in the High Baroque style of garden design from within. A great parterre garden, the Tuileries, lay below the windows and several members of the Mollet and Le Nôtre families worked there. André Le Nôtre was appointed as Dessinateur des Plantes et Parterres of all royal gardens in 1643.[34] He began work on the design of Vaux le Vicomte in 1656 and on Versailles in 1661.

Charles II's period of exile ended in 1660 and he returned to London with an enthusiasm for Baroque garden design. He therefore invited André Mollet to London and asked André Le Nôtre to design a parterre for Greenwich Park. The aim was to make Greenwich an attractive home for his mother. John Evelyn, whose description of the Luxembourg was quoted above, became a trusted advisor on many issues. Charles II held to his father's belief that kings, occupying an intermediate position between God and men, have a Divine Right to rule. Speaking from the scaffold in 1649, his father had told bystanders that 'a subject and a sovereign are clean different things'.[35] Charles II's supporters, many of whom also spent time in France, were known as

5.17 The Mall in St James's Park began as a recreational avenue for playing a type of croquet called pal-mal. On 2 April 1661, Samuel Pepys wrote in his *Diary* that 'I saw the Duke of York playing at Pelemele, the first time that ever I saw the sport'.[36] It is now a busy road, closed to traffic on Sundays and for state events.

5.19 John Evelyn lived a mile from Greenwich Park and may have advised Charles II on its design.

5.18 Greenwich. The Queen's House (1614–17) centre, with Greenwich Park (*c.*1660) beyond, and Greenwich Hospital (1694–1742) in the foreground. They form a Baroque composition. But, in the English way, the axis is pragmatic; it lacks inter-visibility between points.

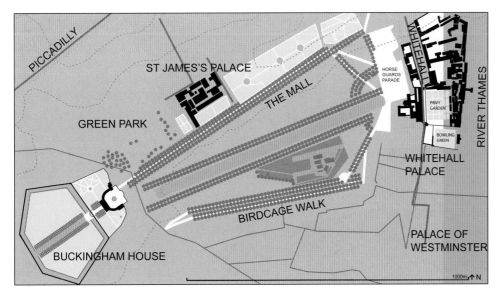

5.20 Plan of St James's Park showing both Whitehall Palace, which was destroyed in 1698, and Buckingham House, which was built after 1703. Celia Fiennes wrote *c.*1701 that the King's Palace in Whitehall had 'the prospect of the Thames on one side and a large Parke on the other, walled in, which is full of very fine walkes and rowes of trees, ponds and curious birds, deer and some fine cows; in this Parke stands another palace, St. James, which is very well and was built for some of the royal family as the Duke of Yorke or Prince of Wales; there is at Whitehall in the privy garden a large pond with a spout of water of a vast height; this of St. James is little but daily building adding may make it great; there is alsoe one Nobleman's house in this, Parke House, which is a very curious building.'[37] Henry Wise designed the canal in the garden of Buckingham Palace.

5.21 a, b Wollaton Hall had a Renaissance garden to which Baroque avenues were appended (see Appendix III).

5.22 a, b Doddington Hall is one of the best surviving examples of a garden drawn by Kip and Knyff, though the planting is much changed.

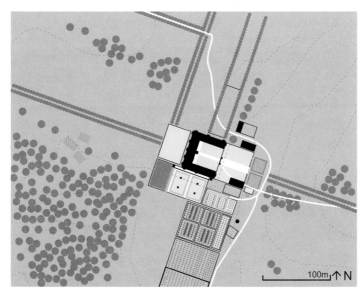

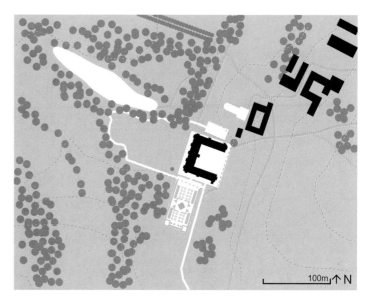

5.23 a, b, c (a) and (b) Temple Newsam in 1707 and 2011. The garden was drawn by Kip and Knyff in 1707. The compartments were removed by Lancelot Brown. A new parterre was built in the nineteenth century, without regard for the original layout. It fell into disrepair and was rebuilt by Leeds City Council Parks Department in the twentieth century, still without regard for the original layout (see also Figure 5.39). (c) The south front of Temple Newsam in 2010.

Royalists, Cavaliers and, after 1678, as Tories. His mother attended the opening of Vaux le Vicomte in 1661. It was the first High Baroque garden with fully integrated terraces, parterres, canals, fountains, statues and avenues.

In London, Charles II commissioned new designs for Greenwich, St James's and Hampton Court, which were walled deer parks. Their designer is unknown but one can guess that André Mollet and/or John Evelyn were consulted. As David Green pointed out, one of the plans in Mollet's *Le Jardin de plaisir* (1651) has a drawing of 'a moated mansion with extensive formal grounds northward to a demi-lune consisting of rank upon rank of trees planted in semicircles'[38] (see Figure 5.16). Green sees this drawing as 'the gist and pith of the resplendent Le Nôtre's teaching' and as the

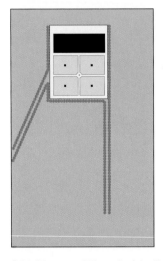

5.24 Diagram of Phase II of the Baroque in England, as found in the drawings of Kip and Knyff's *Britannia Illustrata* (1707).[40]

inspiration for 'the Stuart settings of Greenwich, St. James's, and Hampton Court, all of which showed as main motif a *patte d'oie* of avenues and/or canals radiating from semicircles of trees'.[39] Charles II's reign lasted until 1685 but was marred by a war with Holland, a shortage of money, a Great Plague (1665), a Great Fire (1666) and a popular dislike of Baroque politics and Roman Catholicism. Charles II made avenues by planting single lines of trees in small deer parks, not by cutting avenues through existing forests or by planting new forests. He was changing the design of old parks, not creating new parks.

Phase II, 1688–1714

James II became king in 1685, following the death of Charles II, but was replaced by William III in the Glorious Revolution of 1688. William ruled with his wife, Mary, a daughter of James II. The Baroque seeds which Charles II had planted with his London parks bore fruit during their reigns. William came from another Protestant country but had employed a French garden designer, Daniel Marot, to design his palace garden. Het Loo was made after 1684 with a central axis and a large parterre. Despite its avenues, the palace does not dominate the surrounding landscape. The style of Le Nôtre and Louis XIV had passed its zenith by 1688 and the second phase of Baroque influence on England could almost take the name 'Whig Baroque'. But the Tories were friendlier to royal authority than the Whigs, who had brought him to power, and William had some Tories in his government. Making a distinction between Whig and Tory approaches to gardens involves stretching the evidence.

John Rose had trained with Mollet in St James's Park and later employed George London. Henry Wise may have worked with Rose before going into partnership with George London. The two men established a great nursery and garden design business

5.25 a, b Parts of the layout shown on the Kip and Knyff drawing of Newby Hall survive.

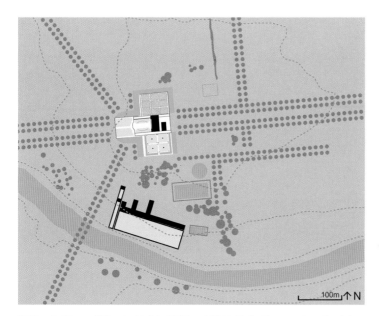
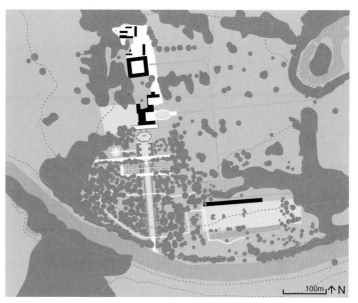

5.26 a, b Plans of Newby Hall in 1707 and 2011. Celia Fiennes described the garden in 1697: 'It looks finely in the approach in the middle of a good parke and a River runs just by it, it stands in the middle and has two large Gardens on each side; you enter one through a large Iron Barr-gate painted green and gold tops and carv'd in severall places, this is fine gravel walks between grass plots 4 square with 5 brass Statues great and small in each Square, and full of borders of flowers and green banks with flower potts; on the other side of the house is just such a Garden, only the walks are all grass, rowl'd, and the Squares are full of dwarfe trees both fruites and green, set cross ways which looks very finely, there is a Flower Garden behind the house, in it and beyond it a Landry Close with frames for drying of cloths, wall'd in …'[41]

at Brompton Park. Stephen Switzer and Charles Bridgeman worked in the nursery. London, Wise, Switzer and Bridgeman designed gardens in many parts of England and spread the second phase of Late Baroque ideas beyond the capital. Historians have examined their drawings and writings but a full history of English Baroque gardens awaits a systematic trawl through estate records. More information is available than for earlier periods. Until this is done, the best overviews of the period are in the diary of Celia Fiennes and the drawings of Kip and Knyff.

The Kip and Knyff garden drawings were discussed in Chapter 4 (see p. 126), because many of them show gardens which are distinctly un-Medieval without being uniformly Baroque. Only a few of the gardens, including Cassiobury, Badminton and Bretby, have classically Baroque central axes. Many of the others have tree-lined walks separating compartments and avenues projecting beyond garden boundaries. The 80 Kip and Knyff drawings published in *Britannia Illustrata* show:

- Less than 5 per cent of the gardens are without tree-lined walks.
- About 25 per cent have avenues within the rectangular compartmented framework.
- About 25 per cent have radiating avenues.

5.27 A painting by Hendrik Danckerts from 1675, believed to show Charles II of England receiving a pineapple from John Rose, with a Baroque parterre garden behind them.

5.28 a, b (a) The Baroque fountain at Chatsworth looks forlorn without the parterre in which it was set (see Figure 5.46 (a)). (b) Paxton's 1843 canal and lake are closer to the French Baroque style than the seventeenth-century layout.

- About 50 per cent have avenues which project the lines of the compartments into the surrounding farmland.

This was a characteristically British approach to avenues – more pragmatic than dogmatic. The plans are dominated by rectangular compartments, many of them previously seen in Renaissance gardens:

- orchards;
- vegetable gardens;
- woodland compartments, probably conceived as 'wilderness';
- bowling greens;
- mounts;
- dovecots;
- fish ponds and canals;
- parterres (mostly cutwork and grass work but with some 'embroidery').

The main Baroque innovations are the avenues, canals and parterres. The information from Kip and Knyff is supplemented by Celia Fiennes's account of her *Journeys*. She belonged to a prominent Whig family and visited every English county between 1684 and 1703, often staying with relatives in great houses. Tough, unmarried and curious about gardens, she travelled on horseback in the company of one or two servants. Fiennes does not use the words 'knot' or 'parterre', and when she sees them, as at Bretby, where the elaborate parterres were drawn by Kip and Knyff, she speaks of 'all sorts of flower trees and greens finely cut and exactly kept'.[42] Fiennes has little to say about avenues and uses the word for a road or a path, not for lines of trees. At Bretby, 'I turned up to ye Earle of Chesterfields parke full of fine Rows of trees running up the avenues to the house',[43] and at Coleshill 'all the avenues to the house are fine walkes of rows of trees'.[44]

Fiennes's description of Chatsworth includes typical Renaissance grass squares, statues and walks but with notable Baroque water features:

> *Before the gate there is a Large parke and Severall fine Gardens one without another with Gravell walkes and squairs of Grass with stone statues in them, and in the middle of Each Garden is a Large fountaine full of images, Sea Gods and Dolphins and sea horses which are full of pipes which spout out water in the bason and spouts all about the Gardens.*[45]

Christopher Ridgway and Robert Williams observe that garden historians tend to emphasise artistic considerations and to neglect the economic situation which made the gardens possible.[46] I agree, and we should distinguish the artistic avenues made in Phase I of English Baroque gardens from the avenues made in Phase III, which were almost rides in forest enterprises. The sixteenth century had seen the rise of gentleman farmers who, as the feudal system drew to its end, converted arable land to pasture, consolidated land holdings, depopulated villages and 'turned farms into capitalist enterprises',[47] often with commercial forests. There was an agricultural depression in the late seventeenth century. The gentry often had to sell out to aristocrats who, having money from other sources (mining, manufacturing, government jobs, etc.) used it to buy land which could be leased to hard-working farmers. This allowed the aristocrats to form compact estates with great mansions, gardens and parks supported by large revenues.[49] Many owners were 'getting rich quickly'.

Charles I's use of the Court of the Star Chamber as an instrument of tyranny has given it a bad reputation. Its original purpose had been to protect the common people from the excesses of the nobility, including the enclosure of open fields and common land. With this constraint removed, there was a rapid increase in the rate of enclosure:

> *So that now the seventeenth century is regarded as having had the fastest rate of enclosure, when about 24 per cent of the country is estimated to have been enclosed compared with only 2 per cent in the sixteenth century, 13 per cent in the eighteenth century and 11 per cent in the nineteenth century.*[50]

Changes in the land ownership pattern were reflected in estate layouts. Everyone knew that Medieval villages belonged to manors. In the seventeenth century, land owners used avenues to show the extent of their holdings. In the eighteenth century, they used avenues to access forestry projects and conceived landscapes as gardens.

5.29 Diagram of Phase III of the Baroque in England, described by Switzer as the 'Forest, or, in a more easy style Rural Gardening'.[48] Grass parterres took the place of embroidery parterres and forestry planting was undertaken within bastioned enclosures and in remote areas.

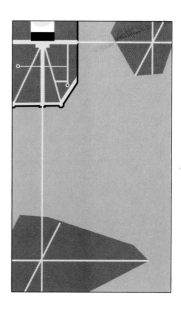

5.30 a, b Cirencester Park, Gloucestershire, was a major forestry enterprise and survives as the best example of the English Forest style.

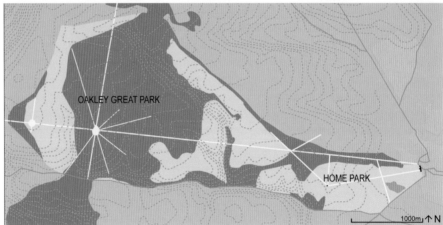

5.31 The frontispiece to Switzer's *Ichnographia Rustica* shows a Baroque grass parterre cut into a forest.

Phase III, 1714–27

Royal leadership in the art of garden design came to an end with the accession of George I in 1714. He lacked the Stuart passions for the arts in general and for gardens in particular. Leadership therefore passed to the nobles, and especially to the Whig nobles. This was the beginning of a creative century for British garden design.

Stephen Switzer published a book which criticised the 'stiff Dutch way' of his former employers (London and Wise) in a book with a long title: *Ichnographia Rustica; Or, the Nobleman, Gentleman, and Gardener's Recreation. Containing Directions for the General Distribution of a Country Seat into Rural and Extensive Gardens, Parks, Paddocks, &C., and a General System of Agriculture; Illus. From the Author's Drawings* (1718).

5.32 a, b St Paul's Walden Bury, Hertfordshire (1720–5), has a grass parterre and bosquet-style hedges skirting the tree canopy (see plan, Figure 5.41 (c)).

Switzer advocated what he called the 'Forest, or, in a more easy style Rural Gardening'. Choosing one of Switzer's terms, the style of design he advocated can be called the Forest style.[51] Switzer admired the magnificent gardens at Versailles, Marly and Fontainbleau and confessed that ''tis to them I owe a great part of that knowledge I have in the designing part of gardening'. He saw himself as the first English author, rather than mere translator, to stress the extensive aspect of the Baroque style, rather than the parterres which London and Wise had taught him to make. Estate forestry had been common since Evelyn's time. Switzer's innovation was the use of forests in giving structure to an estate.

Switzer believed the Forest style was more economical, and more beautiful, than the style of London and Wise. He advised estate owners to spend on forest planting and to save money by reducing the size of parterres or by laying them to grass. Since few avenues could be made by cutting through existing woods in England, extensive tree planting was required to make French-style Baroque gardens. Switzer also thought money was being wasted on levelling hills and filling dales to comply with pre-ordained garden plans. He distrusted paper plans because they often led to noble oaks being felled 'to humour the regular and delusive schemes of some paper engineer'. Switzer also disliked costly garden walls which so easily obstructed views of 'the expansive volumes of nature herself'.[52] These comments come from the 1742 edition of *Ichnographia Rustica* and provide an excellent illustration of the way in which a swing from rationalism to empiricism was affecting the art of garden design. Switzer emerges from his writings as a charming man who may well have played a crucial role in the evolution of British garden design.

5.33 a, b, c Bramham Park, Yorkshire, 1700–31. The recessed space in front of the mansion is now a rose garden. It may have been a small grass parterre with a plat band when first made. Bramham also has outlying forests with radiating avenues.

No complete gardens designed by Switzer survive. There are, however, a number of gardens made between 1700 and 1750 which illustrate the principles of his Forest style. The best surviving examples, none of them directly linked to Switzer, are Bramham Park (1700–31), Cirencester Park (1715–40), St Paul's Walden Bury (1720–5), and Wrest Park (1706–40). Their geometry is Baroque but their other characteristics are sufficiently distinct to justify a separate name. They are quiet rural retreats with extensive woodlands and radiating avenues. The woods are fringed with palisade hedges, like bosquets. Any parterres they had tended to be small and grass-surfaced.

Describing Alan Bathurst, the owner of Cirencester Park, as 'the best of Masters, and best of friends', Switzer wrote that 'the retirement You are pleased to make into your fields and gardens, are evident demonstrations how greatly You prefer solitude before the noise and hurry of public life'.[53] Alexander Pope was a close friend of Bathurst and

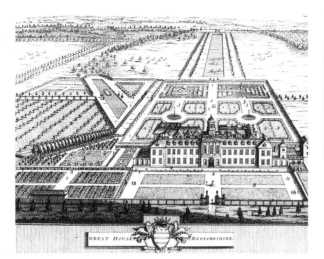

5.34 a, b, c Wrest Park was formed in open country and planted to create a forest setting for the avenues and the canal.

5.35 The avenue at Glamis Castle was originally planted *c*.1683.

5.36 Windsor Castle: the Long Walk was planted by Charles II *c*.1680 and used by Queen Anne, who hunted stags from a wheeled chaise. The avenue bisects the Garden Plott and Little Orchard shown on John Norden's plan (see Figure 3.32 (a)).

had enjoyed a rural retirement lifestyle during his early days in Windsor Forest. Pope expressed the Classical ideal lyrically in his *Ode on Solitude* of 1717:

> *Happy the man whose wish and care*
> *A few paternal acres bound,*
> *Content to breathe his native air,*
> *In his own ground.*
> *Whose herds with milk, whose fields with bread,*
> *Whose flocks supply him with attire,*
> *Whose trees in summer yield him shade,*
> *In winter fire.*
> *Blest, who can unconcern'dly find*

5.37 a, b (a) The avenue at Kinross House was planned by Sir William Bruce between 1675 and 1685. It runs from the entrance gate to the house and from the house towards the island on which Mary Queen of Scots had been imprisoned. Bruce had travelled in France and visited Vaux le Vicomte – with which it has more in common than England's Baroque estates. Bruce was 'both the Scottish Wren and the Scottish Inigo Jones'.[54] (b) The herbaceous borders date from the twentieth century.

5.38 a, b The great avenue at Castle Ashby was part of a radial network planted at the time of William III's visit in 1695. It is over 4,000 m long and there is little inter-visibility between points along its length.

5.39 The undulating avenue at Temple Newsam, like many English avenues, is more pragmatic than dogmatic and is not part of a *patte d'oie* (see plan, Figure 5.23).

Hours, days, and years slide soft away,
In health of body, peace of mind,
Quiet by day,
Sound sleep by night; study and ease,
Together mixt; sweet recreation;
And Innocence, which most does please
With meditation.
Thus let me live, unseen, unknown,
Thus unlamented let me die,
Steal from the world, and not a stone
Tell where I lie.[55]

5.40 a, b, c (a) and (b) Looking west, the avenue at Levens offers no view of the Hall. (c) Looking east, the avenue runs into a hill. It is detached from the layout of the garden, which is a very English approach to the planning of avenues.

Bathurst's park was almost entirely formed by new planting. The avenues which radiate from the house were planned according to aesthetic criteria but their function, like

modern forestry roads, was to give access to the new plantings. Pope asked, 'Who plants like Bathurst?' and invested £4,000 at 4 per cent in his friend's forestry venture.[56] Pope's own garden at Twickenham was small in comparison to Cirencester Park but may be considered an example of the Forest style (see Figure 5.29). It had woods, avenues and grass but no parterres and no topiary. The probability is that Pope was either influenced by Switzer's book or took advice from Switzer's fellow apprentice, Charles Bridgeman.

The relative quiet and economy of Forest style estates indicate another difference from their French predecessors. To Louis XIV, Versailles was a symbol of his sun-like magnificence. Power radiated outwards from Versailles like the great avenues, but extended to the furthest corners of France. All Louis's subjects were drawn into the orbit of his power. Crowds milled through the grounds. On festival days there were masques, garden parties and firework displays. British estates laid out in the Forest style, like Alan Bathurst's park at Cirencester, served a different purpose and were often in the country. Forestry, with avenues and compartments, was used to frame dwellings and as a land use in remote sections of the estate. Forest parks were intended for the Horatian idyll of rural retirement, not for the grandeur of court life. The Golden Age idyll, as discussed in Chapter 4 (see p. 104), outlived the geometry of the Baroque.

Baroque garden features

The Baroque style influenced the design of older features and led to the introduction of new features.

Avenues

The *OED* gives a sentence by John Evelyn as the first use of 'avenue', in English, to mean a 'chief approach to a country-house, usually bordered by trees'. The word derives from the French *avenir* (the future) and the Latin *advenire*. It replaced an older word ('alley', from the French *allée, aller*, 'to go' – see p. 98). In 1645, Evelyn wrote of 'a beautiful avenue of trees' near Santa Maria in Rome, and in 1656 he wrote that at the Palace of Beaulieu he admired 'the fair avenue planted with stately lime trees, in four rows, for near a mile in length'. The name was new but this estate, now called New Hall (near Chelmsford, in Essex) had been the site of Henry VIII's first palace. Nonsuch and Audley End also had tree-lined approach roads. Baroque avenues were aesthetic features creating imposing views from-and-to the principal rooms of a palatial dwelling, also proclaiming the extent of the owner's land ownership.[57]

Avenues became popular additions to English estates after the accession of William III. Some were grand approaches, some had primarily visual roles and some were

CHURCH

100m ↑ N

5.41 a, b, c The avenues at St Paul's Walden Bury are more Baroque than many of their contemporaries. They radiate from near the house and one of them focuses on a church outside the garden boundary, like a Frascati avenue pointing to St Peter's in Rome.

5.42 The avenue at Gibside focuses on a Column to Liberty (built 1750–7).

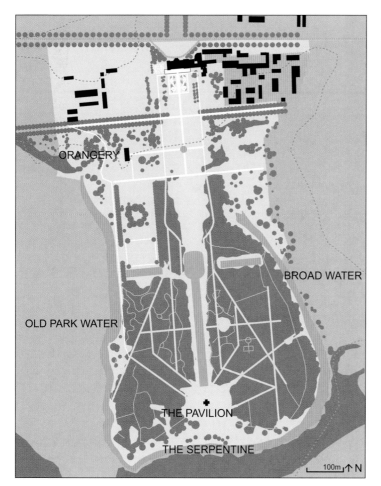

5.43 a, b, c Baroque canals: (a) and (b) in Wrest Park; (c) Westbury Court.

used for hunting. Vehicles require tracks and Louis XIV used comfortable phaetons and cabriolets at Fontainebleu and Versailles. Queen Anne, sister-in-law of William III, used to hunt stags on horseback when young. When older and stouter, she hunted from a large-wheeled chaise drawn by a single horse (see Figure 5.36). Charles II had planted a double avenue of elm trees in Windsor Great Park after 1680 and Queen Anne added a carriage road in 1710. Using this and other drives in Windsor Forest, she could cover 40 or 50 miles on a summer afternoon. Blenheim Palace was designed by Britain's leading Baroque designer, John Vanbrugh, and furnished with a Baroque garden and extensive avenues (see p. 154). A visitor described the scene in 1722:

You have in these gardens nine or ten different prospects through avenues in the park, which generally terminate in some steeple at some miles distance; and from the cupola on the top of the house, you have a view of a delicious country for twenty miles round.[58]

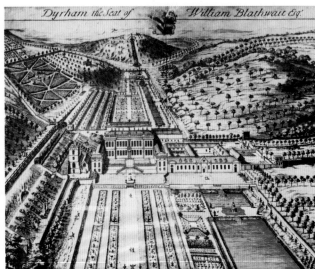

5.44 a, b (a) A fragment of the Baroque canal in the west garden at Dyrham Park survives. (b) It is picked out in blue on a Kip and Knyff drawing which also shows the water cascading down the hill on the east side of the house.

Queen Anne was the last of the Stuarts. She died in 1714 and was succeeded by the Georges, in whose reigns the monarchy lost its power and avenues lost their popularity. Pages 178–80 show the use of avenues in England. They tended to be:

- separate features, sometimes of great magnitude, but added to rather than integrated with the layout of the area adjoining the house or palace;
- often without an axial view from end to end because of undulations in the landform or bends in their alignment.

Focal points

Baroque avenues were planned in conjunction with focal points, within and outside garden boundaries. Robert Morris was a native of Twickenham and an admirer of Lord Burlington and Palladian architecture. In 1734, he described the house and garden he would like to design:

I propose on an eminence about half a mile distant from some public road, or small heath, to which I would have only a foss to separate an avenue leading from thence to the building; each side of that avenue I would plant thick with underwood, and always kept so low, that they might not prevent a prospect from the house to remote objects. About the middle I would propose a canal, or large fountain, to cross the avenue; and from thence to the building, I would have it by a gradual, easy ascent, end in a semicircular, ampitheatrical verdure of ever-greens, in which should be openings to verdant walks, terminated by some distant landscape, a beautiful prospect to a fruitful vale, or some remarkable object.[59]

5.45 a, b The Baroque Fountain Court at Hampton Court, designed by Christopher Wren.

Robert Morris's proposal is for a classic Baroque integration of a mansion with avenues, canals and distant prospects. He wanted to have focal points within and beyond the garden, with a foss (later called a ha-ha) to protect the distant view. The 'semicircular, ampitheatrical verdure of ever-greens' is reminiscent of Burlington's Chiswick House. But full axial planning was never popular in England, and Burlington, as discussed in Chapter 6, was on the cusp of introducing the landscape style which became the accompaniment of Neo-Palladian architecture. Britain does, however, have examples of long avenues, as at Chiswick House, Windsor Castle, Castle Ashby, Glamis Castle, Gibside and elsewhere.

Canals

The *OED* has Pepys's *Diary* as its first example of the word 'canal' being used to mean 'a long and narrow piece of water for the ornamentation of a garden or park'. In 1644, Pepys referred to Somerset House having a canal and in 1666 wrote that he 'Walked to the Park; and there (it being mighty hot, and I weary,) lay down by the Canalle'.[60] This was probably a reference to the canal Charles I had recently made in St James's Park (see p. 167), since Pepys refers to visiting St James's Palace on the same day.

Geometrically shaped water bodies were a characteristic feature of Baroque gardens. They were used for fishing, boating and leisure, as Medieval castle lakes had been, and also had aesthetic roles. Canals impressed visitors and it is reasonable to conclude that this was the intention. Stephen Switzer worked on the design of Dyrham Park and described the appearance and use of the canal in 1718:

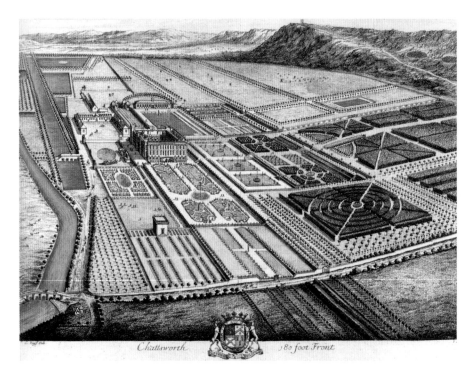

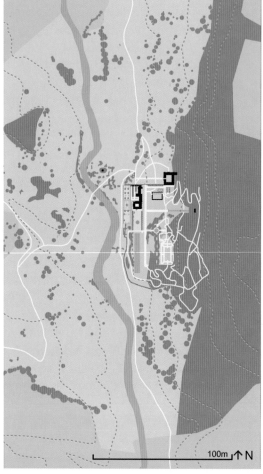

5.46 a, b (a) Chatsworth as a Baroque garden, drawn by Kip and Knyff. (b) As it is today. The circular Baroque fountain south of the house survives (Figure 5.28) but is no longer set in a parterre.

5.47 a, b (a) William Andrews Nesfield's parterre. (b) The Atlas and Prince of Wales fountains at Castle Howard. Though Baroque in conception, they were completed in 1853.

5.48 a, b (a) The water cascade in Bushey Park was built in 1710 and restored in 2009. (b) The painting by Peter Tillemans is believed to commemorate the visit of Prince George (later George II) and his future wife.

Facing the front of the green-house is a running canal of clear water, about a hundred yards in length; at the upper end, in an enlarged circle, with a high head of fine stone, is a fountain which casts water above sixty foot in height, and great variety of small pipes playing all round, which entirely fill the circle or head of the canal. In this canal several sorts of fish are confined, as trout, perch, carp, &c. of a very large size, and though it is deep, yet the water is so transparent that you may easily discover the scalely residents, even those of the smallest dimensions: and this canal is so very much freqented in the summer, that the fish will not be disturbed at your approach; but are almost as tame as the swans.[61]

The canal shown in Kip and Knyff's drawing of Dyrham (see p. 184) is in fact more like a water-filled compartment than a Baroque canal integrated with an avenue and aimed on the principal rooms.

Fountains

Fountains were key components of Baroque gardens in continental Europe but were expensive to build and maintain. In 1700, John Worlidge recognised the importance of fountains to the Baroque style:

Fountains are principal ornaments in a garden; scarce a famous garden in Europe without its fountains, which were primarily intended for bathing, and are in the more southern countries used for that purpose to this day. The Italians bestow very great cost in beautifying them for that use: The French are very prodigal in their expenses about fountains, and several curious gardens in England have them, but here only for ornament. They are generally made of stone, some square, others round or oval, and of divers other forms, some flat in the bottom, others round like a bason.[62]

5.49 The cascade at Chatsworth was completed in 1696.

5.50 The Privy Garden at Hampton Court, carefully restored from old plans in 1995, is the most authentically Baroque parterre in England.

Chatsworth had a great fountain and other Baroque garden features, drawn by Kip and Knyff in 1707 and described by William Stukeley in 1724:

> *The Gardens abound with green houses, summer-houses, walks, wildernesses, orangeries, with statues, urns, greens, &c. with canals, basons and waterworks of various contrivance, sea-horses, drakes, dolphins, and other fountains that throw up the water. An artificial willow tree of copper spouts and drops water from every leaf. There is a wonderful cascade. From a neat house of stone, like a temple, out of the mouths of beasts, pipes, urns, &c. a whole river descends the slope of a hill a quarter of a mile in length over steps, with a terrible noise, till it loses itself under ground. Beyond the garden upon the hills is a park, overlooked by a very high and rocky mountain.*[63]

The Baroque fountain at Chatsworth survives, though now set in a grass lawn instead of a parterre (see Figure 5.28). Few great fountains were made in Baroque England,

5.51 a, b (a) The earthworks of Le Nôtre's parterre in Greenwich survive. (b) Le Nôtre's drawing, montaged onto a photograph of its setting.

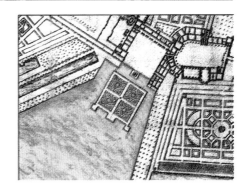

5.52 Mollet designed the 'little garden on the pond at Fontainebleau', using box to make a parterre pattern which involved four rectangles.[64]

because of the expense, and even fewer survive. But when England became wealthy, in the nineteenth century, a number of fountains were made which are stylistically if not chronologically Baroque. William Andrews Nesfield designed great fountains for Castle Howard and Witley Court.

Cascades

Our word 'cascade' derives from the French *cascade* and the Italian *cascata*. Its first use in England was, as with many Baroque garden terms, by John Evelyn. He visited Brussels's Coudenberg Palace in 1641 and wrote that 'here is a stately heronry, divers springs of water, artificial cascades, rocks, grots'.[65] Baroque cascades were made at Chatsworth, Stanway, Bushey Park and elsewhere.

Parterres

Blair Castle was described in 1625 as being 'well beautified with gardens orchards and parterres' ('veill beutified vith gardens orchards and partiers').[66] This is the *OED*'s earliest instance of the word 'parterre'. It comes from Scotland, which had close links with France, and it is possible that the first use of the word 'parterre' was north of the border. John Evelyn is cited by the *OED* as the first man to use 'parterre' south of the border, in his account of a visit to the Coudenberg Palace in Brussels, in 1641 (where Salomon de Caus had worked from 1600–10). In 1644, Evelyn visited the Luxembourg Garden in Paris, assumed to have been designed by Boyceau,[67] and wrote that:

> *The parterre is indeed of box, but so rarely designed and accurately kept cut, that the*
> *embroidery makes a wonderful effect to the lodgings which front it, 'Tis divided into four*

5.53 a, b (a) Cut-work embroidery. (b) The restored cut-grass parterre in the Privy Garden at Hampton Court.

squares and as many circular knots, having in the centre a noble basin of marble near thirty feet in diameter (as I remember), in which a Triton of brass holds a dolphin, that casts a girandola of water near thirty feet high, playing perpetually, the water being conveyed from Arceuil by an aqueduct of stone, built after the old Roman munificence.[68]

The 'circular knots' Evelyn refers to are components of a parterre and, since he speaks of 'squares' to describe other components, he may have seen curved lines as a distinguishing characteristic of knots. Kenneth Woodbridge identifies a book by Liebault (1598) as the first use of 'parterre' to describe a compartment with several component knots. Chapter 47 of *L'agriculture et maison rustique* deals with the 'Parterre, or flower-garden'.[69] Liebault recommends a parterre with a six-foot path. One part is for 'flowers dedicated to bouquets' (e.g. violets, carnations, marigolds, daisies). The other part is for 'fragrant herbs' (e.g. rosemary, jasmine, marjoram, mint). Liebault advised against using box, because of its nasty smell.

Claude Mollet, by his own account, was the first person to use box in making embroidered parterres (*parterre de broderie*). His employer, at Anet, returned from Italy in 1582 wanting Italian-style planting patterns made with flowers and herbs. Mollet recalled that:

At the time I began to make the first compartments en broderie, box was still rarely used, because very few people of rank wished to have box planted in their gardens, so that I planted my compartimens en broderie with several kinds of garden plant which gave a variety of green. But such plants cannot last long in this French climate, because of the extremes of heat and cold that we have. It was the great labour and expense of remaking and replanting the compartments every three years which led me to experiment with the box plant, so as not to have the trouble of remaking so often ... In 1595 the late king, Henry the Great, ordered me to plant the garden of Saint-Germain-en-Laye, and so I made it all of box, and also the garden at Montceaux, together with the little garden on the pond at Fontainebleau.[70]

5.54 Illustrations of topiary from the *Hypnerotomachia Poliphili*, which also has text references, for example: 'Beneath the topiary works and pergolas, the stone paths were the best example of paving that could ever be achieved by human ingenuity and invention'.[71]

The combination of smaller units to make large geometrically integrated patterns, defined by box hedging, became the distinguishing feature of parterres. Box has since been retro-fitted to Italian gardens and to pre-1660 English gardens, confusing visitors about their original character. In France, Jacques Boyceau developed the design of parterres. He probably designed the parterre at the Luxembourg, which Evelyn admired, and he published designs in his *Treaty on Gardening According to the Principles of Nature and of Art, Together with Divers Designs for Parterres, Greens, Bosquets and Other Ornaments*.[72] It has been suggested that Claude Mollet's son, Claude Mollet II, was responsible for the drawings in Boyceau's book.[73] Claude II designed the first *parterre de broderie* at Versailles and his brother, André, worked for Henrietta Maria and then her son, Charles II, in London (see p. 165). Box parterres were popular in England between 1660 and 1730.

The word 'parterre' is French and derives from *par* (meaning 'on' or 'over') and *terre* (meaning 'earth'). The word 'knot' is of Teutonic origin and came to be used in

5.55 a, b Topiary spheres and cones at Westbury Court. 'Why', Shaftesbury asked, 'is the sphere or globe, the cylinder and obilisk preferred?'[74] (a) As re-created by the National Trust (in a different part of the garden). (b) As drawn by Kip and Knyff.

5.56 Levens Hall. Colonel Graham employed Monsieur Beaumont to design the garden 1689–1705. Graham knew John Evelyn and the parterre may have had low box hedging, as it still does. The topiary yews, which now have extravagant shapes, were probably conceived as small cubes, globes and pyramids.

connection with English gardens during the sixteenth century (see p. 135). In seventeenth-century England the words 'knot' and 'parterre' were used almost interchangeably but it is convenient for garden historians to use the words as follows:

- *knot*: a sixteenth-century (Renaissance) garden feature made without box hedging and with the pattern confined to a single rectangle;
- *parterre*: a seventeenth-century (Baroque) garden feature, often with box hedging and with a pattern extending across several rectangles.

London and Wise identified ten types of parterre. They were combinations of embroidery, cutwork and grass with a gravel background. Thierry Mariage and Graham Larkin, discussing the work of Le Nôtre,[75] gave this classification:

5.57 a, b Bosquets at (a) St Paul's Walden Bury and (b) Chiswick House.

- *parterres de broderie:* embroidery parterres;
- *parterres à l'anglais:* cut turf parterres;
- *parterres de pièces coupées:* cut-work parterres in which the design components are flower beds.

'Free embroidery' is made by applying threads without regard to the weave. In making a parterre, comparable patterns can be made with coloured gravel, turf or precision-cut box. 'Cutwork embroidery' is made by cutting holes in the fabric and reinforcing them with buttonhole stitches. In making a parterre, this can be done by cutting out beds and using them for grass or for flowers with box edging.

Topiary

The Romans had cut box in their gardens (see p. 40) but, if this was ever done in Roman Britain, the practice ended when they left. Robert Dallington's 1592 translation of the *Hypnerotomachia Poliphili* is cited by the *OED* as the earliest use of the word 'topiary' in English. Poliphilo is taken to meet the queen of the nymphs and describes her 'noble residence' as having horizontal beams spanning upright posts 'serving as an ideal support for the regularly-spaced topiary work'.[76] Dallington explains in a sidenote that topiary is 'the feate of making Images or Arbours in Trees', by cutting.[77] He does not connect topiary with box or hedging. The *Hypnerotomachia Poliphili* influenced France more than it influenced Britain and it seems likely that the art of clipping evergreens into geometrical shapes reached Britain from continental Europe during the seventeenth century. It came to be called topiary and should probably be classified as a Baroque instead of a Renaissance feature.

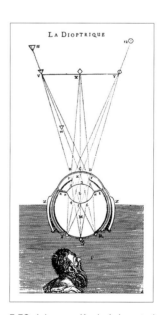

5.58 Johannes Kepler's inverted retinal image as depicted in René Descartes's *La Dioptrique* (1637).[78] Descartes wrote on optics, geometry and philosophy but, though 'Cartesian garden' is a common phrase, he did not write about the design of gardens.

In March 1644, John Evelyn visited Caen and

> *was led to a pretty garden, planted with hedges of alaternus, having at the entrance a*
> *screen at an exceeding-height, accurately cut in topiary work, with well understood*
> *architecture, consisting of pillars, niches, friezes, and other ornaments, with great*
> *curiosity; some of the columns curiously wreathed, others spiral, all according to art.*[79]

Evelyn used *Rhamnus alaternus* (Italian Buckthorn) in his own garden at Sayes Court when he returned to England (see Figure 5.11).

Bosquet

'Thicket' was given as a translation of *bosquet* in the French (1702) and English (1728) editions of the *Royal Dictionary*.[80] In 1707, it appeared in a translation of a French garden book:

> *A bosquet is a small space of ground, inclos'd with palissades of hornbeam, which is fill'd*
> *in the middle with other trees that rise very high, such as elms, and form in the top a*
> *green knot. At the root of these elms, which generally run all along the palissades, at equal*
> *distances, other little wild trees are planted, which rendring the inside very thick and*
> *bushy, form a sort of copse.*[81]

'Palissade' originally meant 'a fence made of wooden pales or stakes' (*OED*). Evelyn used this word as a translation of *espalier*, meaning 'an ornamental hedge, esp. as an edging for an alley' (*OED*). A bosquet was therefore a thicket pierced by avenues bordered with hedges (e.g. of hornbeam). In France, the walks were often gravelled and bosquets were furnished with fountains, sculpture and other features. Philip Miller gave an English interpretation of 'bosquet' in 1733:

> *These are small Compartments of Gardens, which are form'd of Trees, Shrubs, or tall large*
> *growing Plants, planted in Quarters; and are either disposed regularly in Rows, or in a*
> *more wild or accidental manner, according to the Fancy of the Owner: these Quarters are*
> *commonly surrounded with ever-green Hedges, and the Entrance form'd into regular*
> *Portico's with Yews, which are by far the best and most tonsile Trees for this Purpose.*[82]

Perspective

The word 'perspective' originally meant 'the science of optics', which was popular in the Baroque world (see p. 193). It then came to be used for a drawing, of the type Brunelleschi pioneered, made with a knowledge of optics. Brunelleschi is thought to have discovered the principles of geometrical perspective when measuring and drawing Roman buildings. Perspective drawings became a profound influence on the visual arts and encouraged the technique of design-by-drawing, as an alternative to craft design. Philosophically, perspective revealed a mathematical aspect of the visual world, apparently confirming Plato's Theory of Forms. Practically, perspective

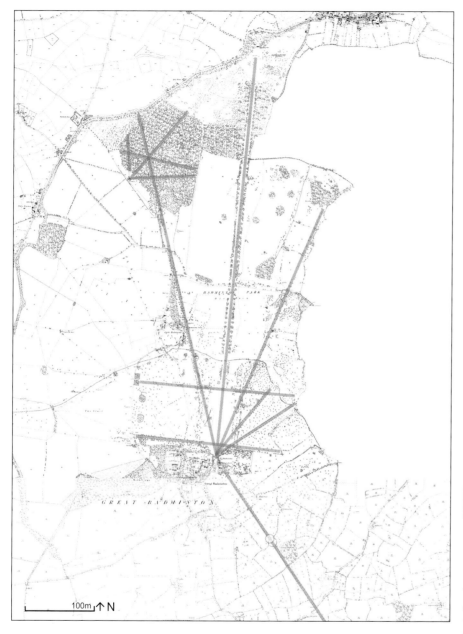

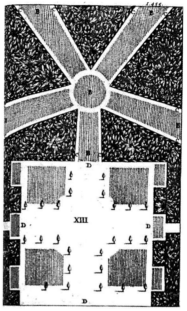

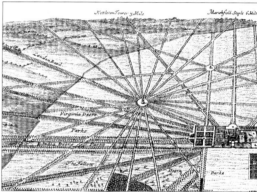

5.59 a, b, c (a) Badminton in the late nineteenth century.
(b) An illustration from *Le jardinier solitaire*, with the
caption 'The Figure of a Patte d' Oye. No. XIII. A. are the
pieces of the Patte d'Oye; and what we see mark'd B are
the other Knots that adorn this. C, are the Gravel walks.
And D. represents the middle of the Patte d' Oye.'[83]
(c) Badminton, as drawn by Kip and Knyff in 1707, had
perhaps the most elaborate *patte d'oie* in England.

provided a new way of designing buildings: on paper and with the help of mathematical calculations. Alberti's example of the mathematics of perspective used paving tiles. The Albertian grid encouraged the integration of architectural design with garden design. Serlio wrote the first architectural treatise with a chapter on perspective (1545), and observed that the best architects of his aquaintance started out as painters.[84]

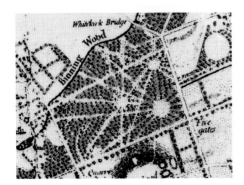

5.60 a, b The Earl of Haddington and his wife designed and planted Binning Wood, on the Tynningham estate, as a 'Wilderness' with a *patte d'oie*. It is still managed for timber.

The *First and Chief Groundes of Architecture* (1563) by John Shute is the book which contains the *OED*'s earliest example of the word 'architect' in English.[85] Contemporary building plans were the work of surveyors. Master masons had responsibility for building construction. Similarly, garden design was the responsibility of master gardeners. A few Renaissance drawings show garden details but it was the Baroque period that formalised the design-by-drawing method. George London held the post of 'Master Gardener of all the Royal Gardens in England'.[86] Christopher Wren and William Talman, working with George London and Henry Wise, used drawings to design and illustrate houses, gardens and parks. Charles Bridgeman was trained by London and Wise and, when he left their employment, worked as a designer and draughtsman, not as tradesman and nurseryman, as they had been. Perspective became a design objective in gardens and Bridgeman can be regarded as Britain's first professional garden designer.

The *OED* gives John Evelyn's use as the first example of the word 'perspective' being used to mean 'a picture drawn or painted according to the rules of perspective ... appearing to enlarge or extend the actual space, or to give the effect of distance'. He was also the first to use the word in connection with gardens, meaning a perspective painting of a garden scene. Evelyn used drawings for the design of his own garden at Sayes Court, which had non-radial avenues (see Figure 5.11). One finds Evelyn involved in many points connected to the arrival of the Baroque garden style in England. Here is Evelyn's description of a garden 'perspective' he had seen on 1 March 1644:

5.61 a, b A reconstructed arbour in the Privy Garden at Hampton Court.

1st March, 1644. I went to see the Count de Liancourt's Palace in the Rue de Seine, which is well built. Toward his study and bedchamber joins a little garden, which, though very narrow, by the addition of a well-painted perspective, is to appearance greatly enlarged; to this there is another part, supported by arches in which runs a stream of water, rising to the aviary, out of a statue, and seeming to flow for some miles, by being artificially continued in the painting, when it sinks down at the wall. It is a very agreeable deceit.[87]

John Dixon Hunt remarks that Evelyn's fondness for *trompe-l'œil* perspectives 'seems to compare oddly to his advocacy elsewhere of natural effects' but points out that Evelyn also saw terraces as a means of providing 'naturall & artificial Perspectives of the Gardens'.[88] Painted perspectives became less valued when planted perspectives became more common and parks became more dramatic.

Patte d'oie

The first use of the term *patte d'oie* in an English book was a translation of Francis Gentil's *Le jardinier solitaire*:

When a patte d'oie is well understood, we may justly say 'tis very ornamental in a garden. This sort of garden-knots has commonly avenues, that lead to it, and these avenues, as well as the other walks which form it, are either of green plots accompanied with paths as above, or gravel-walks, like those represented in the following draught, with the trees planted along them. The middle is commonly a Grafs plot quite round or oval, surrounded with a Gravel Walk as broad as you will.[89]

Patte d'oie refers to 'a number of avenues, roads, paths, etc. (usually three or five) diverging from a common point' (*OED*). It reflects the Baroque enthusiasm for optics.

5.62 a, b, c Raised walks with bastions. (a) Bramham Park. (b) Castle Howard. (c) Grimsthorpe (drawn by William Stukeley in 1736).

5.63 a, b Box hedging at Wrest Park. (a) As shown in Kip and Knyff's drawing. (b) As it was in 2010.

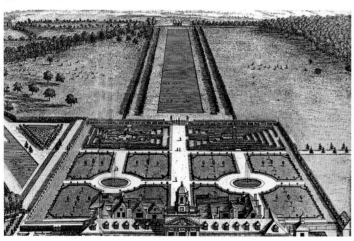

Wilderness

'Wilderness' was used in Old and Middle English, as today, to mean 'wild or unculti-vated land'. But in the seventeenth and eighteenth centuries it took on the specialised meaning of: 'a piece of ground in a large garden or park, planted with trees, and laid out in an ornamental or fantastic style, often in the form of a maze or labyrinth' (*OED*). Garden wildernesses were planted, often with grass paths and an understorey of shrubs. Some were ornamental and some were for timber.

The Earl of Haddington published *A Treatise on the Manner of Raising Forest Trees* which explains that 'I resolved to have a wilderness.'[90] It was a forest plantation (see Figure 5.60) with a *patte d'oie* but not bosquets, and his wife was the driving force behind the project:

5.64 a, b (a) The amphitheatre at Claremont. (b) As engraved by John Rocque in 1738. Like the theatre at the Boboli, it may have been intended for garden entertainments.

in the year 1707, she began to enclose it, and called it Binning-wood. After she had begun to plant it, I thought it would be a pity not to have a centre in it, and walks from it, with the best terminations we could find.[91]

Philip Miller's *Gardener's Dictionary* (1733) advised that straight walks are normal but, aware that the Baroque was becoming unfashionable, advised that curved walks give more pleasure:

The usual Method of contriving Wildernesses is, to divide the whole Compass of Ground, either into Squares, Angles, Circles, or other Figures, ... the Walks are commonly made to intersect each other in Angles, which also shews too formal and trite for such Plantations, and are by no means comparable to such Walks as have the Appearance of Meanders or Labyrinths, where the Eye can't discover more than twenty or thirty Yards in Length; and the more these Walks are turned, the greater Pleasure they will afford. These should now and then lead into an open circular Piece of Grass; in the Center of which may be placed either an Obelisk, Statue, or Fountain.[92]

Wilderness plantations became components of Baroque gardens after *c.*1688 and a framing element of Forest style gardens after *c.*1714.

Arbours

Arbours, as places to walk and places to relax (see p. 197), became more sophisticated during the Baroque period. John Norris wrote a poem about the solace to be obtained from *Sitting in an Arbour* (1699):

> *Thus ye good Powers, thus let me ever be*
> *Serene, retir'd, from Love and Business free;*
> *The rest of your great World I here resign*
> *To the Contentions of the great;*
> *I only ask that this Retreat,*
> *This little Tenement be mine.*[93]

Bastions

The first sunken walls and bastions in English gardens were made to provide views of the surrounding countryside. In this, they compare to the walks and views from wall-walks (see p. 198) on Medieval castles. Examples can be seen at Stowe, Castle Howard, Bramham, Levens Hall and elsewhere. The Bagot family, which owns Levens Hall, claim that:

In the map of the Garden, the sunk fence or 'ha-ha' with its 'bastion' on the west side, are the first known to have been constructed in England, well before Bridgeman, who is popularly thought to have introduced these features. These were constructed in the year 1694–5.[94]

But the word 'ha-ha' came into use at a later date (see p. 228).

Box hedging

Buxus sempervirens was little used in Italian Renaissance gardens and not for hedges (see p. 191). The idea of using box to make parterres is described by Mollet and may have come to England from him or with him. William III used box hedging at Het Loo and Harris's 1699 account of the garden refers to 'some plain Parterres bordered with Box'.[95] Box hedging became a feature of English Baroque gardens and they are now retro-fitted, anachronistically, to Renaissance and even Medieval gardens in England.

Theatres

Stephen Switzer knew of outdoor theatres in the gardens of Frascati and Versailles,[96] but few were made in England. The best-known example is at Claremont (see p. 199). Stage drama moved indoors in the seventeenth century and, as remains the case, plays came to be performed on indoor stages separated from the audience by proscenium arches.

Kitchen gardens

Kip and Knyff drawings often show vegetables growing in compartments integrated with the geometry of the land around a house. They became separate in the Baroque period, hidden from the noble family's gaze by walls, hedges or trees. Switzer, writing in 1718, was in two minds about separating vegetable gardens from pleasure gardens:

5.65 The walled vegetable garden at Castle Fraser is tucked behind a Baroque avenue and set apart from the castle.

5.66 Badminton Park came closer to the spirit of the Baroque than most English estates. But Worcester Lodge is by the Neoclassical designer of Chiswick Park, William Kent.

If we would mix the utile [utility] *with the* dulce [sweet] *the quarters may be stocked with such sorts of kitchen-stuff as are not offensive, as are cabbages, etc. for peas, beans, artichokes, etc. being kept clean, will look as well as anything, and pay for their keeping.*[97]

Four decades later, Miller's *Gardener's Dictionary* was definite about the need for separation. He wrote that a kitchen garden should be 'placed out of the View of the House' and that:

as it will be proper to inclose the kitchen garden with walls, and to secure the gates, that no persons may have access to it, who have no business in it, for the sake of preserving the product, so these walls will answer the purposes of both.[98]

The separation of kitchen gardens from pleasure gardens became normal practice in the eighteenth and nineteenth centuries, resulting in the great walled vegetable gardens of Victorian Britain. We could call them Baroque vegetable gardens.

Conclusion

Though the Baroque style of garden design influenced Britain, it did not become a dominant style and garden historians have paid it less attention than they might have done. Those who have studied the period have shown more interest in searching for the early 'wriggles' of Naturalism than in the study of avenues, parterres, fountains, bastions, sunk fences and the expansive views that characterised the Baroque approach to garden design. In garden design, as in literature, the Baroque merges into the Neoclassical:

> Both Baroque and neoclassical are labels from the history of the arts. The latter is used generally to mean art which imitates the classics and stresses order, restraint, the rational, the lucid; the former, art which stresses disorder, excrescence, exhuberance, the irrational, the grotesque, the cryptic. The chronology of the use of the terms as indicating period styles varies from art to art and country to country. But most who use them usually see them as succeeding each other, Baroque to neoclassical, between the middle of the sixteenth and the end of the eighteenth century.[99]

Chapter 6 deals with Neoclassical gardens.

Neoclassical gardens and landscapes, 1730–1800

6.0 Claude Lorrain's *Landscape with Aeneas at Delos* (1672) illustrates a story from Ovid with a West Asian origin. Aeneas, in red, is on the sacred island of Delos. '[He] showed his city, the new-erected shrines and the two sacred trees beneath which Latona had once brought forth her children ... according to the customary rite, they slaughtered cattle and burned their entrails in the altar-fire; then sought the palace-hall and, reclining on the high couches, they partook of Ceres' bounty and the wine of Bacchus.'[1]

Introduction

Tim Richardson used the title *Arcadian Friends* for a book on the development of landscape gardens. He wrote:

> The basic and aesthetic premise of this book is that the English landscape garden is the greatest artform ever to have been devised in the British Isles. What is more, it is an artform that has gone on to influence the rest of the world like no other in our history. The only genre of comparable stature in British art is Perpendicular Gothic architecture – all those wonderful cathedrals and churches which were built in the fifteenth and sixteenth centuries.[2]

Frank Clark had a similar view of the period, and introduced me to garden history at the University of Edinburgh. As the author of a book on *The English Landscape Garden* he was asked to give evidence at an inquiry into a Ministry of Transport plan to drive the M6-to-Kendal link road through a historic landscape park. I can still see him

6.1 The M6 link road to Kendal was originally routed through Levens Park. It had been a Medieval deer park before it became a Baroque park and then a landscape park. Frank Clark told his students that this landscape represents an English contribution to world culture of greater importance than Milton's poetry or Shakespeare's plays.

6.2 a, b Neoclassical landscape theory evolved into a comprehensive theory of environmental planning and design.

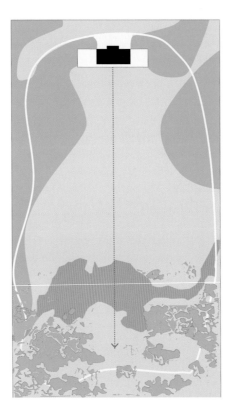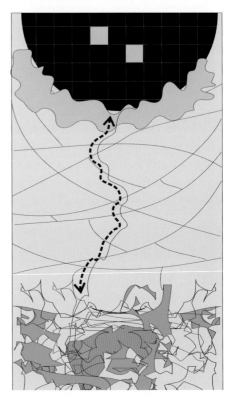

gazing out of the window, to George Square, and telling his students that 'You can, if you wish, claim that Dante or Goethe are greater poets than Shakespeare or Milton. But you cannot claim that another country has produced a better theory of environmental design – because no other country *has* produced a comprehensive theory of environmental design.'[3] The first application of the theory was to gardens. Then, as Christopher Hussey explained in *The Picturesque*, it had a dramatic impact on other arts, ranging from poetry itself, to painting, literature, architecture, town planning, landscape planning and, we may add, global planning.[4] The theory can be set forth as a set of principles:

- Study the principles of landscape painting.
- Make a survey and analysis of the site's character.
- Bring the works of man into harmony with the works of nature.
- Compose buildings with landform, water, vegetation and paths.
- Take pleasure, as Horace and Virgil did, in richly productive agricultural land.
- Use rational, benevolent and far-sighted principles to manage land.
- Do not squander money on vain ostentation or formal gardens.

Nikolaus Pevsner argued that these principles developed into a 'national' planning theory[5] which may be summarised as follows:

6.3 a, b Edinburgh is a compact town with an agricultural hinterland and views of wild nature beyond. The Neoclassical monument to Dugald Stewart, in both photographs, stands on Calton Hill. Based on the Choragic Monument in Athens, it was designed by William Henry Playfair in 1831. Stewart was a leading Enlightenment philosopher and Sir Walter Scott was one of his students.

- Towns should be compact.
- Agricultural land should be beautiful, productive and conserved.
- Wild nature should be protected from development, with clear separations between town, country and wilderness.

6.4 a, b Christopher Wren's 1682 design for the Royal Hospital in Chelsea can be classified as English Baroque, Palladian or Neoclassical. It is less melodramatic than the continental Baroque.

The evolution of these principles, which will be traced through Chapters 7 and 8, is summarised in the diagrams. Figure 6.2 (a) shows their application to private estates and Figure 6.2 (b) shows their application to urban and rural landscapes.

The cultural context

This chapter will review the ideas which underlie the development of landscape gardens in the eighteenth century. They are Neoclassical in the sense of looking back to the ideal landscapes of antiquity but they also looked forward with increasing confidence to the creation of 'new landscapes for our new lives'.[6] The three phases will be described as:

1   *the Classical landscape garden*, looking back to the landscape of Augustan Rome and the Campagna (e.g. Castle Howard, Chiswick, Painshill, Rousham and Stourhead);
2   *the Serpentine landscape garden*, looking back to the imagined simplicity of Arcadian Greece, with temples set in open country (e.g. Blenheim, Prior Park, Petworth, Bowood, Sherborne Castle);
3   *the Picturesque landscape garden*, looking to the ruggedness of wild nature as represented in landscape paintings (e.g. Scotney Castle, Wakehurst Place, Sheffield Park).

6.5 a, b Painswick, described as a Rococo garden, has been restored since Christopher Thacker wrote, 'In England, the gardens of a rococo kind have all perished entirely'.[7] The restoration was based on a 1748 painting by Thomas Robins.

The three phases of the landscape garden can be thought of as 'Back to Rome', 'Back to Greece' and 'Back to Jerusalem'.[8] They relate to the Classical cultures of the Eastern Mediterranean and West Asia.

Having dominated the first half of the seventeenth century, Baroque culture broke up between 1650 and 1750 and was followed by a new Classicism. The change affected different arts in different countries at different times. Typical dates are: Neoclassical architecture (1640–1850), Neoclassical painting (c.1750–1860), Classical music (1750–1830), Neoclassical gardens (1730–1800). The eighteenth century is also the Age of Enlightenment, in which reason became the primary source of intellectual authority.

In continental Europe, the Baroque period was followed by a Rococo phase, in which princes lavished money on ornamentation, and then by a Neoclassical phase, in which there was a return to the purity and restraint of Classical times. Since Rococo attitudes were unpopular in Britain (see p. 251), Neoclassicism made an early appearance, affecting architecture from c.1640 onwards. In gardens, it led to the Romantic evocation of Classical times which grew into a full-blown Romanticism. The Italian aspect, though important, should not be over-estimated: there was a general enthusiasm for the Classical world and Judaeo-Christian civilisation.

The social context

The eighteenth century was a time of flux with people looking back to tradition and forward to an emerging modernity. Empiricism challenged rationalism; science challenged religion; democracy challenged aristocracy; garden designers challenged each other; parliament challenged monarchy; enlightenment advanced. Aristocrats, though jealous of their privileges, were involved in the agricultural and industrial revolutions which promoted change, enriched the country and diminished their ascendency. Party politics, dominated by the landed elite, took hold in Britain. The Tory Party emerged from the Royalist faction of the seventeenth century and was opposed by a Whig Party, which emerged from the factions which supported the political revolutions of the 1640s and 1680s. It would be convenient for garden historians if the Tory landowners had upheld the old styles and the Whigs had promoted new styles. Richardson summarised the political affiliations of mid-eighteenth-century garden makers as follows:

> These gardens were made by dissident Whigs openly allied with Prince Frederick's court and Lord Cobham's Patriot opposition; by Tories or Roman Catholics who had not yet given up the ghost; by disappointed Whig ideologues; or by country gentlemen of independent views.[9]

Most families had one eye on the past and another eye on the future. Sir Walter Scott used an old garden as a symbol of the society then passing. *Waverley* was written in 1814 and set in the Scottish Borders at the time of another revolution, in 1745:

> The solitude and repose of the whole scene seemed almost monastic; and Waverley, who had given his horse to his servant on entering the first gate, walked slowly down the avenue, enjoying the grateful and cooling shade, and so much pleased with the placid ideas of rest and seclusion excited by this confined and quiet scene, that he forgot the misery and dirt of the hamlet he had left behind him. The opening into the paved courtyard corresponded with the rest of the scene. The house, which seemed to consist of two or three high, narrow, and steep-roofed buildings, projecting from each other at right angles, formed one side of the inclosure. It had been built at a period when castles were no longer necessary, and when the Scottish architects had not yet acquired the art of designing a domestic residence ... Two battlemented walls, one of which faced the avenue, and the other divided the court from the garden, completed the inclosure.[10]

Traquair House is a possible model for Scott's description of Tully-Veolan.[11] The combination of a Baroque avenue with Renaissance compartments remained common in the first half of the eighteenth century. But a different style of estate layout had become the norm by 1800 and the manner of its enjoyment is described in Jane Austen's *Pride and Prejudice* (1813):

6.6 a, b, c Traquair House is one of several possible models for Sir Walter Scott's Tully-Veolan. It has a long avenue, several enclosures – and a Bear Gate which has been shut since the 1745 Jacobite Rising.

The park was very large, and contained great variety of ground. They entered it in one of its lowest points, and drove for some time through a beautiful wood stretching over a wide extent. Elizabeth's mind was too full for conversation, but she saw and admired every remarkable spot and point of view. They gradually ascended for half-a-mile, and then found themselves at the top of a considerable eminence, where the wood ceased, and the eye was instantly caught by Pemberley House, situated on the opposite side of a valley, into which the road with some abruptness wound. It was a large, handsome stone building, standing well on rising ground, and backed by a ridge of high woody hills; and in front, a stream of some natural importance was swelled into greater, but without any artificial appearance. Its banks were neither formal nor falsely adorned. Elizabeth was delighted. She had never seen a place for which nature had done more, or where natural beauty had been so little counteracted by an awkward taste. They were all of them warm in their admiration; and at that moment she felt that to be mistress of Pemberley might be something![12]

The change from walled gardens and avenues to naturalistic compositions of woods, water and hills was a 'great revolution in taste' (see Figure 6.94) and has exercised

6.7 Chatsworth is thought to have been the model for Jane Austen's Pemberley, where: 'They gradually ascended for half-a-mile, and then found themselves at the top of a considerable eminence, where the wood ceased, and the eye was instantly caught by Pemberley House, situated on the opposite side of a valley.'[13]

the minds of historians accordingly. They agree that many factors were involved but, as with the causes of the French Revolution and the First World War, there is little agreement about a primary cause. People have looked, rightly, to the histories of ideas, politics, economics, agriculture, literature, art, gardens and elsewhere. My own view, as prejudiced as any other, is that while the pen is mightier than the sword, the idea is mightier than either the pen or the sword. Scott, who had a powerful pen,

6.8 a, b Sir Walter Scott's own house, at Abbotsford, has something of the character of an old Scots garden and something of the character of an eighteenth-century landscape garden.

made a garden at Abbotsford, 26 km from Traquair House. Its character draws something from Tully-Veolan and something from Pemberley. He cared about the past, the present and the future. As Edmund Burke reflected on the French Revolution, society is 'a partnership not only between those who are living, but between those who are living, those who are dead, and those who are to be born'.[14]

The following account of the Great Revolution in Garden Taste begins with individuals but concentrates on the history of ideas and associated changes in design styles. For fuller accounts of what happened on the ground, I recommend Christopher Hussey's *English Gardens and Landscapes, 1700-1750* and David Jacques's *Georgian Gardens*.[15] For a witty, careful and extensive treatment of the people, books and events which feature in the revolution, I recommend Tim Richardson's *Arcadian Friends*. For more examples, I recommend the Gardenvisit.com website.

Early proponents of a new style?

Though Temple, Shaftesbury and Switzer were discussed in preceding chapters, with regard to Renaissance and Baroque gardens, they are best known to British garden historians as the forerunners of the eighteenth-century approach to garden design. Variously described as the 'natural', 'irregular', 'informal', 'English' or 'landscape' style, it is contrasted with the 'geometrical', 'regular', 'Dutch', 'stiff', 'French' or 'formal' style of the seventeenth century (see Appendix II for a discussion of style

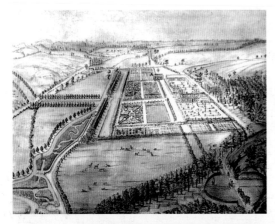

6.9 a, b, c Sir William Temple's own garden at Moor Park in Surrey is an English Renaissance garden – in which Pevsner detected 'the first suggestion ever of a possible beauty fundamentally different from the formal, a beauty of irregularity and fancy'. The serpentine river survives and the walks could be re-created.

names). Pevsner only expressed a popular view rather boldly when he praised the last section of Temple's essay:

> *This passage is one of the most amazing in the English language. It started a line of thought and visual conceptions which were to dominate first England and then the World for two centuries. It is the first suggestion ever of a possible beauty fundamentally different from the formal, a beauty of irregularity and fancy.*[16]

Here is what Temple actually wrote: 'There may be other forms wholly irregular, that may, for aught I know, have more beauty … They must owe it … to some great race of fancy or judgement in the contrivance.'[17]

In a similar vein, Shaftesbury was described by Joseph Burke as 'the first philosophical sponsor of a new movement in gardening',[18] and Switzer, by Hunt and Willis, as 'the first professional gardener in England to write about the new style'.[19] There is a puzzle in the fact that Switzer, Shaftesbury and Temple are so widely believed to have promoted a new style of garden design.

Switzer was trained in the Baroque style by London and Wise. He greatly admired D'Arganville's book on French gardening practice (which had recently been trans-

6.10 The Villa Poggio Reale in Naples had a 'formal' logia and *jettes d'eau*.

lated into English) and, with Versailles in mind, wrote of Louis XIV , ''tis certain that gardening was by his means brought to the most magnificent height and splendour imaginable'.[20] Switzer saw himself as the first English author, rather than mere translator, to advocate the style of Louis XIV in England. Can it really be that Switzer was mistaken in thinking himself an advocate of a French style? Or are we mistaken in thinking he advocated a new style for England?

A similar puzzle arises in connection with Shaftesbury. His writings are considered a major influence on the new style but the fine garden he described in the year before his death was in the Late Renaissance style. Writing from Naples, Shaftesbury praises:

> *The disposition and order of one of their finer sort of gardens or villas: the kind of harmony to the eye from the various shapes and colours agreeably mixed and ranged in lines intercrossing without confusion and fortunately coincident; a parterre, cypresses, groves, wilderness, walks; statues here and there ... with all those symmetries that silently express such order, peace, and sweetness.*[21]

It is sometimes thought that when Shaftesbury wrote of 'the formal mockery of princely gardens' he was mocking the 'formal' style of princely gardens. It is more likely that he was criticising such gardens only for being a substitute for peace and harmony in the minds of their owners: he speaks rhetorically of 'a coach, liveries, parterre and knolls? cascades, jettes d'eau? – how many rattles?'[22] Shaftesbury saw

6.11 Chinese gardens, with extensive use of stone and roofed corridors, have few similarities with the gardens made in eighteenth-century England (the Jing Xin Zhai).

grand gardens, like other Baroque trinkets, as unimportant 'rattles'. In another passage he asks, 'How can the rational mind rest here, or be satisfied with the absurd enjoyment which reaches the sense alone?'[23] His conception of a fine garden was, however, as geometrical as Switzer's. The last year of Shaftesbury's life was spent in Naples and Poggio Reale may have been his target.[24]

The puzzle also arises with Temple. He has been hailed as a prophet of the new style since 1712, but his description of 'the perfectest figure of a garden I ever saw'[25] is formal and geometric. This garden and the plan of his own garden, which was also geometric, will be described below. Before considering why, in the face of such evidence, Switzer, Shaftesbury and Temple are seen as prophets of a new style, let us review the reasoning behind the claim.

The first reason given for Temple's originality is his remark that there may be other forms of gardens which are 'wholly irregular'. Shaftesbury and Switzer join in the praise of irregularity. Shaftesbury refers to 'all the horrid graces of the wilderness itself, as representing nature more'[26] and Switzer to 'the beauty of rural and extensive gardening, when compared with the stiff Dutch way'.[27] But the taste for nature's irregularity was not new at the end of the seventeenth century. Bacon had written, in 1625, that a part of his ideal garden would be a 'natural wilderness'.[28] And in 1642 Wotton had written that a garden 'should be irregular'.[29] Thus, we cannot say that it was original for Temple, Shaftesbury or Switzer to praise irregularity at a later date.

A second reason for hailing Temple as the originator of a new style is his much-quoted praise of Chinese gardens. Temple wrote that 'our walks and trees ranged so as to answer one another, and at exact distances. The Chinese scorn this way of planting.'[30] But Temple had not visited China, or seen a drawing of a Chinese garden, and the new style had almost passed maturity before any Chinese garden ornament appeared in England. It was doubtless important to know that a different style of garden design was possible but, in its early stages, the new style owed nothing to China. Nor was there anything Chinese about Temple's own garden, Shaftesbury does not mention Chinese gardens and Switzer only refers us to Temple on the subject. Chinese classical gardens were most 'irregular' but not in the manner of England's eighteenth-century gardens.

The third and most important reason for believing that Temple, Shaftesbury and Switzer contributed to the development of a new style is that they conceived garden design as an art which should *imitate* nature. Temple wrote that it was not possible to design a good garden 'if nature be not followed', adding that he took this principle 'to be the great rule in this, and perhaps in everything else'.[31] Shaftesbury stated that, 'I shall no longer resist the passion growing in me for things of a natural kind',[32] and Switzer wrote that 'a design must submit to nature'.[33] The three authors were thus united in praise for nature. But the meaning of the word 'nature' was in a state of flux.

The principle that 'Art should imitate Nature' derived from Plato's Theory of Forms and influenced Renaissance gardens (see p. 159). But the consequence of the axiom depends on the meaning attached to nature. Consider these alternatives:

- If 'nature' is used to mean 'essence', as in 'the nature of the case' and 'human nature', then the axiom exhorts designers to base their proposals on the essential geometrical forms – the circle, the square and the straight line.
- If 'nature' is used to mean 'unaffected by man' or 'the natural world', then the axiom exhorts designers to produce irregular and non-geometrical designs.

A series of different conceptions of nature was slotted into the ancient axiom that 'Art should imitate Nature' between 1700 and 1800, generating new styles of garden

6.12 Rationalism tends to the view that art should represent the perfect world of the forms, including straight lines and circles. Empiricism tends to the view that art should represent the experiential world of imperfection, curves and jagged lines.

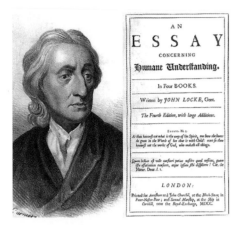

6.13 John Locke believed in a divine creative spirit but did not believe that humans are born with innate ideas. This is reflected in the passage from Ecclesiastes 11.5 on the title page of his *Essay Concerning Humane Understanding*: 'As thou knowest not what is the way of the Spirit, nor how the bones do grow in the womb of her that is with child: even so thou knowest not the works of God, who maketh all things.'[34] Locke therefore directed the attention of natural philosophers to the empirical world.

6.14 Zeuxis chose the best features of five models for an image of Platonic female perfection. The text, lower left, may be translated as: 'Zeuxis, not relying on art, believed he could produce a true image by examining the beauty of the chosen maidens.'

design.[35] But the evolving conceptions of nature did not replace one another in English usage and to explain how they affected the course of garden design something more must be said about seventeenth-century aesthetics, empiricism and the Neoplatonic axiom.

Empiricism

Empiricism holds that our knowledge of the world comes primarily from experience. Rationalism holds that reason is the fundamental criterion of truth. Epistemological rationalists argue that we are born with innate ideas tucked up in our minds, and that we only come to know the world in the light of this knowledge. Empiricists, on the other hand, believe that our minds contain nothing at birth and we acquire knowledge only by seeing and experiencing the world. When applied to aesthetics, rationalism tends towards the view that art should represent the world of the forms. Empiricism tends to the view that art should represent the world of experience. Rationalist art makes great use of regularity, proportion and mathematics, while empiricist art delights in wildness, irregularity and unexpected details. The two conceptions of art depend on two views of how man comes to know the 'nature of the world' – and the 'world of nature'.

John Locke was the most important empiricist philosopher to influence eighteenth-century garden design. He was not an extreme empiricist and his approach to philosophy was rational. Locke was, however, more empiricist than preceding British philosophers and was interested in gardens. His book on gardening contains nothing on aesthetics but a good deal of information about cultivating the vine.[36] Locke's influence on garden design came about through his patron, the First Earl of Shaftesbury, and through his pupil, the famous Third Earl of Shaftesbury.

The Third Earl held to the Neoplatonic theory of art. He believed that an artist should represent the simplest and purest forms. 'Why,' Shaftesbury asks, 'is the sphere or globe, the cylinder and obilisk preferred; and the irregular figures in respect of these, rejected and despised?' His answer to the question was Neoplatonic. Simple and pure shapes are preferred because 'the beautiful, the fair, the comely were never in the matter ... but in the form or forming power'.[37] It is clear that Shaftesbury has assigned each of the geometrical shapes a hierarchical position, with the sphere and cylinder having high positions and the irregular forms having lowly positions. Neoplatonists have often interpreted Plato in this way and seventeenth-century gardens used spheres, squares and cones in gardens (see Figure 5.55).

It is noteworthy that Shaftesbury, like Pope, uses the word 'nature' in several different senses. In the following passage Shaftesbury describes the painter who 'strictly copies life' as 'unnatural':

> *A Painter, if he* have *any Genius, understands the Truth and Unity of Design; and knows he is even then unnatural, when he* follows *Nature too close, and strictly copies Life.*[38]

Is the injunction not to copy life too strictly in conflict with Shaftesbury's oft-quoted remark that 'I shall no longer resist the passion growing in me for things of a natural kind'?[39] No. The apparent conflict is explained by the current of empiricism running through Shaftesbury's essentially rationalist philosophy. Like Plato, he believed that our knowledge of the forms can be increased by a study of the particulars which comprise the visible world. A visual symbol of this truth could be provided by a Palladian villa, based on the circle and square, set in a wild and irregular landscape. Had Shaftesbury lived for another twelve years (i.e. until 1725), he could have seen beautiful examples of this idea at Mereworth Castle in Kent (designed by Colen

6.15 a–d The design of Palladian villas was based on circles and squares. The imitation of these 'Platonic Forms' was a way of making buildings partake of the 'nature' of the world. (a) Andrea Palladio's Villa Capra, near Vicenza. (b) Mereworth Castle in Kent. (c) and (d) Chiswick House, in London: the area between the house and the canal is thought to be the site of William Kent's first exercise in Neoclassical landscape design.

Campbell) and at Chiswick House (designed by Lord Burlington and William Kent). Both are closely based on Andrea Palladio's design of 1552 for the Villa Capra at Vicenza. The small Palladian temples which were later used to adorn Stourhead and many other English landscape gardens also illustrate Shaftesbury's point.

In the middle years of the eighteenth century, when Stourhead was being laid out and Lancelot Brown was the Royal Gardener at Hampton Court, there was a balance between rationalist formality and empiricist irregularity. By the end of the century an empiricist conception, of wild nature, had won the hearts and minds of Britain's gardeners.

6.16 a, b Sir Uvedale Price's *Essay on the Picturesque* fostered an appreciation of wild landscapes and an approach to the making of Picturesque gardens.[40]

Formality and aesthetic theory

According to the *OED*, 'formal' can mean:

> *Marked by extreme or excessive regularity or symmetry; stiff or rigid in design; wanting in ease or freedom of outline or arrangement.*

The *OED* gives *A Lover's Complaint* (1597), attributed to Shakespeare, as the first instance of the word 'formal' being used to refer to regularity in design. 'Informal garden' is a nineteenth-century term. The earliest example I have found of 'formal' being used in connection with Baroque gardens comes from a 1706 translation, by London and Wise, published as the *Compleat Florist*, of Louis Liger's *Le jardinier fleuriste* (1704).[41] The translators, who were assisted by John Evelyn, wrote that: 'A good Nursery of Flowers does not necessarily require your large *formal* Parterres; your simple Flower Beds will do.'[42]

Marc Treib described the use of 'formal' by garden and landscape historians as 'a particularly nasty linguistic problem'.[43] But the problem exists only if one forgets the origin of the usage: it derives from the second of Aristotle's Four Causes.[44] Applying

6.17 The *OED* has Shakespeare's *Lover's Complaint* (1597) as its earliest instance of 'formal' as an antonym for 'careless': 'Her hair, nor loose nor tied in *formal* plat, Proclaim'd in her a careless hand of pride' (illustration by Henry Corbould).

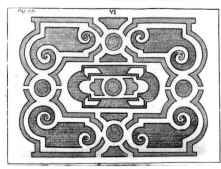

6.18 a, b (a) An early use of 'formal' in connection with gardens was in the *Compleat Florist* by London and Wise. The drawing is of parterre with cutwork beds. (b) C.F. Ferris's coloured plan, published in 1837, shows 'The figure of a Parterre of nothing but cut-work and plots of grass'.[45]

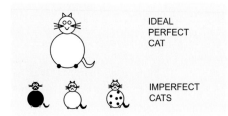

6.19 Plato's Theory of Forms encouraged the idea that artists and designers should represent the perfect forms in their work, not the imperfect everyday world.

Aristotle's theory of causality to gardens we could say that:

- The *material cause* is that out of which the garden is made (soil, water, plants, etc.).
- The *formal cause* is the shape of the garden (the design drawing).
- The *efficient cause* is the garden maker (the owner or builder).
- The *final cause* is the objectives for which a garden is made (use and beauty).

Aristotle's Theory of Causality is related to Plato's Theory of Forms, as is most European aesthetic theory, and the Theory of Forms rests on the difference between particulars and universals. Particulars are the individual things which comprise the visible world. They can be animal, vegetable or mineral, but all are imperfect and all are subject to change. Universals are general concepts such as straightness, yellowness, beauty and justice. They are perfect and they are not subject to change. Take straightness as an example. It refers to a line which is absolutely and perfectly straight, though no such line exists. Every particular example of a straight line deviates from the universal idea of 'straightness' because of imperfections in the drawing instrument and the surface upon which the line is drawn. Plato reasoned that since the visible world is made entirely of particulars, and since we know that universal concepts exist, there must be another realm of existence which contains the Forms of the natural world. He called universals 'forms' or 'ideas' and his theory about their nature and existence is known as the Theory of Forms.

Because the world of the Forms is perfect and changeless, Plato thought it superior to the visible world. He believed that the more we know and love the Forms, the better we will conduct our lives and govern our societies. From this standpoint, the Forms, of Beauty, Truth and Justice, are more important than such Forms as straightness and yellowness. The Forms can therefore be arranged in a hierarchy with the most important Form at the top and the least important Form at the bottom. In Plato's view, the Good is the most general and most important Form. 'Goodness' is a difficult quality to define but an understanding of its meaning is of the first importance for the conduct of our lives and the production of works of art, including gardens.

Among philosophers, there are numerous and ancient disputes concerning Plato's theory. Some doubt whether Plato believed in the separate existence of the world of the Forms. Aristotle, who spent 20 years in Plato's Academy, and Plotinus, who incorporated Plato's ideas into Christian theology, believed that he did. Others believe the Theory of Forms was intended as a simile. Plato loved similes and used them, including the famous simile of the cave, to explain the Theory of Forms.

A.N. Whitehead remarked that 'the safest general characterisation of the European philosophical tradition is that it consists in a series of footnotes to Plato'.[46] A lengthy footnote would be required to deal with Plato's influence on aesthetic theory and the

6.20 The hierarchy of forms, as implied by Plato's Theory of Forms, applied to landscape and garden design. It shows the nature of the world, comprising universals and particulars.

6.21 Socrates, through his influence on Plato and Aristotle, deserves a place in the history of garden design (photograph of the author's green roof).

work of practising artists. The discussion of mimesis (imitation) in *The Republic*, *The Timaeus* and *The Laws* was taken up by Aristotle and by countless later philosophers. They argue that since the world of the Forms is better than the everyday world, artists should refer to the ideal Forms in their work: 'Art,' they said, 'should imitate Nature.' In the course of its long history, the consequences of this axiom have varied according to the different interpretations which have been placed upon 'imitation' and 'nature'.

Aristotle's influence displaced that of Plato during the Middle Ages but the works of Plato were rediscovered in Renaissance Italy. Lorenzo de Medici founded a Platonic Academy in his garden at Carregi outside Florence, in 1439, and from this point

6.22 a, b Lorenzo de Medici founded a Platonic Academy at Careggi and put Plato's works in the mainstream of European culture. The ceiling of the loggia has the form of a garden with paintings of arbours and vignettes of Classical landscapes.

6.23 John Serle's plans of Pope's garden and his grotto (inset, top right) were diagrammatic. His drawing is shown with a site based on Anthony Beckles Willson's book.[47]
The key identifies: 1 the grass platt before the house next the Thames; 2 the house; 3 the underground passage; 4 the road from Hampton Court to London; 5 the Shell Temple; 6 the large mount; 7 the stoves; 8 the vineyard; 9 the obelisk in memory of his mother; 10 the small mounts; 11 the bowling green; 12 the grove; 13 the orangery; 14 the garden house; 15 the kitchen garden.

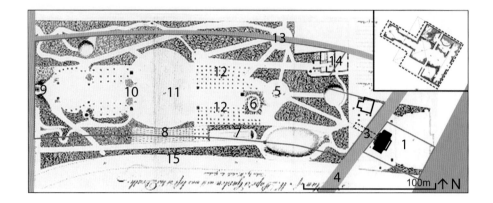

onwards Plato had a strong influence on Renaissance art. Humanist architects, such as Alberti and Palladio, studied Classical architecture in the light of Plato's theories and rediscovered the fact that Greek and Roman architecture was based on mathematical proportions. The relationship between the width of a column and its height, for example, was found to be based on Plato's conception of harmonic proportion. This was taken to be an example of architecture imitating the Forms. Wittkower described how Palladio was inspired by Neoplatonism.[48] Palladian architecture was based on the circle, the square and the principle of harmonic proportion. Palladio believed them to represent the Forms of the Good, Justice and Harmony.

Similar beliefs underlie the mathematically calculated 'Cartesian' gardens of the seventeenth century. Descartes did not write on aesthetics or gardening but his use of the geometrical method in reasoning led philosophers and artists to seek self-evident axioms on which to base aesthetic decisions. The axiom that 'Art should imitate Nature' fitted Cartesian philosophy. 'Nature' was understood once again as the set of essential and universal forms underlying the visible world. We can find the 'geometrical method' in Poussin's use of grids,[44] in Racine's plays, in Le Nôtre's garden designs and in the formulae which Boyceau gives for calculating the correct relationships between the length, height and width of an avenue. The latter correspond to the formulae used by Palladio to work out the mathematical relationship between a pavement and its adjacent arcade.

Neoplatonic ideas had wide currency in seventeenth- and eighteenth-century England. They are found in the writings of Dryden, Shaftesbury, Pope, Johnson and Reynolds. In one way or another, these authors all tell us that 'Art should imitate Nature'. The theory was taken up by gardening authors and became commonplace. It was expressed by Pope in his famous lines:

> *To build, to plant, whatever you intend,*
> *-- To rear the Column, or the Arch to bend,*

6.24 Pope's Villa, montaged onto a panorama of the Twickenham waterfront. (The turret of Radnor House School can be seen above the villa.)

> *To swell the Terras, or to sink the Grot;*
> *In all, let Nature never be forgot.*[50]

Pope's garden in Twickenham was Late Baroque and presents us with another example of the puzzle discussed in connection with Temple, Shaftesbury and Switzer. Pope is renowned as one of the prophets of the new English style but his garden had this character only in the slightest degree, if at all. When Pope writes that 'all art consists in the imitation and study of nature', the 'nature' he has in mind is mathematical, methodised and Neoplatonic. As Thacker observed, 'Pope's words, like Addison's, must be read with caution':[51]

> *First follow Nature, and your judgement frame*
> *By her just standard, which is still the same:*
> *Unerring NATURE, still divinely bright,*
> *One clear, unchang'd, and universal light, ...*
> *Those Rules of old discover'd, not devis'd,*
> *Are Nature still, but Nature Methodiz'd;*
> *Nature, like Liberty, is but restrain'd*
> *By the same Laws which first herself ordain'd.*[52]

Early Naturalism

English historians have spent a great deal of time scrutinising the gestation of landscape gardens. They have examined literary sources, as discussed above, and they have scoured the work of Late Baroque designers for green shoots presaging a new style. It has not been easy and many of the shoots which have been found are examples of authors using 'nature' in an empiricist sense, rather than developments in garden design. Pevsner (see p. 214) believes Temple introduced the first wiggle.

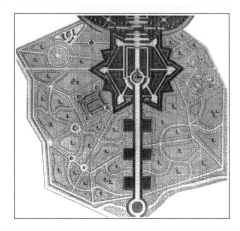

6.25 Switzer's design for the 'Manor of Paston', which is generally taken to be a design for Grimsthorpe Castle, shows no sign of an empiricist 'feeling for nature'.

6.26 The Lake Pavilions at Stowe, designed by John Vanbrugh in 1719, are connected by a ha-ha designed by Charles Bridgeman (see Figure 6.28).

Others have looked to the work of Bridgeman and Switzer.

Stephen Switzer was born in 1682, eight years before Bridgeman. He died in 1745, seven years after Bridgeman. In 1718, in, *Ichnographia Rustica*, Switzer quotes Classical authors, including 'the Divine Virgil' on the merit of 'studying nature's laws',[53] and Vitruvius for his 'excellent directions relating to situations'.[54] With regard to his design ideas, Hunt and Willis comment that his frontispiece (see Figure 5.31) displays 'a vaguely French manner' but that his text 'already announces the sensitivity to scale and proportion and the feeling for nature that distinguish the English landscape garden'.[55] It is not an easy distinction to sustain and it receives no support from the plans in Switzer's book.

Charles Bridgeman (1690–1738) was on good terms with Alexander Pope. He shared Switzer's taste for extensive prospects and his willingness to make a pragmatic response to the Genius of the Place. It is for these reasons that Peter Willis describes Bridgeman as a pioneer in 'the transition from the geometric layouts

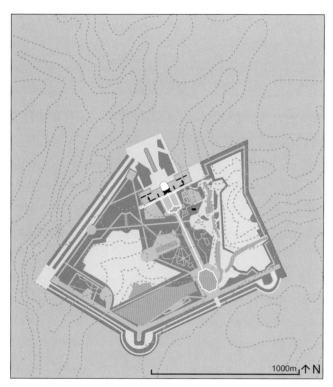

1000m ↑ N

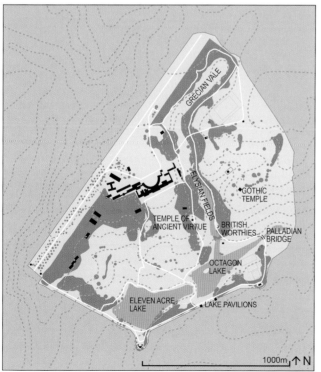

GRECIAN VALE

ELYSIAN FIELDS

GOTHIC TEMPLE

TEMPLE OF ANCIENT VIRTUE

BRITISH WORTHIES

PALLADIAN BRIDGE

OCTAGON LAKE

ELEVEN ACRE LAKE

LAKE PAVILIONS

1000m ↑ N

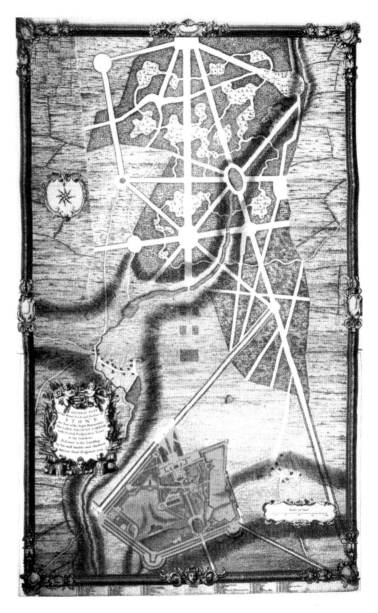

6.27 a, b, c (a) Stowe as a Baroque park. (b) Stowe as a Neoclassical park. (c) Bridgeman's plan of Stowe, as it appeared in *Views of Stowe* (1739) shows a Late Baroque layout with forestry at some distance from the house.

6.28 A ha-ha, running between two small temples, separates the garden at Stowe from the parkland and the Monumental Arch.

of the early 1700s to the freer designs of Capability Brown'.[56] But the evidence is thin. Bridgeman's most important project was Stowe. A plan of the park was published by his wife in 1739, the year after her husband's death. It is a Late Baroque design but with an interesting use of bastions and sunken walls, later given the name 'ha-ha'. Bastions were characteristic of both Bridgeman's and Switzer's work. They commanded wide views of the surrounding countryside and protected the garden from sheep and cattle. Forest style bastions can also be found at Bramham Park and Levens Hall, and there are examples of long avenues at Castle Howard and Studley Royal.

The desire of Bridgeman and Switzer to open up views and respect the *genius loci* can be seen as a move towards a more empirical approach to estate layout, if not as a fresh design style. But at Stowe and elsewhere, most of Bridgeman's work was swept away to make room for later and freer garden designs. There is a parallel with Pope's poetry. It was regarded as 'natural' during his lifetime but came to be described as 'artificial' by Wordsworth and the Romantic critics. The poems survive but Pope's garden, like Bridgeman and Switzer's work, has almost gone.

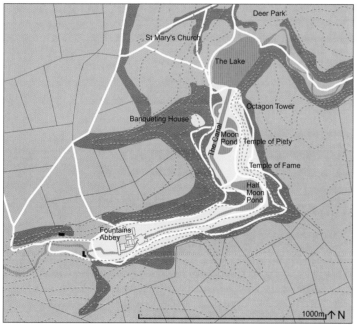

6.29 a, b, c Studley Royal, Yorkshire, is a fine example of a Neoclassical landscape garden. It has both Baroque geometry and irregular geometry, reflecting two conceptions of 'nature'.

Classical landscapes

The re-discovery of Classical literature was accompanied by a passion for the art, architecture, landscapes and gardens of the ancient world. Always believing their work should 'imitate nature', artists sought to discover the essential nature of the world. One way of investigating essences was to determine what had been valued since ancient times. Painters therefore copied antique models. 'The best artists,'

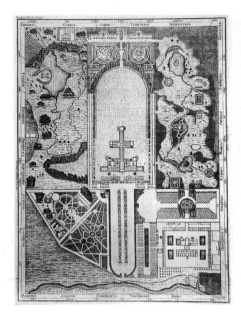
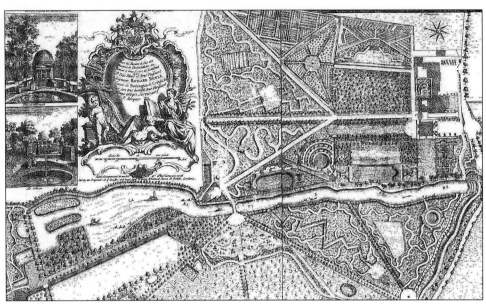

6.30 a, b (a) Robert Castell's *Villas of the Ancients* tells us little about Roman gardens but much about how they were conceived when Lord Burlington paid for its publication in 1728.[57]
(b) Lord Burlington's Chiswick House (1729) resembles Castell's plan (see Figure 6.33).

6.31 Statues by the best ancient sculptors were considered 'a better rule than the perfectest human bodies could afford' (Aphrodite, from Ephesus).

Shaftesbury tells us, 'are said to have been indefatigable in studying the best statues: as esteeming them a better rule than the perfectest human bodies could afford'.[58] Nothing was more *natural* than for garden designers to discover how the landscape of antiquity had looked. Just as Palladio studied Classical buildings, his English admirers interested themselves in the Classical landscapes in which temples had been set. Classical literature, landscape painting and personal visits to archaeological sites helped artists and designers compose images of antiquity. Classical landscapes became the natural settings for Palladian architecture.

William Kent travelled to Rome in 1710 and in the next decade had opportunities to see the relationship between Roman buildings, Palladio's Roman-inspired villas and the Classical landscapes in which they stood. Visiting Greece was very difficult, because of the Ottoman Empire, but there were similar temple-and-landscape compositions in Italy and information about Ancient Greece could be had from books. Ovid's *Metamorphosis* retold the Greek myths. Pausanias's *Description of Greece* had been available since the fifteenth century. It contained information about temples, landscapes, springs, groves and statues, with some mention of gardens. Beside a temple in the Garden District of Athens, 'the statue of Aphrodite in the Gardens is the work of Alcamenes, and one of the most noteworthy things in Athens'.[59] The Greek and Roman practice of siting temples in significant landscapes relates to the ancient cities of the Eastern Mediterranean and West Asia.

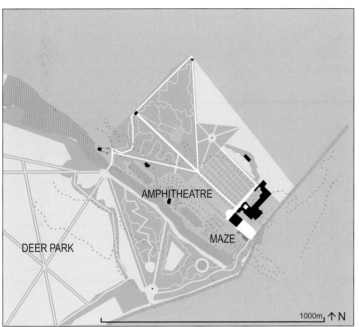
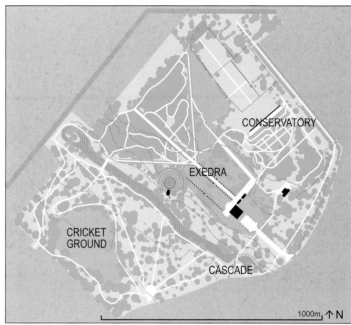

6.32 a, b Lord Burlington's villa, (a) as a Neoclassical Augustan garden and (b) as it is today.

6.33 The gardens at Chiswick House were a symbolic re-creation of the form Roman gardens were believed to have had. The *exedra*, designed by William Kent, is thought to have contained statues of Caesar, Pompey and Cicero.

6.34 *Templa quam dilecta* ('How beautiful are thy temples') was the Temple's family motto and their garden, at Stowe, contains many Classical temples.

William Kent returned to England after a decade in Italy and helped Lord Burlington design one of the most Palladian buildings in England. This was followed by a partial transformation of its setting into a Classical landscape. Chiswick became a place for rural retirement from Burlington House in Piccadilly. Burlington's circumstances were entirely different from those of a Hindu holy man (*rishi*) but his attitude of mind relates to that of his Indo-European predecessors. After settling in India the Hindus rhapsodised the gods, mountains, forests and holy places that their ancestors had known. Burlington, with assistance from William Kent, rhapsodised, and 'retreated' to a re-creation of a Graeco-Roman sacred landscape. Palladio's re-creation of Graeco-Roman architecture contributed to Burlington's Chiswick landscape and Lord Cobham's Stowe landscape.

Claude and Poussin were seen to be illustrating Classical landscapes and the rural retirement theme which Horace, Virgil and England's Augustan authors celebrated. Claude painted scenes from Italy, Greece, North Africa and the Bible lands. Sir Kenneth Clark described these Classical landscapes as paintings of 'the most enchanting dream which has ever consoled mankind, the myth of a Golden Age in which man lived on the fruits of the earth, peacefully, piously, and with primitive simplicity'.[60] The dream was of an 'earthly paradise ... a harmony between man and nature'. A seventeenth-century gardening author's version of the dream is shown on the frontispiece of Timothy Nourse's *Campania Felix*.[61] Nourse had been a bursar at Oxford but lost his job after becoming a Roman Catholic. He suffered during the Popish Plot and died in 1699, the same year as Sir William Temple. Like many of their contemporaries, Nourse and Temple came to believe that rural retirement allowed a better life in which the fruits of the earth could be enjoyed. The frontispiece of Nourse's book shows a toga-clad Happy Husbandsman ploughing his furrow towards a seventeenth-century garden.

6.35 a, b, c Circular temples at Delphi, Tivoli and Stowe. Hadrian visited Delphi and William Kent visited Tivoli.

6.36 Claude's painting of a scene from Ovid's *Metamorphosis* in which Argus, disguised as a cowherd, is guarding Io, who has metamorphosed into a cow.

6.37 a, b (a) An illustration from Dryden's translation of Virgil (1697 edn), subscribed by the best-known English garden designer of the period, George London.[62] (b) The frontispiece to Timothy Nourse's *Campania Felix* (1700).

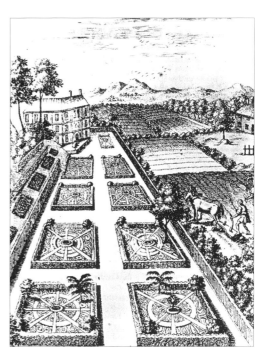

No longer content to dream of 'earthly paradises', the owners of eighteenth-century estates set about giving reality to their dreams. These were the lords who effected the 'great revolution in taste'. Some analysts have tried to single out one factor, such as 'love of nature', 'a revolt against formality', 'Romanticism' or 'Chinese influence' as *the* cause of the great revolution. This is misleading. The objective was to make ideal landscapes and it is not surprising that ideas were gathered from many sources to construct the ideal. They came from philosophy, art, politics, economics, horticulture, agriculture, forestry and science; from Greece, Italy, Holland, England, France and China. The grand coalition was then assembled in an English garden.

It appears that the political genius who first brought the coalition together was Joseph Addison. Dobrée describes him as 'a very able, very well-read, and intelligent popu-lariser of astonishing literary skill', who made known 'the most advanced thought of his time, both philosophically and aesthetically'.[63] Addison's essays of 1712 on *The Pleasures of the Imagination* contain most of the key ideas which were combined to make ideal landscapes. The assembly of the following ideas was particularly significant: rural retirement, Neoplatonism, Lockeian empiricism, eclecticism, landscape painting and the idea that pragmatic improvements to a country estate can be achieved through gardening, forestry and agriculture. None of the ideas was new but several were new bedfellows in 1712. The coalition gained strength from Addison's clear formulation, and the resultant impetus launched garden and landscape design onto a path of dynamic change.

6.38 a, b (a) The gorge of the River Aniene at Tivoli was much visited by Grand Tourists. Joseph Addison wrote, 'The villa de Medicis, with its water-works, the cascade of the Teverone, and the ruins of the Sibyl's Temple, (of which Vignola has made a little copy at St Peters de Montorio,) are described in every Itinerary.' The first-century Temple of Vesta, also called the Sibyl's Temple, is on the skyline. (b) The gorge is now called the Parco Gregoriana.

In what Richardson describes as Addison's 'greatest poetic flourish',[64] he wrote:

> *For wheresoe'er I turn my ravish'd eyes,*
> *Gay gilded scenes and shining prospects rise,*
> *Poetic fields encompass me around,*
> *And still I seem to tread on classic ground.*[65]

Addison's familiarity with the Classics 'transports him back in time' so that 'his imaginative recollections of literature merge with the evidence of his eyes':[66]

> *Tivoli is seen at a distance lying along the brow of a hill ... The villa de Medicis [the Villa d'Este], with its water-works, the cascade of the Teverone, and the ruins of the Sibyl's Temple, (of which Vignola has made a little copy at St Peters de Montorio,) are described in every Itinerary ... But the most enlivening part of all, is the river Teverone, which you see at about a quarter of a mile's distance throwing itself down a precipice, and falling by several cascades from one rock to another, till it gains the bottom of the valley, where the sight of it would be quite lost, did it not sometimes discover itself through the breaks and openings of the woods that grow about it. The Roman painters often work upon this landscape, and I am apt to believe that Horace had his eye upon it in those two or three beautiful touches he has given us of these seats. The Teverone was formerly called the Anio:*
>
> *...*

6.39 Sir Uvedale Price wrote of: 'The peculiar excellence of the painter, who most studied the beautiful in landscape, is characterised by *il riposo di Claudio*, and when the mind of man is in the delightful state of repose, of which Claude's pictures are the image, — when he feels that mild and equal sunshine of the soul, which warms and cheers, but neither inflames nor irritates, — his heart seems to dilate with happiness, he is disposed to every act of kindness and benevolence, to love and cherish all around him.'[68]

Resounding with her water-falls,
And Tivoli's delightful shades,
And Anio roiling in cascades,
That through the flow'ry meadows glides,
And all the beauteous scene divides.[67]

This was the scenery which travellers remembered and owners wished to re-create on English estates.

Gardens as Classical landscapes

The reason for describing the first phase of the Classical landscape garden as 'Augustan' is that it equates with Augustan literature. Horace and Virgil celebrated the Roman Emperor Augustus's age of peace and security after civil war. The English Augustans celebrated a second Golden Age following the troubles of the seventeenth

6.40 a, b Sir Francis Dashwood embarked on a Grand Tour at the age of 18, in 1726. After acquiring an appreciation of Classical art, he created a Classical landscape at West Wycombe.

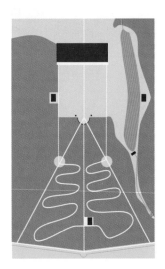

6.41 Diagram of the Classical landscape, Augustan style.

century. Laurence Eachard, in 1695, wrote that: 'Augustus made the World happy, and was happy in the World.'[69]

Understandably, George I wanted to be a new Augustus. Writers, artists, architects, gardeners and others sought to relive and make anew the glories of Rome in the time of its first emperor, who, according to Suetonius, boasted that 'I found Rome built of sun-dried bricks; I leave her clothed in marble.'[70] Augustus's reign from 27 BCE to 14 CE saw a great flowering of the arts. In eighteenth-century England, Palladian architecture, heroic couplets and Augustan gardens were the products of looking 'back to Rome'. The diagram of the Augustan style (Figure 6.41) has a kinship with the drawings in Castell's *Villas of the Ancients* (Figure 6.30).

Alexander Pope was England's foremost Augustan poet and a significant influence on garden design. In 1713, Pope stated that 'the taste of the ancients in their gardens' was for 'the amiable simplicity of unadorned nature, that spreads over the mind a more noble sort of tranquility'.[71] Eighteen years later he devoted an epistle, in heroic couplets, to the man who had become the leading English patron of Palladianism, Lord Burlington:

> *In you, my Lord, Taste sanctifies Expense,*
> *For Splendour borrows all her Rays from Sense,*
> *You show us, Rome was glorious, not profuse,*
> *And pompous buildings once were things of use.*[72]

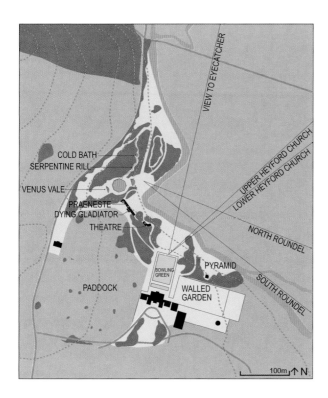

6.42 a, b (a) William Kent 'leaped the fence' at Rousham and placed an Eyecatcher beyond the garden boundary. (b) The plan has Baroque aspects and is predominantly Neoclassical.

Burlington's friend and protégé William Kent became the foremost Augustan garden designer. Horace Walpole gave this account of his achievement:

> At that moment appeared Kent, painter enough to taste the charms of landscape, bold and opinionative enough to dare and to dictate, and born with a genius to strike out a great system from the twilight of imperfect essays. He leaped the fence, and saw that all nature was a garden. He felt the delicious contrast of hill and valley changing imperceptibly into each other, tasted the beauty of the gentle swell, or concave scoop, and remarked how loose groves crowned an easy eminence with happy ornament, and while they called in the distant view between their graceful stems, removed and extended the perspective by delusive comparison.[73]

Though much-quoted, Walpole's remark lacks circumspection. Baroque gardens had been outward-looking and, as Timothy Mowl and Brian Earnshaw remark, 'Burlington allowed no leaping of fences at Chiswick. It was, and even now remains, an enclosed, even slightly claustrophobic Arcadia.'[74]

Kent worked with Bridgeman on some estates and in succession to Bridgeman on others. The historical records are incomplete but it is likely that when they worked

6.43 a, b At Rousham, the Praeneste, named after the home of a Roman oracle, and Venus's Vale were inspired by William Kent's decade in Italy.

together, Kent provided the ideas and Bridgeman the technical expertise. The best surviving examples of their work are at Claremont, Chiswick House, Rousham and Stowe. The avenues in these gardens are Baroque. The delightful lakes and glades are among the earliest examples of the Serpentine style. Kent loved to give canals, basins and water bodies a 'natural' shape. In Walpole's words, 'the gentle stream was taught to serpentise seemingly at its pleasure'.[75] Kent saw landscapes as pictures, not as plans. 'The great principles on which he worked were perspective, and light and shade.'[76] But as with the landscape painters of his time, the places which really interested him were the landscapes of antiquity. The gardens designed by Kent and

6.44 a, b At Stowe, the Temple of British Worthies looks across the Elysian Fields to the Temple of Ancient Virtue.

6.45 Venus looks over the Brownian lake at Sherborne Castle.

6.46 The *exedra* at Chiswick Park.

Bridgeman were redolent of ancient times, full of statues, temples, grottoes, baths and a hermit's cave.

At Chiswick House, the statues in the *exedra* were said to have come from Hadrian's Villa and to represent Caesar, Pompey and Cicero. Another of Kent's exedra, at Stowe, has niches for eight British Worthies. Their derivative genius is shown by making them look allegorically upwards to a Temple of Ancient Virtue set in the Elysian Fields. The design of the temple was itself derived from the Temple of Vesta which overlooks the Tivoli gorge outside Rome (see Figure 6.38). At Rousham, Kent designed a Venus's Vale and an arcade named the Praeneste, after the Roman resort where an oracle resided. At Claremont, Bridgeman designed a Graeco-Roman amphitheatre, made out of grass instead of stone, and not intended for bloody spectacles. He placed a circular pond in front of the amphitheatre which Kent changed into the natural lake which occupies the centre of the valley today (see p. 199).

This was the age when garden design became a 'nobleman's recreation', when noblemen had a love of antiquity and when landscape painting exceeding that of professional designers. Lord Carlisle was the leading figure in the creation of the park at Castle Howard. Hussey calls it 'the masterpiece of ... the Heroic Age of English landscape architecture'.[77] In 1733, an anonymous poet wrote that 'Carlisle's genius ... form'd this great design' and compared Wray Wood to an Italian scene:

> *This Wood with Justice Belvidere we name.*
> *Statues at proper Views enrich the Scene,*
> *Here chaste Diana and the Paphian Queen,*
> *Tho' Opposites in Fame, tho' Rivals made*
> *Contented stand under one common Shade.*[78]

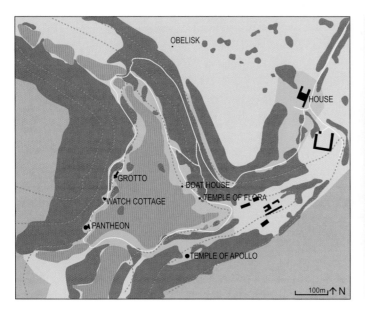

6.47 a, b Stourhead is the best example of a Classical landscape garden in England. Reyner Banham wrote, 'The purely visual aesthetic of Stourhead, free of sentimentality and allusion, is what puts it in the class of European masterpieces.'[79]

The Temple of the Four Winds at Castle Howard was inspired by Palladio's Villa Capra which Colen Campbell adapted at Mereworth and Lord Burlington at Chiswick.

Charles Hamilton and Henry Hoare were less noble but had been on the Grand Tour and acquired a passion for the landscapes of antiquity. At Painshill, Charles Hamilton installed a Grecian statue of Bacchus in a temple, built a Roman Bath House and assembled a set of busts of the Roman emperors.

Henry Hoare II, known to his family as 'the Magnificent', returned from Italy in 1741 to take possession of the Stourhead estate. He made the lake in 1744 and surrounded it with a walk conceived as an allegory of Aeneas's voyage after the fall of

6.48 a, b The lake at Painshill Park, viewed from the Gothic Temple. The Gothic style was associated with the Classical landscapes of Medieval Italy.

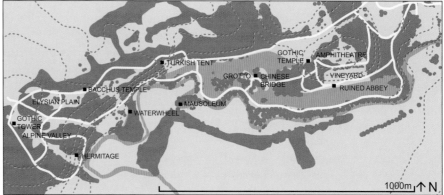

6.49 The Serpentine park at Holkham Hall was designed by William Kent and improved by Lancelot Brown.

Troy. The grotto marks a stage in his journey. The Temple of Flora is inscribed with the caution uttered by the Cumaean Sybil, in Virgil's *Aeneid*, before she led Aeneas into the underworld to hear the prophecy of Rome's founding: 'Begone! You who are uninitiated, begone!' Hoare based his design for the bridge on Palladio's five-arched bridge at Vicenza and expressed the hope that the whole composition would resemble a painting by Gaspar Poussin.

British patrons and designers sought to re-create the landscape scenery of antiquity. Their visions of how this landscape might have appeared were formed from Latin poetry, from places visited on Grand Tours and from the Neoclassical landscape paintings of Claude, Poussin and others. William Kent had met Lord Burlington on a Grand Tour. Charles Hamilton went to Italy after leaving Oxford and returned home to design Painshill. Henry Hoare was in Italy when he inherited Stourhead. These men admired the Augustan Age and, in the course of making gardens which reflected this taste, the geometry of garden plans became increasingly serpentine.

Gardens as Serpentine landscapes

The adjective 'Serpentine' is used here to describe the famous style associated with the name of Lancelot 'Capability' Brown. Repton wrote of 'modern serpentine gardening',[80] which is good authority for naming the mid-century style 'Serpentine' (alternatives are considered in Appendix II). Richardson groups the styles reviewed in this chapter as 'Arcadian'. The term comes from a Greek province in which shepherds and shepherdesses were believed to live in pastoral harmony with nature, free from pride and greed but not immune to lust. The domain of Pan was imagined full of beautiful nymphs frolicking in lush forests:

6.50 a, b (a) Nicolas Poussin's *Et in Arcadia ego* ('I too [was] in Arcadia', meaning that there was death even in Arcadia). Though born in France, Poussin spent most of his life in Rome and sold paintings to noblemen on the Grand Tour. (b) Pousin's *Landscape with the Ashes of Phocion.*

> *Brown effectively drained the landscape of meaning and dissent. His gardens were emphatically Arcadias, where mortals could enjoy the rural scene, rather than the Elysiums, symbolic domains of gods and heroes.*[81]

Classical landscape gardens had been rich in allegory. Serpentine landscapes were essentially pastoral and, with gleaming Palladian houses, symbolised parliamentary democracy, frugal government and the Enlightenment:

> *The landscape gardens of the type 'improved' by Capability Brown implied not only a different aesthetic, based on a different metaphysics of nature, but also a new economics. Not that they were inexpensive; rather, they looked inexpensive because they looked as if they were nature. In the Baroque scheme of things, bullion might be converted into flowing water, cascades, spouts, water mirrors, and water theatre. In the Enlightenment scheme, bullion was thought better applied to agricultural improvement, trade, and manufacturing. Beauty was perceived less in what artists called the 'general nature,' or the 'ideal nature,' the model of the classical landscape painters, than in the given, empirical, experienced nature, a piece of land which might be improved so as to yield not only a truer beauty but also an increased net product.*[82]

The steps by which the Augustan Style evolved into the Serpentine style constitute a fascinating episode in the history of taste. It has occupied the attention of many historians and is best chronicled by Christopher Hussey in *English Gardens and Landscapes, 1700–1750*. One of the most celebrated steps in the progression was the

6.51 a, b Castle Howard. (a) The path on the north front fizzles out, instead of driving into Wray Wood. (b) The path on the south front, Henderskelf Lane, follows the serpentine curve of an ancient track.

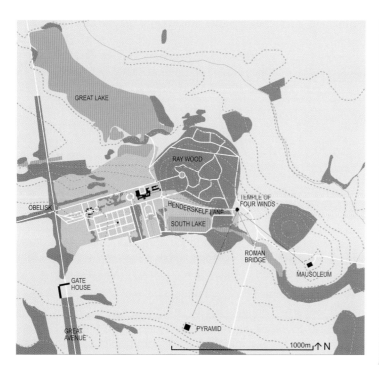

6.52 a, b, c Christopher Hussey described Castle Howard as 'the masterpiece of ... the Heroic Age of English landscape architecture'.[83]

6.53 a, b Duncombe is 21 km from Castle Howard and has a serpentine terrace which, it is thought, the owner might have wished to link with the serpentine terrace at Rievaulx, 4.5 km west.

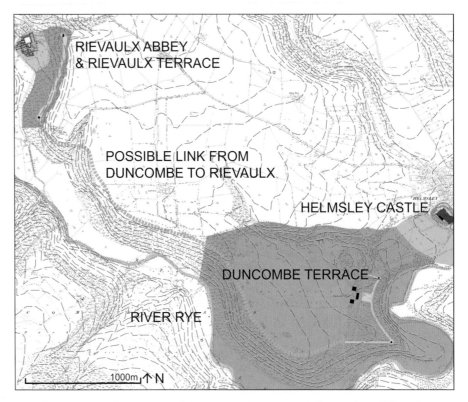

6.53 There may have been a plan to link the serpentine terraces at Duncombe and Rievaulx.

retention of Wray Wood and Henderskelf Lane at Castle Howard. Hussey comments that the low hill on which they lie is 'historic ground, since it became the turning-point of garden design not only at Castle Howard but in England'.[84] 'And,' he could have added, 'the Western hemisphere'.

The low hill at Castle Howard was occupied by a stand of mature beech trees. Wray Wood (now Ray Wood) lies east of the new house which Vanbrugh and Hawksmoor designed between 1699 and 1712. George London advised on the layout of the grounds until his death in 1714 and his apprentice, Stephen Switzer, is assumed to have advised Lord Carlisle after London's death. London wished to drive avenues from the front of the house up the hill and into Wray Wood. Switzer described the idea, in 1718, as 'a star' and wrote that London's proposal 'would have spoil'd the Wood, but that his Lordship's superlative genius prevented it'.[85] Instead of becoming a bosquet and a *patte d'oie*, Wray Wood was retained and furnished with waterworks and labyrinthine paths to make what Switzer judged an 'incomparable Wood the highest pitch that Natural and Polite Gardening can possibly ever arrive to'.[86] Hussey suggests that since Switzer was both a modest man and an expert in waterworks, it may in fact have been he, rather than Lord Carlisle, who had the idea of conserving

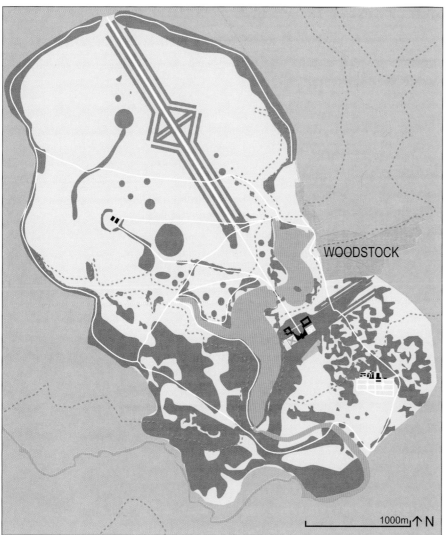

6.54 a, b (a) Blenheim Palace was designed as a place of retirement and harmony for a Classical hero: the first Duke of Marlborough. His descendant, Sir Winston Churchill, wrote that 'he never fought a battle that he did not win, nor besieged a fortress that he did not take'.[87] (b) Plan of Blenheim Park.

WOODSTOCK

1000m N

6.55 The eponymous Serpentine in London's Hyde Park was designed by Charles Bridgeman.

6.56 a, b A ha-ha was a way of having an uninterrupted view of farmland without animals being able to enter the garden. (a) The ha-ha at Wallington Hall. (b) Only the change in the character of the grass reveals the existence of a ha-ha at Kedleston Hall.

6.57 Lancelot Brown started out as a garden labourer at Kirkharle in Northumberland and, after losing his popularity, was disparaged for his humble origins.

6.58 The Temple of Concord and Victory, at Stowe, overlooks the Grecian Vale, designed by William Kent and Lancelot Brown.

Wray Wood. Today the waterworks have disappeared and the beechwood is recovering from being clear-felled in 1940 and being managed as a woodland garden in the Gardenesque style.

Henderskelf Lane survives intact as a path skirting the southern flank of Wray Wood. It links Castle Howard to the Temple of the Four Winds. The lane was an ancient track which, according to the logic of George London's layout, should have been eliminated or straightened. Instead, it was retained and made into a broad meandering grassy walk which commands a heroic prospect of a Classical landscape. It resembles the grass terrace at nearby Duncombe, but it is not known which of the two terraces was made first. A visual comparison of the two terraces leads one to think that Henderskelf is the prototype. Thomas Duncombe married a Howard and is said to have considered extending his serpentine walk for five kilometres along the hillside to Rievaulx Abbey in the 1740s.

Some of the other famous steps in the evolution of the Serpentine style are as follows: Vanbrugh's suggestion that £1,000 could be saved by keeping Old Woodstock Manor in Blenheim Park as a picturesque feature in the view; the acceptance of site irregularities at Bramham Park so that the garden has an axis of its own and is not dependent on the axis of the house; the formation of the irregular grove at Melbourne Hall which Hussey describes as 'the classic example in England of the first movement away from an entirely regular conception of garden-design which eventually led to landscape'[88] (as at Bramham, the axis of the garden was not related to the axis of the house); the use of the accidental diagonal provided by an old lane at Stowe to form the 'Great Cross Lime Walk' (it crosses at 70 degrees instead of the usual 90 degrees), the extensive use of a ha-ha (sunk fence) at Stowe to bring the view of the countryside into the garden; and Charles Bridgeman's design for joining up a series of small ponds in Hyde Park to form the large lake which is now known, very appropriately, as the Serpentine.

Each of these evolutionary steps, taken between 1709 and 1748, marks a slight swing of the pendulum from rationalism to empiricism and from geometrical regularity to asymmetry and serpentine curves. Some of the finest eighteenth-century gardens were made when the pendulum reached a mid-point between the two poles. Duncombe (1713–50), Studley Royal (1715–30), Rousham (1726–39) and Stourhead (1726–39) are brilliant examples of the way in which a disciplined and imaginative design concept can be developed from an intuitive response to the prevailing genius of a place. But it is not sufficient to analyse the first phase of the Serpentine style in geometrical terms alone: it was rich in symbolism, allusion and allegory.

The maturity of the Serpentine style was heralded by the start of Lancelot Brown's career as a freelance designer. Brown began as a garden labourer at Kirkharle in the north of England, a background which left him well suited to an Enlightenment pursuit of practicality. His education was basic; he had no knowledge of the Classics and had not been on a Grand Tour. But he was 'competent, reliable, honest, and easy to deal with', which appealed to his clients.[89] Brown moved south in 1739. By 1751, he had been head gardener at Stowe for ten years and had seen great works under the overall direction of William Kent. They probably worked together on the design of the Grecian Vale. It had Classical overtones but was executed with more feeling for the abstract composition of landform and woods than most of Kent's work. Serpentine curves became Brown's hallmark. He was not averse to including the occasional temple when it improved the composition but there is no reason to think he regarded them as anything other than ornaments. Modern visitors see them as 'follies'.

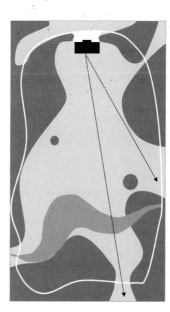

6.60 Diagram of the Serpentine landscape style.

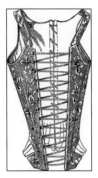

6.61 a, b (a) A 'formal' straight corset, *c.*1720.
(b) This illustration from Hogarth's *Analysis of Beauty* shows serpentine lines applied to chair legs and women's stays. *The World* complained about 'breasts compressed by a flat straight line'.

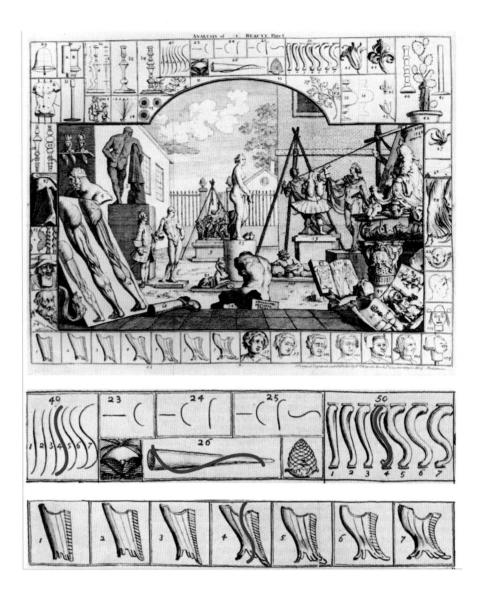

6.62 Lady Luxborough, with serpentine curves and Classical scenery in the background.

For the 32 years of his career as an independent designer Brown's style hardly changed and is represented on the Serpentine style diagram (see Figure 6.60). One could think of it as a 1,000-hectare estate. The characteristic features of Brown's style are the circular clumps of trees, the grassy meadow in front of the mansion house, the serpentine lake, the enclosing tree-belt and the encircling carriage drive. Hussey remarked that Brown was a practical man in the grip of a theory. The diagram shows the theory. *The World*, ever with its finger on the pulse of the nation's taste, was quick to recognise Brown's interest in serpentine shapes and drew a comparison between Hogarth's line of beauty, the profile of a woman's body and a Brownian park.

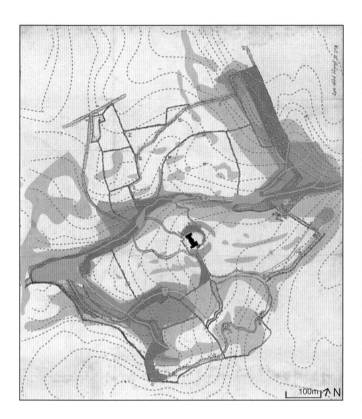

6.63 a, b (a) Dodesley's plan of the Leasowes with (1) his planting in dark green; (2) mid-nineteenth-century planting in mid-green; (3) present-day planting in light green. (b) The Leasowes is now a golf club.

In 1753, the editor wrote that 'a young lady of the most graceful figure I ever beheld' had come to London:

"To have her shape altered to the modern fashion". That is to say, to have her breasts compressed by a flat straight line. I protest, when I saw the beautiful figure that was to be so deformed by the stay maker, I was as much shocked, as if I had been told that she was come to deliver up those animated knowls of beauty to the surgeon – I borrow my terms from gardening, which now indeed furnishes the most pregnant and exalted expressions of any science in being. And this brings to mind the only instance that can give an adequate idea of my concern. Let us suppose that Mr Brown should, in any one of the many Elysiums he has made, see the old terraces rise again and mask his undulating knowls, or straight rows of trees obscure his noblest configurations of scenery.[90]

The comparison between serpentine lines and women's stays comes from Hogarth's *Analysis of Beauty* (1753). Hogarth commented on the 'elegant degree of plumpness to the skin of the softer sex',[91] and drew diagrams to show how the ideal stay resembled the line of beauty. The beautiful Lady Luxborough borrowed William Shenstone's copy of the book and envied the shape of the letter with which his name began. She wrote in 1754 that she was 'sorry I have not now an S in my name to claim any

6.64 a, b Lancelot Brown used mounds and clumps to soften the crags and make Alnwick Castle a feature in a Neoclassical landscape. (a) As painted by Canaletto in 1752. (b) As Serpentined by Brown after 1769.

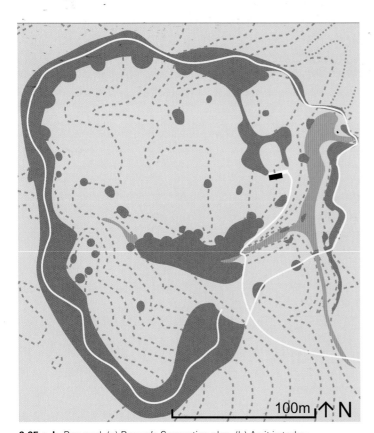
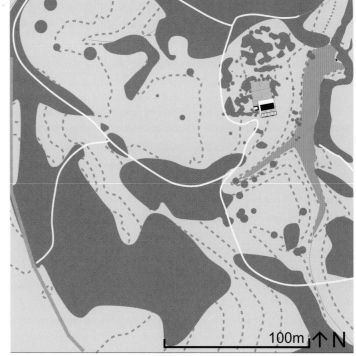

6.65 a, b Bowood. (a) Brown's Serpentine plan. (b) As it is today.

6.66 Bowood has a serpentine lake and a Doric temple (see also Figure 6.65).

share in it'.[92] Shenstone's own park at the Leasowes attracted famous visitors and prevented him from visiting Lady Luxborough as often as she would have liked. There is a Rococo flavour to *The World*'s comment but, though Brown's style is curvy and chronologically belongs to the Rococo period, the adjective is unhelpful for several reasons: the Rococo was essentially an indoor style; it was never strong in England; it has more affinity with the Baroque than the Enlightenment. But for these facts 'the inventive, ornate Rococo style should, in the natural course of events, have been Britain's prevailing decorative style' between 1710 and 1770.[93]

Dorothy Stroud attributes 211 designs for English parks to Brown. A surprising number remain in good condition, often because they have been adapted to modern use as public parks, farms, golf courses and schools. The best of them are magnificent, probably more so today than when seen by Brown's critics in the 1790s. My own favourites are the Arcadian glade at Prior Park, the Grecian valley at Stowe, the lakes at Luton Hoo and Blenheim Park, the parkland outside Alnwick Castle, Chatsworth Park and the grand views at Petworth and Harewood which J.M.W. Turner painted.

Some of Brown's other designs are so 'naturalistic' and 'English' that it is difficult to appreciate them without a survey of the site as it was and a plan of the works executed by Brown. His lakes lie in comfortable depressions, his woods clothe hills which would resist the plough and his green pastures roll to the rhythm of the English countryside. A large collection of Brown's professional papers, which might have provided more information on what he actually did, was given to Repton by Brown's son and have since disappeared. The paucity of documentation on so many

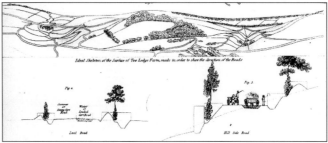

6.67 a, b Great Tew in Oxfordshire. (a) Looking south to the village. (b) Loudon's drawing of his *ferme ornée*.

sites makes Bowood a park of special interest. Here the plan and the estate survive in reasonable condition (see p. 250).

A variant of the Serpentine style, known as the *ferme ornée*, is of particular interest to historians of the rural retirement theme. Maren-Sofie Rostvig comments that 'Instead of penning yet another version of Horace's second epode, Southcote translated the literary ideal into a living reality',[94] at Woburn Farm near Chertsey (*c.*1735). It was a working farm ornamented with trees, shrubs and temples, and is usually described as a *ferme ornée* despite the fact that Switzer did not invent the term until 1742. '*Ornée'* does not convey the fact that these farms were intended to satisfy the widest possible range of human needs and aspirations. 'Ideal farm' would be a better description. The term *ferme ornée* was first applied to the Leasowes in 1746 but it is significant that Shenstone did not include it in the threefold classification of types of gardening which he made in 1764 (kitchen-gardening, parterre-gardening, and landscape-gardening).[95] He refers to Burke in the following paragraph and it may be that Burke's empiricist aesthetics discouraged Shenstone from using the term. Burke believed there was no connection between use and beauty. He pointed out that however useful the wedge-like snout of a pig or the bared teeth of a wolf may be, they are not beautiful.[96] Shenstone may have thought the utility of his farm would be judged a detraction from its beauty.

In practice, use was combined with beauty on many estates laid out in the Serpentine style. They were run as ideal farms whatever the aesthetic beliefs of their owners and designers. This fact was apparent to the French observer R.L. Girardin whose *Essay on Landscape or, on the Means of Improving and Embellishing the Country Round*

6.68 a, b Thomas Robins illustrated flower gardens in the mid-eighteenth century.

Our Habitations of 1783 became popular in England. He admired the Leasowes and, with honed Enlightenment sensibility, wrote:

> *This change of things then, from a forced arrangement to one that is easy and natural will bring us back to a true taste for beautiful nature, tend to the increase of agriculture, the propagation of cattle, and, above all, to more humane and salutary regulations of the country, by providing for the subsistence of those, whose labour supports the men of more thinking employments who are to instruct, or defend society.*[97]

John Claudius Loudon took these remarks to heart and at the beginning of the nineteenth century made an ornamented farm at Great Tew in Oxfordshire. On completing the project, he said that 'Time alone is requisite to render Tew Lodge the most magnificent *ferme ornée* in England.'[98] Loudon must have thought his belief well justified when he sold the lease after four years work, and made the magnificent profit of £15,000 (equivalent to £900,000 in 2008 using the Retail Price Index). Like the Leasowes, it survives and deserves to be restored as a monument to the fact that farmers need not sacrifice beauty to profit. Loudon drained the land, improved the shapes of the fields, made new roads, planted new hedgerows and strengthened the old tree-belt on the skyline to create a delightfully secluded valley.

Flowering plants were an important aspect of the *ferme ornée* and, as John Harris and Mark Laird pointed out, they were not excluded from the Serpentine style to the degree which has been supposed. A main feature of Woburn Farm was a walk planted with broom, roses, lilac, columbine, peonies and sweet William. It wound its way through the fields. Shenstone wrote to Lady Luxborough that he had a copy of

6.69 An engraving of Chatsworth from Watts's *Seats of the Nobility and Gentry*.[99] A comparison with Figure 5.46 gives a measure of the great revolution in taste between 1707 and 1782.

Philip Miller's *Gardener's Dictionary* and that 'if there arrive a flowering shrub; it is a day of rejoicing with me.'[100] Flower gardens were protected from livestock with a ha-ha[101] and were also separated from utilitarian enclosures (kitchen gardens, melon grounds, etc.). The flower garden was not necessarily separated 'from areas of specialized horticulture (hothouses, scientific collecting grounds, etc.)' but:

> *Very often it contained one spot primarily devoted to shrubs, the shrubbery, as well as one spot principally dedicated to flowers, what we shall here call the flower garden (i.e., the delectable as opposed to rare flower garden).*[102]

Loudon had a great collection of flowering plants at Tew Lodge and there is a superficial resemblance between his drawings of the garden and the paintings by Thomas Robins which Harris used to establish the presence of flower gardens in eighteenth-century estates. Flower gardens were the most Rococo feature of eighteenth-century gardens.

The astonishing degree to which the Serpentine style of estate layout became fashionable between 1740 and 1780 can be seen by comparing the engravings in Kip and Knyff's *Britannia Illustrata* with those in Watts's *Seats of the Nobility and Gentry*. Kip and Knyff show every house surrounded by rectangular compartments. Watts shows every house in a grazed field with forest trees framing views near the house. The popularity of the Serpentine style reached fever pitch in the 1780s and its creators believed the style to be completely natural. The next generation disagreed. A further move to empiricism led to the depreciation of Brown and thoughts of a new style.

The appreciation and depreciation of Lancelot Brown

Dramatic changes in the appreciation of Lancelot 'Capability' Brown as a designer provide a second illustration of the consequences which different uses of 'nature' and 'landscape' have for garden and landscape design theory.

During his career as an independent designer Brown was hailed as a near-genius and arbiter of taste. His work was seen to be uniquely British and in the most 'natural' style conceivable. This status was publicly recognised by Brown's appointment as Royal Gardener at Hampton Court in 1764. The naturalness of his style was praised in an anonymous poem on *The Rise and Progress of the Present Taste in Planting Parks, Pleasure Grounds, Gardens, Etc*, with the author giving fulsome praise to Brown and emphasising the naturalness of his work:

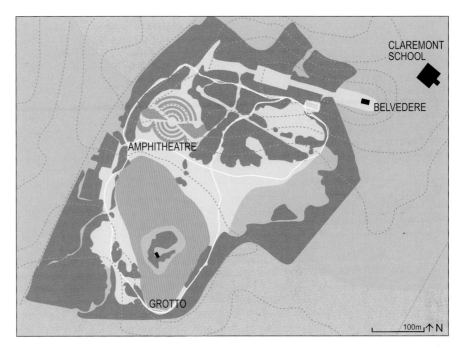

6.70 a, b, c (a) Brown planned the house which is now Claremont School, with Henry Holland doing the drawings. (b) Brown also modified the garden, making it more of a landscape. (c) Plan of Claremont (see also p. 199).

> *He barren tracts with every charm illumes,*
> *At his command a new Creation blooms;*
> *Born to grace Nature, and her works complete,*
> *With all that's beautiful, sublime and great!*
> *For him each Muse enwreathes the Laurel Crown,*
> *And consecrates to Fame immortal Brown.*[103]

The poet's conception of Nature was gentle and pastoral. As the empiricist philosopher David Hume had written in 1748, 'the eye is pleased with the prospect of corn-fields and loaded vineyards, horses grazing, and flocks pasturing: but flies the view of briars and brambles, affording shelter to wolves and serpents'.[104] Hume died, in 1776, shortly before scenes of briars and brambles became wildly popular.

Further praise for Brown's conception of nature came from two books written before 1770. The first was Thomas Whately's *Observations on Modern Gardening*, which Loudon proclaimed 'the grand fundamental standard work on English gardening'.[105] It contains detailed descriptions of several of Brown's designs and practical advice on how to achieve similar effects with ground, woods, water, rocks and buildings. The second book, Horace Walpole's essay 'On the history of modern taste in gardening'

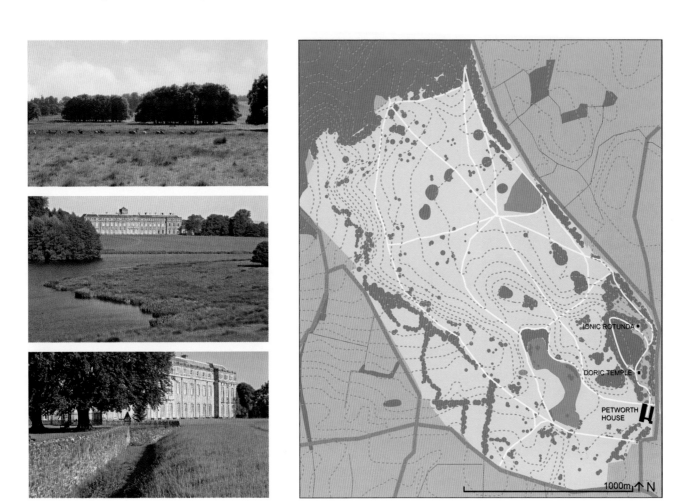

6.71 a–d Petworth is a classic Brownian Park, with clumps in the deer park, grass sweeping to the main rooms, an enclosing tree belt with a circuit walk, a serpentine lake and a pleasure ground protected by a ha-ha.

was completed in 1770 but not published until 1780. It has had a preponderant influence on garden historians. Walpole praises Whately's book as 'a system of rules pushed to a great degree of refinement, and collected from the best examples and practice'. After debating some points raised by Whately, Walpole concludes:

In the meantime how rich, how gay, how picturesque the face of the country! The demolition of walls laying open each improvement, every journey is made through a succession of pictures; and even where taste is wanting in the spot improved, the general view is embellished by variety. If no relapse to barbarism, formality and seclusion is made, what landscapes will dignify every quarter of our island, when the plantations that are making have attained venerable maturity! A specimen of what our gardens will be may

be seen at Petworth, where the portion of the park nearest the house has been allotted to the modern style.[106]

Petworth Park was laid out by Brown in 1752. Walpole's praise for the design was a way of celebrating the designer, despite his resolve to exclude 'living artists' from the essay. It is noteworthy that Walpole praises the 'modern style' for its lack of 'formality and seclusion'[107] – because the main charges against Brown, when the reaction set in, were his excessive 'formality' and lack of 'naturalness'. Taste had moved on and the public had come to appreciate 'briars and brambles' and even the wild scenery of the Lake District. The once-praised 'natural' style of Brown was beached by the tides of taste. It was deprecated as 'artificial', 'stiff' and even 'formal'.

The first serious criticism of Brown, in this vein, came from Sir William Chambers in his *Dissertation on Oriental Gardening*, published in 1772. Chambers criticised Brown's style:

In England ... our gardens differ very little from common fields, so closely is common nature copied in most of them; there is generally so little variety in the objects, such a poverty of imagination in the contrivance, and of art in the arrangement, that these compositions rather appear the offspring of chance than design; and a stranger is often at a loss to know whether he be walking in a meadow, or in a pleasure ground, made and kept at a very considerable expense.[108]

Chambers also praised the Chinese for introducing some of the terrible in nature to their gardens:

6.73 The Pagoda at Kew is the most visible symbol of Sir William Chambers's enthusiasm for Chinese gardens. It was not long before British designers were making gloomy woods, deep valleys, dark caverns and impetuous cataracts.

6.74 a, b William Gilpin (1724–1804), described as the 'Master of the Picturesque and Vicar of Boldre', painted these scenes and observed that 'In a mountain-scene what composition could arise from the corner of a smooth knoll coming forward on one side, intersected by a smooth knoll on the other; with a smooth plain perhaps in the middle, and a smooth mountain in the distance. The very idea is disgusting. Picturesque composition consists in uniting in one whole a variety of parts and these parts can only be obtained from rough objects.'[113]

6.75 a, b (a) Thomas Hearne's drawing of the rough track below Downton Castle. (b) A recent photograph of the track.

Their scenes of terror are composed of gloomy woods, deep vallies inaccessible to the sun, impending barren rocks, dark caverns, and impetuous cataracts rushing down the mountains from all parts. The trees are ill formed, forced out of their natural directions, and seemingly torn to pieces by the violence of tempests.[109]

Chambers wondered, with sense and prescience, if there could be a new style of garden design which did not involve returning to the 'ancient style'. He considered it 'impertinent as well as useless to start a new system of one's own' and hoped 'without offence to others [to] offer the following account of the Chinese manner of Gardening; which is collected from my own observations in China':[110]

The Chinese Gardeners take nature for their pattern; and their aim is to imitate all her beautiful irregularities. Their first consideration is the nature of the ground they are to work upon ...[111]

Their surprizing, or supernatural scenes, are of the romantic kind, and abound in the marvellous; being calculated to excite in the minds of the spectators, quick successions of opposite and violent sensations.[112]

Chambers was ridiculed for filling Kew gardens with small buildings, including a Chinese Pagoda, but his substantial point that 'our gardens differ very little from common fields' was soon being made by other authors.

The Reverend William Gilpin aimed to 'derive rules of picturesque beauty'. A visit to Painshill led him into sketching designed landscapes and then un-designed

landscapes.[114] Gilpin saw landscapes as God's work and quoted Cowper with approval, before making a point about the spiritual value of nature:

Nature is but a name for an effect,
Whose cause is God.

If however the admirer of nature can turn his amusements to a higher purpose; if it's great scenes can inspire him with religious awe; or it's tranquil scenes with that complacency of mind, which is so nearly allied to benevolence, it is certainly the better.[115]

Gilpin gave a ruthless account of how gardens could be made Picturesque:

Turn the lawn into a piece of broken ground: plant rugged oaks instead of flowering shrubs: break the edges of the walk: give it the rudeness of a road; mark it with wheel-tracks; and scatter around a few stones, and brushwood; in a word, instead of making the whole smooth, make it rough; and you make it also picturesque. All the other ingredients of beauty it already possessed.

You sit for your picture. The master, at your desire, paints your head combed smooth, and powdered from the barber's hand. This may give it a more striking likeness, as it is more the resemblance of the real object. But is it therefore a more pleasing picture? I fear not. Leave Reynolds to himself, and he will make it picturesque by throwing the hair dishevelled about your shoulders. Virgil would have done the same.[116]

Since Claude put wild foregrounds in his paintings, Gilpin took the correctness of his taste to be established beyond reasonable doubt. Gilpin became known as 'the High Priest of the Picturesque' and published a series of *Picturesque Tours* after 1782. The books did much to popularise the type of scenery which Chambers had admired in China and Gilpin had seen in the wilder parts of Britain. In an essay, *On Picturesque Beauty* (1792), Gilpin wrote that the smoothness of a garden was of no use in making a picture. It should therefore be roughened with 'rugged oaks instead of flowering shrubs' and by scattering stones and brushwood in the foreground.

Sir Uvedale Price even thought that 'the tracks of the wheels contribute to the picturesque effect of the whole'. He wanted his garden to be picturesque but acknowledged that:

Near the house picturesque beauty must, in many cases be sacrificed to neatness ... It is not necessary to model a gravel walk or drive after a sheep track or a cart rut, though very useful hints may be taken from them both.[117]

Price's friend and neighbour Richard Payne Knight had the incautious hauteur of an immensely rich man. At Downton Castle, 'large fragments of stone were irregularly thrown amongst briers and weeds, to imitate the foreground of a picture'.[118] Repton

6.76 Gilpin praised Joshua Reynolds for his picturesque portraits. The Countess of Harrington, in 1778–9, is shown with strands of hair blowing in harmony with the drama of the sky.

6.77 a, b (a) A Brownian scene from *The Landscape*. Knight considered this type of scenery dull, vapid and smooth. (b) A Gilpinesque scene from *The Landscape*. Knight loved broken banks and shaggy mounds.

saw this as an 'experiment' but Loudon was there ten years later and reported that fragments of rock were still 'scattered in front of Downton Castle ... quite unconnected with each other'.[119] In his maturity, Knight decided that it was more convenient to have a neat terrace in front of a castle. Downton Vale is Gilpinesque and one of the most Romantic 'improved places' in England. The estate, and Knight's views on terraces, will be further described in Chapter 7 (see p. 284).

Price and Knight directed Gilpin's line of criticism against Brown, with withering effect, after 1793. The first blast came from Knight in a didactic poem *The Landscape*:

> *See yon fantastic band,*
> *With charts, pedometers, and rules in hand,*
> *Advance triumphant, and alike lay waste*
> *The forms of nature, and the works of taste!*
> *T'improve, adorn, and polish, they profess;*
> *But shave the goddess, whom they come to dress;*
> *Level each broken bank and shaggy mound,*
> *And fashion all to one unvaried round;*
> *One even round, that ever gently flows,*
> *Nor forms abrupt, nor broken colours knows;*
> *But, wrapt all o'er in everlasting green, makes one dull, vapid,*
> *smooth, and tranquil scene.*[120]

Brown's contemporaries would have been amazed to find him lampooned for destroying nature. But Knight's criticism was supported by Sir Uvedale Price and echoed by other critics for a century, often embellished with dismissive remarks on

6.78 The River Derwent at Chatsworth has the placidity of a Brownian lake – it is no longer a 'turbulent mountain-stream'.

Brown's humble origins or lack of education. Price was particularly critical of Brown's handling of water. He wrote, 'Mr Brown grossly mistook his talent, for among all his tame productions, his pieces of made water are perhaps the most so.'[121] In Price's judgement, the serpentine curves of Brown's lakes, and the lack of vegetation on their banks, made them look too like canals:

> In Mr Brown's naked canals nothing detains the eye a moment, and the two sharp extremi-
> ties appear to cut into each other. If a near approach to mathematical exactness was a
> merit instead of a defect, the sweeps of Mr Brown's water would be admirable.[122]

Even Repton, who normally supported Brown, thought he had erred in taming the River Derwent:

> Where a rattling, turbulent mountain-stream passes through a rocky valley, like the
> Derwent at Chatsworth, perhaps Mr Brown was wrong in checking its noisy course, to
> produce the glassy surface of a slow moving river.[123]

Loudon admired Gilpin, Price and Knight in the first phase of his professional career and surpassed them in advocacy of wild irregularity in gardens. He made a sharp attack on Brown in 1802:

> What first brought him into reputation was a large sheet of water which he made at Stowe,
> in which, as in all his other works, he displayed the most wretched and Chinese-like taste.

6.79 Sir Walter Scott's favourite view, of the Eildon Hills, exemplifies the Picturesque taste which led to the overthrow of Brown's style.

Wherever his levelling hand has appeared, adieu to every natural beauty! see every thing give way to one uniform system of smoothing, levelling and clumping of the most tiresome monotony, joined to the most disgusting formality.[124]

Sir Walter Scott wrote that Brown's imitations of nature had 'no more resemblance to that nature which we desire to see imitated, than the rouge of an antiquated coquette, bearing all the marks of a sedulous toilette, bears to the artless blush of a cottage girl'.[125]

Criticism of Brown continued in the first decade of the twentieth century. Thomas Mawson, in 1901, remarked that 'had Brown and his followers been content to imitate nature, they would simply have perpetrated so many absurd and expensive frauds, but this imitation did not meet the whole of their misguided practice'.[126] Even the wise and generous Gertrude Jekyll disliked Brown:

> The long avenues, now just grown to maturity in many of England's greatest parks, fell
> before Brown's relentless axe, for straight lines were abhorrent to the new 'landscape'
> school. Everything was to be 'natural' – sham natural generally, and especially there was
> to be water everywhere ... Possibly his avowed dislike of stonework arose from his incapac-
> ity of designing it; certainly when he did attempt anything architectural ... his ignorance
> and want of taste were clearly betrayed.[127]

A revival of Brown's popularity began when Marie-Louise Gothein recognised his work as a distinct style rather than a failed attempt to imitate nature's wildness. She declared, in 1913, that 'Brown was the original advocate of Hogarth's line of beauty.'[128] The point was taken up by Christopher Hussey 17 years later in his seminal book *The Picturesque*. Hussey observed that Brown attempted 'to create landscapes that should arouse emotions, by means of the recipes for beauty evolved by Hogarth and Burke.'[129] He supported his observation with a lovely quotation from Burke which appears to describe a Brownian park:

> Most people have observed the sort of sense they have had of being swiftly drawn in an
> easy coach on a smooth turf, with gradual ascents and declivities. This will give a better
> idea of the Beautiful than almost anything else.[130]

In 1950, writing an introduction to Dorothy Stroud's monograph on Brown, Hussey went further and spoke of Brown as 'the most celebrated English landscape architect of the eighteenth century'.[131] The association of Brown with Hogarth, Burke and Eng-lishness proved irresistible to later critics. Brown became a national hero. The final seal of approval, for the twentieth century, came from Pevsner in an edition of his *Outline of European Architecture* which makes no reference to Repton or Loudon or Lutyens:

> The great name in the history of mid-eighteenth century gardening is Lancelot Brown
> (Capability Brown, 1715–83). His are the wide, softly sweeping lawns, the artfully scattered
> clumps of trees, and the serpentine lakes which revolutionised garden art all over Europe
> and America.[132]

W.G. Hoskins, in the *Making of the English Landscape*, praised Brown and remarked:

> In 1764 he created at Blenheim the most magnificent private lake in the country by dam-
> ming the little river Glyme: 'there is nothing finer in Europe,' says Sacheverell Sitwell. He
> manipulated square miles of landscape in the park, planting trees on a scale consonant
> with the massive Vanbrugh house.[133]

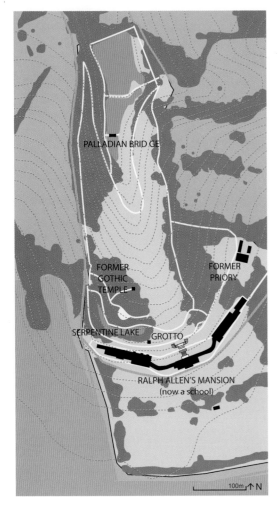

6.80 a, b (a) Plan of Prior Park. (b) Prior Park is a Neoclassical landscape and one of Lancelot Brown's most successful projects. It can be read as a symbol of the desire to create Arcadian harmony between the works of man and the works of nature.

Nan Fairbrother even defended Brown's clumps: 'this was how Capability Brown established the superb trees in his landscape parks, by planting a close group of saplings and protective shrubs and thinning them as they grew'.[134] The only criticism of Brown in recent years has come from those writers who, understandably, lament the loss of the Renaissance gardens destroyed in order to make way for Brownian parks.

The astonishing appreciation/depreciation/appreciation of Brown as a landscape designer is a consequence of the development of garden history as an academic discipline. Designers were muddled but historians and theorists could see that Brown was a stylist, and that the 'nature' he sought to imitate was not the wildness of briars, brambles and the Lake District. The 'nature' Brown loved was found in the English lowlands, with feminine wiles and smoothly flowing curves. Serpentine lines can be conceived to occupy an intermediate position in the Neoplatonic hierarchy of Forms. They are not so perfect as the circle or the square but they have more generality than the random patterns and jagged lines that characterise wilderness and mountains.

So how should we judge Brown? Were his contemporaries right to adulate him? Were his nineteenth-century critics right to damn him? Was the twentieth century right to re-crown him? I have seen a few excellent designs with which Brown was involved – and many places which are distinguished only by association with the famous man, leaving me with the suspicion that Brown has been periodically over-rated.

Gardens as picturesque landscapes

Travellers feared wild scenery at the start of the eighteenth century. When passing through the Alps they would close their eyes or close the blinds in their coaches – to hide the jagged cliffs, the torrents and the imminent prospect of catapulting over precipices. This fear had so far diminished by the century's end that a positive liking for 'Salvator Rosa and Sublimity' had taken its place. Travellers now sought ever-wilder locales. Garden designers responded to the new visual taste. In the 1790s they invented the Picturesque style, and in the following century they made 'wild', 'rock' and 'woodland' gardens to accommodate plants, notably rhododendrons, from far-flung lands and even from 'the eaves of the world'.

As the eighteenth century progressed, the passage of the Alps changed from a genuinely terrifying experience to one which induced awe and fear at the time but which could be recalled at home with excitement and youthful pride at the dangers overcome. The effects of Alpine scenery on the traveller were a special interest of Frank Clark:

For what in fact the gardeners were trying to do ... was to recapture the emotions experienced during the Grand Tour when, after leaving the sunny plains of France and Italy, they had ascended the Alps to the very roof of Europe. Suspended between earth and sky they had seen with fearful fascination the complex pattern of the earth at their feet. Mountains,

6.81 A terrifying alpine scene: the Devil's Bridge on the St Gotthard Pass. As the eighteenth century progressed, the emotions aroused by the passage of the Alps changed from fear to excitement.

6.82 Frank Clark wrote that 'scandalous legends of lawlessness' became encrusted around Salvator Rosa and his paintings.

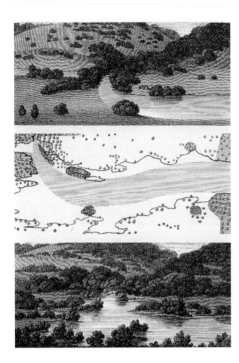

6.83 a, b Loudon's design for converting the lakeshore at Harewood House from the Serpentine style to the irregularity of the Picturesque style. The proposal was not based on an accurate site survey but Loudon's design intentions are very clear.

6.84 a, b The Duke of Atholl's Pleasure Ground (the Hermitage), near Dunkeld, was made *c.*1758. Loudon knew it to be a Romantic glen and Gilpin wrote that 'This grand view, which I scruple not to call the most interesting thing of the kind, I ever saw, is exhibited through the windows of a summer-house.' He objected that 'knots of shrubs and flowers … in scenes, dedicated to grandeur and solitude are incongruous'.[135]

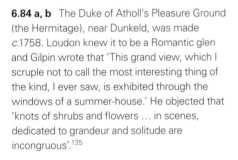

6.85 a, b Loudon knew the Water of Leith as a boy and thought it much more 'natural' than Lancelot Brown's supposedly 'naturalistic' design. The temple was designed, in 1789, by a portrait painter who became known as the 'father of Scottish landscape art', Alexander Nasmyth.

roaring cascades, the evidences of the convulsive forces of nature in these vast ranges, filled them with sensations of awe which they never afterwards forgot. The painter who had best been able to translate this experience into the idiom of paint was Salvator Rosa. Rosa, or Savage Rosa, as he was called, round whose life scandalous legends of lawlessness had become encrusted, the outlaw and friend of those banditti who had threatened their safety in the mountains, became the romantic hero, the pre-Byronic hero, of the age. His canvases, peopled with hermits and banditti and filled with twisted trees, tumbled rocks, cliffs, ruins and racing skies, enabled the traveller to re-experience the delightful horror of such scenery and to appreciate its significance when met with in poetry, the paintings of other artists and in landscape. The correct associational link was made by Walpole in a letter during his tour with Gray in 1739: 'Precipices, mountains, torrents, wolves, rumblings, Salvator Rosa![136]

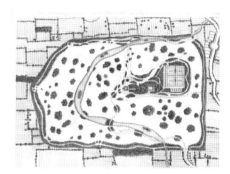

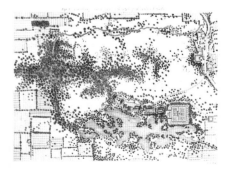

6.86 a, b (a) London's caricature of a Brownian plan. (b) Loudon's diagram of the wild, irregular, 'modern' and Picturesque style advocated in *Country Residences* (1806).[138]

The young Loudon, an ardent admirer of Price, Knight and frenzied irregularity, announced to the world in his first book that:

I believe that I am the first who has set out as a landscape gardener, professing to follow Mr Price's principles. How far I shall succeed in executing my plans, and introducing more of the picturesque into improved places, time alone must determine.[137]

Loudon was the son of a Scots farmer. He had not been on a Grand Tour when he arrived in London at the age of 20 but did have memories of the picturesque charm of the Water of Leith in Edinburgh, and of a park outside Edinburgh which had been

6.87 a, b, c Barnbarrow (Barnbarroch). (a) Loudon's drawing of the house as a Brownian scene, in 1806. (b) Loudon's design for creating a Picturesque landscape. (c) The house as it was in 1985.

designed by a pupil of Lancelot Brown's. A tree-belt hid the view of Craigmillar Castle and Arthur's Seat, and the brook which ran through an estate which had been, as Sir Walter Scott later observed, 'twisted into the links of a string of pork-sausages'.[139] Scott, the arch-Romantic, was also an admirer of Price and Knight. When judged by the principles of Price and Knight, Loudon complained that Brown's style was 'productive of the most tiresome monotony joined to the most disgusting formality'.[140]

Loudon's early work shows his interpretation of Price and Knight's plea for the picturesque. His mentors drew no plans but their admirer was a skilful draughtsman.

The sketches and plans Loudon published in *Country Residences* show 'Mr Brown's style' and 'the modern style' as practised by himself. It is plain that 'the modern style' is more deserving of the description 'irregular' than any other style in the history of British garden design. Loudon employed the Picturesque style for a large number of commissions in the first decade of his professional life, and published designs for numerous country residences, including Ditchley Park in Oxfordshire, Harewood House in Yorkshire and Barnbarrow (now Barnbarroch) in Wigtownshire. Next to nothing survives of his work but on some estates, including the grounds of Barnbarroch and parts of the lakeshore at Harewood, nature has been allowed to take her course and has created some of the effects which Loudon wished to attain by art.

Picturesque planting

The Picturesque style had, and has, a profound influence on British planting design. It offered a theory about the use of foreign plants in gardens and provided a system of compositional principles which could be used to harmonise exotic and native plants. As will be discussed in Chapter 7, this developed into the Gardenesque style.

Book III of Knight's poem *The Landscape* has a versified discussion of planting design. Knight was enchanted by the romance of the English landscape:

> *O waft me hence to some neglected vale;*
> *Where, shelter'd, I may court the western gale;*
> *And, 'midst the gloom which native thickets shed,*
> *Hide from the noontide beams by aching head!*
> *For though in British woods no myrtles blow, ...*
> *No prowling tiger from the covert springs;*
> *No scaly serpent, in vast volumes roll'd,*
> *Darts on the unwary loiterer from his hold.*[141]

6.88 'Let then of oak your general masses rise/ Wher'er the soil its nutriment supplies' (Knight, *The Landscape*).

Knight liked to see plants growing in luxuriant good health and without signs of regret for 'the comforts of a warmer sky'. This led him to prefer 'trees which nature's hand has sown', or which had adapted to the British climate. His favourites were the English stalwarts, oak and beech:

> *Let then of oak your general masses rise,*
> *Wher'er the soil its nutriment supplies:*
> *But if dry chalk and flints, or thirsty sand,*
> *Compose the substance of your barren land,*
> *Let the light beech its gay luxuriance shew,*
> *And o'er the hills its brilliant verdure strew.*[142]

Should time or fortune damage an ancient oak, then Knight wished to keep its gnarled remains as one would a ruined abbey:

> *If years unnumber'd, or the lightning's stroke*
> *Have bared the summit of the lofty oak*
> *(Such as, to decorate some savage waste,*
> *Salvator's flying pencil often traced).*
> *Entire and sacred let the ruin stand.*[143]

Despite his love of native plants, Knight wished to see exotic plants in gardens – providing they were planted near the house or near water and not in the midst of a natural wood:

6.89 'The rich laburnum with its golden chain … Should near to buildings, or to water grow' (Knight, *The Landscape*).

6.90 Rhododendrons and 'choice American plants' at Scotney Castle. Price was the first author to advocate the use of exotic flowering shrubs in naturalistic groups and outside the confines of walled gardens.

6.91 a, b (a) Edward Kemp's design for a quarry garden. (b) The rock garden in Birkenhead Park, designed by Paxton with Edward Kemp as superintendent of works.

The bright acacia, and the vivid plane,
The rich laburnum with its golden chain;
And all the variegated flowering race,
That deck the garden, and the shrubbery grace,
Should near to buildings, or to water grow,
Where bright reflections beam with equal glow,
And blending vivid tints with vivid light,
The whole in brilliant harmony unite …
But better are these gaudy scenes display'd
From the high terrace or rich balustrade;
'Midst sculptured founts and vases, that diffuse,
In shapes fantastic, their concordant hues.[144]

Knight's exposition of the principles for selecting and using plant species were complemented by Price's ideas on how they should be composed to produce a 'brilliant harmony' with 'concordant hues'.

Price was the first author to write openly in favour of using exotic flowering shrubs outside the narrow confines of an enclosed garden. He said that if the improver seeks 'an infinite number of pleasing and striking combinations', then he should 'avail himself of some of those beautiful, but less common flowering and climbing plants'.[145] Plantings of furze, wild roses and woodbine might, he suggests, be enlivened with 'Virginia Creeper, pericoloca, trailing arbutus' and 'the choice American plants … such as kalmias and rhododendrons'. Price was much read during the nineteenth century and this remark appears to have been widely influential, especially with regard to the planting of rhododendrons.

Price was willing to allow flowering plants to be moved from their traditional positions 'in borders or against walls' but insisted that they should be grouped to form painterly compositions. He believed that the eye of the landscape painter with its understanding of nature and the principles of natural composition was the best guide to good planting design. The painters he most admired were Claude, Poussin and Rosa. This idea assumed great importance during the nineteenth century and produced the Romantic woodland gardens which grace so many of England's stately homes. Scotney Castle in Kent is an outstanding example. Christopher Hussey writes that it was planted by his grandfather as a deliberate application of the principles of Sir Uvedale Price.[146]

The Picturesque style (see Figure 7.61) is of theoretical interest as an extreme application of the idea that 'Art should imitate Nature'. As can be seen from the diagram, it made great use of jagged irregular lines and represents the furthest possible remove from geometrical regularity. In the second half of the nineteenth century the Picturesque style was used in the making of woodland gardens. Garden owners on the western shores of the British Isles acquired an enthusiasm for rhododendron woods arranged in 'painterly compositions'. Sir Joseph Hooker's *Rhododendrons of Sikkim-Himalaya* (1849–51) illustrated and popularised the genus.[147]

One consequence of the desire for Picturesqueness was an enthusiasm for rock gardens.

6.92 Scotney Castle: picturesque planting with picturesque rocks in a former quarry.

Depreciation of the Picturesque

John Claudius Loudon, as quoted above, remarked that 'time alone' would determine how Picturesque gardens became. He helped determine the outcome by finding an inherent absurdity in 'the Principles of Mr Price'. As discussed in Chapter 7, this led him to invent the Gardenesque style of planting design. Quatremère de Quincy (1755–1849) wrote an *Essai sur la nature, le but et les moyens de l'imitation dans les beaux-arts*, which was published in 1823 and led an assault on the 'irregular system of landscape gardening':

> *What pretends to be an image of nature is nothing more nor less than nature herself. The means of the art are reality. Every one knows that the merit of its works consists in obviating any suspicion of art. To constitute a perfect garden, according to the irregular system of landscape gardening, we must not have the least suspicion that the grounds have been laid out by art.*[148]

6.93 Sawrey Gilpin believed that a day in the New Forest would convince anyone of nature's fundamental irregularity.

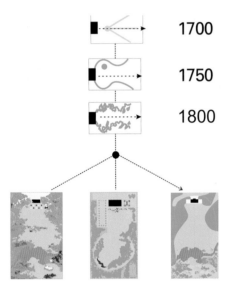

6.94 A philosophical conundrum led to a Great Turning Point in the history of garden and landscape design.

Loudon took the point and expressed it as follows:

> *There is not a single writer, as far as we are aware, from Shenstone to Knight, Price, and Gilpin, who does not adopt the imitation of nature as a principle; and who has not, at the same time, forgotten, or failed to see, that, in so far as landscape-gardening is to be considered one of the fine arts, the principle of the imitation of nature must be rendered subordinate to that of the Recognition of Art. If the imitation of nature were the sole principle of guidance, then the perfection of park scenery would be, that it should be so like the scenery of a natural forest, as that it might be mistaken for it ... Henceforth it may be considered as an established principle, that there can be no landscape-gardening in the natural style, where only indigenous trees and shrubs are used.*[149]

Loudon supported the idea of arranging trees geometrically so that they could not be mistaken for natural forest, as did Sir Henry Steuart in his *Planter's Guide*:

> *There is no man whose taste has been formed on any correct model, which does not feel and acknowledge the beauty of these elegant forms, the Oval, the Circle, and the Cone ... and there are few well-educated persons, who will for a moment compare to them a multitude of obtuse and acute angles, great and small, following each other, in fantastical and unmeaning succession.*[150]

This was in direct opposition to William Gilpin. His nephew, William Sawrey Gilpin, expostulated: 'Did nature ever bound plantations by a circular or oval form?' and 'Are they to be traced in Claude or Poussin – in Wilson or in Turner?'[151] Sawrey Gilpin invoked the names of his famous uncle and Sir Uvedale Price, who had done so much to popularise Picturesque irregularity, and of Sir Walter Scott, who had reviewed Steuart's book in the *Quarterly Review*.[152] The truly maddening thing for Sawrey Gilpin was that Steuart had claimed, in full accord with Neoplatonism, that the circle and the oval are 'prevalent in all the most beautiful objects in nature' (see p. 160).[153] 'It appears singular,' says Gilpin, 'that the advocates on each side of the question before us, should appeal to nature as the foundation of their diametrically opposite systems.' Gilpin recommended the author of the *Planter's Guide* to 'spend a day amidst the splendid scenery of the New Forest'[154] and discover that 'nature' is fundamentally irregular.

It can be seen from the controversy between Gilpin and Steuart that by the nineteenth century the 'nature' which Gilpin, and most landscape gardeners, believed they should imitate was located near the bottom of the Neoplatonic hierarchy of forms (see Figure 6.20). 'Nature' had become the empirical world of everyday experience: not the world of the forms. This created a Great Turning Point in the history of garden and landscape design. The steady advance of empiricism, exerting its influence through the axiom that 'Art should imitate Nature', became the engine which drove the aesthetic development of garden and landscape design in the eighteenth century. The engine faltered after the turn of the century but flickered back to life towards the end of the nineteenth century in the work of Robinson and Jekyll. Indeed, if Abstract art is conceived as an attempt to analyse the nature of the visible world, then it might be said that a derivative of the engine is chugging away in the garden to this day (see p. 358).

Wordsworth (1770–1850), discussed at greater length in Chapter 7, shared Price's and the young Loudon's enthusiasm for wild nature. In his 'Lines composed a few miles above Tintern Abbey, on revisiting the banks of the Wye during a tour, July 13, 1798', Wordsworth wrote of his youthful passion for nature:

> *For nature then ...*
> *To me was all in all – I cannot paint*
> *What then I was. The sounding cataract*
> *Haunted me like a passion: the tall rock,*
> *The mountain, and the deep and gloomy wood.*[155]

When the still-Romantic poet returned to the Wye Valley, he had learned to 'look on nature, not as in the hour/Of thoughtless youth' but with an almost Classical perception:

> *Of elevated thoughts; a sense sublime*
> *Of something far more deeply interfused,*
> *Whose dwelling is the light of setting suns,*
> *And the round ocean, and the living air,*
> *And the blue sky, and in the mind of man,*
> *A motion and a spirit, that impels*
> *All thinking things, all objects of all thought,*
> *And rolls through all things.*[156]

Wordsworth, who was influenced by the Picturesque and who became a leading Romantic poet, is discussed further in Chapter 7.

6.95 Coming from Scotland, Loudon knew how wild 'nature' could be.

6.96 Tintern Abbey in the Wye Valley, where Wordsworth learned to 'look on nature'.

Romantic gardens and landscapes, 1794–1880

7.0 Caspar David Friedrich's *Wanderer Above the Sea of Fog* (1818). Nineteenth-century Europeans gazed and travelled beyond their shores after the Napoleonic Wars, wishing to see, to understand and to experience the world and its plants.

Introduction

'Romantic means precisely that it oversteps all bounds' (Kierkegaard).[1] It is indefinable – but an opposite of Classicism, which was bounded by history, geography and rules. Caspar David Friedrich captured the spirit of Romanticism with his *Wanderer Above the Sea of Fog*. A cultured man gazes at the wonder of nature and the mystery of the universe. Knowing the world became easier during the nineteenth century. Ships brought plants and artefacts to Europe from far-off lands. Draughtsmen, and then photographers, illustrated everything. Authors wrote about foreign countries. One can imagine that Friedrich's *Sea of Fog* conceals a wealth of exoticism. Garden owners grew to love exotic plants and features but were puzzled how 'Art should imitate Nature' as knowledge of nature grew (see p. 309). Combining unity with variety became a serious challenge and the most influential response came from Picturesque theory.

The *OED* defines four uses of 'picturesque' as an adjective, two uses as a noun and one 'special use', in a combination:

> **picturesque gardening** *n. Hort. (now* hist.*) the arrangement of a garden so as to make it resemble a picture; a romantic style of gardening, aiming at irregular and rugged beauty.*

This definition contains three ideas: making gardens resemble pictures, making them Romantic and making them 'irregular'. The first idea prevailed in the early eighteenth century[2] and the third idea in the late eighteenth century. William Gilpin promoted both uses. He was a clergyman, a teacher, a painter and a travel writer who had the idea that gardens could and should be organised like landscape paintings with a 'foreground, middleground, and background'.[3] The idea became very influential but, unfortunately, was not appreciated by John Claudius Loudon. Closer to a polymath than anyone who has yet given their attention to garden and landscape design theory, Loudon was brilliant, energetic, a skilled draughtsman, a systematic historian, a scientist, a technologist and a prolific author. Perhaps he was less strong as an artist. Whatever the reason, he seems not to have appreciated one of the most important design ideas of his time: that of creating a *picturesque transition* from the works of man to the works of nature (see Figure 7.2).

7.1 Romanticism led designers to wonder at the mysteries of nature and the universe. The dome at the Swiss Garden at Old Warden Park soars above a secret world of exotic rocks and ferns.

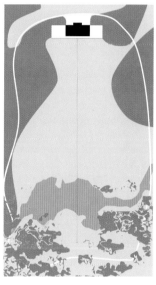

7.2 Diagram of the picturesque transition, in a landscape garden.

The picturesque transition

The Classical and Neoplatonic theory that 'Art should imitate Nature' had been the bedrock of seventeenth- and eighteenth-century aesthetic theory. In 1772, William Gilpin wrote: 'Nature is the great book of God; in every page is instruction to those

7.3 Humphry Repton's painting of Leigh Court shows the three stages in a picturesque transition: (1) a 'polished' foreground, with terrace, balustrade and exotic garden plants; (2) a Neoclassical middleground, with livestock and trees beneath which shepherds might play flutes; and (3) a wild background in the hazy distance.

7.4 Repton considered the view from Uppark dull and recommended a foreground terrace. He wrote, wisely, that: 'The lawn or park which forms the foreground, is part of that broad and extensive summit on which the house is built, and which is generally so amply enlivened by the numerous herds of deer, that it requires no further embellishment, but when the deer are in other parts of the park, it is bleak and bald, and seems to call for some line of separation betwixt the palace and the pasture by which it is surrounded.'[6]

who read.'[4] He meant that 'every page' makes us better informed about the nature of Nature: 'The nearer we approach the character of nature in every mode of imitation, no doubt the better: yet still there are many irregularities and deformities in the natural scene, which we may wish to correct.'[5] Learning about nature through empirical study was not the same as learning about nature through prayer and reason. The 'nature' to be imitated became the everyday pages of visible nature. This created a problem for garden designers. Should they 'imitate' weeds and wilderness in their gardens?

In 1762, Lord Kames had advised that:

> Regularity is required in that part of a garden which joins the dwelling-house; for being considered as a more immediate accessory, it ought to partake the regularity of the principal object ... In an extensive plan, it hath a fine effect to lead the mind insensibly from regularity to a bold variety giving an impression of grandeur.[7]

Gilpin went further and, in 1791, described the idea of creating a picturesque transition from the works of man to the works of nature:

> As the park is an appendage of the house, it follows, that it should participate of its neatness, and elegance. Nature, in all her great walks of landscape, observes this accommodating rule. She seldom passes abruptly from one mode of scenery to another; but generally connects different species of landscape by some third species, which participates of both. A mountainous country rarely sinks immediately into a level one; the swellings and heavings of the earth grow

7.5 A Beautiful foreground. Repton admired Watteau and would have enjoyed the *Plaisir du bal*.

7.6 John Constable painted Wivenhoe Park as a Picturesque middleground.

7.7 J.M.W. Turner's painting of *The Lake of Thun* is Sublime.

gradually less. Thus as the house is connected with the country through the medium of the park; the park should partake of the neatness of the one, and of the wildness of the other.[8]

This transition idea was applied to gardens by three great landscape theorists: Sir Uvedale Price, Richard Payne Knight and Humphry Repton. Their writings looked back to the literature and practice of the eighteenth century and established the base from which most nineteenth-century garden theorists began their deliberations.

Price and Knight were wealthy landowners, old friends and Herefordshire neighbours. Repton came from Norfolk and they met through an invitation to design an estate at Ferney Hall in Herefordshire, belonging to a friend of Knight's. In 1794, each of the three friends was preparing to publish a book on landscape design.[9] Knight was first off the mark and hurried the others into print. Repton succeeded in getting his book printed in 1794 but did not manage to publish until early in the following year. He required the services of a small army of women and children to colour up the illustrations. The measure of agreement between the opinions expressed by the three men was considerable and a modern textbook editor might have persuaded them to put their names to a single treatise. The sparkle of individuality would have been lost but the three would surely have agreed – had they any conception of how seriously readers would overstate their differences and misunderstand their intentions. It has been blown up into 'the Picturesque controversy'.

7.8 a, b, c (a) and (b) Before and after drawings showing Repton's proposal for Bayham Abbey, with the meadow becoming a lake and the fields becoming parkland. (c) The lake and house as built. Repton often recommended sites on rising ground, but below the crest of a hill, as in his proposal (not as built, at a later date). He wrote: 'The aspect of a house requires the first consideration, since no beauty of prospect can compensate for the cold exposure to the north, the glaring blaze of a setting sun, or the frequent boisterous winds and rains from the west and south-west.'[10]

Many of the differences between Price, Knight and Repton can be resolved by distinguishing between the specialised and ordinary meanings of the words 'beautiful', 'sublime' and 'picturesque'. In this book the words are capitalised when they are used in a particular eighteenth-century sense:

- 'Beautiful' refers to smoothness, delicacy and gradual variation (appropriate to foreground scenery).
- 'Sublime' refers to the great, terrible and awe-inspiring (appropriate to background scenery).
- 'Picturesque' refers to the intermediate aesthetic category of roughness, wildness and irregularity (appropriate to middleground scenery). The scope of 'Picturesque' ranged from parkland (with native trees, pasture and animals) to wild scenery with rocks, waterfalls and unmanaged habitats.

When using the words in other senses they will be written with the first letter in the lower case. The *OED* definitions which come closest to the special meanings are:

- 'beautiful': 'excelling in grace of form, charm of colouring, and other qualities which delight the eye'.
- 'sublime': 'affecting the mind with a sense of overwhelming grandeur or irresistible power'.
- 'picturesque': 'irregular and rugged beauty'.

7.9 a, b Repton produced a Red Book for Hatchlands and the terrace, as designed by H.S. Goodhart-Rendell, has the relationship of foreground:middleground which Repton advised. The house dominates the foreground but is only an incident in the middleground and background (see also Figure 7.13).

To bring out the points of agreement between the three men, we can consider the advice which they might have given to a friend who had recently inherited a country seat. Knight and Price occasionally gave advice to their friends but did not charge for their services. Repton was an impoverished squire who asked a fee for his advice and summarised his opinion in beautiful hand-written volumes, known as Red Books, illustrated with his own watercolours and bound in red morocco leather. Let us assume then, that having come into possession of a 500-hectare estate in 1795, we have asked the three literary squires for their opinion on how his estate could be improved in the modern taste. Their collective advice is expressed in modern English except for the words 'Beautiful', 'Sublime' and 'Picturesque':

Good morning. We have walked your estate and would like to recommend a site for your house below the brow of the hill. This will provide both shelter and good views. Mr Repton has made sketches from numerous points of view in order to appraise its present character. The changes which we propose are designed to fit in with the existing site and to make improvements which will create a landscape that is both useful and beautiful.

It is highly desirable that there should be a picturesque transition between your house and the natural landscape. We can best explain this idea by referring to the work of the great landscape painters who inspired our art. The foreground of the view from your house should be a terrace garden with a profusion of flowers. It should be Beautiful and well-kept for your family's use, with something of the character of a garden scene by Watteau or, if you decide to have a lake, a Claudian seaport. The middleground of the view should be a noble park, laid out with a view to picturesque effect but available for agricultural use. Claude and Poussin show how Picturesque scenes can be when they contain sheep, cattle and herdsmen. The background of your view should be Sublime and we recommend felling some trees to open up the view of the waterfall and the forest scenery. You have the makings of a Salvator Rosa on the fringes of your estate and should most certainly keep the ancient oak and shepherd's cottage which lie at the foot of the hill.

7.10 The rose shows how the Beautiful may be combined with the Picturesque (*Rosa gallica*, painted by Pierre-Joseph Redouté).

Each of the three grounds in the scene can contain more than one aesthetic quality but the Beautiful should predominate in the foreground, the Picturesque in the middleground and the Sublime in the background. Nature shows us how to combine these qualities when we see the Beauty of a rose set off by the Picturesque setting of its sharp thorns and serrated leaves. Nature and the landscape painters can also teach us how to combine unity with variety. New planting will unify the scene, like the light of the setting sun, while also providing shelter from cold winds.

Your new mansion must be carefully placed to enjoy a good microclimate and fine views. The house should dominate the foreground but should only be an incident in the background. Lancelot Brown was too much interested in middlegrounds but he had excellent taste in the selection of sites and in the composition of landform with woods. It is very important that a balance should be achieved between the competing demands of prospect and aspect: a good view is pleasant but a good microclimate is essential. A well-designed garden will lengthen the summer by catching winter sun and will also have shady groves in which the family can relax on summer afternoons.

7.11 Grecian buildings are suited to Poussinesque sites. Italian buildings are suited to Claudian sites.

The principle of association which helped us to plan your grounds can also guide the design of your house. It should look like a building which belongs to the age, country and place in which it is built. The materials should be of a colour and texture which suit the style and the site – preferably a local stone. Since all the rooms and outbuildings should be planned to meet the needs of your family and servants, we think an irregular floor plan is more convenient than strict symmetry.

Our next task is to recommend an architectural style. We think an Italian style is best for a Claudian site, a Grecian style for a Poussinesque site and an English style for a classically English site. It is also important for your house to look its part; it should not resemble a church, a university or a temple. Since your estate is near the Welsh Border and your dwelling will be larger than a house but smaller than a palace, we think that the English Castle style would be a very appropriate choice. A circuitous carriage drive will let you and your visitors experience all the views and qualities which we aim to create: congruity, utility, order, symmetry, picturesque effects, intricacy, simplicity, variety, novelty, contrast, continuity, association, appropriation, animation, grandeur and the ever-changing seasons, weather and daylight.

7.12 Repton advised on Hylands Park, which has a Grecian façade and a Reptonian park, made after 1814.

7.13 'Let us have a small temple in the park where we can join you ... on hot summer days.' At Hatchlands, Surrey, there is a transition from the terrace to the temple. Repton produced a Red Book for the estate, c.1797. The terrace and temple were built in the 1920s.

Finally, let us have a small temple in the park where we can join you for an outdoor repast on hot summer days. It should be sited on the brow of the hill which can be seen from your drawing room window and we suggest that you inscribe it with the famous lines by Alexander Pope which have guided the design of your estate:

> *To build, to plant, whatever you intend,*
> *To rear the Column, or the Arch to bend,*
> *To swell the Terras, or to sink the Grot;*
> *In all, let Nature never be forgot.*
> *Consult the Genius of the Place in all*
> *That tells the waters or to rise, or fall ...*
> *Joins willing woods, and varies shades from shades*
> *Now Breaks, or now directs, th'intending*
> *Lines; Paints as you plant, and as you work, Designs.*[11]

Eleven key ideas are embodied in the above opinion: existing character, nature, utility, the picturesque transition, landscape painting, planting, unity in variety, a balance of prospect with aspect, appropriation, irregular architecture and the principle of association. If the three squires' views were set out individually and then compared, we would find some cases of complete agreement, some of differing emphasis and some of near disagreement.

They would have been in complete agreement over the importance of existing character, nature, planting, irregular architecture and the combination of unity with variety.

7.14 'The mouldering remains of obsolete taste and fallen magnificence'. The quotation is from Knight, and the drawing of a Picturesque ruin is from the 1842 edition of Price's *Essay on the Picturesque*.[14]

7.15 a, b 'Mouldering remains of obsolete taste and fallen magnificence' are used as garden features at Sudeley Castle.

Cases of differing emphasis would be found over prospect and aspect, appropriation, the picturesque transition and the principle of association. Repton[12] and Price[13] give the fullest accounts of how to form a transition between a terrace and wild nature. Repton was the first of the three to propose the reintroduction of terraces to English gardens but the demand for a paved area near the house had been growing since the 1760s. Price and Knight argued on *visual* grounds that a terrace would be an asset in composing the foreground of the view. Repton originally recommended terraces for utility but came to agree with his friends on this point.

From 1794 onwards, each of the three advocated a transition from regularity to wilderness. As shown in Figure 7.2, it runs from a 'regular' terrace beside the house, through a serpentine park to a wild forest or other sublime feature. Repton, as the only professional designer in the trio, has the best advice on how to achieve a balance between a good prospect and a good microclimate.[15] He was also, perhaps for the same reason, the only one to recommend the idea of appropriation.[16]

Knight, as the most philosophically able, gives most attention to the principle of association which underlies each of the author's aesthetic views. Knight believed that our aesthetic judgement of phenomena is governed by an understanding of their associations, history and symbolic significance. For example:

> *Ruined buildings, with fragments of sculptured walls and broken columns, the mouldering remnants of obsolete taste and fallen magnificence, afford pleasure to every learned beholder, imperceptible to the ignorant, and wholly independent of their real beauty.*[17]

Knight collected Greek and Roman coins and believed their vivid sexual imagery gave them more interest than a merely abstract design would have had.

The cases of near disagreement between Repton, Price and Knight would have arisen over their interpretation of utility and landscape painting. These disagreements have received much attention from commentators but are of more philosophical than practical consequence. They turn on the precise meaning and significance given to the words 'picturesque' and 'utility'.

Price wished to restrict the word 'Picturesque' to the sense we have distinguished with a capital P, and to use it to describe the aesthetic pleasure which we receive from rough, shaggy and irregular scenes.[18] Knight disagreed with the restriction and believed that 'picturesque' should be used to describe a scene which resembled a landscape painting.[19] Repton misunderstood the Herefordshire squires. He thought that Price advocated the Picturesque in preference to the Sublime and the Beautiful, and that Knight advocated the picturesque in disregard of utility.[20]

Neither charge is substantiated by a close reading of Price and Knight – but it is easy to see how the mistakes arose. Price does concentrate on the Picturesque. Knight may have said too little about utility. Price's reason for giving more attention to the Picturesque was that earlier writers, especially Burke, had not explained the term. Price insisted that he was 'by no means bigoted to the Picturesque or insensible to the charms of Beauty'.[21] His favourite instance of the Picturesque was a river with rocks, overhanging trees, rushing water and reedy swamps.

The difference between the three squires over utility arose because Repton misunderstood his friends' books. Repton thought that Price's *Essay* of 1794 had advocated a wild, rugged and Picturesque area near the house, and that the idea was preposterous. When Price wrote in favour of terraces in his 1795 *Letter*,[22] Repton declared the dispute settled. Price's remarks, he wrote, 'left no room for further controversy'.[23]

The lake at Wingerworth, Derbyshire, was designed by Repton to be beautiful and

> *so managed as to admit of being occasionally drawn down two or three feet to supply canals, and other circumstances of advantage, in this populous and commercial part of the kingdom; exclusive of the increased supply of fish, where such food is in constant requisition.*[24]

It is a good example of Repton's admiration for landscapes which are useful as well as beautiful. Repton criticised Knight for disregarding utility in his advocacy of the picturesque. In fact, Knight's position was close to Burke's: he believed that utility and

7.16 Repton used the lake at Wingerworth to illustrate his point that a landscape could be useful as well as beautiful; it fed local canals and was available for fishing.

7.17 The river below Downton Castle is Picturesque in the sense of 'shaggy and irregular' and is also a suitable subject for a picturesque landscape painting (see also Figure 7.3).

7.18 Knight persuaded the owner of Powis Castle to keep the terraces which step down the hillside. Knight believed that a terrace creates a foreground which can have the same role in a landscape garden as it does in a landscape painting.

7.19 a, b Richard Payne Knight lived at Downton Castle enjoying a view of the Picturesque valley of the River Teme.

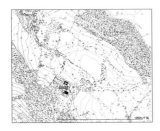

7.20 a, b (a) Sir Uvedale Price's estate at Foxley in Herefordshire in the mid-nineteenth century (with a new house). (b) The view from the Foxley estate.

aesthetic pleasure are both good things, but unconnected. Of the qualities which a herdsman and a poet see in a field of grass, Knight asks 'Who shall presume to decide that the one are more truly and properly beauties than the other?'[25] His dispute with Repton was over what to say, not over what to do. They agreed that there should be a terrace between the house and the fields. Indeed, Price tells us that the owner of Powis Castle was persuaded by Knight not to destroy the great terraces which step down the hillside in front of the castle.[26]

Repton, Price and Knight each put the picturesque transition theory into practice. Little is known of Price's design for his own estate at Foxley, though the remains of what may have been a garden terrace survive. Knight's estate at Downton Castle remains in good condition. Repton wrote in 1806 that Downton provided 'consummate proof'

7.21 a, b Repton designed a Beautiful foreground for his own cottage at Hare Street in Essex.

of Knight's good taste but that 'it is impossible by description to convey an idea of its natural charms, or to do justice to that taste which has displayed these charms to the greatest advantage'.[27] Knight appears to have laid out the park in a wholly Picturesque style during his youth and to have converted it to a picturesque transition by placing a terrace between the house and the park. Comfort and convenience assume greater importance as one grows older.

Repton lived in a cottage in the village of Hare Street. He treated the garden as the foreground to a view of the village and a wood can be seen on a hill in the background. The picturesque transition also formed the basis of Repton's extensive practice. He was unfortunate in that the prime years of his professional career, between the publication of his first book in 1793 and the collapse of his health in 1815, coincided with the Napoleonic Wars. For a country fighting a major war, the number and extent of Repton's commissions were extraordinary. But the scale of the projects was modest by peacetime standards. Repton was skilled in the design of forests, parks and lakes but in most cases his clients did little more than enrich the foreground of an existing scene with a terrace or garden.

Once the fashion for sweeping agricultural land to living room windows had passed, there was a demand for comfortable terraces near dwellings. At Ashridge, which Repton considered one of his major works, a Beautiful foreground was added to a park designed by Brown. At Sherringham, Repton had a rare opportunity to lay out a completely new estate, though a modest one by peacetime standards. Repton also designed the house with the help of his sons and preferred this project 'over every other in which I have been consulted'.[28] The foreground at Sheringham is occupied by a small terrace garden which is separated from the park by a low wall and fence. The

7.22 a, b, c Sherringham in Norfolk. The house and garden, designed by Repton, are a fine example of the Picturesque landscape style. It has the North Sea as a Sublime background; the terrace in front of the house as a Beautiful foreground and an agricultural landscape as a Picturesque middleground. As built, the balustrade is less substantial than in Repton's drawing.

7.23 At Ashridge, Repton proposed a 'paved terrace' and an 'embroidered parterre' to be enjoyed in conjunction with the house.

middleground is interesting: it is a straightforward Serpentine park such as Brown might have designed. The North Sea forms a Sublime background to the park but cannot be seen from the house. Repton would have liked the sea to be visible but did not recommend a site in full exposure to the north wind for climatic reasons. The North Sea, he observed, 'is not like that of the Bay of Naples'.[29]

There is a clear statement of how nineteenth-century designers interpreted the transition idea in Charles M'Intosh's *Book of the Garden* (1853):

> Sir Uvedale Price clearly recognises a threefold division of the domain, which we have
> already referred to – namely, the architectural terrace and flower-garden, in direct connec-
> tion with the house, where he admits the formal style; the shrubbery or pleasure-ground,
> a transition between the flowers and the trees, 'which we would hand over', says the writer
> in the Quarterly Review *already quoted, 'to the natural style of Brown and his school'; and
> thirdly, the park, which he considers the proper domain of his own system.*[30]

Influence of the picturesque transition

The picturesque transition has old roots. Like the English language, it brought together Medieval, Renaissance, Baroque and Romantic elements into a new entity. Like a Buddhist palace mandala, it represented an ideal landscape and an interpretation of the structure of the cosmos.[31] The theory on which the transition concept rests is described as 'picturesque' because it involves the composition of landscape scenery, like landscape paintings, into three stages:

1   *foreground*: like a Renaissance garden – regular, geometrical and designed
    for human use;

7.24 a, b, c Hampstead Garden Suburb has a Reptonian terrace and a picturesque transition from the town centre square to a distant view.

7.25 The Duke of York steps are an incident in a picturesque transition which runs from St James's Park to Regent's Park, which was on the edge of London in the early nineteenth century.

2   *middleground*: a landscape park, symbolising a Golden Age of Arcadian harmony between the natural and the man-made;

3   *background*: as wild and as little affected by man as possible, in the senses now described as 'natural' and 'ecological'.

Conceptually simple, but vast in scope and scale, these ideas are the best support for the claim that British designers made a unique contribution to Western culture during the eighteenth century (see p. 205). Nikolaus Pevsner made the claim in his 1955 Reith Lectures and identified an 'English picturesque theory' which 'lies hidden in the writings of the improvers from Pope to Uvedale Price, and Payne Knight'. Pevsner saw it as the foundation of an 'English national planning theory' which gives English planners 'something of great value to offer to other nations'. Asking whether 'the same can be said of painting, of sculpture, and of architecture proper?', Pevsner's answer was that Henry Moore and other contemporary sculptors had 'given England a position in European sculpture such as she has never before held', but that painting and architecture were of a lower order of excellence.[32]

The first application of the picturesque theory was to architectural and landscape design. It provided a rationale for irregular floor planning, to suit a building's functional requirements, and for the design of buildings as picturesque features in the landscape. When applied to urban design, the theory led to the picturesque planning of streets to create a sequence of visual experiences. In London, John Nash, with help from Repton's son, designed a picturesque transition from St James's Park to Regent's Park. In Boston, Frederick Law Olmsted designed the 'Emerald Necklace' as a picturesque transition from Boston Common to Franklin Park. When applied to regional planning, the theory led to the idea of creating a grand transition from an urbane city centre to a distant wilderness. It extended through:

- healthy suburbs planned on garden city lines;
- protective and productive green belts;
- agricultural landscapes protected from urban sprawl;
- National Parks, undeveloped coasts and other natural areas.

From the perspective of the 1980s, the picturesque theory was a precursor to the conservation movement: it provided sound reasons for preserving ancient buildings, for conserving natural vegetation and for designing new buildings which fitted into their surroundings. I have discussed the ramifications of the picturesque transition in previous books.[33] The three stages of the transition in private estates are discussed in the following sections on foregrounds, middlegrounds and backgrounds. Few English estates had Sublime background scenery but the distinction between foreground and middleground scenery became characteristic of English estates in the nineteenth century. Repton was a leading advocate of the idea and it influenced many other designers.

7.26 Repton designed a terrace at Cobham Hall.

7.27 A nineteenth-century transition, from house to lake to lawn (at Biddulph Grange – see plan, Figure 7.53).

7.28 A Reptonian balustrade separates the 'formal garden' at Sudeley Castle from a Brownian middleground and a Priceian background.

7.29 A balustrade separates the 'formal garden' at Castle Ashby from a Brownian park. The Latin inscription on the balustrade can be translated as 'To Theodosia, sweetest of wives'.

Foregrounds: terraces and flower-beds

The Serpentine landscape style of Lancelot Brown had pastures sweeping to the main rooms of a dwelling (see p. 247). When this idea became unpopular, for both utilitarian and aesthetic reasons, a range of features was interposed between the mansion and its park: terraces, flower gardens and historicist garden components. Geometrically, this was a partial return to the arrangement of Renaissance gardens. Terraces became places for ladies and gentlemen in fine clothes to take the air before or after a meal. The difference was that Renaissance compartment gardens had been enclosed and almost square. Nineteenth-century terraces flanked great houses with rectilinear geometry and outward views. Meason wrote, in 1828, that, 'The regularity of gardens is, as it were, an accompanying decoration and support to the architecture.'[34]

Foreground terraces

The idea of making terraces derived from villas on the hills around Florence. John Evelyn had seen them and written that 'the Terrasses adjoyning to a House can hardly ever be too broad'[35] (see pp. 124–5). In the nineteenth century, better transport made Italy a relatively easy country to visit and it was admired politically. France, before the Revolution, had been 'a byword for poverty and for effete and despotic values'.[36] Liberal England 'increasingly saw its own mission (as it developed in the nineteenth century) reflected in the Italian past'.[37] In *Childe Harold* (1818), Lord Byron trumpeted:

> *The commonwealth of kings, the men of Rome!*
> *And even since, and now, fair Italy!*
> *Thou art the garden of the world, the home*
> *Of all Art yields, and Nature can decree.*[38]

A comment on this canto pointed out that 'the love of Nature now appears as a distinct passion in Lord Byron's mind', and makes the correct observation that 'Lord Byron had, with his real eyes, perhaps, seen more of Nature than ever was before permitted to any great poet.'[39] *Childe Harold* was an international success and John Claudius Loudon cannot have been unaware of it when deciding that he should visit the gardens of France and Italy. He 'proceeded by way of Calais and Abbeville to Paris, where he arrived on the 30th of May, 1819 ... afterwards he proceeded to Marseilles, and thence to Nice, from which city he sailed in a felucca for Genoa'.[40] Loudon was preparing the world's first illustrated and comprehensive history of garden design, for inclusion in the *Encyclopaedia of Gardening* (1822). He knew that England's leading garden designer, Humphry Repton, was recommending terraces. Sometimes adorned with urns, they can be described as 'Italianate', but Repton did not design full-blown Italian gardens with flights of steps, statuary, fountains and terraces integrated round a central axis.

7.30 a, b The garden at Drummond Castle was designed by Lewis Kennedy, and his son George, between 1818 and *c.*1840. Charles M'Intosh was an apprentice in the garden.

7.32 The Italian terrace at Trentham Hall, designed by Charles Barry. The house has been demolished.

7.31 a, b Loudon visited, admired and sketched Isola Bella.

Loudon became the first British garden writer of the period to admire pre-eighteenth-century gardens. He praised their style as 'ancient or geometrical' and his opinion of contemporary British gardens was correspondingly diminished. The first edition of Loudon's monumental *Encyclopaedia of Gardening* was published in 1822 and included the comment that:

> *To say that landscape gardening is an improvement on geometric gardening, is a similar misapplication of language, as to say that a lawn is an improvement of a cornfield, because it is substituted in its place. It is absurd, therefore, to despise the ancient style ... It has beauties of a different kind, equally perfect in their kind.*[41]

Most of the Italian gardens made in Victorian England were conceived as a stage in a transition. Charles Barry, who was a contributor to Loudon's *Architectural Magazine*, designed an Italianate terrace at Trentham Hall, in 1834, which set the fashion for adding Italian terraces to Brownian parks. Barry designed terraces at Holkham, Cliveden and Harewood, also adapting the idea for the design of a balustraded terrace in Trafalgar Square. In 1848, Barry designed an Italian garden with a full axial layout for Shrubland Hall in Norfolk. William Andrews Nesfield, who worked at Trentham with Barry, designed the terrace in front of the plant house at Kew and the parterre on the south side of Castle Howard, in 1853. George Kennedy designed the lower terrace at Bowood in 1851.

Joseph Paxton was an enthusiast for the Italian style and the man who most completely took on 'Loudon's mantle'. He designed his first lake at the age of 19 in

7.34 Charles Barry designed a foreground terrace for Trafalgar Square.

7.35 The Italian garden at Bowood, Wiltshire, was designed by George Kennedy in the 1860s as a foreground for a Brownian park (see Figure 7.29).

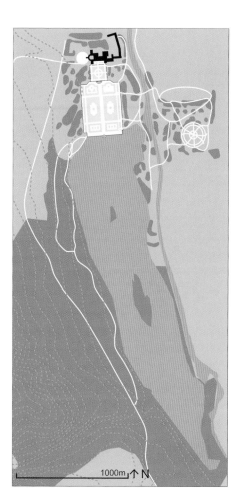

7.33 Trentham has an extensive picturesque transition from house to terrace to park to forest.

7.36 a, b Paxton designed foreground terracing at Tatton Park. It leads the eye to a Serpentine park designed by Lancelot Brown.

7.37 a, b, c The Crystal Palace, now decayed, had a picturesque transition from terrace to garden to a now-ruined park.

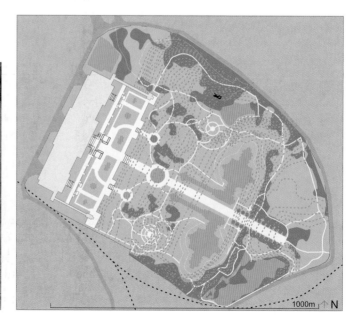

7.38 The People's Park, Halifax, designed by Joseph Paxton, has a transition from a terrace to parkland, woodland and a view.

7.39 Miller Park by Edward Milner, who had worked for Joseph Paxton at Chatsworth and the Crystal Palace.

the year (1822) which saw the publication of Loudon's *Encyclopaedia of Gardening*. Loudon had a chapter on the 'Education of Gardeners' which contained the following advice for young gardeners:

> *Suppose, for example, a man desires to be a king; that is a desire sufficiently extraordinary; but if he will first make himself acquainted with the history of men who have raised themselves from nothing to be kings ... he may very likely attain his object ... Let no young gardener, therefore who reads this, even if he can but barely read, imagine that he may not become eminent in any of the pursuits of life ... to desire and apply is to attain, and the attainment will be in proportion to the application.*[42]

Four years later, Paxton was appointed head gardener to the Duke of Devonshire at Chatsworth and Loudon commenced publication of his *Gardener's Magazine*. The *Magazine* contained voluminous advice on self-education for gardeners. Paxton worked with Jeffry Wyatville on the Italian gardens at Chatsworth, which divide the house from the Brownian park (see p. 196), and in 1831 he launched a horticultural periodical to rival Loudon's.

In 1850, Paxton used Loudon's method of greenhouse construction to build the Crystal Palace and in the following year he set up a company which spent £1.2m on moving the Crystal Palace to Sydenham and installing it in a grandiloquent Italian garden. This was as near as an apprentice gardener from a poor home could get to becoming a king in Victorian England. The waterworks at Sydenham were intended to outshine Versailles, with wide terraces stepping down the hill on both sides of a long central axis. Paxton included an irregular lake at the far end of the axis and a Sublime

7.40 a, b Warwick Castle has a classic Victorian transition from a conservatory to a terrace to a flower garden to an open landscape.

7.41 a–d Waddesdon Manor has a great Victorian flower garden and other exotic foreground features.

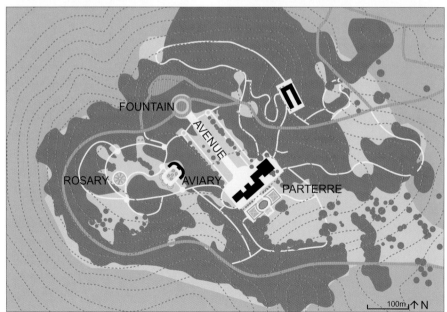

7.42 a, b, c The art of floral bedding, or mosaiculture, disappeared from private gardens but survived in public parks: (a) Cannizaro Park; (b) Avenham Park; (c) Guildford Castle.

7.43 a, b Garden restoration projects, as at Brodsworth and Sledmere, are restoring geometrical bedding to English gardens. Loudon recommended that 'the dwarfish Dutch box' should be planted 'where turf is not used as a ground or basis out of which to cut the beds and walks'.[43]

7.44 Repton's design for the Flower Garden at Valleyfield, in Scotland.

7.45 The Rose Garden in Regent's Park is in the spirit of Repton.

FLOWER GARDEN, VALLEY-FIELD.

7.46 Illustrations from Loudon's *Encyclopaedia of Gardening*. Loudon wrote: 'In general, the materials which form the surface of flower-gardens (Figs. 393. and 394.) are gravel (a), turf (b), and dug-borders (c), patches (d), or compartments (e), and water (f); but a variety of other objects and materials may be introduced as receptacles for plants, or the surface of walks; as grotesque roots, rocks, flints, spar, shells, scoriae; in conglomerated lumps, sand and gravel of different colours; besides works of art introduced as decorations, or tonsile performances, when the old French style (Fig. 395.) is imitated.'[44]

7.47 a, b Circular beds in Bath.

7.48 A design for geometrical carpet bedding by Charles M'Intosh (from *The Book of the Garden*, 1853).[45] He worked for the Duke of Buccleugh at Dalkeith Palace and for the King of the Belgians at Claremont in Sussex. Patterns of this type were published in books and journals and gardeners competed to produce schemes which would delight their employers and excite the admiration of friends.

7.49 Loudon admired the circular beds at Hoole House.

7.50 Prince Albert, with help from Ludwig Gruner, designed the terrace garden at Osborne House. The parterre has Late Baroque cut-work with annual bedding plants set in grass.

feature: a Romantic island inhabited by models of prehistoric monsters. Paxton also designed terraces for large houses, such as Mentmore, and for public parks, including Baxter Park in Dundee and the People's Park in Halifax. The conservatory he designed at Somerleyton Hall framed a terrace garden designed by another successful designer of terraces and parterres: William Andrews Nesfield.

Foreground flower gardens

A 1778 dictionary of gardening noted that parterres had been 'almost banished [from] English gardens; substituting in their stead spacious grass lawns and rural shrubberies'.[46] Little had changed by 1824 and a friend of Sir Walter Scott complained that the flowers grown beside mansions 'in the ancient system' had been banished to out-of-sight vegetable gardens. This left the mansion 'a cold dry specimen of architecture, placed on a cold, dry, shaven, and polished lawn, where not even a daisy is suffered to raise its head'.[47] Repton was alive to the problem and designed flower gardens for Valleyfield, Woburn, Ashridge (see Figure 7.58) and many later projects. The idea became popular and by the mid-century a new craze for flower gardens was underway.

Repton used flowers in borders, where shrubs and herbaceous plants were intermixed, and also designed geometrical rose gardens. To make this type of planting more colourful, plants were grown in pots and set into borders. Loudon described this in his 1822 *Encyclopaedia of Gardening* as a 'changeable flower garden':

> All the plants are kept in pots, and reared in a flower nursery or reserve ground. As soon as they begin to flower, they are plunged in the borders of the flower-garden, and, whenever they show symptoms of decay, removed, to be replaced by others from the same source.[48]

Loudon was very interested in glasshouses, in the application of industrial technology to greenhouses and in the new plants which plant hunters were making available. These developments came together:

> Sheet glass was invented in 1833, and when the removal of the glass tax by 1845 reduced its price, greenhouses proliferated. It became within the means of quite modest gardeners to prepare massed annuals and tender plants many of them, such as petunias, calceolarias, salvias and verbenas from South and Central America, with bright tropical colour – as well as prized South Africans, until now only grown in stove houses.[49]

Gardeners vied with each other to produce new and ever more dazzling displays. Jane Loudon compared geometrical flower gardens to carpets and the term 'carpet bedding' became current in the second half of the century. She wrote:

> As a flower-garden in the geometric style consists of a number of beds, arranged in a regular form, so as to make a sort of pattern, like that of a carpet, it is essential that each bed

7.52 a, b (a) The Swiss Garden at Old Warden Park. (b) Humphry Repton recommended the Hindu style for Brighton Pavilion.

7.51 a, b (a) The Japanese garden in Tatton Park. (b) Paxton's prehistoric monsters at the Crystal Palace.

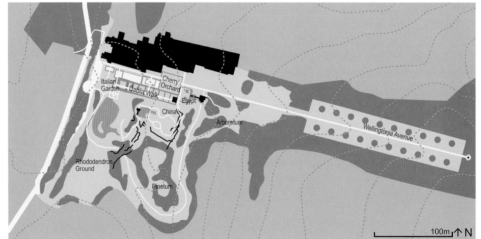

7.53 a, b, c Biddulph Grange has an Italian garden (see Figure 7.27), an Egyptian garden and a Chinese garden.

should be planted with flowers of the same kind, and, as nearly as possible, of the same height, so that each bed may form a mass of colour, and strike the eye at once.[50]

Jane Loudon's husband, John, preferred to see bedding plants in circular beds. He considered the circle to be the purest geometrical shape and also the most practical:

We wish we could strongly impress on the mind of every amateur, and of every gardener, that, for all general purposes of planting beds of shrubs, or beds of flowers on a lawn ... the best form is the circle, provided that it be always kept of small size, say from 18 in. to 6ft., in diameter, one circle never placed nearer to another than 2ft., and these beds be thrown together in groups or constellations, as stars are in the firmament.[51]

Loudon's wish was granted. The circular flowerbed survives in public parks and a few suburban gardens. The star and the moon have also been brought down from the firmament and used to shape flowerbeds.

Joseph Paxton excelled in the art of floral bedding and filled the grounds of Chatsworth, Mentmore and the Crystal Palace with elaborate displays. They were one of the chief attractions of the Crystal Palace and Paxton was annoyed when publicly financed parks departments started making displays of bedding plants which could be viewed without paying an admission charge. Edward Kemp and Charles M'Intosh, who succeeded Loudon as popular writers on garden design, included patterns for carpet-bedding in their books. M'Intosh even wrote a learned section on the application of the principles of colour harmony to the design of bedding schemes. It contained references to Repton, Loudon, Newton and Chevreul.

Middlegrounds: the world's plants and the world's garden

When landowners became as interested in the entire world as their predecessors had been in the Greek and Roman worlds, they made middlegrounds with exotic plants and historical re-creations of design styles and features from everywhere. The world's plants and the world's gardens were assembled in the gardens of Victorian England. Without leaving home, people could 'see the world'.

Sir Joshua Reynolds advocated history painting for the traditional Neoplatonic reason that 'the whole beauty and grandeur of the Art consists, in my opinion, in being able to get above all singular forms, local customs, particularities, and details of every kind'.[52] He therefore advised artists to select and paint subjects which are 'commonly supplied by the Poet or Historian ... [such as] the great events of Greek and Roman

7.54 a, b Spanish and French style gardens. (a) The Spanish garden at Newstead Abbey was commissioned by Geraldine Webb in *c.*1896, after she had seen a parterre on a visit to Spain. (b) The French garden at the Bowes Museum.

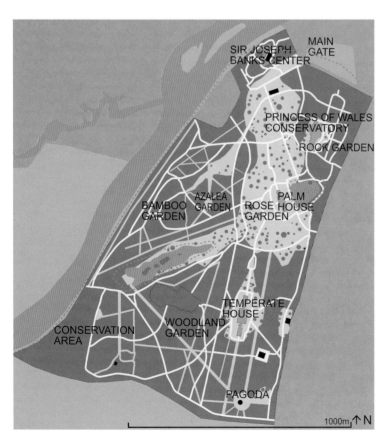

7.55 a, b, c Kew Gardens claims to have one in eight of the world's known plant species in its gardens, conservatories and herbarium (see Figure 6.73).

fable and history, which early education and the usual course of reading, have made familiar and interesting to all Europe'.[53] 'This idea of the perfect state of Nature, which the Artist calls the Ideal beauty, is the great leading principle by which works of genius are conducted. By this Phidias acquired his fame.'[54] Reynolds thought the road to a full appreciation of Nature was as long as it was hard, adding that 'I know but of one method of shortening the road; this is, by a careful study of the works of the ancient sculptors.'[55] Architecture also became historicist and *The Gentleman's Magazine* observed that:

In the ages that have passed, we can scarcely ever discover the adoption of a diversity of styles, at one and the same time; and we cannot but remark, that it has been reserved for the nineteenth century, and especially for [our] own country, to exhibit to the world the every day occurrence, of buildings being unceasingly constructed, in styles that in a chronological point of view are the most remote from each other, as well as on principles which are diametrically opposite.[56]

Garden designers took to historicism. Plants and design styles from around the world and from history were amassed to create incidents and scenes from 'the world's garden'. Byron and Bulwer Lytton both used this phrase and it encapsulates the spirit of nineteenth-century garden historicism. *The Gardener's Monthly and Horticulturist* reported, in 1868:

'Alton Towers,' is a complete Italian villa, with Italian gardens, filled with a succession of beautiful terraces, vases, statues, fountains and flowers. In fact the variety and beauty of the conservatories, orangeries, greenhouses and flowers, the abundance and luxuriance of the trees, especially Evergreens, were enchanting.
....
I hardly dare to undertake a description of Biddulph Grange, 22 acres of ornamental grounds; a Wellingtonia Avenue, a beautiful Pinetum, a rock garden, a stump garden, a Dutch garden and a Chinese garden. Entering the tunnel, we encounter an obscure path on the right, so enshrouded by shrubs as almost to escape notice, and which leads into a wild rocky glen, through which runs a picturesque little brook, filled with aquatic and marshy plants, as well as a complete series of hardy ferns.
....
The next feature of interest is the Chinese garden, very difficult of access, so that strangers may wander about for hours without being able to find either of two narrow passages by which it is approached. The best mode of entering it, however, is from the rocky glen just mentioned. Through a long irregular dark tunnel, apparently excavated from the living rocks, and flanked by grottoes of considerable extent ... The garden is filled only with plants, indigenous to China. Such as Yulan, (Magnolia Conspicua,) the Tea plant, the funebral Cypress, and many more requiring protection of a house in the winter. When to all this is added, an Italian Garden, for the drawing room windows, a quaint Dutch Garden for the Library, and a rose and verbena garden for the breakfast room, and

7.56 a, b, c The Indian garden at Sezincote, for which Repton made recommendations, is part-Muslim and part-Hindu.

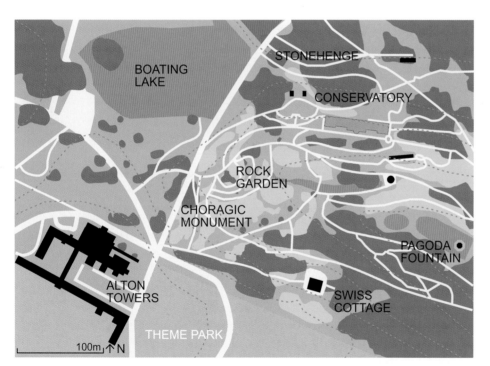

7.57 a, b, c The exoticism of Alton Towers is associated with Loudon, despite his sharp criticism of its wanton eclecticism.

an Egyptian court, connected with a conservatory, your readers may gather some slight idea of Biddulph Grange.[57]

The 'world's garden' in Victorian Britain drew plants and ideas from many countries, including: America, China, Egypt, France, India, Italy, Japan and Switzerland. Glasshouses accommodated tropical plants and scenes. 'Historicism' refers to the use of styles from the past. When two or more historicist styles are used in single garden, the result can be described as 'eclectic' or 'mixed'. Since the term 'Mixed style' was used by Edward Kemp and others during the nineteenth century, it is an appropriate name. It is sometimes thought, wrongly, that John Claudius Loudon invented the Mixed style and that Alton Towers is the best surviving example of his taste. The reasoning appears to be that Alton Towers is described in the *Gardener's Magazine*, which Loudon edited, and that it looks like a physical counterpart to his encyclopaedias on gardening and architecture: a vast assemblage of plants and garden buildings in styles from all parts of the known world.

Alton Towers is a good example of an eclectically Mixed garden but Loudon was appalled by the mixture of styles. It offended him in the same way that an encyclopaedia entry on 'typhoid and triangles' would have offended him. His account of the owner and garden, after a visit in 1831, was as follows:

This nobleman, abounding in wealth, always fond of architecture and gardening, but with much more fancy than sound judgement, seems to have wished to produce something different from everything else. Though he consulted almost every artist, ourselves among the rest, he seems only to have done so for the purpose of avoiding whatever an artist might recommend. After passing in review before him a great number of ideas, that which he adopted was always different from every thing that had been proposed to him.

...

The first objects that met our eye were, the dry Gothic bridge and the embankment leading to it, with a huge imitation of Stonehenge beyond and a pond above the level of the bridge alongside of it, backed by a mass of castellated stabling. Farther along the side of the valley, to the left of the bridge, is a range of architectural conservatories, with seven elegant glass domes, designed by Mr Abraham, richly gilt. Farther on, still to the left, and placed on a high and bold naked rock, is a lofty Gothic tower or temple ... consisting of several tiers of balconies, round a central staircase and rooms; the exterior ornaments numerous, and resplendent with gilding. Near the base of the rock is a corkscrew fountain of a peculiar description ... below the main range of conservatories are a paved terrace walk with a Grecian temple at one end ... The remainder of the valley, to the bottom, and on the opposite side, displays such a labyrinth of terraces, curious architectural walls, trelliswork arbours, vases, statues, stone stairs, wooden stairs, turf stairs, pavements, gravel and grass walks, ornamental buildings, bridges, porticoes, temples, pagodas, gates, iron railings, parterres, jets, ponds, streams, seats, fountains, caves, flower-baskets, waterfalls, rocks, cottages, trees, shrubs, beds of flowers, ivied walls, rockwork, shellwork, rootwork,

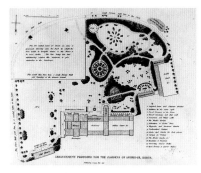

7.58 a–d Repton's design for Ashridge had 'no less than fifteen different kinds of gardens', including a Rosary and a monk's garden. (a) Repton's plan. (b) Repton's drawing of the Rosary. (c) The Rosary. (d) The conduit in the monk's garden.

7.59 a, b Shendish, Hertfordshire, is a good example of Edward Kemp's work in the Mixed style.

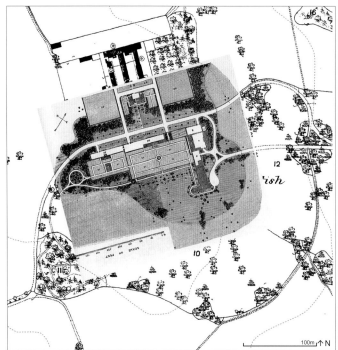

moss-houses, old trunks of trees, entire dead trees, &c., that it is utterly impossible for words to give any idea of the effect ... in one place we have Indian temples excavated in it, covered with hieroglyphics; and in another, a projecting rock is formed into a huge serpent, with a spear-shaped iron tongue and glass eyes.[58]

Loudon concluded that: 'we consider the greater part of it in excessively bad taste, or rather, perhaps, as the work of a morbid imagination, joined to the command of unlimited resources'.[59]

The most influential advocate of historicist garden design was Humphry Repton. His last book contains proposals for a variety of 'different kinds of gardens'. They were restrained by the standard of Alton Towers but very Mixed by the refined standards of the eighteenth century. Repton described Ashridge as 'the child of my age and declining powers' and his 'youngest favourite'. He said that few other projects had 'excited so much interest in my mind', and published a fragment from the Ashridge Red Book in which he justified the mixture of features as follows:

The novelty of this attempt to collect a number of gardens, differing from each other, may perhaps, excite the critic's censure; but I will hope there is no more absurdity in collecting gardens of different styles, dates, characters, and dimensions, in the same inclosure, than in placing the works of a Raphael and a Teniers in the same cabinet, or books sacred and profane in the same library.[60]

Declining, Repton's powers may have been, but his reasoning had a potent influence on Victorian gardens, encouraging ornamented terraces and overt historicism. He praised the 'artificial and truly magnificent style of gardening in former times', in the Ashridge Red Book,[61] and was proud to remember 'having been present' when Mrs Siddons remonstrated with Sir Joshua Reynolds for the way he painted the ringlets in her hair. Sir Joshua had answered, 'Madam, pray allow me the dignity of one straight line.'[62] The Ashridge Red Book proposed 'no less than fifteen different kinds of gardens'.[63] They included a holy well in an enclosure of rich masonry, a winter garden, a monk's garden, a sheltered garden for foreign trees, an American garden, raised beds and a rosarium which was 'supplied from the holy well, and then led into the grotto, from whence it is finally conducted into the drinking-pool in the park'. At Woburn Abbey, Repton proposed an American garden and a Chinese dairy 'decorated by an assemblage of Chinese plants, such as the Hydrangea, Aucuba, and Camellia japonica'. Repton's *Fragments on the Theory and Practice of Landscape Gardening* appeared in 1816.[64] Alton Towers was made between 1814 and 1827. It is therefore likely that Repton, as the most famous landscape designer and gardening author of his day, was the predominant influence on the Earl of Shrewsbury.

Edward Kemp published the first edition of his successful book on garden design in 1850 and included a number of Reptonesque designs by his own hand. He advocated

7.60 Underscar in the Lake District, designed by Edward Kemp.

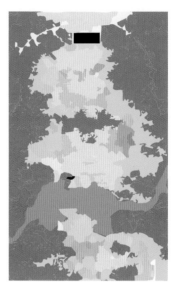

7.61 a, b The main difference between Picturesque and Gardenesque lies in the use of exotic plants.

7.62 a, b Gardenesque planting at Wakehurst Place and Sheffield Park, in Sussex. The composition of the planting is Picturesque but the use of exotic plants makes the gardens 'recognisable' as works of art – and therefore Gardenesque. Wakehurst Place is run by the Royal Botanic Gardens so the plants are well grown and well labelled, as Loudon would have wished.

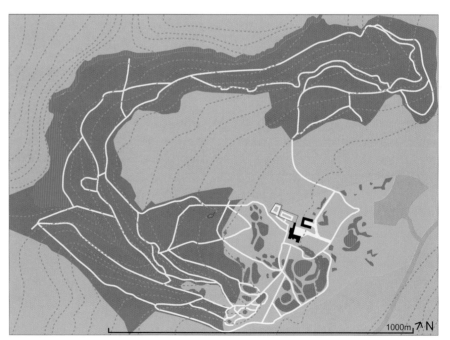

7.63 Wakehurst Place has a transition from a modest foreground terrace, through a large Gardenesque middleground to a Picturesque background in the valley below.

'the mixed style, with a little help from both the formal and the picturesque'.[65] Fearing that this might not be sufficiently Mixed, he went on to say that 'an absolute adherence to one style ... is not to be reckoned among the paramount virtues of the art'.

Believers in stylistic purity may never appreciate the Mixed style but its popular appeal cannot be doubted. In Victorian England, one could see many of the world's garden cultures without boarding a ship. Today, we can turn to the TV, the web, a book or a plane to see the world's gardens.

Gardenesque planting: the world's plants

The aesthetic considerations which led Loudon to praise geometrical gardens also led him to devise a new approach to planting design. He saw three ways of avoiding the absurdity of 'gardens' which are indistinguishable from 'nature':

1   Base their layout on abstract shapes (especially circles, see Figure 7.49).
2   Make exclusive use of plants which are foreign to the country in which the garden is located.
3   Keep plants well separated from each other so that they can be recognised as exotics. This is the intellectual origin of the 'specimen' trees and shrubs which are still dotted about in British gardens.

The word 'Gardenesque' meant 'a Picturesque composition using garden plants' and is shown on the diagrams.

Loudon described the basis of Gardenesque planting as the Principle of Recognition. He asserted that 'Any creation, to be recognised as a work of art, must be such as can never be mistaken for a work of nature.' The rules were rigorous:

The brook, lake, or river, is readily appropriated as a work of art, by planting exotic, woody, and herbaceous plants along the margins, in a natural-looking manner; carefully removing all that are indigenous.

Even the turf should be composed of grasses different from those of the surrounding grass fields.[66]

Loudon wondered how a natural outcrop of rocks could be made to look artificial:

By what means are the perpendicular rocks on the banks of the river Wye, at Piercefield in Monmouthshire, to be rendered a work of art? By substituting another kind of rock for the indigenous one? No; for not only is the scale too large to render this practicable, but, if it were accomplished, the very largeness of the scale would make it be still considered as the work of nature; unless, indeed, rocks, which every one knew did not exist in the country at all, were substituted for the natural ones.[67]

7.64 Specimen trees, at Nymens. A range of species is used and the plants are not allowed to grow together, so that their characteristics are recognisably the result of human intervention.

7.65 a, b The Isabella Plantation in Richmond Park is Gardenesque in the sense of a Picturesque composition using exotic plants.

7.66 At Piercefield Park, Loudon considered replacing the native plants with exotic plants, so that the park would be 'recognisable' as a work of art. Piercefield extends for 3 km west from Chepstow Castle.

7.67 a, b The Derby Arboretum, designed by Loudon in 1839. The mounds were planned to create orderly walks through which plants could be viewed in the correct botanical sequence.

Loudon's solution was to remove all indigenous vegetation and replace it with 'foreign vegetation of a similar character'. Given the impracticality of the idea, it is no cause for wonder that Loudon preferred regular gardens. However, he also liked to see exotic plants arranged in naturalistic groups – providing they were well grown and well labelled.

Loudon's passionate interest in the plants, which made his Gardenesque style possible, brought him close to financial ruin. His wife gave the following account of his labours:

> From the year 1833 to Midsummer 1838 Mr Loudon underwent the most extraordinary exertions both of mind and body. Having resolved that all the drawings of trees for the Arboretum *should be made from nature, he had seven artists constantly employed, and he was frequently in the open air with them from his breakfast at seven in the morning till he came home to dinner at eight in the evening, having remained the whole of that time without taking the slightest refreshment, and generally without even sitting down ... In addition to the large sums in ready money he paid to the artists and other persons employed during the progress of the* Arboretum, *he found at its conclusion that he owed ten thousand pounds to the printer, the stationer, and the wood-engraver who had been employed on that work.*[68]

The *Arboretum et Fruiticetum Britannicum* was eventually published in eight volumes with 'upwards of 2,500 engravings'. Professor Sir Joseph Hooker wrote:

> There is not a naturalist in Europe who could have executed the task with anything like the talent, and judgement, and accuracy, that is here displayed by Mr Loudon ... In short, nothing is omitted, either in the descriptive or pictorial matter, which can tend to illustrate the history and uses of trees and shrubs ... it will be seen at once of what vast importance must such a work be to this country, to every part of Europe, and the temperate parts of North America; and we may even say, to all the temperate parts of the civilised world.[69]

Loudon's Gardenesque principles have been widely adopted in botanical gardens. Hooker became the first Director of Kew Gardens two years after reviewing the book and set about arranging the trees and shrubs in accordance with Loudon's principles. The exotic trees and shrubs at Kew are arranged in naturalistic groups and great attention is paid to botanical accuracy – though Hooker and his successors have not stopped the plants from being 'pressed on during their growth'. The same idea was employed by Paxton in the arboretum at Chatsworth and was repeated in many Victorian arboreta. Woodland gardens can now be found, as Hooker predicted, in 'all the temperate parts of the civilised world'. Collections of exotic animals were also popular. A turtle house was built at Wotton between 1820 and 1830 and Sir Edmund Loder made a collection of wallabies at Leonardslee.

7.68 a, b (a) The fernery at Tatton Park was made for a botanical collection. (b) The greenhouse at Wallington Hall was made for 'pelargoniums and other small plants in pots'.[70]

7.69 a, b Gardenesque planting in Edinburgh's Botanic Gardens.

7.70 a–d Rock gardens at (a) Brighton; (b) Holehird; (c) Cragside; (d) Wisley. They are compositions of exotic plants using principles derived from mountain scenery. Though a Romantic idea, their form is usually un-Romantic.

Heated glasshouses facilitated growing the world's plants in a stormy climate. Glass was used for growing exotic fruits and exotic flowers, as well as being used for botanical collections and for winter gardens with collections of fabulous flowers. John Evelyn called a place for conserving plants in winter a 'conservatory' and this term came to be used for glazed garden structures. Loudon wrote, in 1839, that 'A conservatory is for the growth of trees and shrubs, not, like a green-house, for mere pelargoniums and other small plants in pots; and trees and shrubs, to look well, must have room, and especially breadth, to expand themselves.'[71]

Loudon's encyclopaedic approach to gardens imparted a range of enthusiasms to his readers. It became fashionable to have extensive glasshouses, Gardenesque plant collections, pinetums and plants with 'informal' and 'formal' arrangements. These features are evident in the great estates, like Waddesdon Manor.

Geographical gardens

Historicist gardens relied more on ornament than planting. Geographical plant collections became a way of dealing with the influx of plants from around the world. Despite their names, the geography of geographical gardens related more to growing conditions than regional origins. Repton had recommended a 'Magnolia and American Garden' at Ashridge. Later American gardens became places for acid-loving plants and bog. Charles M'Intosh explained:

> There seems, however, to be some incongruity in the term, as a great majority of the plants and trees found in such a department are in reality not of American origin, but from most extra-tropical quarters of the globe; though the types of some of the most important of them are found in America, as Azaleas, Rhododendron, Mangolia, &c., while individuals of even these genera are also natives of China, India, &c. The term is, however, sanctioned both by long custom and also by cultivators.[72]

Alpine and Rock gardens became places for low-growing plants which can tolerate cold conditions with sharp drainage, peaty soils and protection for their roots. In 1834, Loudon wrote of the rock gardens at Blenheim, Syon House and Hoole House that 'The styles of the three rockeries are totally different, though their object is the same, viz. that of displaying to advantage alpine plants.'[73] Rock gardens use Gardenesque principles. When plant collectors ventured to the Himalayas, the concept of Alpine gardens was expanded and Reginald Farrer wrote a series of popular books including *My Rock Garden* (1907) and *On the Eaves of the World* (1917).[74] Despite their often spotty appearance, Alpine gardens were a Romantic idea which caught my imagination at the age of 23. Working in a Rock, Bog and Alpine Nursery, I spent my lunch breaks reading these books and dreaming of high mountains and the type of scenery in Caspar David Friedrich's *Wanderer Above the Sea of Fog* (see Figure 7.0).

Vegetable gardens

As in the eighteenth century (see p. 201), the practice of the nineteenth century was to hide vegetable gardens behind walls and shrubberies. Repton explained the reasoning in his proposals for White Lodge in Richmond Park:

> I was, therefore, driven to suggest a third expedient, which, in these Fragments, has, or will be, frequently mentioned, viz. to adopt a decided artificial character for the garden; boldly reverting to the ancient formal style, which, by some, will be condemned as departing from the imitation of nature: and, by such treatment, is now secured to these premises an ample portion of ground for fruit and vegetables of every kind; yet, these are so enveloped, in screens of shrubbery and garden-flowers, as to be nowhere visible, or offensive. At the same time, by preserving the inequalities in the ground, which were about to be levelled, the walk is made to take advantage of views into the park; and, thus, neither beauty nor utility is banished by the enclosure.[75]

7.71 Clumber Park. The typical nineteenth-century arrangement was to grow vegetables in a high-walled enclosure with greenhouses on the south-facing walls and fruit trees trained on the other walls.

7.72 West Dean has an arbour for apple trees in the walled vegetable garden.

7.73 James Brown, author of *The Forester: A Practical Treatise on the Planting, Rearing and General Management of Forest-Trees*, worked at Arniston estate and wrote that 'no man ought to attempt the laying out of land for [a plantation] who is not naturally possessed of good taste for that sort of landscape scenery which is based upon the laws of nature'.[76] The Forestry Commission in Britain could have avoided much criticism by taking his advice.

7.74 Drumlanrig Castle looks over a Victorian flower garden, in the foreground, and dramatic forest scenery, in the background.

7.75 Dalmeny House looks over the Firth of Forth to Fife and the Scottish Highlands.

In Medieval and Renaissance gardens, growing fruit and vegetables had been a foreground activity, and the primary use of garden compartments (see p. 91). In Romantic gardens, fruit and vegetables were considered un-Romantic.

Backgrounds: scenery and scenic parks

Scenery

The word 'scenery' came from the theatre and was first applied to natural scenes in the late eighteenth century.[77] William Cowper saw Brown as an 'omnipotent magician'.[78] Cowper loved 'the Freeman, whom the truth makes free' who therefore 'looks abroad into the varied field of Nature' and

> *Calls the delightful scenery all his own.*
> *His are the mountains, and the valleys his,*
> *And the resplendent rivers.*[79]

Sir Uvedale Price spoke of 'natural scenery' as a contrast to the artificial scenery made by Brown and others. This implies a theatrical perspective. John Barrell writes that the word 'scene', when applied to a landscape, 'assumed also that what was being described lay opposite the observer, en face: and this sense came with it from its theatrical origin'.[80]

Scenic parks

The history of the nature conservation movement can be traced to the forest conservation movement in Germany, from whence the ideas were transmitted to the Indian Forest Service, the American Forest Service and elsewhere. In Britain, forest management developed on the great landed estates, managed for trees and animals. James Brown, who became the first president of the Royal Scottish Forestry Society, was trained as a gardener and went on to write the most successful nineteenth-century book on forestry. Brown stated:

> *It is admitted by every person of refined taste, that no object is so ornamental upon a*
> *landed estate as an extensive healthy plantation, situated upon a well chosen spot and*
> *having a well defined tastefully bending outline ... no man ought to attempt the laying out*
> *of land for [a plantation] who is not naturally possessed of good taste for that sort of*
> *landscape scenery which is based upon the laws of nature.*[81]

By 'refined taste', Brown meant the picturesque taste of Gilpin and Price:

> *A country without trees is as repulsive to the eye of taste as a picture of landscape would*
> *be without one shown upon it. In short, I would ask, what adds beauty and natural effect*
> *to a fine mansion-house? What constitutes the charm and pleasure of country scenery in*

7.76 Sir Uvedale Price advised garden designers to observe 'small ledges of rocks, and stones of various sizes … some of them in the sides of the bank itself, some below it, and near the edge of the water' (illustration from the 1842 edition of Price's *Essay on the Picturesque*).

general? What gives rise to the ecstasy felt on viewing a cascade, or a lake with its islands? What is it that renders the homeparks of our landed proprietors so cheerful, so enlivening, so rich in beauty, and so much praised by the most cultivated minds? … I have a feeling approaching to respect for them, more especially when I look upon gigantic specimens of them that have stood over four and five hundreds of years, and have witnessed many generations of feeble men pass away.[82]

Brown worked on the Arniston estate, outside Edinburgh, and had learned to view forest scenery as a necessary part of a gentleman's estate.

Sir Uvedale Price recognised the importance of animals in creating picturesque scenery and his advice on treating the bank of a river is like that in a twentieth-century conservation manual:

The general form of the bank, that is, of the mere ground, being made out in this rude manner, the improver would next observe what were the other circumstances, independently of trees and vegetation, which gave picturesque effect to the bank of the natural river which he was endeavouring to imitate, and produced varied reflections in the water. These, he might probably find, were old stumps and trunks of trees, with their roots bare and projecting; small ledges of rocks, and stones of various sizes, either accompanied by the broken soil only, or fixed among the matted roots; some of them in the sides of the bank itself, some below it, and near the edge of the water; others in the water, with their tops appearing above it. In another part again, there might be a beach of gravel, sand, or pebbles, the general bank being there divided and a passage worn through it, by animals coming to drink, or to cool themselves in the water.[83]

Biodiversity was not on the agenda in 1794 – though game was conserved. Price's views relate to the 1971 Ramsar Convention on Wetlands.[84] It calls for 'the maintenance of their ecological character, achieved through the implementation of ecosystem approaches'. The modern conservation movement grew from the scenic conservation movement. James Brown's concern with animals was traditional. As he wrote:

Landed proprietors, generally speaking, look upon their enclosed plantations as so many game preserves, and in reality they are so, as on most estates game lie quiet, and therefore breed there; and on most not even the forester himself is allowed to prosecute the necessary operations of thinning, for fear of disturbing the animals.[85]

The world's first report on the management of a National Park, by Frederick Law Olmsted in 1865, provides a valuable clue to 'the motivations behind Yosemite's secession to the State of California'.[86] Olmsted, familiar with English parks and with the writings of Gilpin and Price, wrote a report which echoes the above quotation from Price. He reported that Yosemite had

7.77 a, b (a) Yosemite is Picturesque in the Pricean sense and has the highest waterfalls in North America. (b) Olmsted Point, Yosemite National Park, offers a view into the valley and is a reminder that Olmsted produced the world's first management plan for a national park.

magnificent trees, and meadows of the most varied, luxuriant and exquisite herbage, through which meanders a broad stream of the clearest water, rippling over a pebbly bottom, and eddying among banks of ferns and rushes; sometimes narrowed into sparkling rapids and sometimes expanding into placid pools which reflect the wondrous heights on either side ... The stream is such a one as Shakespeare delighted in, and brings pleasing reminiscences to the traveller of the Avon or the Upper Thames.[87]

Olmsted was profoundly affected by 'the deepest sublimity with the deepest beauty of nature' in Yosemite. His account of the Sublime derives from the English landscape movement and Olmsted further reported that:

It is a universal custom with the heads of the important departments of the British Government to spend a certain period of every year on their parks and shooting grounds, or in travelling among the Alps or other mountain regions.[88]

Olmsted's involvement with Yosemite was consequent upon his work on Central Park and, as the name tells, Yosemite was regarded as a National *Park*. It has been called 'America's best idea'[89] and it led to the creation of national parks in half the world's countries.

7.78 a, b, c (a) The view from Lintertis House resembles the view from Foxley (see Figure 7.20), with the cedar a fragment of the old garden. (b) and (c) A drawing and a photograph of the house (now demolished). It was designed by Archibald Elliot in 1833 for Gilbert Laing Meason. Inspired by the great painters of Italy, including Gozzoli and Raphael, Lintertis can be regarded as 'the home of landscape architecture'. It was later owned by Sir Hugh Munro, famous for his list of Scotland's highest mountains.

7.79 a, b (a) A drawing from Meason's *On the Landscape Architecture of the Great Painters of Italy*. The design is attributed to Benozzo Gozzoli. (b) Gozzoli's fresco the *Three Wise Men*. Gozzoli was a pupil of Fra Angelico.

7.80 'Castellated Gothic is easily known, at first sight, by the line of battlements cut out of the solid parapet wall, which surmounts the outline of the building in every part. ... The Castellated style never appears completely at home except in wild and romantic scenery.'[90]

Landscape architecture

The picturesque transition was concerned with outward views from private estates. It was a way of organising an owner's worldview into foreground, middleground and background. The aim was to create visual harmony between architecture and landscape, reflecting a deeper harmony between indoor and outdoor space, as between man and nature. Gilbert Laing Meason put forward this view in a book entitled *On the Landscape Architecture of the Great Painters of Italy* (1828). He was a wealthy Scotsman who had not had 'the opportunity of visiting Italy' but loved the country from art and books. With regard to the landscape, he wrote that 'it is due to the talents and taste of Mr Payne Knight'. Meason admired Price's Picturesque ideas about the proper relationship between landscape and architecture. He was familiar with Vitruvius and recommended a careful study of 'Raphael, Dominichino, Titian, Julio Romano, and Michael Angelo', adding, with regard to foreground and middleground scenery, that 'The exterior decorations of terraces, parterres, stairs of communication, and different gardens, filled with groups of the many flowering shrubs and plants introduced lately into Britain, are admirably in harmony with this style of architecture.'[91]

Meason is the grandfather of the modern world's landscape architecture profession, which has Olmsted as its father. Meason had a conceptual vision of the need to relate the works of man to the works of nature and viewed this relationship as what is now called a public good: 'The public at large has a claim over the architecture of a country. It is common property, inasmuch as it involves the national taste and character.'[92] Meason's vision of the need to relate architecture to landscape influenced the development of urban design and public parks, through Loudon, Olmsted and Andrew Jackson Downing. Olmsted was the first to use 'landscape architecture' in connection with a public sector project (for Central Park in New York). William Andrews Nesfield had been the first person to use 'landscape architect' as a professional title, when designing a garden for Buckingham Palace.[93] The relationship between architecture and landscape was a key factor in the development of an Arts and Crafts approach to landscape.

CHAPTER 8

Arts and Crafts gardens, 1880–1970

8.0 John Ruskin loved the landscape and architecture of country cottages. He wrote: 'You must over and over again have paused at the wicket gate of some cottage garden, delighted by the simple beauty of the honeysuckle porch and latticed window.'[1]

Ruskin's landscape architecture

John Ruskin was a picturesque traveller. From an early age he liked nothing better than exploring, sketching and writing about picturesque places. Since this 'work' was so enjoyable, Ruskin believed everyone should be able to take as much pleasure in their daily toil. It would, he believed, convert discontented workers into idealistic craftsmen. Ruskin attributed the richness of Medieval architecture to the fact that each workman was also an artist and a designer. He explained the dullness of Classical architecture by the subservience of labourers to the imperious diktat of drawings. Ruskin had learned to draw from picturesque artists[2] and, though he does not mention Gilpin, fully took on his belief that 'The art of sketching is to the picturesque traveller, what the art of writing is to the scholar. Each is equally necessary to fix and communicate its respective ideas.'[3]

John Dixon Hunt observes that Ruskin's earliest tastes for architecture and landscape were 'formed by the picturesque movement'[4] and comments on 'the huge role that landscape gardening played in shaping his early visual theories'.[5] Ruskin is believed to have assisted Loudon in preparing *The Landscape Gardening and Landscape Architecture of the Late Humphry Repton Esq.*[6] Published in 1840, the book had been in preparation during the years Ruskin was writing for Loudon. After a visit to his house in 1837, Ruskin told his father:

8.1 An enthusiasm for country cottages and gardens influenced the Art and Craft of making gardens. (*At the Cottage Door* by Myles Birket Foster).

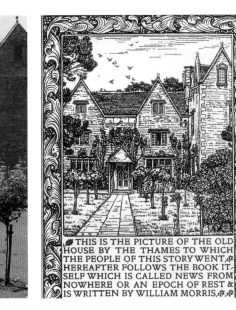

8.2 Kelmscott Manor in 2010 and as shown on a woodcut (by C.M. Gere) in the 1893 edition of William Morris's *News from Nowhere*.[7]

8.3 Philip Webb wrote that Kelmscott Manor's garden 'is tiny and ornamental, set out in little paths where two cannot walk abreast, bordered by low box hedges, and walled with mellow Cotswold stone and great ramparts of yew'.[8]

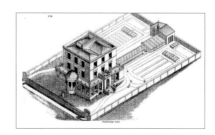

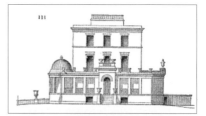

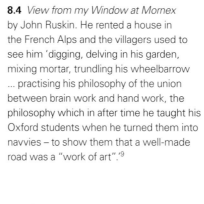

8.4 *View from my Window at Mornex* by John Ruskin. He rented a house in the French Alps and the villagers used to see him 'digging, delving in his garden, mixing mortar, trundling his wheelbarrow ... practising his philosophy of the union between brain work and hand work, the philosophy which in after time he taught his Oxford students when he turned them into navvies – to show them that a well-made road was a "work of art".'[9]

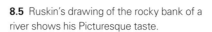

8.5 Ruskin's drawing of the rocky bank of a river shows his Picturesque taste.

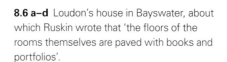

8.6 a–d Loudon's house in Bayswater, about which Ruskin wrote that 'the floors of the rooms themselves are paved with books and portfolios'.

Mr Loudon's house, as I have often remarked, is to the eye of the casual observer, what the extent of the work he goes through proves that it cannot be to the master or presiding genius thereof, a chaos of literary confusion ... the floors of the rooms themselves are paved with books and portfolios.[10]

Loudon's edition of Repton contains only a footnote by Ruskin but 'Repton's writings have a peculiarly intimate relationship' with the essays on the *Poetry of Architecture*, about which Ruskin said, 'I could not have put in fewer, or more inclusive words, the definition of what half my life was to be spent in discoursing of.'[11]

Loudon published Ruskin's first article (on 'Enquiries on the Causes of the Colour of the Water of the Rhine; by J. R.') in his *Magazine of Natural History* (1834). Later articles on 'The Poetry of Architecture' appeared in Loudon's *Architectural Magazine*. The editor was deeply impressed and wrote to the father of the 19-year-old:

Dear Sir
Your son is certainly the greatest natural genius that ever it has been my fortune to become acquainted with, and I cannot but feel proud to think that at some future period, when both you and I are under the turf, it will be stated in the literary history of your son's life that the first article of his which was published was in Loudon's Magazine of Natural History.
Yours very sincerely,
J.C. Loudon[12]

Loudon's estimation of Ruskin's talent was accurate. The two men had shared interests in architecture, the natural world and sketching. Because he was still an undergraduate, Ruskin took the pen name Kata Phusin for contributions to Loudon's *Architectural Magazine*. The pen name came from Aristotle. *Kata phusin* meant *'according to nature'*, as distinct from *para phusin*, 'contrary to nature'. The pen name embodied Ruskin's approach to architecture and landscape. The subtitle of the young Ruskin's articles explains their central concern: 'The Architecture of the Nations of Europe considered in its Association with natural Scenery and national Character'. In spirit, the articles are close to Meason's *Landscape Architecture* (see pp. 318–19). 'One reads but a very few pages of *The Poetry of Architecture* before he realises that Ruskin is not interested in architecture, but in prospects of external nature.'[13] Ruskin may have read Meason's book, or Loudon's review of Meason's book, or he could have absorbed the ideas from books Loudon admired, by Gilpin, Price and Knight. Ruskin's youthful opinions included the use of local styles, the transition from art to nature and the Vitruvian design objectives. Ruskin wrote:

The whole glory of the design consists in its unison with the dignity of the landscape, and with the classical tone of the country.

8.7 Ruskin thought of Brantwood as 'the cottage ... near the lake-beach on which I used to play when I was seven years old'.[14]

[W]e have obtained a link between nature and art, a step of transition, leading the feelings gradually from the beauty of regularity to that of freedom.

[T]he climate must always be considered; for, as we saw, the chief beauty of these flights of steps depends upon the presence of the sun; and, if they are to be in shade half the year, the dark trees will only make them gloomy, the grass will grow between the stones of the steps, black weeds will flicker from the pedestals, damp mosses discolour the statues and urns, and the whole will become one incongruous ruin, one ridiculous decay.[15]

The articles Ruskin wrote for Loudon's *Architectural Magazine* dealt with English vernacular architecture in its environmental and cultural context and with regard to the 'craftsmanship and social being in relation to architecture and fine art'.[16] This was Ruskin's main subject and be became a pioneer of what is now called 'environmental' thinking.[17]

Cottages and gardens

Love of cottages may have been the starting point for Ruskin's interest in the relationship of architecture to landscape. He wrote:

> Of all embellishments by which the efforts of man can enhance the beauty of natural scenery, those are the most effective which can give animation to the scene, while the spirit which they bestow is in unison with its general character ... It is for this reason that the cottage is one of the embellishments of natural scenery which deserve attentive consideration. It is beautiful always, and every where; whether looking out of the woody dingle with its eye-like window, and sending up the motion of azure smoke between the silver trunks of aged trees; or grouped among the bright corn fields of the fruitful plain; or forming grey clusters along the slope of the mountain side, the cottage always gives the idea of a thing to be beloved: a quiet life-giving voice, that is as peaceful as silence itself.[18]

Gilpin had written of 'the wastes of Derbyshire ... without a cottage to diversify the scene'.[19] Price wrote that 'a cottage of a quiet colour half concealed among trees, with its bit of garden, its pales and orchard, is one of the most tranquil and soothing of all rural objects'.[20] Knight compared 'dressed cottages' to 'a shepherdess in a French opera' and asserted that:

> The real character of every object of this kind must necessarily conform to the use, to which it is really appropriated; and if attempts be made to give it any other character, it will prove, in fact, to be only a character of imposture: for to adapt the genuine style of a herdsman's hut, or a ploughman's cottage, to the dwellings of opulence and luxury, is as utterly impossible, as it is to adapt their language, dress, and manners to the refined usages of polished society.[21]

Knight's *Analytical Inquiry into the Principles of Taste* advised: 'The best style of architecture for irregular and picturesque houses, which can now be adopted, is that mixed style, which characterizes the buildings of Claude and the Poussins.'[22] Ruskin did not like the idea of adapting Italian styles to England. His articles on the *Poetry of Architecture* grew from his studies of cottages in Italy, Switzerland and Westmoreland. His theme was Wordsworthian: 'that landscape should condition local building, and that local should be the bedrock of national architecture'.[23] Wordsworth wrote his best poetry in a cottage with a garden:

> It seemed the home of poverty and toil,
> Though not of want: the little fields, made green
> By husbandry of many thrifty years,
> Paid cheerful tribute to the moorland house.[24]

Wordsworth was decidedly middle-class, though relatively short of money during the time (1799–1808) he rented the former Dove and Olive Branch Inn beside Grasmere.

8.8 Wordsworth's 'Dove Cottage' was so-named by the National Trust, in 1890.

8.9 A *cottage ornée*, in Old Warden, built by the landowner as a picturesque addition to his local village.

More than 'touched' by Romanticism, he wrote in 1802 of its

Sweet Garden-orchard, eminently fair,
The loveliest spot that Man hath ever found,
Farewell! — we leave thee to Heaven's peaceful care
Thee, and the Cottage which thou dost surround.[25]

The name 'Dove Cottage' was a dash of National Trust Romanticism, applied when it bought the property in 1890. Wordsworth had paid a rent of £5/year and the Trust paid £650 for the freehold. 'Real' cottage gardens were different – the word was a Medieval term for a small feudal dwelling (see p. 57).

The rural retirement dream, the *ferme ornée* and the Picturesque aesthetic gave birth to the *cottage ornée*, meaning 'a residence in the country'. Horace Walpole had an ornamental cottage at Strawberry Hill and wrote:

I showed them my new cottage and garden over the way, which they had never seen, and
with which they were enchanted. It is so retired, so modest, and yet so cheerful and trim,
that I expect you to fall in love with it. I intend to bring it a handful of treillage and
agremens from Paris; for being cross the road, and quite detached, it is to have nothing
gothic about it, nor pretend to call cousins with the mansion-house. [26]

The *Penny Cyclopaedia* (1845) explained how this use of the word 'cottage' evolved:

The term cottage has for some time past been in vogue as a particular designation for
small country residences and detached suburban houses, adapted to a moderate scale of

8.10 a, b (a) Horace Walpole lived at Strawberry Hill. (b) He also had a 'Cottage in the Woods' to which he retreated from his mansion.

living, yet with all due attention to comfort and refinement. While, in this sense of it, the name is divested of all associations with poverty, it is convenient, inasmuch as it frees from all pretension and parade and restraint.[27]

One has to check, when reading about cottage gardens in the nineteenth century, whether the reference is to a gentleman's cottage or a labourer's cottage. Jane Austen lampooned the upper-class cottage in *Sense and Sensibility*:

I am excessively fond of a cottage … The dining-parlour will admit eighteen couple with ease; card-tables may be placed in the drawing room; the library may be open for tea and other refreshments; and let the supper be set out in the saloon.[28]

Friedrich Engels knew the character of an artisan's cottage:

An ordinary cottage, in Leeds, extends over no more than about five yards square, and consists usually of a cellar, a sitting-room, and a sleeping chamber. This small size of the houses crammed with human beings both day and night, is another point dangerous alike to the morals and the health of the inhabitants.[29]

Loudon described the character of middle-class and upper working-class cottage gardens in the 1835 edition of his *Encyclopaedia of Gardening*:

Labourers' gardens
The extent of the garden of a labourer ought never to be such as to interfere with his regular employment; unless it is sufficiently so to enable him to dispose of part of the produce in the manner of a market-gardener or to keep a cow, and dispose of her produce

8.11 Gustave Doré shows the kind of garden a prosperous artisan, like my great-grandfather, had in London.

... In the management of cottage-gardens, no opportunity should be neglected by the cottager of collecting manure from the highways, from the grass, weeds, and mud of ditches and lanes.[30]

Artisans' gardens

The cottage-gardens of artificers, that is, of operative mechanics and manufacturers, small tradesmen, and other country artisans, differ from those of the common labourer in being somewhat larger, and in having a larger portion of the space devoted to the culture of fruit trees and flowers ... They are generally an intelligent, industrious class of men, who take great delight in their gardens, and the point of practice in which they excel is in the production of florists' flowers. Norwich is, or used to be, noted for carnations. Spittalfields is still noted for all the competition flowers, but especially for auriculas and tulips. Manchester for auriculas and polyanthuses, and also for the production of new varieties, and large specimens of gooseberries; and Paisley and Glasgow for pinks.[31]

Small suburban gardens

They differ from the former in being almost always gardens of pleasure, consisting of a grass-plat (complot, Fr. a design or device), with a border, or a few patches of flowers in front of the house, and a grass-plat or gravel walks behind, with beds for culinary vegetables and small fruits. Their extent may be from an eighth to half an acre, and they are managed by jobbing-gardeners by the day or year. The plants and turf are soon injured by the smoky and confined atmosphere incident to their situation, the finer plants and trees do not thrive in them, and the sorts which do succeed, and even the turf, require frequent renewal. Evergreens and early spring flowers, both of the tree and herbaceous kinds, are most to be desired as permanent plants for these gardens; and in summer, a display of annuals is made from transplanted plants furnished by the jobber, whose great object ought to be to keep up a succession of flowers, to have the grass and gravel in order, and to keep the whole perfectly neat.[32]

The middle class had Picturesque tastes but no more desire to live in hovels than to sleep on the pavements of Bologna. Ruskin confessed:

Yesterday, I came on a poor little child lying flat on the pavement in Bologna – sleeping like a corpse – possibly from too little food. I pulled up immediately – not in pity, but in delight at the folds of its poor little ragged chemise over the thin bosom – and gave the mother money – not in charity, but to keep the flies off it while I made a sketch. I don't see how this is to be avoided, but it is very hardening.[33]

Robinson and Naturalism

William Robinson claimed a friendship with Ruskin and saw him as a powerful ally in Nature's cause. Bisgrove suggests they may have met only once but Robinson was familiar with the *Seven Lamps of Architecture*, in which Ruskin identified nature as one of the main sources of beauty:

> *I do not mean to assert that every happy arrangement of line is directly suggested by a natural object; but that all beautiful lines are adaptations of those which are commonest in the external creation ... The pointed arch is beautiful; it is the termination of every leaf that shakes in summer wind, and its most fortunate associations are directly borrowed from the trefoiled grass of the field, or from the stars of its flowers.*[34]

Robinson emphasised the dependence of art upon Nature with a capital N but one wonders if his taste for cottages may have developed in London. Robinson's first job had been as a garden boy on the Marquess of Waterford's grand Curraghmore estate, where he may have lived in a labourer's cottage with an earth floor and straw roof. Robinson moved from Ireland to London at the age of 23 (in 1861) and established himself as a horticultural journalist and gardening author. The *Gardener's Chronicle* sent him to Paris (in 1867) and he published books about its gardens and parks in 1868. The books have quotations from Ruskin's *Stones of Venice* (1851, 1853) and Robinson appears to be familiar with Ruskin's 1837–8 articles on the 'Poetry of architecture' in which he discussed villas on the shore of Lake Como.

Ruskin described the Villa Carlotta and the Villa Bellaggio, specifically noting: statues and urns ('graceful in their outline, classical in their meaning, and correct in their position'); grottoes ('agreeable objects seen near, because they give an impression of coolness to the eye'); terraces ('dignified in their character'); formal rows of trees ('right in this climate'); the transition from art to nature ('from the beauty of regularity to that of freedom').[36] But Ruskin had some reservations in his praise for regular gardens. First, 'there can be no barbarism greater than the lozenge borders and beds of the French garden'. Second, Italian garden features would 'be out of place in any country but Italy':

> *The whole glory of the design consists in its unison with the dignity of the landscape, and with the classical tone of the country. Take it away from its concomitant circumstances, and, instead of conducting the eye to it by a series of lofty and dreamy impressions, bring it through green lanes, or over copse-covered crags, as would be the case in England, and the whole system becomes utterly and absolutely absurd, ugly in outline, worse than useless in application, unmeaning in design, and incongruous in association.*[37]

If only at the start of his career, William Robinson accepted the merits of 'architectural embellishments, costly fountains, and statues' in gardens, providing they were in

8.12 'Here is an engraving of a very small cottage garden in Oxfordshire to show what is an artistic garden in its simplest expression. There was very little in this beyond the Monthly Rose and a few Pansies and the tree beyond, and yet it was right and beautiful.'[35]

8.13 Helen Allingham's painting of an Irish cottage illustrates the type of cottage Robinson would have known as a young man.

8.14 a, b The Villa Carlotta (also called the Villa Somma and Villa Somariva), as drawn by Ruskin and as it is today. Ruskin considered the terraces, outward views, statues and urns well suited to the locality – but unsuited to England.

countries 'where people can live out of doors the greater portion of the year' so that 'along the shores of the Mediterranean – it is more desirable to have the nude form in marble in the open air, independently of the fact that the lichens and moss do not so soon begin to embellish the carving'.[38] But Robinson lashed Versailles, where 'there is nothing more appalling than the walls, fountain basins, clipped trees, and long canals', and he detested Paxton's design for the Crystal Palace where 'a more horrid impression is received than in any part of Versailles'.[39]

The summer weather of 1867 was dismal and English gardeners were grumbling about their floral bedding being ruined by 'cold nipping winds ... followed almost continuously by cold nights, and an unusually heavy rainfall'.[40] Various suggestions were sent to the *Gardener's Chronicle* for breeding tougher plants, for using foliage plants which would survive bad weather and for making new arrangements of circles and stars to delight the eye and ensure that 'our employers will inspect their neighbour's floral decorations again with pleasure'.[41] Robinson thought M. Barillet-Deschamps had a solution to the problem. He was experimenting, in Paris, with palms, tree ferns and other sub-tropical foliage plants. They were less affected by the weather because they did not depend on flowers for effect. Also, they were being used in more natural groups than British floral beds. Robinson was impressed and in 1867 John Gibson deployed the system in Battersea Park, where it proved popular but expensive. Robinson remarked, in his *Gleanings from French Gardens* (1868), that the idea would work better with hardy plants: 'We have no doubt whatsoever that in many places

8.16 Robinson admired the bold foliage of 'subtropical planting' but wanted to find a way of achieving a similar effect at a lower cost. He particularly recommended the use of Pampas Grass, Yuccas, Bamboos, Crambe and Rheum.

8.15 William Robinson thought the Crystal Palace gave a 'horrid impression'.

as good an effect as any yet seen in an English garden from tender plants, may be obtained by planting hardy ones only!'[42]

This idea led to a book with a brilliant title: *The Wild Garden* (1870). Ruskin had despised Claude's 'formalism' and 'foolish pastoralism' but praised Sir Walter Scott for his 'delight in those wild scenes of nature which had so long been despised'[43] and had drawn attention to the 'rambling briars and wild grasses' in Tintoretto's *Crucifixion*.[44] Robinson took up the idea of 'Nature' being essentially 'wild' and, thinking of gardens, criticised the 'vast quantities of flowers, covering the ground frequently in a showy way, and not unfrequently in a repulsively gaudy manner'.

Asking 'What is to be done?' Robinson found an answer in 'the little cottage gardens in Kent, Sussex, and many other parts of England'. He called them 'little Elysiums, where the last glimpses of beautiful old English gardening may yet be seen' and recommended

naturalizing or making wild innumerable beautiful natives of many regions of the earth ...
I allude to the Lilies, and Bluebells, and Foxgloves, and Irises, and Windflowers and
Columbines, and Aconites, and Rock-roses, and Violets, and Cranesbills, and countless
Pea-flowers, and mountain Avens, and Brambles, and Cinquefoils, and Evening Primroses,
and Clematises, and Honeysuckles, and Michaelmas Daisies, and Feverfews, and Wood-
hyacinths, and Daffodils, and Bindweeds, and Forget-me-nots, and sweet blue Omphalodes,
and Primroses, and Day Lilies, and Asphodels, and St. Bruno's Lilies.[45]

8.17 a, b (a) William Robinson joked that shaving one's grass is as foolish as shaving one's face. (b) There are 'wild' sections at Gravetye Manor but the area beside the house is a traditionally 'formal' terrace.

8.18 a, b Robinson advocated the use of hardy flowers composed like wild plants.
(a) The frontispiece to Robinson's *The Wild Garden*.[46] (b) 'A colony of myrrhis odorate, established in a shrubbery with harebells here and there.'

A new style of planting was born of the English weather, nature and economy. Robinson's ideas were illustrated with engravings of plants in *The Wild Garden* and then with engravings of plants growing around picturesque cottages in *The English Flower Garden*. The cottages belonged to the middle classes. They were not peasant hovels and might now cost a million pounds each.

Robinson's references to Nature and Elysiums remind us that his design philosophy was an unwitting return to the planting design principles of the Picturesque theorists. Christopher Hussey remarked upon the ancestry of Robinson's wild planting and was summoned to Robinson's manor house, Gravetye, to be told that he had 'never' heard of Sir Uvedale Price.[47] It is all too likely. Robinson saw Loudon as his predecessor and devoted a series of articles to him in the first issues of his own periodical, *The Garden*. Loudon had in fact followed Price's taste in the natural composition of plants, but wanted them to be well-grown and well-labelled and he also had a fondness for circular beds (see p. 298).

The Neoplatonic and Neoclassical principle that gardens should 'imitate nature' was misunderstood by gardeners during the middle years of the nineteenth century. They paid their respects to Dame Nature but failed to see how gardens could imitate her without imitating the wildness of empirical nature. Edward Kemp's attitude is representative:

> *Readers who have travelled with me thus far will have perceived that I have had occasion more than once to refer to Nature as the great school of landscape gardening. It may be worth while, then, specifically to inquire how far the imitation of nature is possible and right. I profess not to be [one] of those who would carry this principle very far, or into minor matters ... A garden is for comfort, and convenience, and luxury, and use, as well as for making a beautiful picture. It is to express civilisation, and care, and design, and refinement ... In these respects, it is fundamentally different from all natural scenes.*[48]

Robinson became a militant protagonist for naturalistic planting and a determined foe of floral bedding. There was a kindly mention of circular beds in his 1871 book on *Hardy Flowers* but he subsequently turned against this favourite device of Loudon, Kemp and M'Intosh. M'Intosh had written that: 'circular figures ... in laying out flower-gardens' were 'strongly advocated by the late Mr Loudon'.[49] The former garden boy from Curraghmore may have come to resent the idea of arranging plants in circles and stars for an employer's delight – and, when the Arts and Crafts generation became active as amateur gardeners, people came round to Robinson's point of view.

8.19 a, b The gentlefolk of the nineteenth century employed humble tradesmen to look after their gardens – but gardening has become one of Britain's most popular hobbies.

Amateur garden craft

The popularity of amateur gardening grew in the nineteenth century. Historically, gardening had been the work of garden labourers and the job was sometimes hereditary.[50] John Selden (1584–1654) wrote:

> *Just as a gardener brings his lord and master a basket of apricots, and presents them, his lord thanks him, perhaps gives him something for his pains; and yet the apricots were as much his lord's before as now.*[51]

The celebration of rural retirement and Happy Husbandmen led to a gradual appreciation of honest toil, as Wordsworth had known it (see pp. 325–6). Fanny Burney (1776–1828) was a novelist and Wordsworth's contemporary. She received a letter

8.20 Sir Winston Churchill built the garden wall at Chartwell with his own hands. His ancestors, the Dukes of Marlborough, would not have done so.

8.21 An amateur gardener with his cabbages, by Frederick Walker.

from her father noting that her husband will be 'not only his own architect, but intends being his own gardener'. Fanny replied, 'He dreams now of cabbage-walks, potato-beds, bean-perfumes, and peas-blossoms. My mother should send him a little sketch to help his flower-garden, which will be his second favourite object.'[52] An 1842 edition of Burney's diary described her husband as an 'amateur gardener' and the suburban villas of the nineteenth century made ornamental gardening as popular with the middle class as it had been with the upper class. Weeding was less popular and in 1843 the *Gardener and Practical Florist* remarked that:

> The amateur gardener—the occupier of a small rural villa—the more humble cottager—every one, indeed, who loves ornamental gardening as an active pursuit, is more or less attached to a shrubbery; but many find it irksome or difficult, from want of time, to keep the ground about the shrubs in neat and trim condition.[53]

Use of the term 'amateur gardener' in a much-read book on *The Miseries of Human Llife, or, the Last Groans of Timothy Testy and Samuel Sensitive* (1807) helped popularise the term. Beresford wrote about the misery of visiting an amateur gardener who 'detains you among his pines and melons, till you are in danger of being forced, too!'[54]

Ruskin's attitude to work encouraged tending plants as well as admiring them. Though his own preferred work was sketching, Ruskin wrote of the 'fatal error of despising manual labour':

> we want one man to be always thinking, and another to be always working, and we call one a gentleman and the other an operative; whereas the workman ought often to be thinking, and the thinker often to be working, and both should be gentlemen, in the best sense.[55]

William Morris practised what Ruskin preached. Always thinking and always working, Morris became a poet, an artist, a skilled craftsman, a founder of the Socialist League and a leader of the Arts and Crafts movement. He was sympathetic to Robinson's criticism of floral bedding and wrote in *Hopes and Fears for Art* (1882) that:

> Another thing also too commonly seen is an aberration of the human mind, which otherwise I should have been ashamed to warn you of. It is technically called carpet bedding. Need I explain further? I had rather not, for when I think of it even when I am not quite alone I blush with shame at the thought.[56]

Gardening was one of the many types of work Morris enjoyed, as he explained in a letter, written at Kelmscott, to Mrs Burne-Jones:

> I am just going to finish my day with a couple of hours work on my lecture but will first write you a line ... Yet it sometimes seems to me as if my lot was a strange one: you see,

8.22 The Red House, designed by Philip Webb for William Morris, was built in an old orchard. This was a good setting for a Medievalising Arts and Crafts garden but little is known of its original design.

8.23 Taking a pride in an orchard was perhaps the most authentically Medieval aspect of Arts and Crafts gardens.

I work pretty hard, and on the whole very cheerfully, not altogether for pudding, still less for praise; and while I work I have the cause always in mind ... Well, one thing I long for which will certainly come, the sunshine and spring. Meantime we are hard at work gardening here: making dry paths, and a sublimely tidy box edging.[57]

In 1859, William Morris commissioned Philip Webb to design the Red House in Bexleyheath. The house takes its name from the unpretentious red brick and tiles with which it was built. The garden survives. Regrettably little is known about its original planting but it was made in an old orchard and has comfortable proportions which are better suited to homely use than Victorian display. A subsequent owner, Ted Hollamby, made the garden which survives. The Arts and Crafts movement embodied an approach to life and work which is especially close to the historic gardening ideal of combining use with beauty, profit with pleasure and work with contemplation. Gardening became a craft, as it had been in Medieval England.

Formality and informality

Morris looked back to the glories of Medieval England, imagining it filled with contented craftsmen living in charming cottages adorned by flower-filled gardens. He wanted craftsmen to be artists and these attitudes were embodied in the Art Workers' Guild, founded in 1884. Morris was not a founder member but became its Master in 1892. Many of the architect members were involved with the design of country houses and two of them published books on garden design: John Dando Sedding and Reginald

8.24 Sedding's drawing has a Hestercombe-esque geometry and a transition relationship with the landscape beyond.

8.25 Brickwall exemplified the type of garden Blomfield advocated in *The Formal Garden in England*.

Blomfield. These books form a sharp contrast to mid-century garden design books by Kemp and M'Intosh, which had been weak on history and theory but well supplied with sample designs in Loudon's manner.

Sedding knew Morris from having worked with him in G.E. Street's office and gave his book the title *Garden-Craft Old and New* (1891). The Preface summarises most of what the book has to say: 'The old-fashioned garden ... represents one of the pleasures of England, one of the charms of that quiet beautiful life of bygone times that I, for one, would fain see revived.'[58] On the question of how the resulting garden might look, he quotes the Reverend Thomas James, who had written in 1852:

> *If I am to have a system at all, give me the good old system of terraces and angled walks, and clipt yew-hedges, against whose dark and rich verdure the bright old-fashioned flowers glittered in the sun. I love the topiary art, with its trimness and primness, and its open avowal of its artificial character.*[59]

James explained his design theory with greater clarity than Sedding:

> *[Uvedale Price] seems to recognise a three-fold division of the domain – the architectural terrace and flower-garden in direct connection with the house, where he admits the formal style; the shrubbery or pleasure-ground, a transition between the flowers and the trees, which he would hand over to the 'natural style' of Brown and his school; and, thirdly, the park, which he considers the proper domain of his own system. This is a distinction which it would be well for every proprietor to keep in view ... Our present subject of complaint is the encroachments which the natural and picturesque styles have made upon the regular flower-garden.*[60]

Sedding called this 'graduated formality' and recognised 'the general composition of landscape-scenery' as 'landscape architecture'.[61] But the 'clipt yew-hedges, against whose dark and rich verdure the bright old-fashioned flowers glittered in the sun' is not a Medieval idea.

Reginald Blomfield's book entitled *The Formal Garden in England* appeared in 1892. It was primarily a history book. Blomfield was a good historian who used engravings of named historic gardens to illustrate the type of garden he advocated. In effect, they are illustrations of the above quotation from the Reverend Thomas James. The last paragraph of Blomfield's book explains his deepest concern:

> *The best English tradition has always been on the side of refinement and reserve ... the inexpressible sweetness of faces that fill the memory like half-remembered music. This is the feeling that one would wish to see realised in the garden again, not the coarse facility that overwhelms with its astonishing cleverness, but the delicate touch of the artist, the finer scholarship which loves the past and holds thereby the key to its meaning.*[62]

Hitherto, 'formal' had been used by ill-wishers. Blomfield acknowledged this in his Preface but used the word as a term of praise. It was a brilliant marketing pitch and paid off. Formality had an innate appeal to the Victorians and Blomfield makes the entirely correct point that good design requires design talent. The problem with the horticulturalists Blomfield disparaged was not their expertise in horticulture: it was the all-too-obvious lack of design talent revealed in the work of Kemp, M'Intosh and Milner. Blomfield had a bombastic design verve and received a string of commissions for country house gardens. On large estates, he tended to treat gardens as settings for buildings, as in the French Baroque gardens he so admired. But on smaller projects, he was able to treat garden compartments as outdoor rooms and did this very successfully.

The difference between Blomfield's best and worst work left fertile ground for misunderstandings and a vituperative argument arose between Blomfield and Robinson. The issues at stake were: which profession should design gardens? Should gardens contain straight lines? Should gardens have terraces? Is planting design important? Should gardens be natural? Robinson went too far in opposing geometry and terraces. Blomfield went too far in opposing Robinson's Naturalism and horticultural enthusiasm. It was a surprising recurrence of an argument which had been settled in the 1790s, by an idea Blomfield and Robinson scarcely appreciated: the picturesque transition (see p. 275). A mediator stepped forward in the 1890s, destined to fulfil Loudon's prediction that nothing was likely to have such a good effect on the art of garden design as the fact that so many young ladies were taking up landscape painting.

8.26 a, b Blomfield's design for Mellerstain has a transition from 'formal' to 'informal' but the garden's primary role is that of a setting for the mansion.

8.27 a, b Blomfield's design for Godinton House has a charming enclosure but the main garden is ponderously 'formal'.

8.28 a, b Athelhampton, designed by Reginald Blomfield and F. Inigo Thomas, is one of the best examples of the style recommended in *The Formal Garden in England*, which was illustrated by Thomas.

Gertrude Jekyll was born in the year Loudon died (1843). She studied painting at the Kensington School of Art and became an admirer, later a friend, of John Ruskin. Her approach to life and work was that of the Arts and Crafts movement. Had the Art Workers' Guild permitted lady members, she would doubtless have joined and might have restrained the pugilistic Blomfield at an earlier date. Skilled in many arts and crafts, Jekyll practised them with a loving care for naturalness and beauty. One of her skills was gardening. She made a garden for herself, began to give advice on other gardens and, with Robinson's help, to write for the horticultural press. This was done with great authority and Jekyll became an admired figure in the gardening world.

In 1896, Jekyll considered the arguments advanced by Robinson and Blomfield and pronounced judgement: 'both are right, both are wrong'. You could, Jekyll believed, have a terrace near the house, but you should arrange your plants in naturalistic compositions. She thought both the disputants hot-headed but was somewhat more inclined to Robinson's side, adding the comment that Blomfield seemed to be saying 'There is no garden but the formal garden and I am its prophet.'[63] Blomfield accepted her judgement and in the third edition of his book sheepishly referred to 'a somewhat acrid controversy' between landscape gardeners and architects in which 'there was a good deal of truth on both sides'.[64] Robinson bought an estate at Gravetye in Sussex which needed a terrace and Blomfield found that his own garden required naturalistic planting (see p. 332).

Robinson's and Blomfield's gardens both had a picturesque transition from a terrace near the house to an open lawn, a woodland garden and a distant view. The elements of this sequence are shown on the diagram. It represents a garden of about 5 hectares. Jekyll considered this to be 'small'. Her Munstead Wood garden was 7 hectares, which she was just able to manage with the help of 11 men. Not many property agents would consider 7 hectares 'small' but even 107 hectares would have been pinched for the estates on which the Landscape Transition evolved. Since Repton was the chief professional advocate of the transition, it is worth noting what Jekyll and Sedding said about him. Jekyll wrote that Repton teaches us 'to see how to join house to garden and garden to woodland';[65] Sedding that 'the best advice you can give to a young gardener is – know your Repton'.[66]

Through her wisdom, artistry and good sense, Jekyll became a powerful influence on the revival of British garden design at the turn of the twentieth century. Her own taste for terraces probably dated from her youthful tours of Italy and the Mediterranean. Jekyll's second book, *Wall and Water Gardens*, contains photographs of the Villa d'Este and a plan for 'one small section' of a garden which 'I have ventured to describe and figure in detail.'[67] The design was for an elaborate terraced garden with rills of water running down both sides of a flight of steps in the Italian manner. The geometry of Italian gardens, then as now, was softened by evergreen plants. The delightful combination of regular and irregular lines attracted Jekyll's eye and became a feature of the Arts and Crafts style. An indication of how it was interpreted in an English context, with a different vernacular tradition, can be gained by comparing Robinson and Blomfield's drawings of Haddon Hall. Blomfield shows the types of space which characterised the style and Robinson the vocabulary of hardy plants in natural groupings which were used to adorn the spaces.

Jekyll's influence on garden design came about through her books and through her partnership with a third Arts and Crafts architect: Edwin Lutyens. They met in 1890 when Lutyens was 21 and Jekyll was 47. A friendship developed into a productive working partnership. It was founded on a genuine 'closeness of minds' and a shared

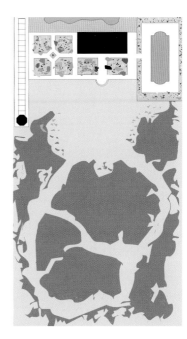

8.29 Diagram of the Arts and Crafts style.

THE TERRACE: HADDON HALL: DERBYSHIRE

8.30 a–d Haddon Hall in Derbyshire was admired by both Blomfield and Robinson. (a) Blomfield's illustration emphasises the architectural terrace. (b) Robinson's illustration emphasises the cloak of Romantic planting. (c) and (d) As the photographs show, the current planting design is more Robinson than Blomfield.

Ruskinian belief in 'the divinity of hard work'.[68] Jekyll, having absorbed Repton, Price, Knight and Ruskin's ideas on outdoor design (Chapter 7), passed them on to the young Lutyens. When merged with their joint love for local arts and crafts, it produced an approach to house and garden design which is well described by Christopher Hussey:

The whole approach of the young Lutyens to architecture, through his study of the landscape, traditions, and vernacular techniques of his home county, was in the romantic tradition that regards buildings as properly the product of their soil and of the country

8.31 a, b, c Gertrude Jekyll's own garden, at Munstead Wood, became a profound influence on Arts and Crafts gardens.

craftsman's lore; and their planning as properly ordered by the circumstances of the site and the needs of their inhabitants. At the beginning and again at the end of the nineteenth century these principles were habitually qualified by another, that the resulting building should possess the qualities of picturesqueness, that is, 'compose' picturesquely both as a design and in its setting.[69]

The idea is Neolithic, Neoclassical and Romantic. Jekyll and Lutyens toured Surrey in a pony cart, discussing the materials, design and construction of the things they saw. Later, Jekyll asked Lutyens to help design a new house in her garden at Munstead

8.32 Christopher Hussey wrote: 'Hestercombe's gardens represent the peak of the collaboration with Miss Jekyll and his first application of her genius to classical garden design on a grand scale.'[70]

8.33 a, b The garden Jekyll designed for Lindisfarne Castle is delightful. Walled and surrounded by the kind of meadow land from which garden turf used to be cut, it was made for a Late Medieval castle re-built by Edwin Lutyens for the publisher of *Country Life*.

8.35 a, b The Salutation was designed in 1911 for a banker and 'is a comfortable upper-middle-class country home, serene, confident, and assured in its elegant solidity. It is the perfect house that many in Britain aspire to.'[71]

8.34 Snowshill Manor was designed by Charles Wade and Baillie Scott, both of whom were artists and architects.

Wood. Construction began in 1895 and the project was a great success. It is facile to think that Lutyens designed the house and Jekyll designed the garden. Nor does this appear to have been the case: it was a joint project. Lutyens had the drawing skills and Jekyll knew the character, functions and proportions of the spaces which should be made. This applied equally to house and garden.

The close working relationship which produced Munstead Wood grew more distant as the years passed. But in the decades before the First World War, Jekyll and Lutyens created some of the most adored houses and gardens which have ever been made in Britain. They have a charm which satisfies a deep-felt yearning for a civilised life in the country. One can place them in the same quality bracket as the gardens of sixteenth-century Italy and seventeenth-century France. When compared to the stately pleasure grounds of pretentious mansions, Arts and Crafts gardens come closer to the Homeric and Virgillian idyll of rural retirement in lands of bounteous peace. Abraham Cowley, in the seventeenth century, wrote of his dream that:

> *I might be master at last of a small house and large garden, with moderate conveniencies joined to them, and there dedicate the remainder of my life only to the culture of them and the study of nature.*[72]

Cowley would surely have found contentment at Munstead Wood, Orchards, Deanery Garden or Hestercombe. They are rural retreats and gardens of a Golden Age. Jane Brown describes them as 'the gardens of a golden afternoon', and contrasts them with the later projects on which Jekyll was less involved and often supplied no more than a planting plan, sometimes without visiting the site.[74] Without his partner's guiding influence Lutyens's garden designs tended to become bleak and formal. Grandeur took the place of charm. At Gledstone Hall (1922) and Tyringham (1924), the gardens are ornaments to the buildings with little use or beauty of their own – Lutyens did not enjoy gardening, or even sitting about in gardens.

8.36 a, b The sundial at Graythwaite Hall (1896) provided the motif for the cover of the first garden design book to use 'Arts and Crafts' in its title – and T.H. Mawson dedicated it to the hall's owner.[73]

Other Arts and Crafts garden designers

Jekyll and Lutyens deserve the attention they receive from garden historians but so do many of their contemporaries. Professional designers and owner-designers, attracted by Arts and Crafts ideals, contributed to making the half-century after 1880 one of the best periods in the history of British garden design. They can be divided into three groups: horticulturalist designers, architect-designers and owner-designers.

Horticulturalist designers

Thomas H. Mawson, Percy Cane, Richard Sudell, Ralph Hancock, George Dillistone, Brenda Colvin, Sylvia Crowe and many others came to garden design from a

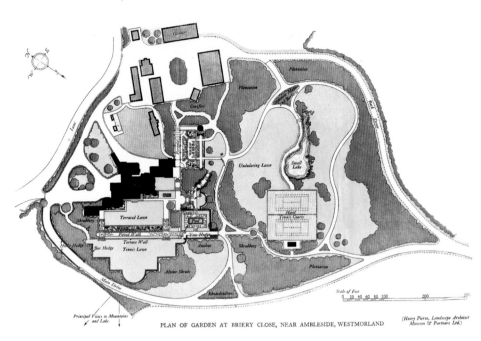

8.37 Mawson's plan for Briery Close in Westmoreland.

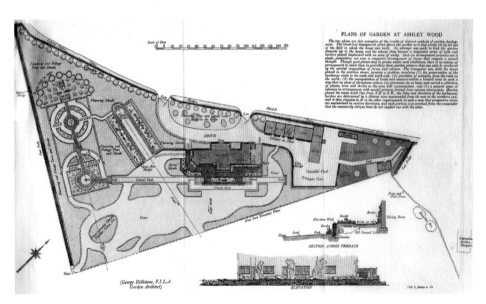

8.38 George Dillistone FRHS was an early member of the Institute of Landscape Architects (ILA).

8.39 In the Potteries, Mawson made good use of local materials in his design for Hanley Park (Stoke on Trent).

8.40 Roynton Cottage (now called Rivington Terraced Gardens) used local stone to make a gargantuan 'cottage garden' for Lord Leverhulme.

8.41 The Hill Garden, Hampstead, was designed by Mawson for Lord Leverhulme in a Mediterranean spirit.

8.42 a, b Mawson designed Kearsney Abbey for the owner of a nearby paper mill. The canal is parallel to the front of the house and in the valley below.

8.43 a, b Mawson worked with John Cory, his patron, on the design of Dyffryn. They visited Italy and the design is more axial than Mawson's earlier work.

horticultural background. Influenced by the Arts and Crafts movement, they believed in combining 'informal' planting design with 'formal' designs for what came to be called 'hard landscaping'. Mawson was the most prolific garden designer of the period and the first, in a book title, to associate gardens with the Arts and Crafts movement.[75]

Mawson was eight years older than Lutyens and started his career as a garden designer at almost the same time (*c.*1890). He lacked Lutyens's genius but became a leading exponent of the Arts and Crafts style. Mawson took Repton and Kemp as his models and quoted Repton on the desirability of 'formality near the house, merging into the natural by degrees, so as to attach the house by imperceptible gradations to the general landscape'.[76] In 1900, Mawson published a book on *The Art and Craft of Garden Making* which caught the mood of the day and provided the current name for the style: he related contemporary gardens to the Arts and Crafts movement. The book was handsomely produced and, as the publishers boasted on the title page, was

8.44 a, b Percy Cane, who designed the garden at Sutton Park, had studied both horticulture and architecture. The scale of the spaces, and the planting, are better than in most architect-designed Arts and Crafts gardens.

8.47 Harold Peto owned and designed Iford Manor.

8.45 a, b Polesden Lacey was designed by J. Cheal & Sons, for an Edwardian hostess, Mrs Margaret Greville, who lived in Berkeley Square and brought guests here for country house parties.

8.48 The terrace garden at Manderston was designed by John Kinross. Asked how much he might spend, the client told him, 'It simply doesn't matter'.[77]

8.46 a, b Arley Hall, as painted by George Elgood in the 1890s and as it survives: a time-capsule for the garden taste of its day and age. In 1904, Jekyll considered it had the best planting in England.

8.49 The garden of Cottesbrooke Hall was designed by Robert Weir Schultz, an architect member of the Art Workers' Guild.

'Illustrated by photographic views and perspective drawings by C.E. Mallows and others, also chapter headings designed by Mr D. Chamberlain, and one hundred and thirty plans and details of gardens designed by the author.'

The use of photographs in a book on garden design was a novelty and, along with a great series of garden picture books from *Country Life*, *The Studio* and other publishing houses, they have left historians with a visual record of the state of British gardening at a time when vast resources were available for the construction and maintenance of country houses and gardens. It was the twilight hour of that wealthy landowning class which had so long patronised the arts of garden and landscape design. Like ageing fruit trees, not destined to survive the season, the country landowners of England produced one last crop of magnificent new gardens before succumbing to income tax, estate duty, war and another flirtation with Italian gardens.

Architect-designers

Many architects followed Blomfield and Sedding in the design of Arts and Crafts gardens, for their own houses and for their clients.

Inigo Triggs was a country house architect and garden designer. His major study of *Formal Gardens in England and Scotland* (1902) contains examples of gardens made during the seventeenth- and nineteenth-century phases of enthusiasm for Italian gardens.[78] They stimulated both historical research and new garden designs. Clients were attracted to the Italian style by its air of grandeur. It was adopted by many Arts and Crafts designers, including Inigo Thomas, H.A. Tipping, Oliver Hill, Clough Williams-Ellis and Harold Peto. Thomas Mawson became a member of the RIBA and laid out an elaborate Italian garden for Lord Leverhulme which survives in good condition (now known as The Hill Garden) (Figure 8.41). Mawson also designed an enormous 'cottage garden' for him in Lancashire. Previously known as Roynton Cottage, and now as Rivington Terraced Gardens, it was built in the Arts and Crafts style but with an inventive use of stone (Figure 8.40).

Owner-designers

William Morris and Gertrude Jekyll, as discussed above, led the way in using their own gardens as places to enjoy design and gardening as hobbies. They were followed by wealthy owner-designers of whom the best known are Vita Sackville-West and Major Lawrence Johnston, for their work at Sissinghurst and Hidcote.

Sir George Sitwell knew that his family had owned a Renaissance compartment garden in the seventeenth century. He spent many years studying Italian gardens, wrote a book on the subject and then spent a fortune laying out two gardens in an Arts and Crafts version of the Italian style at Renishaw in Derbyshire and at Montegufoni in Italy.

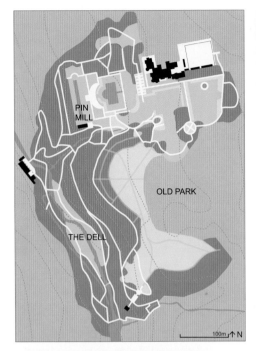

8.50 a, b, c The garden at Bodnant was made by Lord and Lady Aberconway.

8.51 a, b, c Sissinghurst Castle Garden was designed by its owners: Vita Sackville-West and Harold Nicolson.

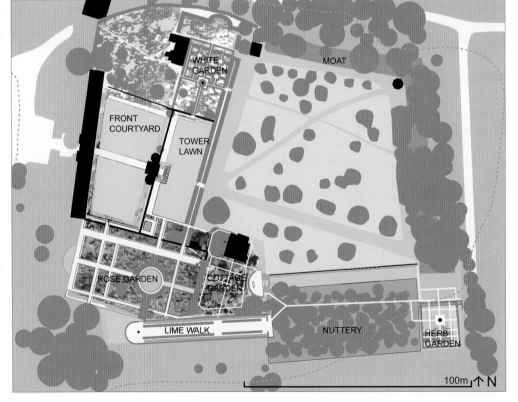

8.53 Hinton Ampner was designed by its owner Ralph Dutton, the Eighth Baron Sherborne.

8.52 a, b, c Hidcote Manor Garden was designed by its owner, Major Lawrence Johnston.

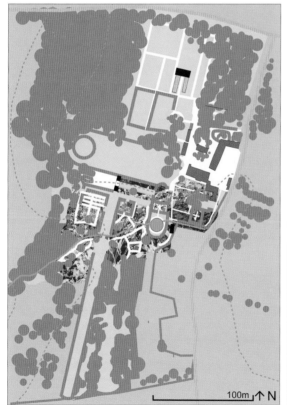

8.54 a, b The garden of Crathes Castle was designed by Lady Sybil Burnett and her husband, Sir James Burnett of Leys.

8.55 Borde Hill was laid out after 1892 by Colonel Stephenson Clarke.

8.56 a, b Coton Manor was laid out by its owners in the 1920s and the wildflower meadow was developed in the twenty-first century.

8.57 a, b The garden of Kellie Castle was designed by Robert Lorimer and painted by George Elgood.

Many architects, like Reginald Blomfield, became owner-designers. Robert Lorimer made his first design for Kellie Castle, Fife, Scotland, in 1880, at the age of 16. Jekyll described the garden he made:

> The castle stands at one corner of the old walled kitchen garden, a door in the north front opening directly into it. The garden has no architectural features. There are walks with high box edgings and quantities of simple flowers. Everywhere is the delightful feeling that there is about such a place when it is treated with such knowledge and habitation.[79]

Lorimer was a craftsman, an artist, a draughtsman, a garden designer and an architect. He was influenced by William Morris and became a member of the Art Workers' Guild in 1896.

Harold Peto, the son of a wealthy builder, became an architect and went into partnership with Ernest George. When poor health caused him to leave London, be purchased Iford Manor and made an Arts and Crafts garden which incorporated a collection of antiquities. His use of local materials and close integration with the valley landscape were Ruskinian.

8.58 a–e Great Dixter was made by Nathanial Lloyd and his wife, with help from Edwin Lutyens, and then by Christopher Lloyd.

Clough Williams-Ellis, was English-born but proud of his Welsh descent. He trained as an architect and drew extensively on local craft traditions in making a garden for the house he inherited from his father, Plas Brondanw. Williams-Ellis used local stone to create a Welsh Arts and Crafts compartment garden with a long axis and eccentric details.

Charles Paget Wade made the garden at Snowshill Manor with the help of Mackay Hugh Baillie Scott. Wade was an artist, a craftsman, a poet and an architect. Baillie Scott was an artist and an architect. The garden has a series of outdoor rooms which

8.59 The Arts and Crafts style retains its popularity with Britain's owner-gardeners.

'grow' out of the old manor house. Using local materials and traditions, they also had an enthusiasm for Tudor gardens and Renaissance-inspired garden compartments. Wade wrote:

> *A garden is an extension of the house, a series of outdoor rooms, the word garden means – garth – an enclosed space, so the design was planned as a series of separate courts, sunny ones contrasting with shady ones, courts for varying moods.*[80]

Wade's compartment rooms were Renaissance-inspired but his plan for assigning them to 'varying moods' was contemporary. Baillie Scott, in a similar vein, wrote that:

> *It is not a case of first designing a house and then lay out its immediate surroundings a garden bearing a certain relation to it, for house and garden are here the product of a single initial idea which comprehends the whole.*[81]

The Arts and Crafts movement encouraged the idea that owners should work in their gardens. This included design work as well as physical work. Many 'amateur gardeners', without a design training, developed a notable skill in garden design. There are famous examples at Hidcote Manor, Sissinghurst Castle Garden and Great Dixter. Talent is the first requirement for a designer: it cannot be learned but it can be fostered by education and experience.

8.60 Gertrude Jekyll's garden at Munstead Wood.

8.61 Purple campanula (from Jekyll's *Some English Gardens*, 1933).

Arts and Crafts planting design

Christopher Hussey described Gertrude Jekyll as 'the greatest artist in horticulture and garden-planting that England has produced'.[82] Her theory of planting design derives from the ideas of Price, Knight and Repton. She brought together: Knight's idea of keeping exotic plants near dwellings, Repton's idea of themed compartments, Price's idea of relating planting design to the compositional principles of landscape painting and the fundamental principle of working with the natural genius of the place. Jekyll's interpretation of these ideas is embodied in the following quotations from her most successful book, *Colour Schemes for the Flower Garden*:

On woods
I am myself surprised to see the number and wonderful variety of the pictures of sylvan beauty that displays throughout the year. I did not specially aim at variety, but, guided by the natural conditions of each region, tried to think out how best they might be fostered and perhaps a little bettered.[83]

On compartments
It is extremely interesting to work out gardens in which some special colouring predominates ... it opens out a whole new range of garden delights ... besides my small grey garden I badly want others, and especially a gold garden, a blue garden and a green garden.[84]

8.62 a, b Jekyll admired J.M.W. Turner and believed the colour sequence from paintings like the *Fighting Temeraire* could be applied to herbaceous borders to create the effect of aerial perspective.

On garden pictures

When the eye is trained to perceive pictorial effect, it is frequently struck by something – some combination of grouping, lighting and colour – that is seen to have that complete aspect of unity and beauty that to the artist's eye forms a picture. Such are the impressions that the artist-gardener endeavours to produce in every portion of the garden.[85]

J.M.W. Turner was the landscape painter Jekyll most admired. Her main border at Munstead Wood and many of her other planting schemes were designed to create a sequence from blood-red in the centre, to golden yellow, to lemon yellow, to the white of the moon and the pale blue of the sky. This sequence can be found in *The Fighting Temeraire* and many of Turner's later paintings. The influence of the French Impressionists on Jekyll's planting schemes has been exaggerated.[86]

Jekyll's influence on planting design was magnified by her success as an author. Norah Lindsay, the high-society garden designer of her day, was an admirer of Jekyll. Lindsay 'fine-tuned many of the basic tenets of Jekyll's theories by adjusting and tweaking them to produce her own version of the perfect herbaceous border.'[87] Like Jekyll, Lindsay came to her trade as an owner-designer, which is the best way of learning about plants. The owner-designers of Great Dixter (Nathanial and Christopher Lloyd), Sissinghurst (Vita Sackville-West), Hidcote (Lawrence Johnston) and Kiftsgate (Heather Muir) learned planting design in the same way, developing a sustained brilliance in the use of plant material which can scarcely be equalled by a designer who is not in residence.

William Robinson's influence on planting design is less easy to gauge. Since he was a successful magazine publisher, and sold more books than Jekyll, his lifetime influence was probably greater than Jekyll's. He died in 1935, having outlived her by three years. But Robinson's books went out of print and have been superseded by newer books with high-quality colour printing and modern plant names. Jekyll's books have been re-published time and time again since they went out of copyright with colour photographs and effusive introductions. They are appreciated for her attitude to planting design rather than for information on individual plants. Artistic books tend to outlive scientific books.

CHAPTER 9

Abstract Modern gardens, 1925–80

9.0 a, b The Homewood was designed by Patrick Gwynne in 1938, influenced by Le Corbusier's Villa Savoye.
The garden has mildly Expressionist curves and planting which, like the architecture, may have been influenced by Japan.

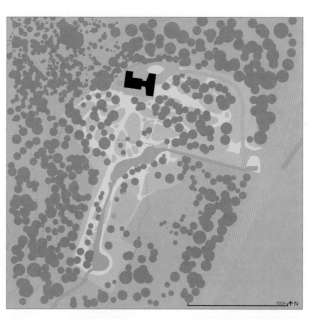

9.1 a, b The Homewood has a Modernist rectilinear terrace leading into a free-form curvilinear garden.

9.2 Though designed at the end of the twentieth century, the Water Garden at Kiftsgate has an Abstract Modern aesthetic.

9.3 The Sackler Crossing in Kew Gardens, completed in 2006, was designed by John Pawson as an Abstract serpentine curve.

9.4 The Noel Baker Peace Garden, designed by Steve Adams, shows how the Abstract style was adapted for public sector projects. It was done with less confidence than in the late twentieth century.

Introduction

The period defined as 'Modern' varies between the arts. Modern painting is dated from 1864.[1] Modern sculpture grew from Rodin's late work but, under the influence of Cubism, took a new direction in 1906.[2] Modern music is dated to the period from 1890–1910[3] and Modern literature to the period 1900–20.[4] Modern architecture began in the 1920s and, according to Charles Jencks, died in 1972.[5]

So what of the Modern garden? It is an elusive subject. Few Modernist designers paid any attention to gardens in the 1920s and 1930s, and those who did also had Pre-Modern and Postmodern concerns, preferring partial abstraction to total abstraction. In 1977, Charles Jencks defined Postmodernism as 'one-half modern and one-half something else' (see p. 380). This chapter reviews the 'one-half modern'. Chapter 10 reviews the 'something else'. A fully Modernist garden would comply with the principles of Modernist design and a Postmodern design would go beyond them. The distinction is sharp in theory but fuzzy in practice. The maxims of Modernism were:

- Form follows function.
- Less is more.
- Truth to materials.
- Ornament is crime.
- The styles are dead.
- Story telling is dead.
- Use modern materials.

The origins of Modernism can be sought in art, philosophy, politics, science, general culture or general history, and traced back, at least, to Descartes's *Discourse on the Method* (1637).[6] It is therefore convenient to have a narrower term to encapsulate the impact of Modernism on garden design. I find 'Abstract' the most useful term. It pinpoints 'the intentional rejection of classical precedent and classical style'[7] which had such a powerful influence on twentieth-century art and design. Abstract art grew out of the nineteenth century, flourished in the early twentieth century and continues to influence art and design in the twenty-first century. The process of abstraction relates to the analytical focus on narrow aspects of reality which characterise the scientific method. In relation to the fine arts, the dictionary definition is that 'Abstract' means 'characterized by lack of or freedom from representational qualities'. The *Cambridge Introduction to Modernism* comments as follows on the relationship between Abstract art and Modern art:

> Abstract, or 'nonrepresentational,' or 'nonobjective,' art has often been taken as the epitome of modern art. As a result, the history of modern art has been understood in terms of an almost scientific set of experiments leading up to the ultimate discovery, abstraction.[8]

9.5 a, b Malevich's *White on White* (1918) could have influenced garden design – and may have influenced Roberto Burle Marx's experiments with patterned grass. Malevich wrote: 'When, in the year 1913, in my desperate attempt to free art from the ballast of objectivity, I took refuge in the square form and exhibited a picture which consisted of nothing more than a black square on a white field, the critics and, along with them, the public sighed, "Everything which we loved is lost. We are in a desert."'[12]

Generalisations about the art of the twentieth century are fraught: a host of -isms resulted from a widespread desire to be in the avant garde of Modern art, as well as being Abstract and Modern. The history of Modern art therefore became 'a cacophony of isms'.[9] The -isms which appear to have had most influence on gardens are Cubism, Constructivism, Expressionism, Neoplasticism and, more recently, Minimalism. The illustrations that accompany the following notes show how Abstract paintings could be translated into garden designs.

Cubism

Cubism was the father of Modern painting, the progenitor of other -isms and a significant influence on garden design. Its starting point is generally taken to be the work of Paul Cézanne and his intention of 'doing over Poussin entirely from nature'. Cézanne spoke of art being 'theory developed and applied in contact with nature' and of treating nature 'by the cylinder, the sphere, the cone, everything in proper perspective so that each side of an object is directed towards a central point'.[10] There is an affinity between this ambition and the Neoplatonic theory of art which, as discussed in Chapter 5, produced the geometrically organised paintings and gardens of the seventeenth century.

Suprematism

Suprematism was promoted by Kasimir Malevich and focused on the primary geometrical forms. He painted a *Black Square* and a *Black Circle* in 1913, followed by his famous Suprematist composition *White on White* in 1918. Suprematism was a utopian movement 'believing staunchly in art's ability to contribute to improving society and all humankind'.[11]

Constructivism

Constructivism originated in Russia after 1919, using the same geometric language as Suprematism, but without the mysticism. The word 'Constructivist' was used in the *Realistic Manifesto* of 1920, written by Naum Gabo and Antoine Pevsner. Aiming to free art from the traditional constraints (line, volume, mass, colour, etc.), the brothers sought to create a social art with a focus on space and time:

> We renounce the thousand-year-old delusion in art that held the static rhythms as the only elements of the plastic and pictorial arts. We affirm in these arts a new element: the kinetic rhythms as the basic forms of our perception of real time.[13]

Gabo's rotating fountains and his use of translucent and transparent materials were a manifestation of this idea and it is surprising that his focus on space, time and kinetics did not attract more interest from garden designers. Gardens are about space and time more than about line and mass. The enclosing elements are less significant than the space they enclose.

Expressionism

Expressionism is both a style of painting, which flourished in early twentieth-century Germany, and a strand in the history of art, which can be traced from prehistoric cave paintings through El Greco to the present. It has the reputation of being 'instantly recognizable' but 'curiously difficult to define'.[14] Friedrich Nietzsche, who was the intellectual force behind German Expressionism, identified two interacting varieties of aesthetic experience:[15]

1   an Apollonian experience which involves order, regularity and repose;
2   a Dionysian experience which involves disorder, irrationality, exuberance and the celebration of nature.

These ideas had a profound influence on the arts and, through sculpture, on architecture. Bruno Taut conceived of a new society in the Alps with luxuriant gardens and delightful buildings. The Bauhaus masters, in Dessau, made sculptural white houses and set them amid pine trees and long grass, establishing a relationship between Apollonian buildings and a Dionysian backdrop. The integration of regular and irregular geometries remains common in garden design.

9.6 The Gabo Fountain beside Westminster Bridge is the best example, in Britain, of a Constructivist approach to garden design.

9.7 a, b Van Gogh's painting, *Wheat Field with Cypresses* (1889), influenced the development of Expressionist painting and was used by Shelley Mosco, in 2011, to design a green wall in front of London's National Gallery.

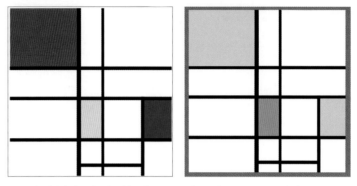

9.9 a, b (a) A drawing by Hay Kranen to show the geometry of Mondrian's Neoplasticism. (b) Its adaptation as a garden plan.

9.8 a, b The front cover of the first issue of *De Stijl* magazine (1917) has a surprising resemblance to a garden plan in the Abstract style. The style can be classified as Neoplasticist, Apollonian and Expressionist. The text may be translated as: 'THE STYLE MAGAZINE FOR THE MODERN VISUAL ARTS EDITOR THEO VAN DOESBURG WITH ASSISTANCE FROM WELL-KNOWN NATIONAL AND INTERNATIONAL ARTISTS. ISSUE 10 HARMS TIEPEN FROM DELFT 1917.'

Neoplasticism

Neoplasticism is the name for an approach to art adopted by a group of Dutch artists between 1910 and 1930. They developed Cubism into a totally non-figurative art which became known as *de Stijl* (the Style). The leading figure in the movement was Piet Mondrian. He had painted realistic landscapes as a young man but came into contact with the Cubist paintings of Georges Braque and Pablo Picasso between 1911 and 1914. At the outbreak of the First World War he returned to Holland and, in association with Theo van Doesburg, developed a rigorously non-figurative art. During his Cubist period, Mondrian gave his paintings titles referring to figurative subjects, such as *The Sea* and *Horizontal Tree*. After formulating the principles of Neoplasticism he used titles which implied no subject, such as *Composition* or *Composition with Red, Yellow and Blue*. The theory underpinning Mondrian's work was developed in conversation with M.H.J. Schoenmaekers, a Dutch philosopher who created a link between the de Stijl movement and Plato's theory of forms (see p. 222). As during the seventeenth century it was believed that art should look beyond the world of the particulars to the world of the universal forms. Theo van Doesburg, the editor of *De Stijl* magazine, explained the basis of the new art:

*As contrasted with traditional painting, where particularisation was of primary impor-
tance, painting in our time considers generalisation, that is to say the uncovering of the
purely aesthetic in plastic features, as its principle value.*[16]

Van Doesburg believed art should look to the primary colours and essential forms,
leaving the interpretation of stories, tales, etc. to poets and writers. The front cover
of the first issue of *De Stijl* magazine resembles an Abstract garden plan (Figure
9.8). It was designed by Vilmos Huszar, a founding member of the de Stijl group,
and published in October 1917. The design could be made into a garden by translat-
ing the black and white pattern into paths, steps, raised beds, pools and stepping
stones. Even the title 'de Stijl', which is above the design, could be used to make a
paving pattern with dark and light slabs. No such literal translation of a graphic
design into a garden plan has been attempted but the geometry of Neoplasticism
has had a profound influence on the design of paved areas. When working with a
T-square and set square, or using CAD software, it is easy to attempt Mondrian-
type patterns.

Minimalism

'Minimalism' is a term which appeared in the 1960s and is now applied to a wide
range of visual and non-visual activities, including music, linguistics, computer pro-
gramming and industrial design. It derives from the Abstract art of the early twentieth
century and is 'a style distinguished by severity of means, clarity of form, and

9.10 A minimalist pool design brings the world
into a garden.

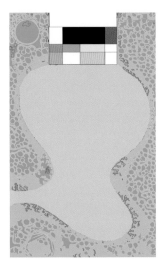

9.11 Diagram of the Abstract style, with de Stijl paving and Expressionist planting.

9.12 New Ways, a Modern house by Peter Behrens standing on a perfunctory Arts and Crafts rockery.

simplicity of structure and texture'.[17] Minimalist architecture and gardens owe much to the de Stijl movement.

Modern planting design has tended to be non-geometric and expressive. Designers have treated plants as abstract shapes and colours, composing them as a foil to the geometry of Neoplasticist and Cubist art. The immediate inspiration for this design idea is uncertain but it relates to the Picturesque theory that planting design should take its lead from painting. Images formed by overlaying vegetation patterns on a structured geometrical background are characteristic of Modern gardens. Two possible contemporary sources for the imagery are Abstract Expressionism (see p. 377) and Abstract sculpture.

Abstract sculpture appears to have influenced the design of landform and the layout of planting areas. It is normal practice to create landform designs with a soft pencil or a clay maquette. Both media lend themselves to the kind of shapes and patterns seen in the work of Jean Arp, Constantin Brancuzi, Henry Moore and Barbara Hepworth. They use what might be called muscular organic curves.

Abstraction in British gardens

The diagram of the Abstract style shows a transition from a rectilinear paved area into a curvilinear planted area. It is intended for comparison with the previous diagrams but represents a garden of perhaps as little as 0.1 hectares while some of the earlier diagrams showed estates of 1,000 hectares and more. In many cases the Modern 'terrace' will be no more than a patio outside a French window but here the use of square slabs with prominent joints reminds one of the de Stijl aesthetic. Parts of the design idea were implemented but, especially in the British Isles, the potential remained largely unrealised in the first half of the twentieth century. Russell Page looked back on British gardens made between 1900 and 1930 in his autobiography and criticised their design strategy, stating that 'a ragbag of styles has nothing to do with real style'.[18] He and other designers recognised the Abstract spatial qualities of Classical gardens, and introduced them into their own work. But they did little to explore the design potential of Modern art and modern materials in garden design.

Christopher Tunnard was one of the first British authors to urge a connection between Modern art and garden design. He published an article on Japanese gardens in *Landscape and Garden* in 1935 and commented that their lack of superfluous ornament has 'a special appeal to the modern mind of all countries'.[19] In 1938, he wrote a series of articles for the *Architectural Review* which attracted attention and were republished as *Gardens in the Modern Landscape*. It became an important textbook

and is often referred to by garden designers who trained in the 1950s as 'the only book we had'. Tunnard opens with the assertion 'A garden is a work of art'[20] and soon reveals himself to be a disciple of the Modern movement. In 1937, he even co-authored a manifesto on garden design with an international comrade. Tunnard and Jean Canneel-Claes proclaimed:

> *We believe in the probity of the creative act ... the reliance of the designer on his own knowledge and experience and not on the academic symbolism of the styles or outworn systems of aesthetics, to create by experiment and invention new forms which are significant of the age from which they spring.*[21]

Tunnard believed that garden designers should 'return to functionalism' and he used quotations from Le Corbusier: 'The styles are a lie', and Adolf Loos: 'To find beauty in form instead of making it depend on ornament is the goal to which humanity is aspiring.'[22] Above all he believed that 'The modern house requires modern surroundings, and in most respects the garden of today does not fulfil this need.'[23] His point was well made by a photograph of a crisp white rectangular Modern house in Northampton, by Peter Behrens, which sits uncomfortably on top of a Jekyllesque dry stone wall and a semi-circular flight of steps which 'fail entirely to harmonize with the character of the house'.[24] The Behrens house was in fact the first in England to be designed in the International style. The public seem to have looked at Tunnard's photograph and decided that the garden was delightful and the house an abomination.

9.13 a–f Abstract Modern landscape architecture. (a) and (b) the Water Gardens, in Edgware, London, designed by Philip Hicks; (c) and (d) the Barbican, by Chamberlin, Powell and Bon; (e) Bishop's Square by Townshend Landscape Architects; (f) More London by Townshend Landscape Architects.

9.14 Modernist architects, thinking 'ornament is crime', often preferred landscapes to gardens as settings for Functionalist buildings.

Garden designers' ambivalent attitude to Modernism presents the historian of Modernist outdoor design in Britain with five anomalies. First, Modernism had little influence on gardens. Second, the designers of Modernist houses had little interest in Abstract gardens. Third, Modernism had a wide influence in the public realm of landscape architecture, which is not the main subject of this book. Fourth, the influence of Abstract art on gardens has been increasing since *c.*1972, which is the date Jencks gives for the death of Modern architecture (see p. 357). This trend could be viewed as another species of revivalism, with Modernism 'a resource to draw on like any other',[25] but it was also a consequence of the fact that designers became more concerned with functions and increasingly adept with modern techniques and materials. They learned to manipulate glass, water and steel with modern cutting, fastening and electronic technology. Fifth, one could argue that Modern gardens were almost Postmodern before they were Modern (see p. 386).

Tim Richardson points out that Modernist architects preferred to design houses in which 'the entrance front consisted either of a large, curving asphalt area for car parking, or else grass running up to the house with small groups of trees or a fringe of shrubs, while the rear garden was generally laid to lawn, again right up to the house'.[26] He regards this taste as left-wing. Architects saw gardens as 'a bourgeois preoccupation'. They were influenced by Le Corbusier, who cared more about the relationship of buildings to landscapes than about the relationship of houses to gardens. Modernist British architects echoed the landscape milieu in the house names

9.15 a, b The Albert Memorial was the bête noire of Abstract Modern designers.

they chose, using 'words such as "hill", "view", "high", "wood", "sea", "orchard", or the names of specific trees such as "beech" or "pine"'.[27] Gardens were seen as ornaments – and potential 'crimes'. Rejecting gardens was seen as a way of rejecting the hated Victorian era of stiff collars, encrusted decoration and social discrimination.

Nineteenth-century garden authors, including Repton and Loudon, had believed in the co-ordination of architectural ornament with garden ornament. Prince Albert, speaking as President of the Royal Horticultural Society in 1861, argued that it was necessary 'to reunite the science and art of gardening to the sister arts of architecture, sculpture, and painting'. He explained:

> *This union existed in the best periods of art, when the same feelings pervaded and the same principles regulated them all; and if the misuse and misapplication of these principles in latter times have forced again upon us the simple study and imitation of Nature, individual arts have suffered by their disjunction, and the time seems now arrived when they may once more combine without the danger of being cramped by pedantic and arbitrary rules of taste.*[28]

Prince Albert died of typhoid shortly after making this speech and the memorial Queen Victoria erected to his memory came to symbolise what the Modernists hated. Completed in 1872, it was historicist, eclectic, highly ornamented and placed like a

365

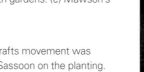

9.16 a, b, c (a) Parque Güell, by Gaudi, and (b) Frank Lloyd Wright's Robie House (1910) showed that a Modern design style was possible, integrating architecture with gardens. (c) Mawson's drawings ridicule Art Nouveau and Art Deco.

9.17 a, b Port Lympne was made in the 1920s when the Arts and Crafts movement was evolving into Abstract Modernism. Norah Lindsay advised Sir Philip Sassoon on the planting.

statue in a Baroque garden. It was built near the site of the original Crystal Palace, which Pevsner identified as one of the sources of Modern architecture. Owen Jones, author of the famous *Grammar of Ornament* (1856), had been Paxton's superintendent of works for the Great Exhibition of 1851 and was appalled at the standard of taste seen in the exhibition and now illustrated by the Albert Memorial. But Jones admired the Crystal Palace itself (see Figure 8.15) and argued that:

All works of the Decorative Arts to be perfect should possess fitness, proportion, harmony, and, as a general result, repose. The great fault of our age was want of purpose in decoration. Walls were ornamented like carpets, and vice versa, without regard to fitness, proportion, or harmony; iron was treated like stone, and wood in the same style as marble. Then, also, construction, he contended, should be decorated – decoration never purposely be constructed. That which was beautiful was sure to be true, at the same time that that which is true must of necessity be beautiful.[29]

The adoption of fitness, proportion and harmony as Abstract design principles rescued garden design from the stylistic confusions of the nineteenth century. But the popularity of Arts and Crafts style gardens in the first half of the twentieth century caused a delay, sheltering their owners and patrons from the explosion of creative energy which generated the Modern movement in art and architecture. In continental Europe and America the response of garden designers to Modern art was faster but still hesitant. By 1900, Gaudi had shown at the Parque Güell in Barcelona that Art Nouveau, then known in Britain as the 'modern style', was suited to the layout of parks and gardens. By 1910, Frank Lloyd Wright's design for the Robie House in Chicago had shown that the lines of Modern structures could extend into the design of outdoor space.

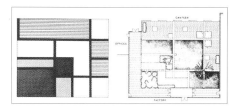

9.18 Abstract diagrams for the Penguin Books courtyard at Heathrow, by John Brookes.

There were social and political aspects to Britain's reluctance to embrace Modernism. High style had a dilettante appeal for some members of the landowning class but they lacked revolutionary fervour. Sir Philip Sassoon included Art Deco features in the Port Lympne garden but the plan style and use of compartments were fundamentally Arts and Crafts. Sassoon was a gay Liberal MP. He was not a socialist and probably saw the Bauhaus as a left-wing organisation. Its Manifesto referred to it being 'the rallying point for all those who, with faith in the future and willingness to storm the heavens, wish to build the cathedral of socialism'.[30] Britain's upper class did not share this wish.

9.19 a, b, c Modern water gardens were made for the 1951 Festival of Britain: (a) on the South Bank; (b) and (c) in Battersea Park (designed by James Gardener, modified by Russell Page, restored by Wandsworth Council).

Nor did garden designers themselves have much interest in Modern art. It was assailed by the leading designers of the day when it appeared over England's skies. In 1916, Thomas Mawson poked fun at the 'art nouveau craze' and lectured on 'the ridiculous ornament and the exaggerated design which this over-enthusiastic cult produced'.[31] In 1934, Reginald Blomfield, knighted in 1919, devoted a whole book to attacking the Modern movement. He believed that 'our younger generation, trained exclusively in our architectural schools, are convinced that they are introducing a new

9.20 a, b Jellicoe's first large-scale garden design was for Ditchley Park. It was Abstract in conception and he described the design as 'a testament to classical values in a world in constant change'.[32]

era in architecture'. Blomfield therefore saw it as his loyal duty 'to do what I can to rescue a noble art from the degradation into which it seems to be sinking'.[33]

Geoffrey Jellicoe and Jock Shepherd had the education Blomfield reviled. After leaving the Architectural Association, the friends toured the gardens of Italy, with more interest in spatial composition than iconography. The beautiful pen and wash drawings in their *Italian Gardens of the Renaissance* (1925) reveal the Abstract spatial qualities of the old gardens they admired. The authors remark, 'The bases of abstract design, running through history like a silver thread, are independent of race and age.'[34] A second book, on *Gardens and Design* by the same authors and published in 1927, illustrated a house and garden by Frank Lloyd Wright and praised him for grasping 'the colossal latent power that lies behind the subject'.[35] A series of articles by Jellicoe appeared in the *Architects' Journal* during 1931 and 1932. The designs were Classical. The discussion was analytical. In 1933, Jellicoe and Russell Page were commissioned by the American-born Ronald Tree to design an Italian garden at Ditchley Park. The owner specifically wanted an Italian garden and Jellicoe comments:

> I had certainly studied the Italian garden in detail, but except for abortive designs for a new landscape at Claremont some years previously, my experience in the actual design and execution of the classics was nil. My aesthetic inclinations, indeed, were wholly for the modern movement in art, fostered by teaching at the Architectural Association's School of Architecture ... Casting aside therefore all thoughts of twentieth-century art, of Picasso and Le Corbusier and Frank Lloyd Wright, I threw myself enthusiastically into a unique study of landscape history made real.[36]

9.21 a, b The Caveman Restaurant (a) in 1934 and (b) in 2009 had an Abstract Modern water garden – which, because of its narrative content, can also be classified as Postmodern (see p. 389). It was designed by Geoffrey Jellicoe and Russell Page.

Ditchley Park was the last major British garden to be designed in the Italian manner. But in comparison with the Renaissance gardens which inspired its design, Ditchley Park is Abstract. It is without a narrative and it lacks the artistic iconography which characterised Renaissance gardens. Page, who worked with Jellicoe at Ditchley, used an abstracted Classicism throughout his career.

Jellicoe received a number of smaller commissions in the 1930s which provided opportunities to introduce elements of the Abstract style. The frontispiece to *The Studio*'s 1932 *Garden Annual* shows a garden by Shepherd and Jellicoe with a distinctly Modern flavour. Then, in 1933, Jellicoe and Page worked together on the design of the Caveman Restaurant and garden in the Cheddar Gorge. The project was widely illustrated in the 1930s as an example of Modern architecture but only part of the garden was built and it has since been wrecked. An interesting aspect of the design, when compared with Ditchley Park, is that it has a narrative (see p. 389).

In 1953, when Peter Shepheard wrote a book on *Modern Gardens*, it was still necessary to look abroad for examples of private gardens that had been influenced by Modern art.[37] His foreign examples included gardens by Thomas Church, Roberto Burle Marx and Jean Canneel-Claes. The most notable British garden in the book was Bentley Wood at Halland, owned by Serge Chermayeff (see p. 370). Its designer, Christopher Tunnard, came closer than any of his contemporaries to both designing a Modern garden and making the case for a radically Modernist approach to garden design and landscape architecture. His influence was stronger in the US than in the

9.22 a, b Christopher Tunnard's design for the garden of Bentley Wood House at Halland.

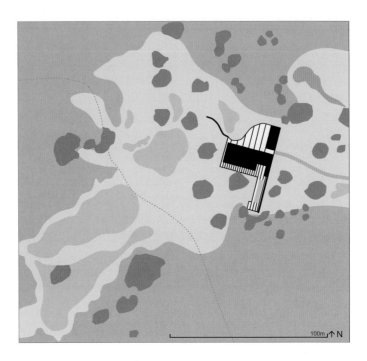

UK.[38] But illustrations in Shepheard's book showed that it was possible to design gardens which could stand as Modern works of art but it would be difficult, even today, to fill a book with examples of wholly Abstract British gardens.

The kind of garden which ought to accompany a Modern building is illustrated by a photograph of Bentley Wood, designed by Tunnard. It was an austerely elegant Modern design. The garden owes nothing to 'the second stone age with its plethora of flagged paths and dry walls'.[39] A sculpture by Henry Moore helped to make another of Tunnard's points:

> *The best of contemporary architecture is closely related to the best of modern sculpture and constructivist painting because architects, sculptors and constructivist painters are in written or personal contact with one another.*[40]

Internationalism, fraternity and socialism were important Bauhaus principles. In 1919, Walter Gropius wrote:

> *Let us create a new guild of craftsmen, without the class distinctions which raise an arrogant barrier between craftsmen and artist. Together, let us conceive and create the new building of the future, which will embrace architecture 'and' sculpture 'and' painting in one unity and which will one day rise toward heaven from the hands of a million workers, like the crystal symbol of a new faith.*[41]

The Bentley Wood project became the crystal symbol of a new faith for British garden designers.

9.23 High Point, Highgate, London, by Tecton. The Constructivist aesthetic of the building is offset by the caryatids and the planting. Jellicoe lived here after leaving his house in Grove Terrace.

9.24 a, b Frederick Gibberd's own garden was Abstract Modern around the house and had Expressionist planting in the garden below.

The most important British design school to adopt the new faith was the Architectural Association (AA) in London. Tunnard was a member of the Modern Architecture Research (MARS) Group which was based at the AA and played an important part in introducing Modern architecture to England. He was probably the author of a 1938 article in *Landscape and Garden* by 'a member of the MARS Group' which proclaimed that if 'lofty buildings, flat roofs, reinforced concrete and a remapping of the country-side' are 'necessary for the betterment of social conditions', then members of the MARS Group 'will not hesitate to advocate them'.[42] For a short time in the 1930s members of the Group had made it possible to say that 'England leads the world in modern architectural activity'.[43] Staff and students at the AA were inspired to create Modern buildings with Modern surroundings. Geoffrey Jellicoe, Frederick Gibberd, Peter Shepheard and Hugh Casson all trained at the AA and later became prominent members of the Institute of Landscape Architects (ILA). Jellicoe and Shepheard became Presidents of the AA and then of the ILA.

9.25 a, b Jellicoe designed the Water Garden in Hemel Hempstead, inspired by the shape of a serpent, and a roof garden for a department store in Guildford, inspired by the launch of the Russian Sputnik.

The future of the Abstract style of garden design after World War II lay with the professional designers who joined the ILA after its formation in 1929. Tunnard left England in 1939 to become a Professor of City Planning at Yale University but his book was republished in 1948 and had a considerable influence on post-war designers in England and America. The first major opportunity for British designers came with the Festival of Britain in 1951. Hugh Casson was the design director of the Festival and landscape architects were employed on its gardens. They included Peter Shepheard, Russell Page, Peter Youngman and Frank Clark. Clark had worked with Tunnard on *Gardens in the Modern Landscape* and led the only full-time landscape design course in the UK, at Reading University. Youngman ran a part-time course at University College in London. A number of photographs of the Festival were included in Peter Shepheard's *Modern Gardens*. The hard detailing was influenced by the de Stijl aesthetic but the way in which it was enlivened by planting and water-washed stones appears to derive from Tunnard's analysis of Japanese gardens. Crisp geometry was offset by natural shapes and patterns.

Many of the designers who joined the ILA before 1939 did so because of their interest in private gardens. After 1946, they found few clients to commission private garden designs. There was, however, a greatly increased demand for landscape designers to work in the public sector: on housing estates, new towns, reservoirs, factories and power stations. It was on these projects that the Abstract style flourished in the 1950s and 1960s. Such projects lie outside the scope of this book but are surveyed by Tony Aldous and Brian Clouston in *Landscape by Design*.[44] There are many public spaces in the new towns which illustrate the style: in Harlow by Gibberd and Sylvia Crowe, in Hemel Hempstead by Geoffrey Jellicoe, in Stevenage by Gordon Patterson and in Cumbernauld by Peter Youngman and William Gillespie.

A number of books illustrating the Abstract style in private gardens were aimed at the general public. In 1953, Lady Allen of Hurtwood and Susan Jellicoe wrote a book on *Gardens* for Penguin Books.[45] Lady Allen had worked with the New Homes For Old group which supported the cause of Modern architecture in the 1930s. The book contained photographs of gardens designed by Thomas Church, Garrett Eckbo, C. Th. Sorensen and other foreign pioneers of the Abstract style.

In 1958, Sylvia Crowe published a book on *Garden Design* which contains a thoughtful analysis of the Abstract qualities of gardens, in the chapters on the principles and materials of design. Her discussion of the Four Faces urn at Bramham Park illustrates the analytical nature of her approach and her belief that 'underlying all the greatest gardens are certain principles of composition which remain unchanged because they are rooted in the natural laws of the universe':[46]

9.26 The Four Faces urn at Bramham Park, West Yorkshire, was used by Sylvia Crowe to illustrate the Abstract qualities of gardens which 'are rooted in the natural laws of the universe'.

> The long vista at Bramham Park, Yorkshire, looks across a pool and the end is marked by a huge urn. The two do not compete, but are complementary, forming together one composition. The dominant vertical figure is completed by the calm horizontal pool which does nothing to prevent the eye travelling easily on its way to the terminal point.[47]

This analysis contrasts with the eighteenth-century associationism of Archibald Alison, who valued the urn at Hagley Hall because it was 'chosen by Mr Pope for the spot and now inscribed to his memory'.[48] Crowe's approach also differs from the stylistic approach of Loudon and Kemp. Loudon advised that urns and statues should be placed only where they can be 'viewed in connection with some architectural production'.[49] Kemp advised that 'statuary, vases, and similar architectural ornaments, are the fitting associates of Grecian and Italian houses, and appear less suitable in relation to every other style'.[50]

John Brookes, who worked for a time in the office of Sylvia Crowe and Brenda Colvin, became well known in the 1970s for applying Abstract principles to garden design. His books achieved a wide readership. They showed that gardens could be Abstract and Modern without resorting to the austerity of the house at Halland. The photographs in his books show warm, friendly and useful spaces. Brookes's plans and diagrams show the Abstract geometrical patterns which led to their spatial organisation.

9.27 a, b Abstract Modernism began to influence designs exhibited at the Chelsea Flower Show after *c*.1980 and by 2000 it had superseded the former dominance of Arts and Crafts ideas.

His design for the Penguin Books courtyard at Heathrow was used in *Room Outside* to illustrate the point that 'looking at modern paintings can also help one to see how areas of colour and texture can be counter-positioned to form a balanced whole'.[51] The design was generated by a Mondrian-type drawing which was geared to the modular pattern of the building and then translated into areas of paving, grass, water and planting (see Figure 9.18).

Planting design

Planting design is a Modern conception. Before the nineteenth century, most garden space was used to grow fruit and vegetables. Other space was used, at various dates, to make herbers, knots, parterres, flower gardens, shrubberies, herbaceous borders and other features. The Modern idea of designing with plants, much as one would use an artist's palette, grew out of the nineteenth century and blossomed in the twentieth century. Plants, like gardens, were abstracted from their historic roles. Designers' attention became focused on planting design as an opportunity to make beautiful compositions involving colour, line, form, texture, rhythm, punctuation and other abstractions. Plant functions were also considered but there was no 'Functionalist' effort to derive the aesthetic quality of plant compositions from their utilitarian roles – and the list of 'functions' rarely included growing fruit and vegetables. Many of the beds and compartments in old gardens were therefore given over to aesthetic compositions of exotic plants. Careless of the solecism,

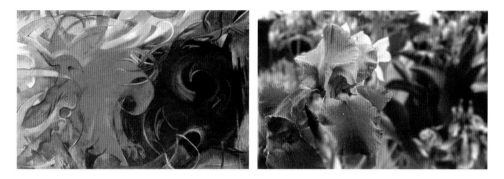

9.28 a, b Non-explicitly, Expressionism has influenced planting designers. (a) Franz Marc's *Fighting Forms* (1914). (b) A garden parallel to Marc's painting.

9.29 a–h British garden designers' enthusiasm for Abstract Expressionism is best seen in their planting designs.

9.30 Henry Moore sculptures in Kew Gardens. His work was inspired by natural forms and, in its turn, inspired the design of Abstract plant and landform compositions.

estate owners began to speak of 'restoring' an 'old walled garden' when they were converting it from a vegetable garden to an Abstract composition of flowers and shrubs.

Sylvia Crowe's *Garden Design* (1958) has a chapter on 'The Contemporary Garden' which refers to a style which 'began to emerge in northern Europe during the first half of the century'.[52] She does not give it a name but associates it with the work of Burle Marx in Mexico, Gustav Ammann in Switzerland, Lawrence Halprin in America, and other international Modernist designers. In subsequent chapters, on 'The Principles of Design', 'Land Form' and 'Plants', Crowe's aim is to abstract design principles from the world's gardens. Her approach to planting design is Abstract and, with narrow limits, Functionalist:

> *Physically, the function of planting is to give shelter, shade and protection, visually, it determines the proportion and form of the garden, the contrast between closed and open space and its division. It provides texture, framing, background, tone and sculptural form.*[53]

Crowe's use of the word 'sculptural' is interesting and it is a pity she did not write more about it. I worked in her office for a time and recall the gestures, vocabulary, phraseology and soft pencil lines she used when talking about plants and planting. Her approach to planting was sculptural and she writes that:

> *The strong affinity between sculpture and landscape evinced by Henry Moore was the forerunner of a marriage between landscape and modern sculpture which can now be seen in many countries. The sculptures take their place within a free-flowing landscape, as an element in the natural scene, conforming to and accentuating the character of the site.*[54]

With regard to colour, Crowe, like Jekyll, advises her readers to 'treat the colour of plants as if they were the colours on a palette and paint pictures with them' (see Figure 9.31).[55] Since the 'pictures' were non-representational, it is an Abstract approach. She writes that herbaceous borders should have 'a backbone of strong form'[56] with the colours planned like 'an abstract painting'.[57] *The Scream*, by Edvard Munch, was a response to seeing 'clouds like blood and tongues of fire hung above the blue-black fjord and the city'.[58] It is an Expressionist painting which, like a planting design, exists at the artistic boundaries between man, nature, expression, abstraction and representation.

Expressionist planting design became the dominant feature of English gardens in the twentieth century. Penelope Hobhouse, after experimenting with colour at Tintinhull House, wrote a book on *Colour in Your Garden*.[59] Nori and Sandra Pope followed her example at Hadspen, and wrote a book on *Colour by Design: Planting the Contemporary Garden*.[60] Tim Richardson writes of

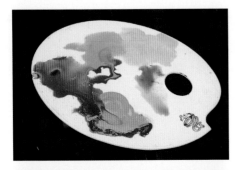

9.31 a, b Palettes: of paint and plants.

a period when theories of colour had become well established and gardens such as Hadspen in Somerset could concentrate on minute, almost scientific gradations of colours in combination; a period when gardeners seemed to vie with each other to produce as many scintillating or unusual plant contrasts as possible. The result was gardens that appeared to be on steroids, so full of 'wow factor' that the attentive visitor came away either exhilarated and in awe of the spectacle of it all, or else exhausted, confused and faintly nauseous.[61]

The planting is best understood as Abstract painting, using plants instead of paints. Its function is purely aesthetic and, since it was the primary component of many twentieth-century gardens, it deserves to be seen as 'more than ornament'.[62]

CHAPTER 10

Post-Abstract and sustainable gardens, post-1980

10.0 a, b Derek Jarman's Prospect Cottage is inscribed with 16 lines from John Donne's *The Sun Rising*, ending with: 'Shine here to us, and thou art everywhere; /This bed thy center is, these walls thy sphere.'[1] Jarman's design is Pre-Modern, Un-Modern and Postmodern. It exemplifies Repton's precept: 'The plan must be made not only to fit the spot, it ought actually to be made upon the spot.'[2] *Crambe maritima* was once a vegetable; it is now an ornamental plant; it is used by Jarman as an element in a work of conceptual art.

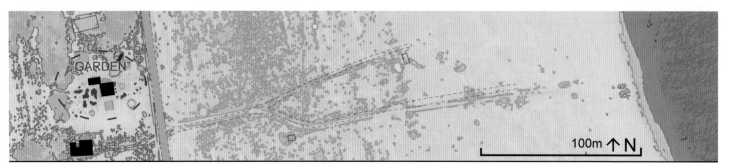

10.1 Derek Jarman's garden is part of one of the largest shingle beaches in the world. It uses pebbles, driftwood, found objects and local plant species, including sea pea, sea kale, sea beet and sea campion.

Introduction

Abstract gardens whisper. Post-Abstract gardens speak their minds. The manifestos which launched Modern art, architecture and even garden design, were far from silent. Artists were screaming for a break with tradition. Designers were dreaming of crystal worlds with clean shapes, white walls, abstract geometry and total freedom from representation. The British public did not heed these cries. Perhaps they heard a cry to reject family, home, country and tradition. Britain's collective response was 'always keep a-hold of Nurse/ For fear of finding something worse'.[3] Architects with public clients were better able to push forward their Modernist agendas and often carried landscape architects with them. Landscape design was silenced. But the Abstract style was disliked by the public and had little influence on private gardens until c.1970 (see p. 364).

Disenchantment with Modernism led to an approach which Charles Jencks categorised as 'Postmodern'. His first definition of the term was 'one-half modern and one-half something else – usually a traditional or regional language of building'.[4] Jencks studied literature before studying architecture and transposed the term 'Postmodern' from literary criticism to design criticism. His clear explanations and sharp illustrations, in *The Language of Post-Modern Architecture* encouraged use of the term, especially by the building designers. Jencks argued that Modernism had failed, because it did not communicate with non-architects. This consideration encouraged designers to explore various styles and devices:

> Often these styles came from the pre-modernist past, as architects turned to history for inspiration, thus marking an emphatic shift away from the modernist obsession with newness. The embellishment and decoration outlawed by the International Style returned in postmodernism, in the form of quotation. A post-modern building was a mix of styles from different historical periods; eclecticism replaced purity as the governing artistic principle, Modernist style was now simply one style among many from which to choose.[5]

Postmodernism embraces aspects of Modernism but aims to move forward, often by looking back. The contrast between the approaches is shown in Table 10.1.

10.2 a, b, c (a) Marco Polo House became a symbol of 1980s Postmodern architecture. Its designer, Ian Pollard, was a non-architect and non-landscape architect who became a non-Modern gardener. The ragwort (*Senecio jacobaea*) is welcome as an adventitious element in an otherwise-banal 'office landscape'. (b) and (c) In his own Post-Abstract garden, in Malmesbury, Pollard transmutes hedging into sculpture and bubbles into baubles.

Table 10.1 **Comparison of Modernism and Postmodernism**

Modernism	Postmodernism
Form follows function	Function follows forms
Less is more	Less is bore
Truth to materials	Wit with materials
Ornament is crime	Decoration is gorgeous
The styles are dead	The styles should be quoted
Story telling is dead	Story telling is fun
Use modern materials	Use modern *and* ancient materials
Minimalism	Maximalism

10.3 Alan Titchmarsh, Britain's best-known gardener, at the 2009 Chelsea Flower Show. Having struggled to come to terms with Abstract design, British gardeners are now struggling with conceptually Post-Abstract design. The Show Catalogue says Luciano Giubbilei's garden is 'dominated by classic lines of yew, box and hornbeam ... exemplifying the relationship between architecture and gardens', with Nigel Hall's sculpture, *Big Bite*, seen to explore 'the connection between geometry and landscape'.[6]

Postmodernism became a key concept in academic and cultural discourse but has been little used in connection with gardens. I was disappointed, when writing this chapter, to find that a web search on 'Postmodern+garden+design'[7] produced little useful information on Postmodern gardens: the first six links on the search results page were to texts I myself had written. The next four links were to pages on Postmodern interiors which happened to include the word 'garden'. A search on 'Modernist+garden+design' was more rewarding, though most of the search returns used 'Modernist' as a synonym for contemporary. The return at the top of the results page, from eHow.com, was the most useful, but relied on architectural ideas to explain the Modernist garden:

10.4 a–d The Diana Memorial Fountain
was designed by Kathryn Gustafson. She is
'a conceptualist landscape designer – that
is, a designer who makes spaces, most of
them public, which are predicated first of all
on ideas opposed to decorative horticulture
or the geometric certainties of architectural
Modernism'.[8] The granite, an ancient material
sculpted like concrete, had to be roughened
when users invented a function for the fountain:
cooling their feet.

10.5 This feature is described on the
West Green House website as 'a dramatic
new Persian water garden in a woodland'.[9]
Geometrically, it is a Postmodern quotation.
Functionally, it has no relationship with Islamic
gardens.

EXISTING SITE 1:500   ▲ July 15 1972

10.6 a, b 'The Rill' at Stillingfleet Garden. The geometry is recent but the name and lack of functionality are Postmodern: in the water channel, the cascade, the use of *Stipa gigantea* and the space itself. In Indian gardens a *chahar bagh* supplies water and a *chadar* relieves the heat and aridity. *Stipa* enjoys double codings: it was not used in Modernist gardens and the plant group (*Gramineae*) was associated with wild nature.

10.7 a, b Scampston Hall. Piet Oudolf reincarnated the vegetable garden with Postmodern planting. It is treated as Abstract art but with quotations from garden history and the natural environment (waves, a mount, etc.).

10.8 a, b Modernist designs were drawn on white paper. Postmodern designs respond to contextual data.

Modernist principles in gardening come from the Modernist style of architecture, which emerged at the beginning of the twentieth century. This made use of the newest technological developments to design buildings that did not have to rely on traditional building techniques. Reinforced concrete could be molded into exciting new forms, creating lighter buildings with bigger interconnected spaces and uncluttered interiors. Today there is a new wave of Modernist thinking, which regards the garden as an outside room that is linked with the house. Key elements of the building's architecture, such as doors and windows, will be repeated as elements of the garden.[10]

The 2006 edition of the *Oxford Companion to Gardens* was equally disappointing. The only two occurrences of the word 'Postmodern' I found were in entries on Hungary and on Slovenia. Despite not adopting the term, garden designers and clients seem more sympathetic to the fecundity of Postmodernism than the austerity of Modernism. Literary theory and design theory are now treating 'Postmodern' as a historical period which has ended, with some talk of post-Postmodernism[11]

10.9 The Penguin Pool in London Zoo, designed by Tecton in 1933, was not popular with the penguins and is now a vacant monument. The concrete was hard underfoot and the pool was too shallow for diving. The form did not, in reality, follow the function. And, unlike the Diana Memorial Fountain (Figure 10.4), the shapes were non-symbolic.

10.10 a, b Brian Yale made a conceptual-contextual garden at Dungeness, near Derek Jarman's garden. He had been an Abstract painter.

and some of Maximalism, as the obvious successor to Minimalism.[12] Maximalism is an approach in which 'ornament is no longer a crime, architecture is more curvaceous, fashion more glamorous, design more decorative'.[13] Garden designers have responded to 'Postmodern' ideas and attitudes, while making little use of the term. This can, for example, be seen in the design of features which 'quote' historic design ideas without trying to create imitations of historic designs.

Abstract architecture began on blank paper and blank screens. This resulted in isolated and self-contained designs which could be equally successful and unsuccessful in any part of any world. But garden and landscape design are inherently place-specific arts. They cleave to an ancient principle: we *must* 'consult the genius of the place' (see p. 40 and p. 281). Roman, Renaissance, Baroque and landscape gardens were always designed in response to, and in a relationship with, their surroundings.

Internationalism was an aspect of the abstractionism which characterised Modernism. Context-sensitive design is a localising principle. It runs against the internationalism, Modernism and *Zeitgeist*-ism. Modernist design theory was based on reason and empirical science. Places were not understood to have intrinsic characteristics which might constrain hot-headed young designers' freedom of expression. Then, since reason was everywhere the same, it was easy to justify an everywhere-the-same design approach. Building forms were generated from internal functions; Abstract

10.11 a, b Derek Jarman saw his stone circles as mini-megaliths (see also p. 379).

design worked from inside to outside. It became a scientific procedure, though largely disregarding the biological and social sciences. Post-Abstract design worked from outside to inside, drawing more from cultural theory than from the sciences.

Derek Jarman, who was a film director, began with the local landscape. He collected local stones, plants, driftwood and rusty iron. His ideas were those of artist and poet, not a scientist or a Functionalist. He wrote:

> *I invest my stones with the power of those at Avebury. I have read all the mystical books about ley-lines and circles – I built the circles with this behind my mind. The circles make the garden perfect – in winter they take over from the flowers.*[14]

10.12 There is a Postmodern aspect to Frederick Gibberd's garden, using re-cycled Classical ornament – as quotations (see also p. 380).

Twentieth-century garden designers were unwilling, and unable, to produce designs which, like cars, office blocks or mobile phones, could be globalised. They were compelled, for example, to consider local conditions when choosing plant material. One can therefore view their work as proto-Postmodern, even in the 1920s, and linguistically this would not be an anachronism. The first use of the word 'Postmodern' was in 1870 and its first appearance in a book title was in 1926. The book was by Canon Bernard Iddings Bell: *Postmodernism and Other Essays*.[15] Bell, who thought secular Modernism had abstracted religion from its fundamentals, argued for a Postmodern re-incorporation of religion with its fundamentals and with science. In a comparable manner, Modern architecture was abstracted from local landscapes and garden designers sought re-incorporation.

Shepherd and Jellicoe's *Italian Gardens of the Renaissance* appeared in 1926 (see p. 368). There is a parallelism between Jellicoe's argument and Bell's. Both men were interested in drawing significant principles from the past and adapting them to current circumstances. Jellicoe wished to abstract historic design principles for his design practice. In books and drawings, which he continued to produce over 70 years, Jellicoe's approach was always Postmodern. He had a bubbling enthusiasm for the modern world but did not want it to be abstracted from history. Jellicoe said that he learned about Modernism from his friend, Frederick Gibberd, and it may be that the historicist strand in Gibberd's Modernism was inspired by Jellicoe. We can group them as proto-Postmodern.

Proto-Postmodernism

Geoffrey Jellicoe

Jellicoe's text, in *Italian Gardens of the Renaissance*, opens as follows:

> *Pandora never loosed a livelier spirit than the one for ever parting Fancy from Design.*
> *In those rare moments when the demon sleeps, is born a work that stands for all time. So*
> *came into being the finest of the Italian gardens, where, in a world of beautiful thoughts,*
> *Fancy and Design roam undivided.*[16]

Jellicoe never wavered from this creed. His belief that Fancy should be married to Design came from a boyhood fascination with the Classics. His love of poetry and the arts was learned on his mother's lap. She smiled on him, as did the goddess Fortuna. He and a friend wrote Latin verse and delighted in allusions to the Greek Myths. Instead of going to the trenches with the generation that preceded his own, Jellicoe turned 18 in 1918 and was able to combine his two loves, for the arts and the Classics: he enrolled at the Architectural Association. In later life he often recalled that 'I received a pretty good classical education'. The remark covered his schooldays, his student life and the long summer of 1923 when he and Jock Shepherd toured the gardens of Italy. Shepherd drew. Jellicoe wrote. Neither could match the other's skill.

'Fancy' was once a standard term in literary criticism. Dr Johnson's *Dictionary of the English Language* (1755) has 'Fancy' as a synonym for 'Imagination'.[17] Both terms referred to the verbal playfulness characteristic of poetry. Reason produced the content; Imagination, or Fancy, gave it form. Under the influence of Coleridge and Romanticism, 'Fancy' and 'Imagination' took on separate meanings. 'Imagination' came to be used for the fundamental creative power which generates works of art: the ability to interpret sensory experience, apprehend order and synthesise form. 'Fancy' came to be used for the less weighty skill of amusing and delighting the public. Often, it involved associative references to the Classics and historic works of art. Coleridge explained that Milton had a highly imaginative mind, while Cowley's mind was fanciful. Jellicoe wished to combine the playfulness of Fancy with the seriousness of Abstract design.

In *Italian Gardens of the Renaissance*, Jellicoe wrote:

> The bases of abstract design, running through history like a silver thread, are independent of race and age. Their one unchanging form of expression is through pattern, both a wholesome admission of human limitation, and a sturdy foundation from which afterwards to build. Pattern is the architectural prototype of the formality of life, and in the same way is modified by the circumstances of moment, principally those governing the relation of formality to informality.[19]

In the Epilogue to *The Landscape of Man*, Jellicoe wrote:

> In landscape design, the first projection of individual personality has been the complex of home, garden and forest tree ... Man's new relation to environment is revolutionary and the landscape designer, unlike the artist, is conditioned by many factors that debar immediate experiment. We must therefore turn to the artists for a vision of the future, gaining confidence in the knowledge that the abstract art that lurks behind all art lives a life of its own, independent of time and space.[20]

Though separated by half a century, these observations are similar. Jellicoe speaks of a creative power, which is a 'projection of individual personality'. He also believes in the existence of principles 'of abstract design, running through history like a silver thread'. At the end of his career, as at the start, Jellicoe believed there were two essential components in a landscape design: individual creativity and the principles of Abstract design. In the 1920s he called them 'Fancy' and 'Design'. Probably, he was more interested in Abstract design at the start of his career and in creativity at the end of his career.

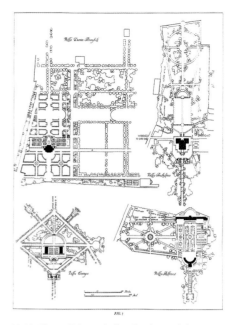

10.13 Figure 7 from *Italian Gardens of the Renaissance*. Jellicoe abstracted the essential nature of Italian gardens as 'long avenues and walks interrupted with open squares, and cross avenues leading to carefully placed climaxes, each considered to the last detail and in their relationship to the whole scene'.[18]

10.14 a, b, c Sutton Place. (a) The Magritte Walk. (b) The Nicholson Wall. (c) The Paradise Garden, inspired by Giovanni Bellini's *Sacred Allegory*.

'Fancy' became progressively trivialised after the Romantic period, leading to the description 'fancy goods', and was at a low ebb in 1925, except perhaps in poetic discourse. Exponents of Modernism saw ornament as crime. Jellicoe's espousal of 'Fancy' reveals a non-Modernist enthusiasm for the history of art. Since the 1920s, partly under the influence of Carl Gustav Jung, there has been a growing interest in symbolism, allegory, anthropology and comparative religion, regarded as aspects of man's collective experience. Philosophical and artistic developments associated with Postmodernism have revived interest in symbolism and allegory.

Saussurean linguistics led artists, writers and architects to a concern for double-coding and multiple-coding. Jellicoe, though he had only a passing knowledge of

Postmodern theory, knew Maggie and Charles Jencks and was at the forefront of this trend in garden design. With trepidation, I once described Jellicoe in *Building Design* as the landscape profession's 'first post-modern designer'. The next day a postcard arrived 'Dear Tom – thanks for the write-up – all the best – Geoffrey.' Since then, I have felt relaxed about applying the label 'Postmodern' to Jellicoe, more or less in Jencks's sense. Its use in architectural criticism is the probable sense in which Jellicoe understood the term. Jellicoe developed a design approach which draws upon the insights of Spencer, Darwin, Freud, Jung and Einstein. A parallel can be drawn with the design thrust of Jencks's *Architecture of the Jumping Universe*. Jencks even shares Jellicoe's interest in Coleridge:

> *The process of creation, as Arthur Koestler has shown in* The Act of Creation *(1964), demands at least two opposite aspects of the personality: critical reasoning and dreaming aside. These complementary aspects, as Coleridge pointed out in his famous discussion of Imagination, produce 'a more than usual state of emotion, with more than usual order', or a work poised between order and entropy.*[21]

Jellicoe can therefore be regarded as a Postmodernist even at the start of his career. One can detect its presence in his first significant designs, for Ditchley Park and the now-wrecked Caveman Restaurant, in the 1930s (see Figure 9.21). Visitors to the restaurant could look up through the glass fish-pond to see the world through a representation of the miasmal mire from which our species evolved. As a designer, Jellicoe was perhaps too literary, theoretical and experimental to become popular. But some of his themes have found echoes in the work of others. Michael Spens wrote a book about him entitled *Gardens of the Mind* and there was a Garden in Mind at Stansted Park in Hampshire, where Ivan Hicks experimented with Surrealism, as Jellicoe did in the Magritte Garden at Sutton Place.[22]

In 1960, Jellicoe published the first of his *Studies in Landscape Design*. They are inspiring books and give examples of the way in which his own design projects were influenced by Modern artists, including Paul Klee, Jean Arp, Henry Moore, Ben Nicholson and Barbara Hepworth. The *Studies* dealt with public sector projects but in 1968 Susan and Geoffrey Jellicoe published a book which examines Modern gardens from a similar standpoint. Jellicoe comments: 'Just as the mind is responding, in abstract art, to shapes which it appears to seek and even to crave, so it responds to shapes in landscapes.'[23] A major opportunity to apply this idea came with an invitation to prepare designs for Sutton Place. Jellicoe described his meeting with the client as follows:

> *My first visit was on 22 July 1980. I remember nearly stumbling over a Henry Moore sculpture on the floor and observing a Ben Nicholson over the mantelpiece, with a huge Monet close by and a Graham Sutherland in the offing. I realised within a few minutes that Stanley Seeger and I were on the same wave-length in thinking that*

landscape art should be a continuum of past, present and future, and should contain within it the seeds of abstract ideas as well as having figurative meaning.[24]

Sutton Place, in Surrey, contains a Paradise garden based on a serpentine grid with fountains at the nodes, a secret Moss Garden with two hidden circles, a Magritte Walk (with urns from Mentmore), a Miro swimming pool, a lake designed as the setting for a Henry Moore sculpture and a marble wall by Ben Nicholson. The latter is a work of great beauty and represents an artistic ideal which has had an overwhelming influence on the Abstract style of garden design.

Ian Hamilton Finlay

Ian Hamilton Finlay's garden, Little Sparta at Stoneypath, became the most important garden to have been made by a poet since Pope's garden at Twickenham (*c.*1719). In the 1970s, Finlay was Scotland's leading concrete poet. As with the work of other concrete poets, the disposition of the words on the page, or another medium, made a significant contribution to the poem's intonation and connotation. Some poets arranged their words to form circles, squares, spirals and triangles on the printed page. Finlay became interested in working with materials other than paper, including wood, stone, glass, aluminium – and then gardens. The resulting poems do not belong on library shelves, but have attracted many authors.

Little Sparta became an anthological garden. It is 'garden poetry'[25] and it is also a flower garden. 'Anthology' derives from 'ἀνθο-ς', flower, and '-λογια', 'collection'.

10.15 a, b Little Sparta, by Ian Hamilton Finlay. His croft became a temple of garden art and poetry. His *Apollon Terroriste* is a blast against Modernism.

Finlay's garden has links with literature, history, art and philosophy. But he preferred to think of himself as a poet. Concrete poetry arose out of avant-garde Modernism. The 'visual shape is, wherever possible, abstract, the words or letters within it behaving as ideograms'.[26] By treating concrete poems as site-specific sculpture, and garden installations, Finlay was making a Postmodern turn. He complies with Jencks's definition of Postmodern as 'as one-half modern and one-half something else'. Little Sparta is rich in the theoretical aspect of Postmodernism identified by Jencks – double-coding:

> *Of the many ways in which Finlay appropriated earlier traditions none is more crucial than both his deployment of mythology and, especially, of the idea and practice of genius loci. The mytho-topography of Arcadia combines the two.*[27]

Glens, burns, shaws, muirs, allays and lochans became settings for inscribed sculpture: tree-plaques, seats, obelisks, tubs, headstones, columns, sundials and bridges. Finlay's interests, in the *genius loci*, mythology, art and poetry place him in a similar Postmodern category to Derek Jarman.

Conceptualist Postmodernism

Sol LeWitt's definition of conceptual art has been influential, partly because it was the first to appear in print, in 1967:

> *In conceptual art the idea or concept is the most important aspect of the work. When an artist uses a conceptual form of art, it means that all of the planning and decisions are made beforehand and the execution is a perfunctory affair. The idea becomes a machine that makes the art.*[28]

Though often quoted, the definition is not universally agreed. Damien Hirst and Tracey Emin assert that if a work is found in an art gallery 'therefore it is art'.[29] This can be extended to works in gardens attached to art galleries. The neon sign in Figure 10.16 is described as an installation. The Landform UEDA in Figure 10.18 is described by its owners as 'a combination of artwork, garden and social space'.[30] Since it was 'presented to an artworld public' and was inspired by chaos theory, they have every reason to regard it as conceptual art. After writing *The Language of Post-Modern Architecture*, Charles Jencks became involved with garden and landscape design. His own gardens, in London and south-west Scotland, are laden with symbolism. In his terminology, they are double-coded. The primary coding is legible to all. The secondary coding is intelligible only to those who share the designer's knowledge of art, mythology and astro-physics. Jencks is the most notable landscape and garden designer to carry forward the 3500 BCE–1800 CE landscape and garden design

10.16 *There Will Be No Miracles Here* is a conceptual installation, by Nathan Coley. It is in the garden of the Scottish National Gallery of Modern Art – which makes it a work of art.

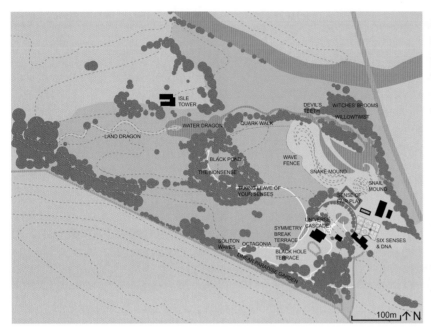

10.17 a, b, c Charles Jencks's Garden of Cosmic Speculation, at Portrack, returns garden design to an ancient root. Plato, in Book X of *The Republic*, wrote that 'God, whether from choice or from necessity, made one bed in nature and one only'.[31] Artists use this as an argument for imitating the essential nature of the world in art. Jencks views natural science as the best way of understanding nature.

10.18 The Scottish National Gallery of Modern Art website states that: 'The lawn at the front of the building was landscaped to a design by Charles Jencks to create Landform UEDA, which comprises a stepped, serpentine-shaped mound complemented by crescent-shaped pools of water. A combination of artwork, garden and social space, the landform was inspired by chaos theory and shapes found in nature.'[32]

agenda (see p. 420). He interprets 'the nature of the world' in garden design. In 2011, Jencks published *The Universe in the Landscape*, seeing Stonehenge as 'part of a ritual landscape, an area conceived in aesthetic and symbolic terms … when I return again and again to the ancient landforms, they convince me of such perennial motives. These nurture my own practice.'[33]

The design in Figure 10.19 has a kinship with Jencks's design and can be claimed for conceptual art. It is described as a 'Folded Landscape' with the idea coming from Gilles Deleuze, directly or indirectly.[34] Deleuze followed Spinoza and departed from Plato, in viewing the world as having a single reality. He was particularly interested in the way it keeps 'folding' as the world evolves:

> *All things are present to God, who complicates them. God is present to all things, which explicate and implicate him … An equality of being is substituted for a hierarchy of hypostases; for things are present to the same Being, which is itself present in things.*[35]

Conceptual artists see ideas as more important than visual form – but this is an approach which has not, so far, appealed to mainstream garden designers.

In 1986, I described the inauguration of a series of Garden Festivals as 'an auspicious pointer to the future of English garden design',[37] but saw the master plans as disappointing interpretations of the Mixed style. As things turned out, the Festivals

10.19 Stephen Schraemmli, of Vogt, designed a Folded Landscape for the Laban Dance School in London. He explained conceptual folding as follows: 'As in a natural landscape, chains of hills and dales form extremely dissimilar situations that can be variously used, for example, the lawn steps as a performance room in the sense of an amphitheatre.'[36]

10.20 a, b The RHS introduced a Conceptual Gardens category at the Hampton Court Flower Show and, in the regulations for entry, suggested that: 'Your brief might be to create a display that promotes (or enhances the image of) a newspaper or magazine. You may be helping to promote a company or a charity, and/or you may be demonstrating how to create a garden for people with special needs. You may be drawing attention to an interesting project, or you may simply be promoting yourself as a talented designer and/or landscape consultant. Be honest, and don't be bashful!'[38]

10.21 a, b, c (a) Building becomes garden and garden becomes building. (b) The planting is 'naturalistic' and Robinsonian, but *Deschampsia cespitosa* ('Golden Dew') is a cultivar while *Allium bulgaricum* and *Cenolophium denudatum* are from Eastern Europe. *Betula pendula* (Silver Birch), though a pioneer species has not been part of the Lea Valley's climax vegetation for thousands of years. The composition is by LDA Design in association with Sarah Price Landscapes. (c) The pomo-ed telephone boxes have lettering to tell a story. The flowery meadows are by Hitchmough and Dunnett.

were a tragic waste. Excepting a few promenades, all five Garden Festivals were destroyed. Their locations were Liverpool (1984), Stoke-on-Trent (1986), Glasgow (1988), Gateshead (1990) and South Wales (1992). Each took two years to build and one year to destroy. The largest sums of money ever spent by a British government on parks and gardens were squandered through bad landscape planning. Equivalent projects in Germany, Holland and France yielded useful parks and dramatic examples of landscape design. Michael Heseltine, a Tory minister and leading advocate of closer relations with continental Europe, was responsible for the great British blunders. When he promoted the Millennium Exhibition site at Greenwich, I wrote a letter which *The Times* did not publish. It proposed the following inscription, either for a slab outside the Greenwich Millennium Dome or as a tattoo on a suitable part of Mr Heseltine's anatomy:

> *In the planning of Festivals, two principles apply. First: the after-use should be planned before the Festival-use. Second: the planning, design and construction process takes 10 years.*

The principle of planning an after-use, now called a legacy, was used in the planning of the 2012 Olympic Park in London. It is a sustainable approach to landscape planning, explained as follows by the organisers:

> *Our job is to harness this potential and create one of the largest new urban parks in Europe for 150 years ... The work can broadly be split into two phases. The first, led by the Olympic Delivery Authority, is focused on the creation of the Park and the development of the venues. The second, led by the London Development Agency, is focused on what the Park is used for after the Games. The two are closely linked, with venues and parklands being designed with their long-term use in mind.*[39]

There was also a sustainable aspect to the landscape design:

> *The southern part of the Park will focus on retaining the festival atmosphere of the Games, with riverside gardens, markets, events, cafes and bars. The northern area will use the*

10.22 The 2012 Olympic Park becomes Queen Elizabeth Olympic Park in 2013. It is part Abstract and part 'something else'.

latest green techniques to manage flood and rain water, while providing quieter public space and habitats for hundreds of existing and rare species, from kingfishers to otters.[40]

The Olympic Park was planned by EDAW/AECOM and designed by LDA Design/ George Hargreaves in association with a number of other landscape and garden design consultancies. Hargreaves explained the design strategy:

The north park is very green, biodiverse, and focused on the river. It seeks to regenerate habitat on the river, and increase visual and physical access to the river. It is much more ecological than the existing London parks but we hope it builds on the legacy by extending the park system into this century. The south park known as the Olympic Gardens is much more urban in character. Certainly a focus for the games, 85% of the visitors move through this area. The concept is to celebrate the British love of gardens and their plant experimentation from the four corners of the world hence our gardens are in four sections: Europe, the New World, the southern hemisphere, and Asia.[41]

10.23 A sustainable chicken looks to a contented future, in gardens.

The historical references are classically Postmodern. Sarah Price took on the historical theme to produce a 2012 Garden which is 'really a giant painting in three dimensions',[42] taking the visitor through four periods in garden history. The sustainability theme adds another 'idea or concept', or 'layer of coding' to the design. It combines excellent landscape planning, for the 'daylighting' of the River Lea, with a Postmodern approach to planting design.

Sustainable Postmodernism

The Brundtland Commission[43] (1987) gave sustainability a high place on the political agenda. In the first decade of the twenty-first century it became an influence on design and management. Gardeners, who could always claim that making compost was helping to save the planet, began to think of other ways of making gardens greener than hitherto. A shift to sustainability can even be found in the work of D.G. Hessayon, said to be the best-selling non-fiction author in British history. His early books were full of advice on chemical warfare against garden pests and diseases, but in 2009 he published *The Green Garden Expert*. Having thought this might be a death-bed conversion, I was pleased to discover the author is in good health but sorry to discover the limited extent of his conversion.

Hessayon's 2009 approach to green gardens was meant to be friendly to plants, animals, people and the environment:

> Our attitude towards gardening has changed in recent years. Nowadays we know that we must look after our plot with some thought for the environment. This calls for such measures as using natural products when we can and not using planet-damaging ones.
>
> In the following pages you will find organic fertilizers and organic pesticides, but this book is not just about organic gardening. The problem is that this concept covers only part of the living things in the garden.[44]

Hessayon then identifies 'Four Features of the Green Garden':

1 *garden friendly*: improving the soil and caring for both the plants it supports and the non-living parts of the garden;
2 *animal friendly*: avoiding harm to pets and wildlife;
3 *people friendly*: avoiding harm to you and your family;
4 *environment friendly*: avoiding harm wherever possible to the environment and to the world's resources of materials in short supply.

It is a valuable classification but the animals Hessayon wishes to befriend are mostly pets and his concern for people is that of a health and safety officer. He does not have a designer's concern for the use and character of outdoor space. Wildflower meadows and wildlife gardens are mentioned but his approach to planting design is 1960s.Two aspects of sustainability are appealing to twenty-first-century garden designers: the image and the reality. The images are of green walls, green roofs, wild-flower meadows, organic vegetables and ecological art. The reality is the difficult task of using gardens to help sustain life on Earth. Sustainable management is thus an approach which could influence any style of garden design. But it is also a style of garden design with identifiable features. Before the agricultural and industrial revolutions, growing food was the primary reason for making gardens. In the nineteenth century, gardens became places of luxury, exoticism and display, instead of work and food. Since then, wars and economic depressions have revived the popularity of home-grown vegetables but, when the good times return, their popularity fades. One cannot know if the rising popularity of food production in gardens, at the time of writing, will prove to be ephemeral.

The imagery of sustainability is Postmodern in the sense that it constitutes a retreat from the silences of abstraction. Communication of ideas and beliefs is back on the agenda of garden design and involves making visual statements about the relationship between Man and Nature. Ian McHarg was keenly aware of this and blamed Genesis 1:26 for Western attitudes to fauna and flora:[45]

10.24 A sacred tree in Ranakpur. Indian faiths influenced the development of a Postmodern and ecological strain in Christianity.

> *And God said, Let us make man in our image, after our likeness: and let them have dominion over the fish of the sea, and over the fowl of the air, and over the cattle, and over all the earth, and over every creeping thing that creepeth upon the earth.*

McHarg's criticism of the Christian attitudes to nature probably came from Lynn White, a troubled churchman, who wrote that:

> *To a Christian a tree can be no more than a physical fact. The whole concept of the sacred grove is alien to Christianity and to the ethos of the West. For nearly 2 millennia Christian missionaries have been chopping down sacred groves, which are idolatrous because they assume spirit in nature. What we do about ecology depends on our ideas of the man–nature relationship. More science and more technology are not going to get us out of the present ecologic crisis until we find a new religion, or rethink our old one. The beatniks, who are the basic revolutionaries of our time, show a sound instinct in their affinity for Zen Buddhism, which conceives of the man–nature relationship as very nearly the mirror image of the Christian view.*[46]

McHarg extended his argument to garden design. He believed that seventeenth-century Baroque gardens subjugated nature while eighteenth-century landscape gardens respected nature. This argument rests on two different conceptions of 'nature' (see pp. 275–6). Christian theologians responded to McHarg and White by arguing that the 'Dominion' given by God to man was in fact stewardship. This led to a

10.25 Christian Ecologists, in the spirit of St Francis, have argued that man's 'dominion' over the world God created should be regarded as a duty of stewardship and should include the conservation of flora and fauna. The wildflowers in country churchyards can be conserved.

Christian Ecology which remembers St Francis of Assisi's love of nature. The debate helped return the man–nature relationship back to the foreground of garden design. It encouraged interests in Buddhism, sustainability and Post-Abstract attitudes to gardens. Faith-based groups in the US subsequently came together with a growing anxiety that 'God's creation was under unprecedented threat.'[47]

A belief in sustainability and conservation is generating new approaches to garden design and new design styles. What Loudon called the 'high keeping' of gardens is becoming less popular. The use of local materials is now seen as an anti-Gardenesque policy. Loudon believed the Principle of Recognition demanded the use of exotic plants and imported materials in preference to local plants and materials. The paradox which troubled Loudon (see p. 271) has been inverted. Designers want their gardens to be 'green' in the sense of 'a political ideology that aims for the creation of an ecologically sustainable society rooted in environmentalism, social liberalism and grassroots democracy'.[48] In many ways, the turn to sustainability is a re-turn to pre-Modern and even Medieval principles.

Sustainably green gardens

To obtain a measure of how gardens might change by 2111, we can review the changes which took place between 1911 and 2011. The main components of a garden in 1911 were detailed in Madeline Agar's book on *Garden Design in Theory and Practice*. Agar studied in America, ran a business, became a teacher and helped educate two of the Institute of Landscape Architects' presidents (Brenda Colvin and Sylvia Crowe).

10.26 a, b These show gardens, on the same plot of land at the Chelsea Flower Show, represent alternative approaches to sustainable garden design. (a) Designed by Paul Stone in 2010, this represents a Low-Tech Sustainability (LTS) approach. (b) Designed by Laurie Chetwood and Patrick Collins in 2011, this represents a High-Tech Sustainability (HTS) approach, and could have had enhanced sustainability credentials if the water table had an aquaponic function.

10.27 a, b Under the influence of Postmodernism, gardens may be recovering their functionality. (a) Sarah Eberle included a swimming pool and a sheltered dining pavilion with a roof garden above in her 2011 design for the Monaco Garden at the Chelsea Flower Show. (b) Mandy Buckland designed an outdoor dining room, which grows apples, strawberries, peaches, lemons, grapes, chillies, tomatoes, salad leaves, peppers, dill, tarragon, parsley, chives, mint and thyme, for Hampton Court in 2010.

Agar's book, aimed at the upper middle classes, has a chapter on 'The Component Parts of a Garden'. Subsections deal with 'The Approach', 'The Kitchen Garden', 'The Orchard', 'Water', 'The Rose Garden', 'The Wild Garden', and 'The Rock and Wall Gardens'. Then, in a chapter on 'Final Considerations', she makes a point which may still command respect in 2111: designers must respond to 'the ground's natural character'.[49] The sustainable components in her chapter titles, written before Functionalism became a recognised design approach, were the kitchen garden and the orchard.

In 2011, the components of a broadly based response to sustainability issues are falling into place. Two approaches may be distinguished: Low-Tech Sustainability (LTS) and High-Tech Sustainability (HTS). The LTS approach draws on the aesthetics of conservation volunteers and rustic gardeners. It uses wild plants, re-cycled materials and DIY construction. Critics might call this a Boy Scout design approach, for the results are amateurish. Advocates remember Henry David Thoreau, John Muir and Aldo Leopold. The HTS approach draws on Modernist principles but makes a Postmodern turn. It goes beyond Modernism and evangelises an approach to the man–nature relationship which is:

- Christian in the manner of St Francis;
- Darwinian in regarding man as just another animal;[50]
- Functionalist in its determination to derive forms from functions;
- Constructivist in its exploration of abstract form to create space with spiritual significance;
- sophisticated in its use of high technology.

So what might a reader expect to find in a book on *The Sustainable Garden Style* published in 2111?[51] The aspect of Modernism I hope will be carried forward is the principle that form *should* follow function. It bore little fruit in twentieth-century gardens, which became decorative accessories with a dearth of functions to follow. Renaissance gardens had been more functional with compartments for herbs, fish yards, garden walks, hunting, chickens, rabbits, vegetables, orchards, theatre, jousting, bowling, archery, etc. The garden functions I was taught to consider as a student (*c*.1970) involved such things as privacy, views, microclimate, desire lines, outdoor rooms and 'planting for year-round interest'. Twenty-first-century gardens, it appears, will have significant environmental roles with regard to the management of energy, water, food, household wastes. There is also likely to be a place for 'the garden as a work of art', which treats functions symbolically.

For garden designers, the challenge of recent years has been to create new design vocabularies and design styles in which functional necessities become aesthetic pleasures, as were fountains in Medieval gardens, water channels in Islamic gardens and garden walls everywhere. A sustainable 'style' will require a visual identity and the identity could come from new ways of viewing, interpreting and representing nature.

10.28 a, b An intensive roof garden, outside Allen & Overy's staff restaurant, provides a calm sunny place which borrows scenery from the City of London.

Sustainable garden features

Green roofs

The first permanent Neolithic dwellings in Britain probably had turf roofs and good examples of old turf roofs survive in Norway and Iceland. The green movement of recent years has given roof vegetation a new lease of life and it is likely to become widespread in the twenty-first century. A useful distinction has been made between extensive green roofs, which receive little human use or maintenance, and intensive green roofs, which are managed as 'roof gardens' and receive intensive maintenance. By 2111 most walls and most roofs are likely be vegetated, making the Environmental Assessment (EA) question I drafted in 1998 obsolete: 'Will the roofs of new buildings be vegetated? If not, why not?'[52] Vegetated roof design may become a key aspect of garden design for small urban sites.

Green walls

Green walls, like green roofs, can be classified as extensive or intensive. Extensive vegetated green walls are normally planted with climbing plants. The use of ornamental plants to complement architecture probably began in the nineteenth century as an offshoot of the Picturesque enthusiasm for making buildings look as if they belong to the land because they have existed for a long time. In twentieth-century Britain this type of planting was associated with the Arts and Crafts movement. *Hedera spp*

10.29 a, b Extensive green roofs, designed for wildlife, water management, insulation and acoustic dampening.

10.30 As Wrest Park reminds us, extensive green walls are as much pre-Modern as Postmodern – and they are even more compatible with modern construction than pre-modern construction.

10.31 a, b, c Intensive green walls, relying on irrigation, provide many benefits: beauty, food, acoustic dampening, biodiversity, dust collection, carbon sequestration, thermal insulation, cooking herbs, etc. Treated as vertical gardens, they give the green wall a Post-Abstract connotation: 'walls can be alive'.

were planted on old stone walls and *Parthenocissus spp* were planted on brickwork. They needed no special care or attention, apart from occasional cutting back. There was, however, a problem: some climbers have tendrils which feed on mortar and cause damage.

Intensive vegetated green walls may have a longer history than extensive green walls. Cultivation of plants on walls probably dates back to the Renaissance and probably began in walled vegetable gardens, because fruiting plants benefit from being trained against walls. As an aspect of the Arts and Crafts movement in the late nineteenth and early twentieth centuries, roses and other flowering climbers were used to 'clothe bare walls' and can often be seen in illustrations of picturesque cottages.

A third category of green wall became popular in the first decade of the twenty-first century and can be described as the super-intensive green walls. It depends on irrigation and a soil substrate suspended in troughs or pockets. They use pumps, irrigation and chemical nutrients but can provide environmental benefits: noise dampening, thermal insulation, wildlife habitats and dust removal (because dust collects on leaves). These benefits may be offset by the disadvantages resulting from energy use (for construction and maintenance) and therefore earn a negative score on sustainability indices.

Three factors are likely to influence the future adoption of green walls. The first is technical. Building science has advanced and the technical problems associated with green walls can be solved. The second is environmental: green walls can produce benefits with regard to noise, dust, surface water management, insulation, food production, aesthetics, etc. The third is cost, because green walls have to be installed and maintained. Fortunately, though intensive green walls can be expensive, extensive green walls can be inexpensive and cost–benefit analysis is likely to show that long-term environmental benefits outweigh the initial costs. Designers can therefore be expected to find ways of incorporating extensive, multi-functional green walls in most buildings in most climatic conditions. They may become a dominant characteristic which will be used to distinguish twenty-first-century cities and buildings from those of previous centuries.

Green food

Food production was the primary reason for making the type of enclosed horticultural space we call a garden (see p. 6). This was so in the ancient world, the Roman world, the Medieval world and the Renaissance world. Old English gardening books are mainly about growing food in gardens. They have some remarks on aesthetics but this is often connected to the growing of herbs, fruit and other edible plants. Even Stephen Switzer, writing in the early eighteenth century, was mainly concerned with how to grow food in gardens and trees in parks.

In 2009, it was reported that the demand for vegetable allotment gardens is soaring with 'almost 6 million people wanting to rent one but only 206,000 plots across the UK'.[53] In 2010, B&Q, a large household retailer, announced that 'sales of seeds for tomatoes, courgettes, beans and other vegetables now outstrip seeds for flowers by

10.32 Myles Birket Foster's painting of a cottage garden shows the walls used for flowers and ground used for vegetables. There is a compost heap beside the shed and the rainwater butt is fed, sustainably, by a pipe from the shed roof.

10.33 a, b The beauty of food is recovering its place in garden design.

10.34 a, b Garden roofs, lawns and ponds can have a role in energy generation, using solar panels, wind turbines and heat pumps.

10.35 Sarah Eberle designed a rainwater detention/attenuation pond which allowed the water to accumulate during a storm event and then discharge slowly (Chelsea Flower Show, 2006).

10.36 This Post-Abstract and sustainable stormwater detention pond, in my garden (1984), takes all the runoff from the house and allows infiltration into the soil. It is dry in dry weather and a rain garden in wet weather. If all urban rainfall was managed in this way then aquifers would be re-charged, fewer reservoirs would be necessary and urban rivers could be released from their concrete jackets. Venus would be pleased and her image symbolises the idea or concept which underlies the 1926 Arts and Crafts design (by Ernest Quilter).

a considerable margin, after the recession and the allotment revival encouraged an increasing number of people to take up their trowels'.[54] The use of gardens to grow food therefore seems to be recovering. Garden owners are exploring the aesthetic potential of food plants and re-learning the cottage gardener's approach to intermixing ornamental and productive plants (see Figure 10.32).

Green energy

Energy will, increasingly, be captured in gardens. It can be done with wind turbines, solar panels, ground source heat pumps, biofuels and other means. Passive solar heating works best when house and garden planning are integrated. Wind turbines can be fixed to roofs and walls or they can be sculptural elements in ponds. Solar panels can be fixed to house roofs and walls or, depending on climatic conditions, can be fixed to the walls and roofs of garden buildings and boundary structures. Ground source heat pumps are a use of garden space without significant visual consequences. They can extract heat from soil or water. Domestic energy generation is a reason for having gardens instead of letting the trend to apartment living continue in the British Isles.

Sustainable water management

Water will, increasingly, be detained, stored, cleansed and then recycled or infiltrated in gardens. It has long been a cliché among design pundits that 'a garden must have a water feature' but the requirements of urban surface water management will make them a necessity. Cities which need to reduce their input of piped water and their output of waste water, can and will use garden space for this purpose.

'Rain garden' is an attractive and commonly used term, from the USA:

> *Bioretention systems are soil- and plant-based facilities employed to filter and treat runoff from developed areas. They are also commonly known as rain gardens.*[55]

As with many aspects of 'green design', the underlying principle, of catching, using and infiltrating water near to where it falls, is old. Roman courtyard dwellings, in Pompeii and elsewhere, used an *impluvium* to store rainwater. Medieval gardens had stew ponds (see p. 94).

Outdoor aquaponic ponds and tanks may become common in gardens, as stew ponds were in Medieval and Renaissance gardens. In principle, aquaponic systems allow fish farming in conjunction with water recycling, organic fertilisation, solid waste disposal and reductions in food miles and the environmental footprint of fish eating. The term 'aquaponics' was formed by combing 'aquaculture' (raising fish and other animals in tanks) with 'hydroponics' (the cultivation of plants in water). Animals and plants have a symbiotic relationship in aquaponic systems. The environmental benefits include water recycling and organic fertilisation. Local food production

10.37 'Thou shalt make compost, unceasingly' remains the First Commandment of Gardening. But there is scope to improve the design of compost heaps.

reduces food miles and thus the carbon footprint, with benefits to food security and food quality.

Green waste management

'Thou shalt make compost, unceasingly' is the First Commandment of Gardening. Waste management has been a municipal function but is becoming a function of home gardens. Some products, like consumer durables, are difficult to recycle in gardens but can be sorted and stored in gardens, ready for infrequent collections or trips to a recycling centre.

Green garden buildings

In several respects, the move to sustainability is a return to the garden philosophy of the Late Middle Ages: the aims combine use (*utile*) with beauty (*venustas*); symbolism is significant; everything is multi-purpose; wastes are re-cycled; gardens are associated with piety and love; small buildings are used for banquets and for contemplation. The placing of spiritually significant buildings in gardens derives from the idea of a temple being a house for a god. It took on a new significance when the idea was secularised. Tudor gardens often had a banqueting house on a mount with a view of the countryside outside the garden (see p. 120). Writers like Roald Dahl worked in garden buildings. Personal offices are built in gardens. Prince Charles, who has made one of Britain's best Postmodern gardens, at Highgrove, has a personal sanctuary in the woods. For many people, as in the Middle Ages, our work is our pleasure and our life. Garden buildings provide opportunities for sustainable living and sustainable construction.

Green construction

Robert Holden and Jamie Liversedge introduce the subject as follows:

> *Concern about humankind's impact on the planet leads to consideration of the sustainable sourcing of materials, as well as the amount of energy required to make and transport a*

10.38 a, b, c Garden buildings can have multiple codings: as places of spirituality, luxury and sustainability.

10.39 a, b At Highgrove, HRH Charles, Prince of Wales, has made one of the most interesting Postmodern gardens in Britain. His introduction to a book on Highgrove describes anti-Modern feelings, a respect for the subconscious and an uncertain destiny. He adopted a philosophical approach with the aim of creating 'a physical reflection of what I feel at a much deeper level'.[56]

10.40 a, b Gabion walls have less embodied energy than equivalent walls built with mortar. They do not use cement and the filling material (e.g. stone, brick or waste materials) can be recycled with ease.

10.41 a, b Natural garden furniture, with low embodied energy, can be made from fallen trees or from boulders (design by Nigel Fenwick).

10.42 Bottles for 'natural spring water' can be recycled as garden buildings.

10.43 a, b Log walls can recycle fallen trees and create wildlife habitats for spiders and other arthropods.

10.44 A Botticelli meadow at Great Dixter.

material and the pollution consequent on its manufacture. Sustainability concerns favour recycling materials.[57]

These concerns have led designers with sustainability concerns to:

- use timber from sustainable sources;
- use oak for timber fencing, furniture and construction, because it does not require chemical treatment to survive in gardens;
- recycle materials on site (e.g. topsoil, subsoil, building materials);
- design structures so that the component materials can be re-used (e.g. by using lime mortar instead of cement mortar);

10.45 Piet Oudolf's 2002 double border at Wisley RHS garden makes use of grasses, herbaceous perennials and other plants. Oudolf gave planting design a Postmodern turn with his remark that 'Dying in an interesting way is just as important as living'.[58]

10.46 Though inspired by natural habitats, Oudolf's planting is not maintenance-free; it is a green design style.

- avoid materials which do not biodegrade (e.g. plastics);
- minimise embodied energy (e.g. gravel has low embodied energy and aluminium has very high embodied energy);
- use paving materials which are permeable to water instead of using impermeable materials;
- use materials with a high albedo ('whiteness') to reflect heat and thus limit global warming;
- prefer local stone to concrete;
- create habitats for insects, birds, fish, reptiles, mammals, etc.

Green horticulture

Postmodernism earned native plants a new place in garden design, symbolising a relationship between man and nature. A.O. Lovejoy explained the Medieval view in *The Great Chain of Being:* man occupies an intermediate position in the chain, below the angels and saints, but above the plant and animal kingdoms.[59] Science, which now has a powerful influence on our world-view, sees man as part of nature. Darwin wrote, in the *Descent of Man* (1871), that 'the human species would have to be considered as just another animal species'.[60] A disappointment in the nineteenth century, this became a point of pride in the twenty-first century. People want to see wild nature in their daily lives and be laid to rest in natural surroundings when they die.

Meadow flowers had been loved in the Middle Ages but disappeared from gardens when exotic plants became available and mowing machines made immaculate lawns

10.47 a, b (a) The Natural History Museum's wildlife garden has more significance as a symbol than as a contributor to biodiversity in London. (b) The sheep help symbolise sustainability.

10.48 The Royal Society for the Protection of Birds (RSPB) has changed an Arts and Crafts garden (at Sandy) into a wildlife garden which attracts birds, insects and wildlife photographers with good kit.

possible. Interest in meadow flowers revived with the Arts and Crafts movement. William Robinson made a case for them (see p. 332) but they did not become fashionable until they came to be viewed in the context of sustainability and biodiversity. Christopher Lloyd believed his mother's love of 'rough grass, was probably derived from Robinson'[61] and, in a book on *Meadows* (2004) recalled that:

10.49 Wildflower meadows, using annual seed mixes, are now sown deliberately (Edinburgh Botanic Garden in 2009).

Here at Dixter, my mother called her first area of planted meadow her Botticelli garden (translated as Bottled Cherry by a small boy staying with us). La Primavera *was her inspiration (my parents visited Florence in the early years of the last century).*[62]

Ecologists see the use of native plants in gardens as a way of creating habitats and fostering biodiversity. Conservation-minded gardeners have learned to combine asceticism with aestheticism. Wildflower meadows help to reduce inputs (water, fossil fuels, embodied energy, fertilisers, composts, equipment, manufactured materials) and to reduce outputs (water, waste energy, chemical wastes, old products, old materials, green wastes). In the Introduction to a book on *Gardening with Grasses* Michael King and Piet Oudolf write that:

The plants in our gardens may serve to excite more than just our visual senses, stirring our memories and promoting a greater consciousness of nature through the associations they

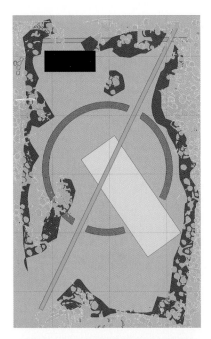

10.50 a, b Diagrams of Post-Abstract and sustainable gardens.

10.51 Gardens may be recovering from a century in which flowers and geometry were the primary consideration of designers.

bring to mind. Grasses sustain modern society, and at the same time symbolize the natural world that modern society seems intent on destroying.[63]

Dan Pearson, who sees Oudolf as 'the father of prairie-planting' and 'godfather of the New Perennial movement', quotes his remark that 'Dying in an interesting way is just as important as living.'[64]

Touring England's gardens in the early 1980s, I was looking for the type of wildflower meadow William Robinson recommended. The only examples I remember were at Gravetye Manor and Great Dixter, both made under the influence of the Arts and Crafts movement. When I re-visited many of the gardens in 2007–11, there was a dramatic increase in the area devoted to wild flowers. The owners of Britain's large gardens have found a way of managing grassland which is beautiful, ecological, economical and fashionable. Understandably, they love it and the public loves it.

Small wildlife gardens are also being made. In 1985, Chris Baines published a book entitled *How to Make a Wildlife Garden*[65] and also made the first wildlife garden exhibited at the Chelsea Flower Show. It was greeted as 'Weeds at Chelsea' and he joked that he had spent his time on a horticulture course in the 1960s 'learning how to kill things'.[66] Wildlife gardens are now recognised as a type and the Natural History Museum has a flourishing Wildlife Garden in Central London.

Green geometry

What forms might Post-Abstract gardens take? Though it is too early to know, I have attempted two diagrams (Figure 10.50). The first, published in 2005, shows a geometry inspired by the Russian Constructivists and, with the possible exception of the planting pattern, does not show a sustainable style. The second, published in 2011, shows an organic fractal geometry, created by *Rhizocarpon geographicum* and a handful of shingle, expresses the idea that forms can, and perhaps should, follow sustainable functions.

Conclusion

In Neolithic times, plants were cultivated in enclosures to produce food. Though flowers and shrubs were also grown, food continued to be the main reason for making gardens in the Roman, Medieval and Renaissance periods. In the grand estates of the seventeeth and eighteenth centuries, vegetable and flower gardens were detached from dwellings, usually in walled enclosures at some remove from the houses they served. The nineteenth century restored flower gardens to their place, near dwellings, but vegetables remained in separate compartments. In the twentieth century, vegetable growing was neglected, because fresh produce was cheaply available. Early Modernist designers turned against flowers and shrubs, because 'ornament is crime'. But garden designers were puzzled by how the principle that 'form follows function' could apply in places with few functions. So flower gardens became opportunities for Abstract Expressionist compositions. Garden and landscape theory separated and lost their way. Since the 1970s, garden designers have been responding to International Modernism while also thinking about historical ideas and about sustainability.

In the twenty-first century, gardens are taking on new functions which are likely to result in new forms and new features. With sustainable landscape design for the space between buildings, cities will require fewer inputs of energy and materials, while also producing less waste.[67] Designers can resume the planning of gardens which satisfy the Vitruvian objectives: *utilitas*, *firmitas* and *venustas*:[68]

- Following functions generates *utilitas*.
- Ingenuity with organic and inorganic materials leads to *firmitas*.
- Wisdom, artistry and imagination create *venustas*.

Gardens and landscapes sustain our flesh, our spirits and our species.

APPENDIX I

Garden and landscape design

ASIA, EUROPE AND THE BRITISH ISLES

AI.0 British landscape and garden design flowered and branched – with seeds, techniques and ideas from the neighbouring continent.

Introduction

British garden and landscape design developed in the context of European gardens, which developed in the context of Asian gardens. To summarise a long evolutionary process, this appendix contains two sets of style diagrams and two lists of design objectives.[1] They are followed by a comment on the development of garden and landscape design theory in the British Isles.

Asian garden and landscape design

The following list of points gives examples of relationships between man, nature and the gods with, in brackets, examples of their visual and physical consequences:

- If gods live on earth, they need houses and gardens (polytheist temple sanctuaries).
- If gods inhabit natural features, sacred places should be venerated (animistic appreciation of sacred landscapes).
- If gods control nature, they should be propitiated through ritual and sacrifice (sacred groves in India and Greece).
- If it is natural for kings to become gods after death, they should be provided with temples and gardens for use in their afterlives (sanctuaries in Egypt).
- If the gods of nature intervene in our daily lives, sacrificial offerings should be made in sacred places, such as altars in woods (hunting parks in China).
- If the circle and square symbolise heaven and earth, they should be incorporated into architectural and landscape design (Hindu and Buddhist temples).
- If gods live in palaces among mountains and lakes, these places should be symbolised in gardens (Daoist-Buddhist gardens in China, Shinto-Buddhist gardens in Japan).
- If the nature of the world is revealed to man through religion, then gardens, as places for contemplation, should symbolise the perfection of nature (Mughal Tomb Gardens).
- If nature is understood through scientific analysis, then gardens should be based on the principles of abstraction (Modern/Abstract gardens).
- If nature is most evident in wild places, then they should be set apart (national parks and nature reserves).

Modified and combined, the above ideas have generated the styles of garden and landscape design represented by the diagrams in Figure AI.1.

Egyptian sanctuaries

Egyptian gardens

Hindu and Buddhist enclosures

Islamic gardens

Daoist-Buddhist parks and towns

Daoist-Buddhist gardens

Shinto-Buddhist gardens

AI.1 Style diagrams for Asian and European garden and landscape design.

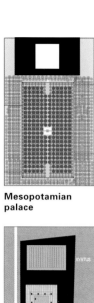

Mesopotamian palace

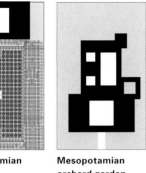

Mesopotamian orchard garden

Egyptian domestic garden

Egyptian palace

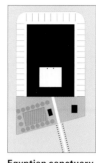

Egyptian sanctuary

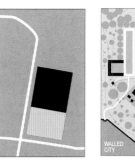

Greek court

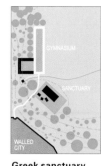

Greek sanctuary

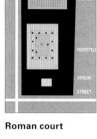

Roman court

Roman villa

Hunting park

Manor garden

Castle garden

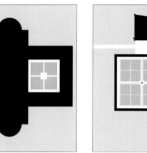

Cloister garden

Early Renaissance

High Renaissance

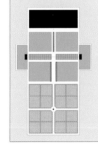

Mannerist

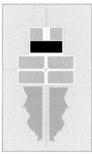

Early Baroque

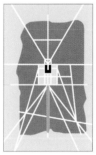

High Baroque

Forest style

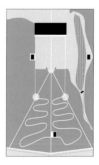

Augustan style

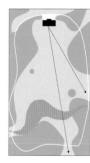

Serpentine style

Picturesque style

Gardenesque style

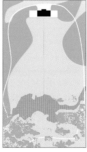

Landscape style

Mixed style

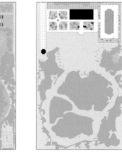

Arts and Crafts style

Abstract style

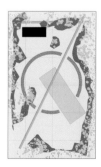

Post-Abstract style

417

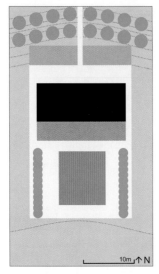

1　LANDFORMS
2　HORIZONTAL STRUCTURES
3　VERTICAL STRUCTURES
4　VEGETATION
5　WATER
6　CLIMATE

AI.2　The six compositional elements of garden and landscape design.

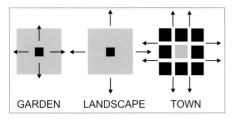

GARDEN　　LANDSCAPE　　TOWN

AI.3　The relationship between garden design, landscape design and urban design.

European garden and landscape design

The design of European landscapes and gardens has been influenced by ideas about the relationships between God, man and nature. The following list gives instances of these relationships and, in brackets, examples of the resultant approach to the design of enclosed outdoor space:

- If gods control the natural world, they should be propitiated through ritual and sacrifice (religious/astronomical compounds).
- If it is in the nature of kings to become gods after death, they should be provided with temples and gardens for use in the afterlife (temple and pyramid compounds in the Ancient World).
- If the gods of nature intervene in our daily lives, sacrificial offerings should be made in a sacred place, such as an altar in a wood (sacred groves, Classical temples, domestic garden shrines).
- If the natural forms have a godlike existence in a perfect world they should be incorporated into architectural and garden design (Graeco-Roman sacred geometry).
- If the nature of the world is revealed to mankind through religion, then gardens, as places for contemplation, should symbolise the perfection of nature (Medieval gardens).
- If the best knowledge of nature comes from the ancients, then modern gardens should be made in the style of ancient gardens (Renaissance gardens).
- If the natural order is revealed to man through reason, then gardens should be based on mathematical ideas and perspective (Baroque gardens).
- If nature is best interpreted through empirical science, then gardens should exhibit a great range of phenomena: natural, artificial and emotional (Romantic gardens).
- If nature is best understood through empirical science, then gardens should be based on the principles of abstraction (Modern/Abstract gardens).
- If our understanding of nature depends on our conceptual framework, then concepts should have a central place in the design of gardens (Postmodern/conceptual gardens).

Modified and combined, the above ideas have generated the styles of garden and landscape design represented by the diagrams in Figure AI.1.

British garden and landscape design

There is no need for a separate 'British' list of design objectives. Since these isles have always formed part of the European cultural sphere, the European list can suffice. A separate style chart could be assembled for British gardens, as it could for most European countries, but the differences would be matters of emphasis and detail, not matters of principle. Baroque and Neoclassical designs, for example, had a special character in Britain, as did Neolithic sanctuaries.

AI.4 The Three Stakes diagram, from *City as Landscape*, shows empiricism, geography and Functionalism piercing the heart of landscape and garden design theory, represented by Repton's trade card.[2]

Garden design, landscape design and urban design involve six compositional elements: landforms, horizontal structures, vertical structures, vegetation, water and climate (Figure AI.2). The distinction is that gardens are enclosed, landscapes are unenclosed and cities are semi-enclosed. Objectives were often shared but in the ancient world, garden design focused on domestic objectives, urban design on community objectives and landscape design on the broad relationship between humanity and the natural world.

In Britain, garden and landscape design objectives began to come together after the Norman Conquest. Medieval, Renaissance and Baroque gardens were planned in relation to landscapes and towns. During the eighteenth century, garden, landscape and urban design objectives were integrated to produce a coherent theory of environmental design (see p. 205). In the nineteenth century, country estates were planned with a transition from the works of man to the works of nature. But design theory faltered and Three Stakes (Figure AI.4) pierced its heart:

1 *Empiricism* muddled the Neoplatonic axiom that 'Art should imitate Nature'.
2 *Geography* adopted the word 'landscape', confusing designers about the nature of their work.
3 *Functionalism*, in the twentieth century, spread further confusion, separating cities from art and nature.[3]

Dazed by these impacts, garden and landscape design returned to their Neolithic separation, suffering from weak design theories and compartmented stockades.

Abstractionism exacerbated the problem but sustainability, if intelligently conceived, could heal the rift between garden, landscape and urban design. Absolute sustainability is not possible.

> *Some say the world will end in fire,*
> *Some say in ice.*
> *From what I've tasted of desire*
> *I hold with those who favor fire.*

But if it had to perish twice,
I think I know enough of hate
To know that for destruction ice
Is also great
And would suffice.[4]

But 'relative sustainability' *is* a practical and desirable proposition. Mammals evolved 200 million years ago. *Homo sapiens sapiens* originated some 200,000 years ago – and seems to be heading for an early exit. We could, however, sustain our species by a thoughtful approach to the most important of all relationships: between the Nature of Man and the Nature of the World. This would involve a conceptually and technically ambitious approach to environmental and design issues. The technical issues relate to sustainable design. Though much discussed, they remain 'abstracted' from the aesthetic issues relating to the character of gardens, landscapes and cities.

Charles Jencks is a leading theorist of Postmodernism in the visual arts and has made significant contributions to garden and landscape design. His approach, in *The Universe in the Landscape* (2011),[5] relates to a historic agenda and the symbolism of ideas. Hence my comment (see p. 391) that 'Jencks is the most notable landscape and garden designer to carry forward the 3500 BCE–1800 CE landscape and garden design agenda'. Jencks designed a small garden in London, followed by a large garden in Scotland and then by many projects in many countries. Like Derek Jarman and Ian Hamilton Finlay, his concerns span gardens, landscapes and the world of ideas. In a Neoclassical sense, Jencks's work exemplifies the axiom that 'Art should imitate Nature' to create *venustas*. He is less concerned with the *firmatas* and *utilitas* of gardens.

Names for styles and periods

Introduction

Our clock strikes when there is a change from hour to hour, but no hammer in the Horologe of Time peals through the universe when there is a change from Era to Era.[1]

Historians borrow names for periods from several sources: chronology (e.g. 'The Eighteenth Century'); military and political events ('Post-Conquest England'); economic periods ('the Agricultural Revolution'); famous individuals ('Victorian'); dynasties ('Tudor'); cultural periods ('Baroque'); intellectual periods ('Enlightenment') and national characteristics ('Italianate'). Though always disputable, period names help with the description and analysis of historical trends. They act as aide-mémoires and they draw attention to the changing habits and ideas which punctuate history.

Names for garden design periods can come from general history or from garden history. My first attempt at diagrams and names for English styles of garden design was in 1986.[2] Their sources included literature, design ideas and the history of art:

- *Enclosed style*: the name came from the phrase *Hortus conclusus*, in the Song of Solomon (which led to the term 'enclosed garden').
- *Forest style*: the name was used by Switzer (in his phrase 'Extensive, Forest and Rural Gardening').
- *Augustan style*: the word 'Augustan' came from literary criticism (as in 'the Augustan poets').
- *Serpentine style*: the word 'serpentine' has long been used by garden writers to identify a key attribute of mid-eighteenth-century design.
- *Irregular style*: the word 'irregular' was much used by Loudon to describe the wildly 'natural' composition he favoured as a young man.
- *Transition style*: the word 'transition' is used by Price and others to identify a key idea (as in 'to go at once from art to simple unadorned nature, is too sudden a transition').

AII.1 a–f Styles of garden design parallel developments in the arts: Medieval, Renaissance and Baroque.

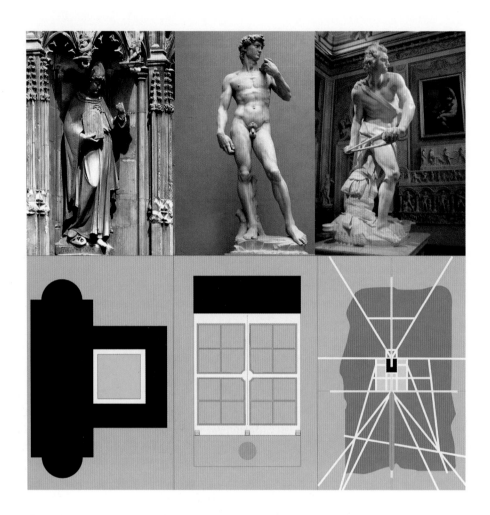

- *Mixed style*: the word 'mixed' was used by Kemp and others to describe the eclectic variety of the nineteenth century.
- *Arts and Crafts style*: the first use I have found of the complete phrase 'Arts and Crafts garden' is in a 1980 book, by Peter Davey, on *Arts and Crafts Architecture: The Search for Earthly Paradise*.[3]
- *Abstract style*: the first use I have found of the phrase 'abstract garden' is in Sylvia Crowe's *Garden Design* (1958)[4] and, since I was working in her office when I began thinking about names for styles, this may be where I got the idea from.

The above list avoids the dynastic names ('Tudor', 'Stuart', 'Georgian', 'Victorian', 'Edwardian', etc.), which are popular with garden historians but which may be thought to over-emphasise royal leadership and imply too much isolation from trends in continental Europe. In the British Isles, this was no more true of gardens than of religion, science, technology, the arts or industry. As an applied art, garden design relates to each of these fields and is closest to the history of art and design.

In 2005, in 2011 and again in this book, I have used names drawn from general history and the history of art as chapter titles. They are a comfortable fit for: Neolithic, Romano-British, Medieval and Renaissance, but less comfortable after that. 'Baroque' is now a widely used term, though less in Britain than in most of Europe and less for gardens than for the other arts. 'Neoclassical' and 'Romantic' are popular categories, though little used in connection with gardens. 'Arts and Crafts' has been accepted as a garden category in the past 30 years. 'Modern' is applied to gardens – though its usefulness is questioned in Chapter 9 of this book. 'Post-modern' is widely used in fields other than garden design but, like 'Modern', must be a label that is due to expire. 'Abstract' and 'Post-Abstract', in the titles of Chapters 9 and 10, are proposed as categories which avoid this problem even if they raise other problems. Possible alternatives for the chapter titles, and for the style names used within chapters, are noted below.

Eleventh to fifteenth century

'Norman', 'Romanesque' and 'Gothic' are possible alternatives to 'Medieval'. If more information comes to light, these terms may be used for sub-categories.

Sixteenth century

Roy Strong used the name 'Renaissance' in connection with English gardens made in the period and I think it is a good choice. The style could be called 'Italian' but 'Tudor' remains popular and 'Elizabethan' is also used and in some respects the period is 'Medieval'.

Seventeenth century

'Baroque' is the most general name for the culture of the period, though dynastic names are often used for architecture and furniture design. The period from 1603 to 1714 has identifiable characteristics, but the dynastic name, Stuart, is little used in connection with garden history. The dynastic period names which could be used are:

- Stuart: 1603–1714
- Jacobean: 1603–25
- William and Mary: 1688–1702
- Queen Anne: 1702–14.

The name 'Formal' is over- used and with little specificity (see p. 159). When the style was least popular, in the eighteenth and early nineteenth centuries, it was also called 'Ancient' or 'Geometric' (see p. 293).

Eighteenth century

'Georgian' is dynastically correct for the period from 1714 to 1830 but explains little about gardens. Hunt uses 'Picturesque' for 'the story that concerns the application of painterly art to the formation of gardens and landscapes'.[5] Others use 'Picturesque' for the Gilpinesque gardens of the late eighteenth century. Richardson uses the attractive word 'Arcadian' for the gardens of the eighteenth century. Others write of 'Landscape' gardens and 'Natural' gardens.

'Rococo', as the art-historical period which comes after 'Baroque', could also be used. 'Neoclassical', with a broad reference to the 'Classical' art and culture of Ancient Greece and Rome, identifies a key influence and explains the initial linkage between painting, dreams of a Golden Age, the ancient world and garden design. Though all these names contribute to an understanding of design intentions and ideas, additional names are required to identify the characteristics of early-, mid- and late-eighteenth-century gardens. Some of the alternatives to the names I have used are as follows:

- *Classical landscape garden*: 'Kentian', 'Palladian', 'Emblematic', 'Poetic', 'Augustan', 'Rococo', 'Elysian';
- *Serpentine landscape garden*: 'Brownian', 'Georgian', 'Landscape', 'Natural', 'Romantic', 'Informal';
- *Picturesque landscape garden*: 'Gilpinesque', 'Irregular', 'Natural', 'Wild', 'Romantic'.

Nineteenth century

'Victorian' is such a useful catch-all label that it is applied even to nineteenth-century architecture in America, where Victoria never ruled. Other architectural terms like 'Gothic Revival', 'Greek Revival' and 'Egyptian Revival' are less relevant to gardens. 'Eclectic' and 'Historicist' characterise design approaches rather than design styles. If seventeenth-century gardens are described as 'Formal', and eighteenth-century gardens as 'Informal', then nineteenth-century gardens could be called 'Formal-Informal'. In a book on *How to Lay Out a Garden* (1858), Edward Kemp advised that:

> On the whole, the mixed style, with a little help from both the formal and the picturesque, is altogether best suited for small gardens. And while the purely geometrical manner may

be adopted under favourable conditions, that which is simply picturesque can never be ap-plied to an entire place, but will be well worthy of use in detached and retired portions.[6]

Not very helpful, but 'Mixed style' remains a useful portmanteau term for the rich variety of ornaments and plants used in Victorian gardens – until the Arts and Crafts movement wrought order from chaos.

Twentieth century

'Modern' is well accepted as the most general name for the art and architecture of the period but has the disadvantages of being out of date and of telling us only a little about the aims and objectives of the designers who created the arts of the period. I remember my mother, in the 1960s, saying that she had bought some 'contempo-rary' furniture. Though used at the time, the term is now recognised as obsolete. The names 'Art Deco' and 'Art Nouveau' are useful but there are disappointingly few examples. One could also pick a name from a category of art which has influenced garden design: 'Non-Objective', 'Non-Figurative', 'Neoplasticist', 'Cubist', 'Construc-tivist', etc. But few gardens would be suitable for inclusion.

Twenty-first century

So long as 'Modern' is used for the dominant theme of twentieth-century art, it is likely that 'Postmodern' will also be used, though with the additional drawback that if 'Modern' lacks specificity, then 'Postmodern' is even less specific. My sug-gested replacements are 'Abstract' and 'Post-Abstract'. Then, as indicated in Chapter 10, 'sustainable' may be the first nameable style of the twenty-first century, more because of its prominence in designers' consciousness than because it has, to date, brought much that is new to gardens: our Neolithic ancestors cultivated enclosures to *sustain* their settlements and used turf for walls and roofs.

Dates

The assignment of dates to periods is at least as difficult as giving them names and other garden historians are likely to use different dates. The dates I have used in the titles of Chapters 1 and 2 come from general history. For Chapters 3, 4 and 5, the dates, but not the names, come from British dynastic history. For Chapters 6–10, the dates come from garden history but are related to the histories of art and architecture.

More specifically: 3500 BCE is a rough archaeological date for the arrival of Neolithic agriculture in the British Isles; 43 is the date of the Claudian invasion and 1066 is the date of the Norman invasion; 1485 saw the start of the Tudor dynasty; 1660 saw the restoration of Charles II; 1714 saw the end of the Stuart dynasty; 1793–4 saw the publication of books by Repton, Price and Knight. Subsequent dates relate to garden history and are based on little more than gut feelings.

Wollaton Hall, Gardens and Deer Park, Nottingham, England

MICHAEL SIMONSEN

Introduction

This study of the park and gardens of Wollaton Hall was undertaken as part of the MA in Garden History at the University of Greenwich.[1] It had three aims. First, a historical analysis of the site's development through 500 years. Second, the preparation of a conservation and management plan for the future. Third, the development of a methodology, with a special focus on drawings and diagrams, for the analysis of historic designed landscapes and gardens.

The present owner of the park and gardens of Wollaton Hall is Nottingham City Council, which describes the park as follows:

AIII.1 a, b At present, Wollaton is managed like a municipal park, not like the great historic park and garden it is.

AIII.2 Assumed location and extent of the Late Medieval deer park.

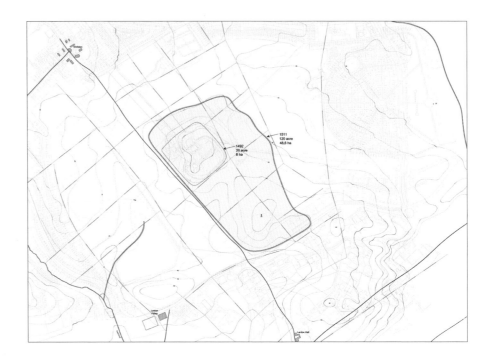

Wollaton Hall is a spectacular Elizabethan mansion in the heart of Nottingham. It is a prominent Grade One Listed building and visitors of all ages are welcome to visit the hall and park ... Wollaton Park is a beautiful open space enjoyed by hundreds of thousands of visitors each year ... The immaculately kept formal gardens provide the perfect spot to sit and think.[2]

The current state of the garden does not, however, match this description. On the contrary: the veteran trees appear to lack professional management; the fences are in poor condition; the golf course is managed separately from the park; the garden walls are decaying; the planting is poorly managed and uncoordinated; the historical 'reconstructions' are not linked to the actual history of the park and gardens. Current management is based on a study which identified four periods in the development of the park and gardens, compared to the eight different phases considered by the author of this study.[3]

Medieval Wollaton

The history of the designed landscape at Wollaton begins with Henry Willoughby (1451–1528), who enclosed a deer park in *c.*1490. It was enlarged some twenty years later to 40.5 hectares. The park is likely to have been located where the palace was subsequently built. The boundaries of this area are, however, unknown.

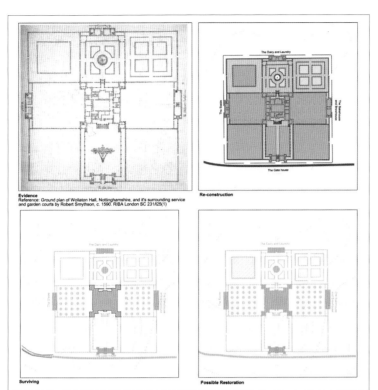

AIII.3 a, b The Renaissance design for Wollaton treated the house and garden as a single entity.

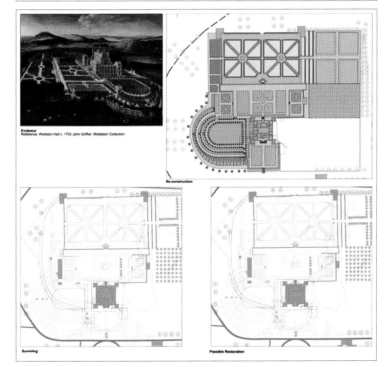

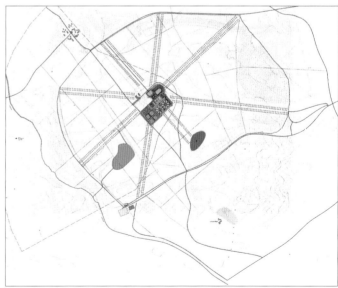

AIII.4 a, b The English Baroque style influenced the gardens and the park (*c.*1720).

Renaissance Wollaton

Francis Willoughby (1547–96) built Wollaton Hall (after 1580) with an incredible landscape view from the top of a hill in a deer park. It was a unique project. The design was developed with the master mason Robert Smythson (c.1534–1614). He used books which provided useful precedents, including du Cerceau's *Les plus excellents bastiments de France* (1576, 1579).[4] The design of the garden was in the Renaissance style, fully aligned with the geometry of the house. The estate was intended to offer Queen Elizabeth I appropriate accommodation for royal visits. This is traceable from the sequence of spaces in the palace, gardens and park. Probably owing to Medieval influence, the gardens were enclosed with walls and there was a knot garden beneath the windows of the royal chamber.

English Baroque Wollaton

Four generations later, another Francis Willoughby (1635–72), known as 'the Naturalist', instigated changes which led to the introduction of Baroque ideas. These were illustrated in detailed paintings by Jan Siberechts (c.1697) and Jan Griffier (c.1710). A bird's-eye perspective by Kip and Knyff (c.1707) showed Wollaton as a classic English Baroque park with grass parterres adjoining the house and avenues projecting into the landscape.

Brownian Wollaton

Another important influence on Wollaton was the style of Lancelot Brown, during the second half of the eighteenth century. The outer park became a Neoclassical landscape in the Serpentine style. It had an enclosing tree-belt, an enlarged lake and a lawn sweeping to the main entrance. The vegetable garden was moved to the north edge of the park and placed behind high walls. Partly due to the enthusiasm for new plantations to support the navy, some avenues were replanted.

Victorian Wollaton

Around 1823, the gardens of Wollaton Hall were given a Romantic Victorian character. The old deer park was now appreciated as a 'natural' landscape and separated from an exotic flower garden with a ha-ha. An iron and glass Camellia House was built and

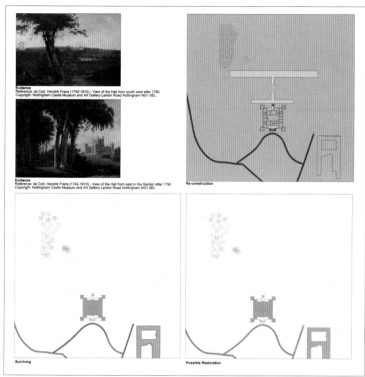

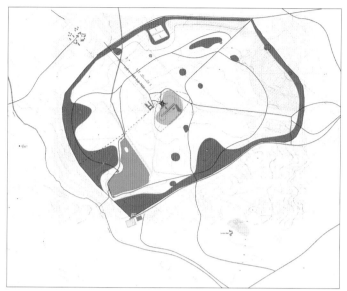

AIII.5 a, b The style of Lancelot Brown influenced Wollaton in the second half of the eighteenth century.

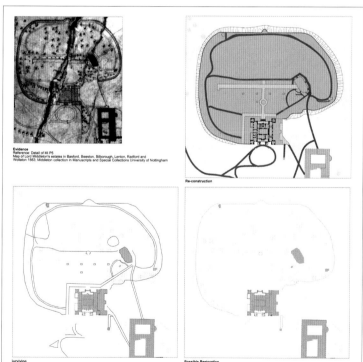

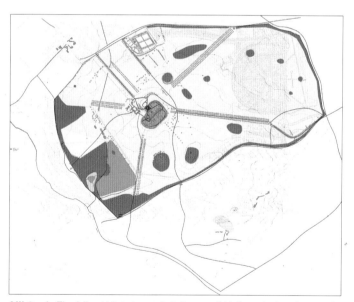

AIII.6 a, b The Mixed Victorian style influenced Wollaton in the nineteenth century.

the compartments on the south side of the Hall were planted with cedars, completely obscuring the view. Digby Wentworth Bayard Willoughby (1844–1922) and Godfrey Ernest Percival Willoughby (1847–1924) were the owners of Wollaton at this time but did not live in the Hall. In 1888, the Royal Agricultural Show took place at Wollaton for the first time. From then onwards Wollaton Park became a place where events were organised on an irregular basis.

Modern Wollaton

After the death of Godfrey Willoughby, the Wollaton estate was sold to Nottingham City Council. A third of the park area was built up for housing. Typically, the park became home to Wollaton Park Golf Club and came to regarded as 'one of the Gems

AIII.7 Wollaton as a municipal park and golf course, *c.*2010.

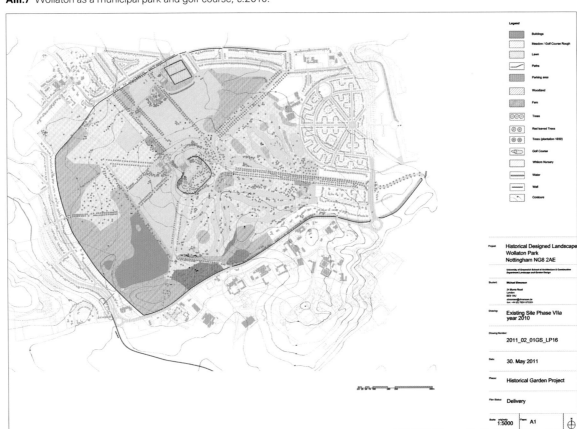

of Midland Golf'.[5] The deer park and gardens were opened as a public park and the Hall became a somewhat strange setting for a natural history museum. The estate continued to be managed as a functional public park.

Of the more than 80 other historic sites in the British Isles that the author visited in 2011, Wollaton Park was the worst managed. It is cared for by a small maintenance team with little understanding of the historical importance of the site. They have adopted a Functionalist-Modernist approach in order to maintain the Victorian character of the 'lawns', 'flower beds', 'shrubberies' and 'specimen trees'. So far, they have not engaged local residents, either as volunteers or as a source of funding for conservation and restoration projects.

Future management of Wollaton

The management plan for the park proposed by the author of this study rests on both design and operational considerations. Following the precedents of Painshill Park after 1981 and Chiswick House after 2005, Wollaton Hall, Gardens and Deer Park could be managed by a charitable trust. Its use as a public park is central to the future of Wollaton. This could be supported by the Public Health Department with a focus on therapeutic use of the gardens. For the future design of the park, the main aim should be to conserve what is important from the different periods in the history of the garden. Geoffrey Jellicoe's approach in his *Guelph Lectures on Landscape Design* is of particular value for a multi-layered garden like Wollaton.[6] It may be summarised as follows:

1   Carry out a thorough analysis of each of the historical layers.
2   Preserve the surviving elements of each layer, including their hidden aspects, and the ideas on which they were based.
3   Plan for the Creative Conservation of the existing elements with some reconstruction and subtle additions to aid interpretation and appreciation of the historical development of the main garden-theoretical ideas.

In this way, Wollaton Park could be changed into a beautiful, useful and well-managed place. Each of the historical layers has its own importance and, with care and imagination, a creative synthesis of these layers is possible:

●   The sixteenth-, seventeenth- and nineteenth-century layers can be integrated in the garden area near the Hall.
●   The seventeenth- and eighteenth-century layers can be integrated in the deer park, possibly with benefits for the twentieth-century golf course.

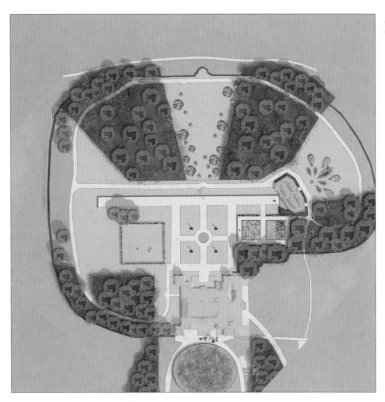

AIII.8 Proposed re-creation of the gardens near the Hall, with outward view through the cedars (which should not be re-planted when they die).

AIII.9 Emperor moth and wild strawberries.

AIII.10 Habitat design by butterflies.

The design of parks and gardens has never stood still and should not be expected to do so. With a look to the future, and in line with the philosophy of Creative Conservation, an approach which integrates biodiversity with aesthetics is recommended for Wollaton. The wildlife conservation aspect of this approach can be symbolised by 'design with butterflies'. It uses the butterfly as an indicator species for habitat development and as a symbol for the configuration of the habitat development plan.

A painting (Figure AIII.9) by Jacques le Moyne de Morgues (c.1533–88) can help to guide the design. He lived at the same time as the man who commissioned Wollaton Hall; he was an enthusiastic botanist and he was highly regarded in Elizabethan London, with Sir Walter Raleigh one of his patrons. Specific butterfly species could be introduced to the gardens and an action plan for biodiversity could be developed. The connection between habitats and historical elements would create a 'mnemonic design' reminding us of the past and guiding us into the future.

Conclusion

The example of Wollaton Hall and Park demonstrates the importance of integrating a textual study of historical documents with an analytical set of maps, plans and diagrams. The historical plans require a consistent scale and graphic style for each development phase.

The identification of modifications and their assignment to specific garden periods allows the preparation of a four-dimensional model of the estate's history. For both visitors and managers, this model provides a basis for interpreting, conserving and developing the site. It manifests the historic and artistic qualities of the park and garden. Comprehension and clarification of the developmental phases, with the aid of current mapping and drawing technology, are an indispensable prerequisite for the care of historic gardens and parks.

Notes

Note all references to *OED* are to the online version: available at: http://oxforddictionaries.com/words/the-oxford-english-dictionary.

Preface

1 Rasmussen, S.E., *London: The Unique City*, London: Jonathan Cape, 1937.
2 Davies, N., *The Isles: A History*, London: Macmillan, 1999, p. 54.
3 Ibid., p. 54.
4 Holland, P. (ed.), *Pliny's Natural History*, book 4, London: n.p., 1847, p. 35.
5 Davies, *The Isles*, p. 204.

1 Prehistoric landscapes and gardening, 3500 BCE–43 CE

1 Hunter, J. and Ralston, I., *The Archaeology of Britain: An Introduction from the Upper Palaeolithic to the Industrial Revolution*, London: Routledge, 1999, p. 13.
2 Saul, N. (ed.), *The National Trust Historical Atlas of Britain: Prehistoric to Medieval*, London: Sutton Publishing, 1997, p. 4.
3 Wells, S., *The Journey of Man: A Genetic Odyssey*, London: Allen Lane, 2002, p. 167.
4 Ibid., p. 168.
5 Peregrine, P.N. and Ember, M., *Encyclopedia of Prehistory: Europe*, vol. 4, New York and London: Kluwer Academic/Plenum, 2001–2, p. 504.
6 Davies, N., *The Isles: A History*, London: Macmillan, 1999, p. 74.
7 Giles, J.A. (trans.), *The Works of Gildas and Nennius*, London: n.p., 1841, Chapter 11.
8 Castleden, R., *The Stonehenge People: An Exploration of Life in Neolithic Britain, 4700–2000 BC*, London: Routledge & Kegan Paul, 1987, p. 16.
9 Giles, *The Works of Gildas and Nennius*, Chapter 12.
10 Hogg, A.H.A., *A Guide to the Hill-Forts of Britain*, London: Paladin, 1984, p. 34.
11 Giles, *The Works of Gildas and Nennius*, p. 8.
12 Exodus 12:12: 'and against all the gods of Egypt I will execute judgment'.
13 Leeming, D.A., Madden, K. and Marlan, S., *Encyclopedia of Psychology and Religion*, New York: Springer, 2009, p. 399.
14 Davies, *The Isles*, p. 76.
15 Eliade, M., *Patterns in Comparative Religions*, London: Sheed & Ward, 1976, pp. 370–1.
16 Renfrew, C., *Before Civilization*, London: Pelican, 1976, p. 259.
17 Castleden, *The Stonehenge People*, p. 26.
18 Hogg, *A Guide to the Hill-Forts of Britain*, p. xi.
19 Ibid., p. 34.
20 Armit, A., *The Archaeology of Skye and the Western Isles*, Edinburgh: Edinburgh University Press, in association with Historic Scotland, 1996, p. 135.
21 Bradley, R., *The Significance of Monuments: On the Shaping of Human Experience in Neolithic and Bronze Age Europe*, London: Routledge, 1998, p. 149.
22 Burl, A., *The Stone Circles of Britain, Ireland and Brittany*, New Haven, CT: Yale University Press, 2000, p. 75.

23 Church, A.J. and Brodribb, W.J. (trans.), *The Agricola and Germany of Tacitus*, London: Macmillan, 1868, p. 2.
24 Castleden, *The Stonehenge People*, p. 18.
25 Green, M., *Animals in Celtic Life and Myth*, London: Routledge, 1998, p. 154.
26 Henig, M., *Religion in Roman Britain*, London: Batsford, 1984, pp. 17–18.
27 Davies, *The Isles*, p. 77.
28 Koch, J.T. (ed.), *Celtic Culture: A Historical Encyclopedia*, Oxford: ABC-CLIO, 2006, p. 1351.
29 Henig, *Religion in Roman Britain*, p. 17.
30 Dowden, K., *European Paganism*, London: Routledge, 2000, p. 104.
31 Lucan, *The Civil War, Books 1–10*, J.D. Duff (trans.), Loeb Classical Library, London: Heinemann, 1928, p. 144.
32 Shakespeare, W., *Richard II*, Act II Scene 1.
33 Turner, T., *Asian Gardens: History, Beliefs and Design*, London: Routledge, 2010 p. vii.
34 Price, D.T. (ed.), *Europe's First Farmers*, Cambridge: Cambridge University Press, 2000, p. 5.
35 Woodard, R.D., *Indo-European Sacred Space: Vedic and Roman Cult*, Urbana, IL: University of Illinois Press, 2006.
36 Barber, C.L., *The English Language: A Historical Introduction*, Cambridge: Cambridge University Press, 2000, p. 75.
37 Ibid., p. 76.
38 Ibid., p. 77.
39 Ó Hógáin, D., *The Celts: A History*, Woodbridge: Boydell Press, 2002, p. 29.
40 Allen, M.J., 'Environment and land use: the economic development of the communities who built Stonehenge; an economy to support the stones', in B. Cunliffe and C. Renfrew (eds), *Science and Stonehenge*, Oxford: Proceedings of the British Academy, 1997, pp. 115–44.
41 Exon, S. *et al.*, *Stonehenge Landscapes: Journeys Through Real-and-Imagined Worlds*, Oxford: Archaeopress, 2000, p. 51.
42 Noble, G., *Neolithic Scotland: Timber, Stone, Earth and Fire*, Edinburgh: Edinburgh University Press, 2006, p. 170.
43 Gimbutas, M., *The Language of the Goddess*, London: Thames & Hudson, 1989, p. 131.
44 Parker Pearson, M., *Stonehenge: Exploring the Greatest Stone Age Mystery*, London: Simon & Schuster, 2012.
45 Turner, *Asian Gardens*, p. 47ff.
46 Ibid., p. 16.
47 Turner, T., *European Gardens: History, Philosophy and Design*, London: Routledge, 2011, p. 68.
48 Bladen, M. (trans.), *Julius Caesar's Commentaries of His Wars in Gaul, and Civil War with Pompeii ... Adorn'd with Sculptures from the Designs of the Famous Palladio*, London: n.p., 1737, p. 85.
49 Davies, *The Isles*, p. 54.

2 Romano-British gardens and landscapes, 43–1066

1 Holland, P. (ed.), *Pliny's Natural History*, book 4, London: n.p., 1847, p. 35.
2 Church, A.J. and Brodribb, W.J. (trans.), *The Agricola and Germany of Tacitus*, London: Macmillan, 1868, p. 2.
3 Gibbon, E., *The History of the Decline and Fall of the Roman Empire*, Bury: John Bagnell, 1896, p. 109.
4 Jones, H.L. and Sterrett, J.R.S., *The Geography of Strabo*, Cambridge, MA: Harvard University Press, 1961, p. 255.
5 'Parcere subjectis et debellare superbos', Virgil, *Aeneid*, Book VI, pp. 847–53.
6 Bradley, K.R., *Slavery and Society at Rome*, Cambridge: Cambridge University Press, 1994, p. 11.
7 Wallace-Hadrill, A., 'Horti and Hellenization', in *Horti Romani*, Rome: "L'Erma" di Bretschneider, 1998, p. 9.
8 Castell, R., *Villas of the Ancients Illustrated*, London: The Author, 1728, p. 103.

9   Humphrey, J.H., *Roman Circuses: Arenas for Chariot Racing*, Berkeley, CA: University of California Press, 1986, p. 568.

10 Columella, *De Re Rustica*, Codice E 39, Biblioteca Vallicelliana, Roma.

11 Myres, J.N.L. and Collingwood, R.G., *Roman Britain and the English Settlements*, Oxford: Clarendon, 1936.

12 Myres, J.N.L and Collingwood, R.G., *Roman Britain and the English Settlements*, Oxford: Oxford University Press, 1998, p. 193.

13 http://en.wikipedia.org/wiki/Fishbourne_Roman_Palace (accessed 12 July 2009).

14 Keil, H.C. (ed.), *Plini Caecili Secundi Epistularum libri novem Epistularum ad Traianum liber Panegyricus*, in *Aedibus*, B.G. Teubneri: Lipsiae, 1870, p. 126.

15 Bean, W.J., *Trees and Shrubs Hardy in the British Isles*, vol. 1, London: John Murray, 1976, p. 460.

16 Beard, M., North, J. and Price, S. (eds), *Religions of Rome: Vol. 2, A Sourcebook*, Cambridge: Cambridge University Press, 1998, p. 103.

17 McCloy, A. and Midgley, A., *Discovering Roman Britain*, London: New Holland, 2008, p. 97.

18 Gibbon, *Decline and Fall of the Roman Empire*, p. 87.

19 Dillon, M. and Garland, L., *Ancient Rome: From the Early Republic to the Assassination of Julius Caesar*, London: Routledge, 2005, pp. 134–5.

20 Browne, R.B. (ed.), *Rituals and Ceremonies in Popular Culture*, Bowling Green, OH: Bowling Green University Popular Press, 1980, p. 90.

21 Cicero, 'On the nature of the Gods', Book I, pp. 46–9, in M. Beard, J. North and S. Price (eds), *Religions of Rome: Vol. 1, A History*, Cambridge: Cambridge University Press, 1998, p. 36.

22 Halliday, W.R., *Lectures on the History of Roman Religion from Numa to Augustus*, Liverpool: University Press of Liverpool, 1922, p. 18.

23 Ibid., p. 20, no. 85ff.

24 Myres and Collingwood, *Roman Britain and the English Settlements*, Oxford: Clarendon, 1936, p. 261.

25 Beard *et al.*, *Religions of Rome: Vol. 2, A Sourcebook*, p. 2.

26 Halliday, *History of Roman Religion*, p. 20.

27 Ibid., p. 20.

28 Koch, J.T. (ed.), *Celtic Culture: A Historical Encyclopedia*, Santa Barbara, CA: ABC-CLIO, 2006, p. 1636.

29 Ingram, J., *The Saxon Chronicle: With an English Translation, and Notes*, London: Longman, 1823. See entry for 982 ad.

30 Laing, L.R. and Laing, J., *Anglo-Saxon England*, London: Routledge, 1979, p. 132.

31 Tertullian, *The Writings of Quintus Sept. Flor. Tertullianus*, vol. 3, Edinburgh: T&T Clark, 1870, p. 218.

32 Giles, J.A. (trans.), *The Works of Gildas and Nennius*, London: n.p., 1841, p. 21.

33 Dowden, K., *European Paganism*, London: Routledge, 1999, p. 91.

34 Giles, J.A., *The Venerable Bede's Ecclesiastical History of England*, J. Stevens (trans.), London: n.p., 1847, p. 55.

3 Medieval gardens and landscapes, 1066–1485

1   Foxe, J., *Actes & Monumentes*, rev. edn, vol. 1, 1590, iii, 204/1.

2   Cartwright, K., *A Companion to Tudor Literature*, Oxford: Wiley-Blackwell, 2010, p. 213.

3   Harvey, J., *Medieval Gardens*, London: Batsford, 1981, p. 4.

4   Ibid., p. 4.

5   Ibid., p. 4.

6   Ibid., p .4.

7   Ibid., p. 4.

8   Ibid., p. 4.

9   Ibid., p. 74.

10 Wild, M.T., *Village England: A Social History of the Countryside*, London: I.B. Tauris, 2004, p. 3.

11 Hamilton. J., *The Norman Conquest of England*, Minneapolis, MN: Twenty-First Century Books, 2008, p. 102.

12 Burnet, G. (trans.), *Sir Thomas More, Utopia*, London: n.p., 1758, p. 51.

13 Ibid., p. 4.

14 *OED*, available at: http://oxforddictionaries.com/words/the-oxford-english-dictionary.

15 Personal email from the Dorking Club of North America: http://www.feathersite.com/Poultry/Clubs/Dork/DorkHome.html, on 7 May 2010.

16 Bailey, M., *The English Manor, c.1200–1500: Selected Sources Translated and Annotated by Mark Bailey*, Manchester: Manchester University Press, 2002, p. 14.

17 Ibid., p. 59.

18 Thatcher, O., *The Library of Original Sources*, vol. 4 (Early Mediaeval Age), New York: University Research Extension, 1907, p. 70.

19 Creighton, O.H., *Castles and Landscapes*, Leicester: Leicester University Press, 2002, pp. 3–33.

20 Mowl, T., *Historic Gardens of Cornwall*, Stroud: The History Press, 2005, p. 21.

21 Giles, J.A. (trans.), *The Works of Gildas and Nennius*, London: n.p., 1841, p. 8.

22 English, E.D., *A Companion to the Medieval World*, Chichester: Wiley-Blackwell, 2009, p. 73.

23 McLean, T., *Medieval English Gardens*, London: Collins, 1981, p. 96.

24 Creighton, *Castles and Landscapes*, p. 20.

25 Taylor, C., *Parks and Gardens of Britain: A Landscape History from the Air*, Edinburgh, Edinburgh University Press, 1998, p. 50.

26 Lubbock, J., *Pre-Historic Times, as Illustrated by Ancient Remains, and the Manners and Customs of Modern Savages*, London: Hertford, 1869.

27 Harvey, *Medieval Gardens*, p. 8.

28 Ibid., p. 74.

29 Ibid., p. 17.

30 Ibid., p. 17.

31 Creighton, *Castles and Landscapes*, p. 72.

32 Allsen, T.T., *The Royal Hunt in Eurasian History*, Philadelphia, PA: University of Pennsylvania Press/Bristol: University Presses Marketing, 2006, p. 16.

33 Ibid., p. 16.

34 Lidiard, R., *Castles in Context: Power, Symbolism and Landscape, 1066 to 1500*, Bollington: Windgather Press, 2005, p. 105.

35 Ashbee, J.A., '"The chamber called gloriette": living at leisure in thirteenth- and fourteenth-century castles', *Journal of the British Archaeological Association*, 157(1), 2004: 24.

36 Colyton, H., *Occasion, Chance and Change: A Memoir 1902–1946*, Wilby: Michael Russell, 1993, p. 68.

37 Lidiard, *Castles in Context*, p. 98.

38 Furnivall, F.J. (ed.), *The Ellesmere MS. of Chaucer's Canterbury Tales*, London: Chaucer Society, 1868–1879.

39 Harvey, *Medieval Gardens*, p. 106.

40 Ibid., pp. 106–7.

41 Colvin, H., in L.L. Howes, *Chaucer's Gardens and the Language of Convention*, Gainesville, FL: University Press of Florida, 1997, p. 25.

42 Johnston, W.M., *Encyclopedia of Monasticism*, London: Fitzroy Dearborn, 2000, p. 960.

43 Athanasius, *Select Works and Letters: Vol. IV, Nicene and Post-Nicene Fathers*, Series II, P. Schaff and H. Wace (eds), Oxford: Parker & Co, 1892, p. 209.

44 Ibid., p. 209.

45 *Rule of Benedict*, Chapter 66, 'On the porters of the monastery'.

46 *Rule of Benedict*, Chapter 48, 'On the daily manual labour'.

47 Ibid.

48 Gilchrist, R., *Contemplation and Action*, London: Leicester University Press, 1995, p. 201.

49 Levi, P., *The Frontiers of Paradise*, London: Collins Harvill, 1987, p. 147.

50 Harvey, *Medieval Gardens*, p. 64.

Notes

51 Crisp, F., *Mediæval Gardens with Some Account of Tudor, Elizabethan and Stuart Gardens, Edited by Catherine Childs Paterson with Illustrations from Original Sources, etc.*, London: John Lane, 1924.

52 Wace, H. and Schaff, P., *A Select Library of Nicene and Post-Nicene Fathers of the Christian Church*, Oxford: Parker & Co., 1893, p. 370.

53 Simpson, E.M. and Potter, G.R., *The Sermons of John Donne*, vol. 4, Berkeley, CA: University of California Press, 1953, p. 227.

54 *The Pearl*, B. Stanton (trans), available at: http://www.billstanton.co.uk/pearl/pearl_old.htm#5, line 38ff (accessed 11 March 2013).

55 Swan, C. (trans.), *Gesta Romanorum, or, Entertaining Moral Stories*, vol. 2, London: n.p., 1824, p. 508.

56 Peck, R.A. (ed.), 'The Pistil of Swete Susan', in *Heroic Women from the Old Testament in Middle English Verse*, Kalamazoo, MI: Medieval Institute Publications, 1991, pp. 82–6.

57 Ingram, J., *The Saxon Chronicle: With an English Translation, and Notes*, London: Longman, Hurst, Rees, Orme & Brown, 1823, p. 70.

58 Chomel, N. and Bradley, R., *Dictionaire oeconomique, or, The Family Dictionary*, 1727.

59 Sidney, P., *The Countesse of Pembroke's Arcadia*, London: printed for William Ponsonbie, 1590, p. 76.

60 Biggam, C.P., *From Earth to Art: The Many Aspects of the Plant-World in Anglo-Saxon England: Proceedings of the First ASPNS Symposium*, Amsterdam: Rodopi, 2003, p. 127.

61 Taylor, C.C., Everson, P. and Wilson-North, R., 'Bodiam Castle, Sussex', *Medieval Archaeology*, 34, 1990: 155–7.

62 Mirk, J. and Erbe, T., *Mirk's Festial: A Collection of Homilies 1905* [S.l.], vol. 1, London: Kegan Paul, Trench, Trubner for the Early English Text Society, 1905, p. 66.

63 Mileson, S.A., *Parks in Medieval England*, Oxford: Oxford University Press, 2009, p. 5.

64 Ibid., p. 6.

65 Webster, K.G.T. and Neilson, W.A. (trans.), *Sir Gawain and the Green Knight*, Cambridge, MA: Riverside Press, 1917, pp. 11–12.

66 Warton, T., *The History of English Poetry from the Close of the 11th Century*, London: Thomas Tegg, 1810, p. 48. The following text was kindly translated by Sarah Wood:

> And wuch so of eny game adde the maystrye,
> The kyng hem of ys gyfteth dyde large corteysye.
> Vpe the alurs of the castles the laydes thanne stode,
> And byhulde thys noble game, and wyche kynjts were god.

67 McLean, *Medieval English Gardens*, p. 92.

68 Mayhew A.L., *A Concise Dictionary of Middle English*, Ware: Wordsworth Editions, 2007, p. 40.

69 Creighton, *Castles and Landscapes*, p. 88.

70 Dunbar, J.G., *Scottish Royal Palaces: The Architecture of the Royal Residences During the Late Medieval and Early Renaissance Periods*, East Linton: Tuckwell, 1999, p. 8.

71 Bates, D.G. and Lees, S.H., *Case Studies in Human Ecology*, New York: Plenum Press, 1996, p. 109.

72 Furnivall, *The Ellesmere MS. of Chaucer's Canterbury Tales.*

73 Milton, J., *The Poetical Works of John Milton: Containing, Paradise Lost, with Mr Addison's Notes*, London: n.p., 1731, p. 180, line 254.

74 Switzer, S., *Ichnographia Rustica: Or, the Nobleman, Gentleman, and Gardener's Recreation*, London: n.p., 1718, p. 196.

75 Bartholomaeus (Anglicus), *On the Properties of Things*, Books XIV–XIX, J. Trevisa (ed.), Oxford: Clarendon Press, 1988.

76 Harvey, *Medieval Gardens*, p. 6.

77 Available at: http://catena.bgc.bard.edu/texts/crescenzi.pdf (accessed 11 March 2013).

78 Mountain, D. [Hill, T.], *The Gardener's Labyrinth*, New York: Garland Publishing, 1982, p. 50.

79 Calkins, R.G., 'Piero de Crescenzi and the medieval garden', in E.B. MacDougall (ed.), *Medieval Gardens*, Washington, DC: Dumbarton Oaks Research Library and Collection, 1986, p. 164.

80 Spenser, E., *The Fate of the Butterfly*, 1590.

81 Markham, G. and Lawson, W., *A Way to Get Wealth: Containing Six Principall Vocations, Or Callings*, London: n.p., 1660, p. 67.

82 Elliott, B., 'Changing fashions in the conservation and restoration of gardens in Great Britain', Centre de recherche du château de Versailles at the Centre Culturel Calouste Gulbenkian, Paris, 3 and 4 December 2007.

4 Renaissance gardens, 1485–1660

1 Hesiod, *Works and Days*, in H.G. Evelyn-White (trans.), *The Homeric Hymns and Homerica*, London: Heinemann, 1914.

2 Bondanella, J.C. and Bondanella, P. (trans.), *Giorgio Vasari: The Lives of the Artists*, Oxford: Oxford University Press, 1991, p. 6.

3 Murray, C. (ed.), *Key Writers on Art: From Antiquity to the Nineteenth Century*, London: Routledge, 2002, p. 66.

4 Neset, N., *Arcadian Waters and Wanton Seas: The Iconology of Waterscapes in Nineteenth-Century Transatlantic Culture*, New York: Peter Lang, 2009, p. 30.

5 Virgil, *L'Énéide de Virgile (Les Bucoliques et les Géorgiques), en Latin et en Français*, Paris: G. de Luyne, 1662.

6 Hesiod, *Works and Days*, ll. 109–20.

7 Neset, *Arcadian Waters and Wanton Seas*, p. 30.

8 Curtius, E.R., *European Literature and the Latin Middle Ages*, Princeton, NJ: Princeton University Press, 1990, p. 193.

9 Ibid., p. 195.

10 Tory, G., *Champ Fleury*, Paris: n.p., 1529.

11 Rossiter, W.T., *Chaucer and Petrarch*, Cambridge: D.S. Brewer, 2010, Chapter 1.

12 Kirkham, V. and Maggi, A., *Petrarch: A Critical Guide to the Complete Works*, Chicago, IL: University of Chicago Press, 2009, p. 295.

13 Robinson, J.H., *Petrarch, the First Modern Scholar and Man of Letters: A Selection from His Correspondence*, London: G.P. Putnam's Sons, 1898, p. 308.

14 Barbour J.D., *The Value of Solitude: The Ethics and Spirituality of Aloneness in Autobiography*, Charlottesville, VA: University Press of Virginia, 2004, p. 44.

15 Pomfret, J., *The Choice*, in *Poems on Several Occasions*, Edinburgh: n.p., 1778.

16 London, G. and Wise, H., *The Retir'd Gard'ner, Vol. I Being a Translation of Le Jardinier Solitaire (by F. Gentil) Containing the Methods of Making a Fruit and Kitchen-garden, Vol. II Containing the Manner of Planting All Sorts of Flowers, Being a Translation from the Sieur L. Liger*, London: n.p., 1706.

17 Columella, *On Agriculture*, H.B. Ash (trans.), Cambridge, MA: Harvard University Press, 1941, p. 5.

18 Virgil, *The Eclogues and the Georgics of Virgil Translated into English Verse by R.C. Trevelyan*, Book 1, Cambridge: Cambridge University Press, 1944, p. 41.

19 Rostvig, M-S., *The Happy Man: Studies in the Metamorphosis of a Classical Idea*, 2nd edn, vol. 1, Oslo: Norwegian Universities Press, 1962, p. 13.

20 Chalmers, A., *The Works of the English Poets, from Chaucer to Cowper*, London: J. Johnson, 1810, p. 199.

21 Milton, J., *Paradise Lost*, 4th edn, London: printed by Miles Flesher for Richard Bently & Jacob Tonson, 1688.

22 Virgil, *The Georgics*, Cambridge: n.p., 1774.

23 Newton, T. (ed.), *Paradise Lost: A Poem in Twelve Books*, vol. 1, Book IV, London: n.p., 1760, p. 274.

24 Temple, W., 'Upon the gardens of Epicurus', in *The Works of Sir William Temple*, vol. 3, London: n.p., 1814, p. 243.

25 Ibid., p. 243.

26 Ibid., p. 214.

27 Ibid., p. 236.

28 Ibid., p. 236.

29 Ibid., p. 236.

30 Ibid., p. 236.

31 Cooper, A.A., Third Earl of Shaftesbury, *Characteristicks of Men, Manners, Opinions, Times*, vol. 2, London: John Darby, 1732, p. 282.

32 Cooper, A.A., Third Earl of Shaftesbury, 'The Beautiful', in B. Rand, *The Life, Unpublished Letters, and Philosophical Regimen of Anthony, Earl of Shaftesbury*, London: Swan Sonnenschein & Co. Ltd, 1900, p. 247.

33 Switzer, S., *Ichnographia Rustica: Or, the Nobleman, Gentleman, and Gardener's Recreation*, London: n.p., 1718, p. 25.

34 Ibid., p. xv.

35 Jones, P.J., *The Italian City-State: From Commune to Signoria*, Oxford: Clarendon, 1997.

36 Kleiner, F.S., *Gardner's Art Through the Ages: The Western Perspective*, Belmont, CA: Wadsworth, 2010, p. 447.

37 Turner, T., *European Gardens: History, Philosophy and Design*, London: Routledge, 2011, pp. 212–13.

38 Ibid., pp. 215–16.

39 Harvey, J., *Medieval Gardens*, London: Batsford, 1981, p. 115.

40 Bushnel, R.W., *Green Desire: Imagining Early Modern English Gardens*, Ithaca, NY: Cornell University Press, 2003, p. 41.

41 Mountain, D. [Hill, T.], *The Gardener's Labyrinth*, New York: Garland Publishing, 1982, p. 51 and p. 53.

42 Austen, R., *The Spiritual Use of an Orchard or Garden of Fruit Trees: Set Forth in Divers Similitudes Betweene Natural and Spiritual Fruit Trees, According to Scripture and Experience*, London: William Pamplin, [1657] 1847, p. vii.

43 Hattaway, M., *Renaissance and Reformations: An Introduction to Early Modern English Literature*, Oxford: Blackwell, 2005, p. 5.

44 London, G. and Wise, H., *The Retir'd Gardener*, London: n.p., 1706, p. 1.

45 Henderson, P., *The Tudor House and Garden*, New Haven, CT: Yale University Press, 2005, p. 76.

46 Groos, G.W., *The Diary of Baron Waldstein*, London: Thames & Hudson, 1981, p. 87.

47 Strong, R., 'The Renaissance garden in England reconsidered', *Garden History*, 27:1 Summer 1999, pp. 2–9.

48 Strong, R., *The Renaissance Garden in England*, London: Thames & Hudson, 1979, p. 7.

49 Girouard, M., *Robert Smythson and the Elizabethan Country House*, New Haven, CT: Yale University Press, 1983, p. 4.

50 Sabillon, C., *On the Causes of Economic Growth: The Lessons of History*, New York: Algora Publishing, 2008, p. 53.

51 Overton, M., *Agricultural Revolution in England: The Transformation of the Agrarian Economy, 1500–1850*, Cambridge: Cambridge University Press, 1996, p. 148.

52 Bacon, F., *The Works of Lord Bacon: With an Introductory Essay*, vol. 1, London: William Ball, 1837, p. 298.

53 Rosenberg, G.D., *The Revolution in Geology from the Renaissance to the Enlightenment*, Boulder, CO: Geological Society of America, 2009, p. 30.

54 Morris, C. (ed.), *The Journeys of Celia Fiennes*, London: The Cresset Press, 1949, p. 9.

55 Colvin, H.M., 'Royal gardens in Medieval England', in E.B. MacDougall (ed.), *Medieval Gardens*, Washington, DC: Dumbarton Oaks Research Library and Collection, 1986, pp. 7–22.

56 Henderson, *The Tudor House and Garden*, p. 36.

57 Ibid., p. 39.

58 Jacques, D., 'The compartment system in Tudor England', *Garden History*, 27(1), 1999: 32–53.

59 Lazzaro, C., *The Italian Renaissance Garden: From the Conventions of Planting, Design, and Ornament to the Grand Gardens of Sixteenth-Century Central Italy*, New Haven, CT: Yale University Press, 1990, p. 33.

60 Morris, *The Journeys of Celia Fiennes*, p. 24.

61 Ibid., p. 29.

62 Mountain [Hill], *The Gardener's Labyrinth*, Chapter 12.

63 Bacon, *The Works of Lord Bacon*, vol. 1, p. 299.

64 Allen, M.J.B., Rees, V. and Davies, M., *Marsilio Ficino: His Theology, His Philosophy, His Legacy*, Leiden: Brill, 2002, p. 259.

65 Lazzaro, *The Italian Renaissance Garden*, p. 47.

66 Saward, J., 'Historic turf labyrinths in England', available at: http://www.labyrinthos.net/turflabuk.html (accessed 1 May 2011).

67 Wright, C.M., *The Maze and the Warrior: Symbols in Architecture, Theology, and Music*, Cambridge, MA and London: Harvard University Press, 2001, p. 219.

68 For example: 'Adjacent to the terrace, a medieval knot garden was designed around an antique wellhead, using boxwood, germander, and gray-leaved santolina for the framework'. Laurie, M. and Church, T.D., *Gardens Are for People*, Berkeley, CA: University of California Press, 1995, p. 240.

69 Abbotsford Club, *The Legend of St. Katherine of Alexandria, Edited from a Manuscript in the Cottonian Library, by J. Morton*, London: n.p, 1841, p. 81.

70 Shakespeare, W., *Love's Labour's Lost*, Act I, Scene I.

71 The *OED* gives W. Horman's *Vulgaria* (1519, xx. f. 172) as the first use: 'The knotte garden serueth for pleasure: the potte garden for profitte.'

72 Elizabeth I (trans.), *The Miroir or Glasse of the Synneful Soul*, 1544.

73 *Les Très Riches Heures du Duc de Berry*, c.1411.

74 Colonna, F., *Hypnerotomachia Poliphili*, Venice: Aldus Manutius, 1499.

75 Lazzaro, *The Italian Renaissance Garden*, p. 21.

76 Godwin, J. (trans.), *Hypnertomachia Poliphili: The Strife of Love in a Dream*, London: Thames & Hudson, 2005, pp. 318–19. The ox-scull (Bucranium) was used by the Romans as altars, often with garlands indicating a sacrificial role.

77 Ibid., pp. 320–1.

78 Lazzaro, *The Italian Renaissance Garden*, p. 52.

79 Harvey, J., 'Medieval garden', in P. Good *et al.*, *Oxford Companion to Gardens*, Oxford: Oxford University Press, 1986, p. 366.

80 Whalley, R. and Jennings, A., *Knot Gardens and Parterres: A History of the Knot Garden and How to Make One Today*, London: Barn Elms, 1998, Chapter 1.

81 Markham, G. and Lawson, W., *A Way to Get Wealth: Containing Six Principall Vocations, Or Callings*, London: n.p., 1660, p. 122.

82 Ibid., p. 12.

83 Miller, P., *The Gardener's Dictionary: Containing the Methods of Cultivating and Improving the Kitchen, Fruit and Flower Garden*, London: n.p., 1733.

84 Switzer, S., *Ichnographia Rustica*, vol. 3, p. 66.

85 London and Wise, *The Retir'd Gard'ner*.

86 Markham and Lawson, *A Way to Get Wealth*, p. 113.

87 Loudon, J.C. (ed.), *The Gardener's Magazine and Register of Rural & Domestic Improvement*, vol. 7, 1831, p. 611.

88 Jones, K., *Gender and Petty Crime in Late Medieval England: The Local Courts in Kent, 1460–1560*, Woodbridge: Boydell Press, 2006, p. 187.

89 Morris, *The Journeys of Celia Fiennes*, p. 119.

90 White, J., *A Lover of Artificial Conclusions: A Rich Cabinet, with Variety of Inventions*, London: n.p., 1658, p. 45.

91 Lazzaro, *The Italian Renaissance Garden*, p. 56.

92 Ibid., p. 57.

93 Bacon, *The Works of Lord Bacon*, vol. 1, p. 299.

94 Longstaffe-Gowan, T., *The Gardens and Parks at Hampton Court Palace*, London: Frances Lincoln, 2005, p. 36.

95 Ibid., p. 37.

96 Morris, *The Journeys of Celia Fiennes*, p. 116.

97 Ovid, *Fasti*, Sir J.G. Frazer (trans.), London: William Heinemann/New York: G.P. Putnam's Sons, 1931, p. 319.

Notes

98 Gifford, W. (ed.), *The Works of Ben Jonson*, vol. 5, London: n.p., 1816, p. 392.

99 Shakespeare, W., *Much Ado about Nothing*, Act I, Scene II.

100 Ibid., Act III, Scene III.

101 Biggs, D. *et al.* (eds), *Traditions and Transformations in Late Medieval England*, Leiden: Brill, 2002, p. 256.

102 Henderson, *The Tudor House and Garden*, p. 184.

103 Dent, J., *The Quest for Nonsuch*, Sutton, Surrey: London Borough of Sutton Libraries & Arts Services, 1970, p. 62.

104 Worsley, L., *Bolsover Castle*, London: English Heritage, 2000, p. 28.

105 Ibid, p. 28.

106 Eusebius Pamphilus, *The Life of the Blessed Emperor Constantine*, London: Samuel Bagster, 1845, p. 353.

107 Ibid., p. 57.

108 Ibid., p. 138.

109 Dryden, J., *All for Love or, the World Well Lost*, 1792.

110 Peacham, H., *Peacham's Compleat Gentleman*, Oxford: The Clarendon Press, [1634] 1906, p. 104.

111 Ibid., p. 107.

5 Baroque gardens and landscapes, 1660–1750

1 Janson, H.W., *A History of Art*, London: Thames & Hudson, 1962, p. 405.

2 Conan, M., *Baroque Garden Cultures: Emulation, Sublimation, Subversion*, Washington, DC: Dumbarton Oaks Research Library and Collection, 2005, p. 14.

3 Quatremère de Quincy, A-C., *Encyclopédie méthodique: Architecture*, vol. 1, Paris: n.p., 1788, p. 210:

> BAROQUE, adj. Le baroque, en architecture, est une nuance du bizarre. Il en est, si on veut, le rafinement, ou, s'il était possible de le dire, l'abus. Ce que la sévérité est à la sagesse du goût, le baroque l'est au bizarre, c'est-à-dire qu'il en est le Superlatif. L'idée de baroque entraîne avec foi celle du ridicule poussé à l'excès.

4 Académie Française, *Dictionnaire de l'Académie Française*, 1765: 'Baroque, fe dit auffi au figuré, pour Irrégulier, bizarre, inégal. Un efprit baroque. Une expreffion baroque, une figure baroque.'

5 Boyer, A., *The Royal Dictionary Abridged, in Two Parts*, London: n.p., 1728, p. 4: 'Baroque, a rough or Scotch Perl.'

6 Wölfflin, H., *Renaissance und Barock: Eine Untersuchung über Wesen und Entstehung des Barockstils in Italien*, München: Theodor Ackermann, 1888.

7 Spielvogel, J.J., *Western Civilization Since 1300*, Belmont, CA/Wadsworth/ London: West, 1999, p. 476.

8 Zamora, L.P., *Baroque New Worlds: Representation, Transculturation, Counterconquest*, Durham, NC: Duke University Press, 2010, p. 98.

9 Mincoff, M., 'Baroque literature in England', in J.L. Halio and J. Limon (eds), *Shakespeare and His Contemporaries: Eastern and Central European Studies*, Newark, DE: University of Delaware Press/London: Associated University Presses, 1993, p. 23.

10 Ibid., p. 32.

11 Marvell, A., *Poetical Works: with a Memoir of the Author*, London: n.p., 1870.

12 Mincoff, 'Baroque literature in England', p. 15.

13 Davidson. P., *The Universal Baroque*, Manchester: Manchester University Press, 2007, p. 1.

14 Turner, T., *Asian Gardens: History, Beliefs and Design*, London: Routledge, 2010, p. 227.

15 Gothein, M.L., *A History of Garden Art*, vol. 1, London: J.M. Dent, 1928, Chapter VII.

16 Zamora, *Baroque New Worlds*, p. 102.

17 Prévôt, P., *Histoire des jardins*, Bordeaux: Editions Sud Ouest, 2006.

18 Hunt, J.D., *Garden and Grove*, Princeton, NJ: Princeton University Press, 1986, p. 169.

19 Russell, B., *History of Western Philosophy*, London: George Allen & Unwin, 1946, pp. 214–15.

20 Hippocrates, G., *Aristotle's Physics, Translated with Commentaries and Glossary*, Bloomington, IN and London: Indiana University Press, 1969.

21 Rogers, K. (ed.), *The 100 Most Influential Scientists of All Time*, New York: Britannica Educational Publishing, 2010, p. 85.

22 Ray. J., *The Wisdom of God Manifested in the Works of the Creation*, London: n.p., 1717 (with spelling and capitalisation modernised, 1st edn, 1691), p. 272.

23 Ibid., p. 106.

24 Goldin, W. and Kilroe, P. (eds), *Human Life and the Natural World: Readings in the History of Western Philosophy*, Peterborough, ON: Broadview Press, 1997, p. 129.

25 Wotton, H., *The Elements of Architecture*, London: n.p., 1685, p. 255.

26 Skrine, P.N., *The Baroque: Literature and Culture in Seventeenth-Century Europe*, London: Methuen, 1978, p. 106.

27 Garnett, R. (ed.), *The Diary of John Evelyn*, Washington, DC and London: M. Walter Dunne, 1901, entry for 1 April 1644.

28 Hunt, J.D., 'Evelyn's idea of the garden: a theory for all seasons', in J. Evelyn, *Elysium Britannicum, or The Royal Gardens*, J.E. Ingram (ed.), Philadelphia, PA: University of Pennsylvania Press, 2000, p. 282.

29 Hunt, J.D, 'Evelyn's idea of the garden: a theory for all seasons', in T. O'Malley and J. Wolschke-Bulmahn (eds), *John Evelyn's 'Elysium Britannicum' and European Gardening*, Washington, DC: Dumbarton Oaks Research Library and Collection, 1998, p. 276.

30 Strong, R., *The Renaissance Garden in England*, London: Thames & Hudson, 1979, p. 196.

31 Switzer, S., *Ichnographia Rustica: Or, the Nobleman, Gentleman, and Gardener's Recreation*, London: n.p., 1718, p. 67.

32 Strong, *The Renaissance Garden in England*, p. 196.

33 Green, D., *Gardener to Queen Anne: Henry Wise (1653–1738) and the Formal Garden*, London: Oxford University Press, 1956, p. 50.

34 Woodbridge, K., *Princely Gardens: The Origins and Development of the French Formal Style*, London: Thames & Hudson, 1986, p. 117.

35 Howell, T.J. *et al.*, *A Complete Collection of State Trials and Proceedings for High Treason and Other Crimes and Misdemeanors*, London: Longman, 1816, p. 1034.

36 Pepys, S., *Diary and Correspondence of Samuel Pepys*, London: Henry Colburn, 1858, p. 204.

37 Morris, C. (ed.), *The Journeys of Celia Fiennes*, London: The Cresset Press, 1949.

38 Green, *Gardener to Queen Anne: Henry Wise (1653–1738) and the Formal Garden*, p. 55.

39 Ibid., p. 50.

40 Kip, J. and Knyff, L., *Britannia Illustrata*, London: D. Mortier, 1707.

41 Morris, *The Journeys of Celia Fiennes*, p. 85.

42 Ibid., p. 172.

43 Ibid., p. 170.

44 Ibid., p. 24.

45 Ibid., p. 9.

46 Ridgway, C. and Williams, R., *Sir John Vanbrugh and Landscape Architecture in Baroque England, 1690–1730*, Stroud: Sutton, in association with the National Trust, 2000, p. 14.

47 O'Brien, J. and Roseberry, W., *Golden Ages, Dark Ages: Imagining the Past in Anthropology and History*, Berkeley, CA: University of California Press, 1991, p. 29.

48 Switzer, *Ichnographia Rustica*.

49 O'Brien and Roseberry, *Golden Ages, Dark Ages*, p. 36.

50 Overton, M., *Agricultural Revolution in England: The Transformation of the Agrarian Economy, 1500–1850*, Cambridge: Cambridge University Press, 1996, p. 148.

51 I have been using this term since 1986 but, since no one else seems to find it useful, the reader might like to consider Rural style and Extensive style as alternatives (see Appendix I).

52 Switzer, S., *Ichnographia Rustica: Or, the Nobleman, Gentleman, and Gardener's Recreation*, vol. 1, London: n.p., 1742, p. xvi.

53 Switzer, S., *The Practical Kitchen Gardener*, London: n.p., 1727, Dedication.

54 Fenwick, H. *Architect Royal: The Life and Works of Sir William Bruce, 1630–1710*, Kineton: The Roundwood Press, 1970, p. xv.

55 Pope, A., *The Poetical Works of Alexander Pope*, vol. 1, New York: Appleton & Company, 1869, p. 43.

56 Hussey, C., *English Gardens and Landscapes, 1700–1750*, London: Country Life, 1967, p. 80.

57 Ridgway and Williams, *Sir John Vanbrugh and Landscape Architecture*, p. 23.

58 Macky, J., *A Journey through England*, London: n.p., 1722, p. 117.

59 Morris, R., *Lectures on Architecture, Consisting of Rules Founded upon Harmonick and Arithmetical Proportions in Building*, London: n.p., 1734, p. 142.

60 Pepys, *Diary and Correspondence of Samuel Pepys*, entry for 15 July 1666.

61 Switzer, *Ichnographia Rustica*, 1718, p. 118.

62 Worlidge, J., *Systema Horti-Culturæ: Or, the Art of Gardening*, J. Worlidge, Gent. London: printed for William Freeman, 1700, p. 41.

63 De La Roche, M., *New Memoirs of Literature*, London: n.p., 1725–7, p. 433.

64 Woodbridge, *Princely Gardens*, p. 106.

65 Bray, J. (ed.), *Diary and Correspondence of John Evelyn*, London: Henry Colburn, 1854, p. 53.

66 Pont, T. and Fullartoun, J., *Topographical Account of the District of Cunningham, Ayrshire*, Glasgow: Maitland Club, 1858, p. 12.

67 Woodbridge, *Princely Gardens*, p. 106.

68 Garnett, R. (ed.), *The Diary of John Evelyn*, Washington, DC and London: M. Walter Dunne, 1901, p. 62.

69 Estienne, C. and Liebault, J., *L'agriculture et maison rustique*, Rouen: n.p., 1625, Chapter 47.

70 Laird, M., 'Parterre, grove and flower garden: European horticulture and planting design in John Evelyn's time', in O'Malley and Wolschke-Bulmahn, *John Evelyn's 'Elysium Britannicum' and European Gardening*, p. 177.

71 Godwin, J. (trans.), *Hypnertomachia Poliphili: The Strife of Love in a Dream*, London: Thames & Hudson, 2005, p. 307.

72 La Brauderie, J.B. de, *Traité du jardinage selon les raisons de la nature et de l'art. Ensemble divers desseins de parterres, pelouzes, bosquets et autres ornements*, Paris: Vanlochom, 1638.

73 Woodbridge, *Princely Gardens*, p. 110.

74 Cooper, A.A., Third Earl of Shaftesbury, *Characteristicks of Men, Manners, Opinions, Times*, vol. 2, London: John Darby, 1732, p. 414.

75 Mariage, T. and Larkin, G., *The World of André Le Nôtre*, Philadelphia, PA: University of Pennsylvania Press, 1999, p. 123.

76 Godwin, *Hypnertomachia Poliphili*, p. 97.

77 The *OED* gives the earliest use of 'topiary' in English as: Dallington, R. (trans.) *Hypnerotomachia: The Strife of Love in a Dreame*, London: printed for Simon Waterson, 1592, f. 51. 'By a turnyng downe the transomes, did ioyne decently one with the other, with a Topiarie woorke.'

78 Descartes, R., *La dioptrique*, Paris: n.p., 1637, Figure 17.

79 Garnett, *The Diary of John Evelyn*, entry for 25   March 1644.

80 Boyer, A., *Dictionnaire royal françois et anglois, et anglois et françois*, Paris: n.p., 1702, and *The Royal Dictionary Abridged, in Two Parts*, London: n.p., 1728.

81 Gentil, F., *Le jardinier solitaire, the Solitary or Carthusian Gard'ner, being dialogues between a gentleman and a gard'ner, containing the method to make and cultivate all sorts of gardens; with many new experiments therein; and reflections on the culture of trees … Also The Compleat Florist; or, the universal culture of flowers, trees and shrubs, proper to imbellish gardens; with the way of raising all sorts of parterres, greens, knots, porticoes, columns and other ornaments. The whole illustrated with many cuts, and with the fable and moral of each plant. By the Sieur L. Liger d'Auxerre … Newly done into English*, London: Benj. Tooke, 1706, p. 454.

82 Miller, P., *The Gardener's Dictionary: Containing the Methods of Cultivating and Improving the Kitchen, Fruit and Flower Garden*, London: n.p., 1733.

83 Gentil, *Le jardinier solitaire*, p. 454.

84 Pérez-Gómez, A. and Pelletier, L., *Architectural Representation and the Perspective Hinge*, Cambridge, MA: MIT Press, 1998, p. 16.

85 Shute, J., *The First and Chief Groundes of Architecture Used in All the Auncient and Famous Monyments*, London: n.p., 1563.

86 *The Gentleman's Magazine*, vol. 2, 1732, p. 174.

87 Garnett, *The Diary of John Evelyn*, p. 54.

88 Hunt, 'Evelyn's idea of the garden', p. 283.

89 Gentil, *Le jardinier solitaire*, p. 454.

90 Hamilton, T., Sixth Earl of Haddington. *A Treatise on the Manner of Raising Forest Trees, &c.* Edinburgh: printed for G. Hamilton & J. Balfour, 1761, p. 3.

91 Ibid., p. 7.

92 Miller, *The Gardener's Dictionary*, entry for 'wilderness'.

93 Norris, J., *A Collection of Miscellanies: Consisting of Poems, Essays, etc.*, London: n.p., 1699, p. 32.

94 Bagot, A., *Levens Hall, the Westmoreland Home of Robin Bagot*, Norwich: Jarrold, 1971, p. 1.

95 Harris, W.M.D., *A Description of the King's Royal Palace and Gardens at Loo. Together with a Short Account of Holland. In Which There Are Some Observations Relating to Their Diseases*, London: n.p., 1699, p. 20.

96 Switzer, S., *An Introduction to a General System of Hydrostaticks and Hydraulicks*, London: T. Astley, etc., 1729, pp. 407–9.

97 Switzer, *Ichnographia Rustica*, 1718, p. 211.

98 Miller, *The Gardener's Dictionary*, entry for 'gardens'.

99 Canfield, J.D., *The Baroque in English Neoclassical Literature*, Newark, DE: University of Delaware Press, 2003, p. 15.

6   Neoclassical gardens and landscapes, 1730–1800

1   Ovid, *Metamorphosis*, Book XIII.

2   Richardson, T., *The Arcadian Friends: Inventing the English Landscape Garden*, London: Bantham Press, 2007, p. 13.

3   The lecture was in 1969 and 'environment', with 1970 designated as European Conservation Year, had recently become a fashionable word.

4   Hussey, C., *The Picturesque: Studies in a Point of View*, London: Frank Cass, 1927.

5   Pevsner, N., *The Englishness of English Art*, Harmondsworth: Penguin, [1956] 1976, p. 168.

6   Fairbrother, N., *New Lives, New Landscapes: Planning for the 21st Century*, New York: Knopf, 1970.

7   Thacker, C., *The History of Gardens*, London: Croom Helm, 1979, p. 175.

8   The classification is from Thompson, J.M., *Lectures on Foreign History, 1494-1789*, Oxford: Basil Blackwell, 1956, who explains that 'Back to Jerusalem' is used to mean influenced by Christian theology.

9   Richardson, *The Arcadian Friends*, p. 329.

10 Scott, W., *Waverley*, Edinburgh: Adam & Charles Black, 1862, p. 32.

11 Traquair House took its final form in 1695. It is identified as the model for Tully-Veolan in Chambers, R., *Illustrations of the Author of Waverley: Being Notices and Anecdotes of Real Characters, Scenes and Incidents, Supposed to Be Described in His Works*, p. 29 but other possible models are noted by Olcott, C.S., *The Country of Sir Walter Scott*, London: Cassell & Co., 1913, p. 109.

12 Austen, J., *Pride and Prejudice*, London: T. Egerton, 1813, Chapter 43.

13 Ibid., Chapter 43.

14 Burke, E., *The Works of the Right Honourable Edmund Burke*, vol. 5, London: n.p., 1803, p. 184.

Notes

15 Hussey, C., *English Gardens and Landscapes, 1700–1750*, London: Country Life, 1967; Jacques, D., *Georgian Gardens: The Reign of Nature*, London: Batsford, 1983.

16 Pevsner, N., *Studies in Art, Architecture and Design*, vol. 1, London: Thames & Hudson, 1969, p. 82.

17 Temple, W., *The Works of Sir William Temple*, vol. 1, London: n.p., 1740, p. 186.

18 Burke, J., *English Art, 1714–1800*, Oxford: Clarendon Press, 1976, p. 40.

19 Hunt, J.D. and Willis, P., *The Genius of the Place*, London: Elek, 1975, p. 9.

20 Switzer, S., *Ichnographia Rustica: Or, the Nobleman, Gentleman, and Gardener's Recreation*, London: n.p., 1718, p. 40.

21 Cooper, A.A., Third Earl of Shaftesbury, *The Life, Unpublished Letters, and Philosophical Regimen of Anthony, Earl of Shaftesbury*, Swan Sonnenschein & Co. Ltd, 1900, p. 246.

22 Ibid., p. 251.

23 Cooper, A.A., Third Earl of Shaftesbury, *Characteristicks of Men, Manners, Opinions, Times*, vol. 2, London: John Darby, 1732, p. 395.

24 http://www.gardenvisit.com/garden/poggio_reale (accessed 11 March 2013).

25 Temple, *The Works of Sir William Temple*, p. 185.

26 Third Earl of Shaftesbury, *Characteristicks of Men, Manners, Opinions, Times*, p. 326.

27 Switzer, *Ichnographia Rustica*, vol. 3, Appendix.

28 Bacon, F., 'Of gardens', in *The Essays, Colours of Good and Evil and Advancement of Learning of Francis Bacon*, London: n.p., 1900, pp. 113–18.

29 Wotton, H., *Elements of Architecture*, London: n.p., 1651, p. 295.

30 Temple, W., *Upon the Gardens of Epicurus, with Other XVII Century Garden Essays*, London: Chatto & Windus, 1908, p. 54.

31 Ibid., p. 235.

32 Third Earl of Shaftesbury, *Characteristicks of Men, Manners, Opinions, Times*, p. 393.

33 Switzer, S., *Ichnographia Rustica*, vol. 2, p. 201.

34 Locke, J., *Essay Concerning Human Understanding*, 4th edn, London: n.p., 1700.

35 Turner, T., *European Gardens: History, Philosophy and Design*, London: Routledge, 2011, p. 24.

36 Locke, J., *The Growth and Culture of Vines and Olives*, London: n.p., 1776.

37 Third Earl of Shaftesbury, *Characteristicks of Men, Manners, Opinions, Times*, p. 405.

38 Ibid., p. 142.

39 Ibid., p. 393.

40 Lauder, T.D. (ed.), *Sir Uvedale Price on the Picturesque: With an Essay on the Origin of Taste, and Much Original Matter*, London: Wm S. Orr & Co., 1842, frontispiece and title page.

41 Liger, L., *Le jardinier fleuriste ou culture universelle des fleurs, arbres, arbustes et arbrisseaux servant à l embellissement des jardins*, Amsterdam: n.p., 1706.

42 Gentil, F., *Le jardinier solitaire, the Solitary or Carthusian Gard'ner, being dialogues between a gentleman and a gard'ner, containing the method to make and cultivate all sorts of gardens; with many new experiments therein; and reflections on the culture of trees … Also The Compleat Florist; or, the universal culture of flowers, trees and shrubs, proper to imbellish gardens; with the way of raising all sorts of parterres, greens, knots, porticoes, columns and other ornaments. The whole illustrated with many cuts, and with the fable and moral of each plant. By the Sieur L. Liger d'Auxerre … Newly done into English*, London: Benj. Tooke, 1706, p. 164. John Evelyn had used the word in connection with a different type of garden when, in a letter of 1657 to Thomas Browne, he wrote of 'the formal projections of our cockney gardens and plots, which appear like gardens of paste-board and marchpane, and smell more of paint then of flowers and verdure'. ('Formal' is used elsewhere by Evelyn to mean 'outward form' and in this quotation probably means 'a projection of the form of the house to create a garden', 'cockney' meant suburban, as opposed to rural, and came to be used for Londoner; 'marchpane', derived from a marzipan cake, was used to mean 'dainty, delicate or fussy'.)

43 Treib, M., 'Formal problems', in *Settings and Stray Paths: Writings on Landscapes and Gardens*, London: Routledge, 2005, p. 87.

44 See http://plato.stanford.edu/entries/aristotle-causality/#FouCau (accessed 11 March 2013):

> *(1) The material cause: 'that out of which', e.g., the bronze of a statue. (2) The formal cause: 'the form', 'the account of what-it-is-to-be', e.g., the shape of a statue. (3) The efficient cause: 'the primary source of the change or rest', e.g., the artisan, the art of bronze-casting the statue, the man who gives advice, the father of the child. (4) The final cause: 'the end, that for the sake of which a thing is done', e.g., health is the end of walking, losing weight, purging, drugs, and surgical tools.*

45 Ferris, C.F., *The Parterre, or Whole Art of Forming Flower Gardens*, London: n.p., 1837, Plate III.

46 Whitehead, A.N., *Process and Reality*, New York: Free Press, 1978, p. 39.

47 Beckles Willson, A., *Mr Pope & Others*, London: n.p., 1986, available at: http://www.twickenham-museum.org.uk/detail.asp?ContentID=19 (accessed 11 March 2013).

48 Wittkower, R., *Architectural Principles in the Age of Humanism*, London: Academy Editions, 1962, pp. 22–3.

49 Rosenberg, R. and Christiansen, K., *Poussin and Nature: Arcadian Visions*, Metropolitan Museum of Art, New Haven, CT: Yale University Press, 2008, p. 37:

> *Examination of the* Abduction of the Sabine Women *at the Metropolitan Museum has revealed that this careful staging was transferred to the canvas by use of an Albertian perspective grid. The grid is visible as an underdrawing with infrared reflectography. A pinpoint in the painted surface marks the vanishing point. Whether a similar system was occasionally used in mapping out the space of a landscape, such as the Landscape with Saint Matthew, with architectural elements dispersed throughout, cannot be said.*

50 Pope, A., *An Epistle to Lord Burlington*, London: n.p., 1731.

51 Thacker, *The History of Gardens*, p. 182.

52 Pope, A., *An Essay on Criticism*, London: n.p., 1711.

53 Switzer, *Ichnographia Rustica*, p. 17.

54 Ibid., p. 26.

55 Hunt and Willis, *The Genius of the Place*, p. 152.

56 Willis, P., *Charles Bridgeman and the English Landscape Garden*, London: A. Zwemmer, 1977, p. 1.

57 Castell, R., *Villas of the Ancients Illustrated*, London: The Author, 1728.

58 Third Earl of Shaftesbury, *Characteristicks of Men, Manners, Opinions, Times*, p. 145.

59 Wycherley, R.E. (ed.), *Pausanias: Description of Greece*, vol. 1, Cambridge, MA: Harvard University Press, 1992, p. 93.

60 Clark. K., *Landscape into Art*, Harmondsworth: Penguin, 1956, p. 67.

61 Nourse, T., *Campania Felix: Or, a Discourse on the Benefits and Improvements of Husbandry*, London: n.p., 1706.

62 Dryden, J. (trans.), *The Works of Virgil: Containing his Pastorals, Georgics and Æneis*, London: n.p., 1697.

63 Dobrée, B., *English Literature in the Early Eighteenth Century, 1700–1740*, Oxford: Clarendon, 1968, pp. 102–4.

64 Richardson, *The Arcadian Friends*, p. 122.

65 Addison, J., 'A letter from Italy, to the Right Honourable Charles Lord Halifax in the year MDCCi', in *The Works of Joseph Addison: The Tatler, The Guardian, Remarks on Several Parts of Italy*, vol. 3, New York: Harper & Brothers, 1837, p. 426.

66 Richardson, *The Arcadian Friends*, p. 123.

67 Addison, *The Works of Joseph Addison*, p. 363.

68 Price, U., *An Essay on the Picturesque, as Compared with the Sublime and the Beautiful*, London: J. Robson, 1796.

69 Eachard, L., *The Roman History, from the Building of the City, to the Perfect Settlement of the Empire by Augustus Cæsar*, London: printed by T. Hodgkin for M. Gillyflower, etc., 1696, p. 451.

70 Suetonius, *The Twelve Caesars*, Harmondsworth: Penguin, 1979, p. 66.

71 Pope, A., 'On gardens', *The Guardian*, No. 173, in *The Works of Alexander Pope esq*, A. Millar and J. Tonson (eds), vol. 4, London: n.p., 1776, p. 264.

72 Pope, *An Epistle to Lord Burlington*.

73 Walpole, H., *The Works of Horace Walpole, Earl of Orford*, London: n.p., 1798, p. 536.

74 Mowl, T. and Earnshaw, B., *An Insular Rococo: Architecture, Politics and Society in Ireland and England, 1710–1770*, London: Reaktion, 1999, p. 65.

75 Walpole, *The Works of Horace Walpole, Earl of Orford*, p. 536.

76 Ibid.

77 Hussey, *English Gardens and Landscapes, 1700–1750*, p. 123.

78 Howard, C., *Castle-Howard: The Seat of the Right Honourable Charles Earl of Carlisle*, London: n.p., 1735, p. 16.

79 Banham, M. (ed.), *A Critic Writes: Essays by Reyner Banham*, Berkeley, CA: University of California Press, 1999, p. 89.

80 Repton, H. and Loudon, J.C., *The Landscape Gardening and Landscape Architecture of the Late Humphry Repton*, Edinburgh: Longman, 1840, p. 235.

81 Richardson, *The Arcadian Friends*, p. 469.

82 Saisselin, R.G., *The Enlightenment against the Baroque: Economics and Aesthetics in the Eighteenth Century*, Berkeley, CA: University of California Press, 1992, p. 13.

83 Hussey, *English Gardens and Landscapes, 1700–1750*, p. 116.

84 Ibid., p. 123.

85 Switzer, *Ichnographia Rustica*, p. 124.

86 Ibid., p. 124.

87 Churchill, W.S., *Marlborough: His Life and Times*, Chicago: University of Chicago Press, 2002, p. 15.

88 Hussey, *English Gardens and Landscapes, 1700–1750*, p. 40.

89 Richardson, *The Arcadian Friends*, p. 471.

90 *The World*, 13 December 1753, No. 50.

91 Hogarth, W., *The Analysis of Beauty: Written with a View of Fixing the Fluctuating Ideas of Taste*, London: n.p., 1753, p. 65.

92 Dodsley, J., *Letters Written by the Right Honourable Lady Luxborough to William Shenstone Esq.*, London: n.p., 1775, p. 379.

93 Mowl and Earnshaw, *An Insular Rococo*, publisher's blurb.

94 Rostvig, M-S., *The Happy Man: Studies in the Metamorphosis of a Classical Idea*, 2nd edn, vol. 2, New York: Humanities Press, 1971, p. 42.

95 Shenstone, W., *Essays on Men and Manners*, London: Parson's Edition of Select English Classics, 1794, p. 63.

96 Burke, E., *A Philosophical Inquiry into the Origin of Our Ideas of the Sublime and the Beautiful*, London: n.p., [1787] 1792.

97 Girardin, R.L., *An Essay on Landscape or, on the Means of Improving and Embellishing the Country Round Our Habitations*, London: n.p. 1783, p. 149.

98 Loudon, J.C., *Designs for Laying Out Farms and Farm Buildings in the Scotch Style Adapted to England*, London: n.p., 1811, p. 24.

99 Watts, W., *The Seats of the Nobility and Gentry*, London: n.p., 1779.

100 Humphreys, A.R., *William Shenstone*, Cambridge: Cambridge University Press, 1937, p. 75.

101 Laird, M., *The Flowering of the Landscape Garden: English Pleasure Grounds, 1720–1800*, Philadelphia, PA: University of Pennsylvania Press, 1999, p. 9.

102 Ibid., p. 13.

103 Anon, *The Rise and Progress of the Present Taste in Planting Parks, Pleasure Grounds, Gardens, &c, from Henry the Eighth to King George the Third; in a Poetic Epistle to the Right Honourable Charles, Lord Viscount Irwin*, London: n.p.,1767.

104 Hume, D., *Essays and Treatises on Several Subjects*, vol. 1, London: n.p., 1757, p. 406.

105 Loudon, J.C., *An Encyclopaedia of Gardening*, London: Longman, 1822, p. 72.

106 Walpole, H., 'On the history of modern taste in gardening', in *Anecdotes of Painting in England*, London: Henry G. Bohn, 1849, p. 810.

107 Ibid., p. 810.

108 Chambers, W., *Dissertation on Oriental Gardening*, London: W. Griffin, 1772, p. 5.

109 Ibid., p. 36.

110 Ibid., p. 9.

111 Ibid., p. 12.

112 Ibid., p. 38.

113 Gilpin, W., *Three Essays: On Picturesque Beauty; On Picturesque Travel; And On Sketching Landscape*, 3rd edn, London: n.p., 1808, p. 19.

114 Jacques, *Georgian Gardens*, p. 97.

115 Gilpin, *Three Essays*, p. 47.

116 Ibid., p. 8.

117 Price, *An Essay on the Picturesque*, p. 37.

118 Repton and Loudon, *The Landscape Gardening and Landscape Architecture of the Late Humphry Repton*, p. 354.

119 Loudon, J.C., *A Treatise on Forming, Improving, and Managing Country Residences*, London: C. Whittingham for Longman, Hurst, Rees, & Orme, 1806, p. 371.

120 Knight, R.P., *The Landscape: A Didactic Poem*, 2nd edn, London: n.p., 1795, p. 83.

121 Price, *An Essay on the Picturesque*, p. 246.

122 Ibid., p. 301.

123 Repton and Loudon, *The Landscape Gardening and Landscape Architecture of the Late Humphry Repton*, p. 510.

124 Loudon, J.C., *Observations on the Formation and Management of Useful and Ornamental Plantations; on the Theory and Practice of Landscape Gardening; and on Gaining and Embanking Land from Rivers or the Sea*, Edinburgh: A. Constable & Co., 1804, p. 210.

125 *The Quarterly Review*, vol. 27, March 1828, p. 315. The article is anonymous but Scott's contemporaries referred to him as the author.

126 Mawson, T.H., *The Art and Craft of Garden Making*, 2nd edn, London: n.p., 1901, p. 2.

127 Jekyll, G., *A Gardener's Testament*, London: Country Life, 1937, p. 13.

128 Gothein's *History of Garden Art* was published in German in 1913. The English edition, from which this quotation is taken (p. 286), was published in 1928 as *A History of Garden Art*.

129 Hussey, C., *The Picturesque: Studies in a Point of View*, London: Frank Cass, 1927, p. 137.

130 Ibid., p. 58.

131 Stroud, D., *Capability Brown: With an Introduction by Christopher Hussey*, London: Faber & Faber, [1950] 1975, p. 13.

132 Pevsner, N., *An Outline of European Architecture*, 3rd edn, Harmondsworth: Penguin, 1945, p. 193.

133 Hoskins, W.G., *The Making of the English Landscape*, London: Hodder & Stoughton, 1955, p. 135.

134 Fairbrother, *New Lives, New Landscapes*, p. 367.

135 Gilpin, *Three Essays*.

136 Clark, H.F., *The English Landscape Garden*, London: Pleiades Books, 1948, p. 19.

137 Loudon, *Observations*, p. 215.

138 Loudon, *A Treatise on Forming, Improving, and Managing Country Residences*, Figures 3 and 4.

139 Scott, W., *The Miscellaneous Prose Works of Sir Walter Scott*, Paris: Baudry's European Library, 1838, p. 392.

140 Loudon, *Observations*, p. 201.

141 Knight, *The Landscape*, p. 83.

142 Ibid., p. 73.

143 Ibid., p. 71.

144 Ibid., p. 81.

Notes

145 Price, *An Essay on the Picturesque*, p. 42.

146 Hussey, C., *A Short History of Scotney Castle*, Kent: n.p., 1963.

147 Hooker, J.D., *Rhododendrons of Sikkim-Himalaya*, London: Reeve, Benham & Reeve, 1849–51.

148 Quatremère de Quincy, A-C, *An Essay on the Nature, the End and the Means of Imitation in the Fine Arts*, J.C. Kent (trans.), London: n.p., 1837, p. 170.

149 Loudon, J.C. (ed.), *The Gardener's Magazine and Register of Rural & Domestic Improvement*, vol. 10, 1834, p. 558.

150 Steuart, H., *The Planter's Guide, Or, a Practical Essay on the Best Method of Giving Immediate Effect to Wood*, Edinburgh: William Blackwood, 1828, p. 422.

151 Gilpin, W.S., *Practical Hints Upon Landscape Gardening: With Some Remarks on Domestic Architecture as Connected with Scenery*, London: T. Cadell, 1832, p. 102.

152 *The Quarterly Review*, vol. 37, 1828, p. 303.

153 Steuart, *The Planter's Guide*, p. 423.

154 Gilpin, *Practical Hints*, p. 108.

155 Wordsworth, W., 'Lines composed a few miles above Tintern Abbey, on revisiting the banks of the Wye during a tour, July 13, 1798', in *Lyrical Ballads*, London: n.p., 1798.

156 Ibid.

7 Romantic gardens and landscapes, 1794–1880

1 Kierkegaard, S., quoted in B.M.G. Reardon, *Religion in the Age of Romanticism: Studies in Early Nineteenth Century Thought*, Cambridge: Cambridge University Press, 1985, p. 1.

2 Pope wrote: 'As nothing can be more natural and affecting than the speech of Patroclus, so nothing is more lively and picturesque than the attitude he is here describ'd in'. John Dixon Hunt comments that: 'Pope took the word [picturesque] to be a French term, denoting what was proper or typical for a painting.' Hunt, J.D., *Gardens and the Picturesque: Studies in the History of Landscape Architecture*, Cambridge, MA: MIT Press, 1992, p. 107.

3 Broglio, R., *Technologies of the Picturesque: British Art, Poetry, and Instruments, 1750–1830*, Lewisburg, PA: Bucknell University Press, 2008, p. 43.

4 Gilpin, W., *Remarks on Forest Scenery, and Other Woodland Views*, London: R. Blamire, 1791, p. 200.

5 Gilpin, W., *Observations, Relative Chiefly to Picturesque Beauty, made in the Year 1772, on Several Parts of England; particularly the Mountains, and Lakes of Cumberland, and Westmorland*, London: R. Blamire, 1792, p. 11.

6 Repton, H., *Sketches and Hints on Landscape Gardening*, London: n.p., 1795.

7 Kames, H.H., *Elements of Criticism*, vol. 3, Edinburgh: n.p., 1762, pp. 305–6.

8 Gilpin, *Remarks on Forest Scenery*, p. 184.

9 Knight, R.P., *The Landscape: A Didactic Poem*, London: n.p., 1794; Lauder, T.D. (ed.), *Sir Uvedale Price on the Picturesque: With an Essay on the Origin of Taste, and Much Original Matter*, London: Wm S. Orr & Co., 1842; Repton, *Sketches and Hints on Landscape Gardening*.

10 Repton, H. and Loudon, J.C., *The Landscape Gardening and Landscape Architecture of the Late Humphry Repton*, Edinburgh: Longman, 1840, p. 278.

11 Pope, A., *An Epistle to Lord Burlington*, London: n.p., 1731.

12 Repton and Loudon, *The Landscape Gardening and Landscape Architecture of the Late Humphry Repton*, p. 365.

13 Price, U., *An Essay on the Picturesque, as Compared with the Sublime and the Beautiful*, London: J. Robson, 1796, pp. 297–300.

14 Lauder, T.D. (ed.), *Sir Uvedale Price on the Picturesque: With an Essay on the Origin of Taste, and Much Original Matter*, London: Wm S. Orr & Co., 1842, p. 147.

15 Repton and Loudon, *The Landscape Gardening and Landscape Architecture of the Late Humphry Repton*, p. 500.

16 Ibid., p. 601.

17 Knight, R.P., *An Analytical Inquiry into the Principles of Taste*, London: n.p., 1805, p.192.

18 Price, *An Essay on the Picturesque*, Chapter 2.

19 Knight, *An Analytical Inquiry into the Principles of Taste*, p. 154.

20 Repton and Loudon, *The Landscape Gardening and Landscape Architecture of the Late Humphry Repton*, pp. 99–100.

21 Price, U., *A Letter to H. Repton Esq.*, London: n.p., 1794, p. 45.

22 Ibid., p. 77.

23 Repton and Loudon, *The Landscape Gardening and Landscape Architecture of the Late Humphry Repton*, p. 352.

24 Ibid., p. 464.

25 Knight, *An Analytical Inquiry into the Principles of Taste*, p. 77.

26 Price, *A Letter to H. Repton Esq.*, p. 77.

27 Repton, H., *An Enquiry into Changes of Taste in Landscape Gardening*, London: n.p., 1806, p. 138.

28 Repton and Loudon, *The Landscape Gardening and Landscape Architecture of the Late Humphry Repton*, p. 577.

29 Ibid., p. 571.

30 M'Intosh, C., *The Book of the Garden*, Edinburgh and London: William Blackwood & Sons, 1853.

31 Turner, T., *Asian Gardens: History, Beliefs and Design*, London: Routledge, 2010, Chapter 5.

32 Pevsner, N., *The Englishness of English Art*, Harmondsworth: Penguin, [1956] 1976, p. 168.

33 Turner, T., *City as Landscape: A Post-Postmodern View of Design and Planning*, London: E. & F.N. Spon, 1996; Turner, T., *Landscape Planning and Environmental Impact Design*, London: UCL Press, 1998.

34 Meason, G.L., *On the Landscape Architecture of the Great Painters of Italy*, London: n.p., 1828, p. 62.

35 Evelyn, J., in J. de la Quintinie, *The Compleat Gard'ner*, i. ii. xviii. 47 (quoted in *OED*).

36 McWilliam, R., *Popular Politics in Nineteenth-Century England*, London: Routledge, 1998, p. 85.

37 O'Connor, M., *The Romance of Italy and the English Political Imagination*, New York: St. Martin's Press, 1998, p. 77.

38 Byron, G.G., *Childe Harold's Pilgrimage*, in F.G. Halleck (ed.), *The Works of Lord Byron, in Verse and Prose*, New York: George Dearborn, 1833, p. 22.

39 Murray, J. (ed.), *The Poetical Works of Lord Byron: Complete in One Volume*, London: n.p., 1846, p. 44.

40 Loudon, J.C., *Self-Instruction for Young Gardeners*, London: Longman, 1845, p. xxv.

41 Loudon, J.C., *An Encyclopaedia of Gardening*, London: Longman, 1822, p. 119.

42 Ibid., p. 1323.

43 Ibid., p. 903.

44 Ibid., p. 794.

45 M'Intosh, *The Book of the Garden*.

46 Mawe, T. and Abercrombie, J., *The Universal Gardener and Botanist: or, A General Dictionary of Gardening*, London: n.p., 1778.

47 MacCulloch, J., *The Highlands and Western Isles of Scotland*, vol. 1, London: Longman, 1824, p. 104.

48 Loudon, *An Encyclopaedia of Gardening*, p. 904.

49 Hobhouse, P., *Plants in Garden History*, London: Pavilion Books, 1992, p. 231.

50 Loudon, J., *Instructions in Gardening for Ladies*, London: John Murray, 1840, p. 321.

51 Loudon, J.C. (ed.), *The Gardener's Magazine and Register of Rural & Domestic Improvement*, vol. 6, 1840, p. 622.

52 Burnet, J., *The Discourses of Sir Joshua Reynolds: Illustrated by Explanatory Notes and Plates*, London: J. Carpenter, 1842, p. 40.

53 Ibid., pp. 52–3.

54 Ibid., p. 41.

55   Ibid., p. 42.
56   *The Gentleman's Magazine*, vol. 13, 1840, p. 409.
57   Meehan, T. (ed.), *Gardener's Monthly and Horticulturist*, vol. 10, 1868, p. 264.
58   Loudon, J.C. (ed.), *The Gardener's Magazine and Register of Rural & Domestic Improvement*, vol. 7, 1831, p. 390.
59   Loudon, J.C., *An Encyclopaedia of Cottage, Farm, and Villa Architecture*, London: Longman, Orme, Brown, Green, & Longmans, 1839, p. 789.
60   Repton and Loudon, *The Landscape Gardening and Landscape Architecture of the Late Humphry Repton*, p. 536.
61   Ibid., p. 533.
62   Ibid., p. 546.
63   Ibid., p. 529.
64   Ibid., p. 552.
65   Kemp, E., *How to Lay Out a Garden*, London: n.p., 1858, p. 126.
66   Loudon, J.C., *The Villa Gardener*, London: n.p., 1850, p. 20.
67   Loudon, J.C., *The Suburban Gardener, and Villa Companion*, London: n.p., 1838, p. 141.
68   Loudon, *Self-Instruction for Young Gardeners*, p. xxxvii.
69   Hooker, J., in *Annals of Natural History, Or Magazine of Zoology, Botany, and Geology*, vol. 3, 1839, p. 188.
70   Loudon, *An Encyclopaedia of Cottage, Farm, and Villa Architecture*, p. 976.
71   Ibid., p. 976.
72   M'Intosh, *The Book of the Garden*, p. 742.
73   Loudon, J.C., *The Gardener's Magazine and Register of Rural & Domestic Improvement*, vol. 10, 1834, p. 103.
74   Farrer, R.G., *My Rock Garden*, London: Edward Arnold, 1907; Farrer, R.G., *On the Eaves of the World*, London: Edward Arnold, 1917.
75   Repton and Loudon, *The Landscape Gardening and Landscape Architecture of the Late Humphry Repton*, p. 481.
76   Brown, J., *The Forester: A Practical Treatise on the Planting Rearing and General Management of Forest Trees*, Edinburgh: William Blackwood & Sons, 1861, p. 45.
77   Marshall, D., 'The picturesque', in H.B. Nisbet and C. Rawson (eds), *The Eighteenth Century*, vol. 4 of *Cambridge History of Literary Criticism*, Newark, NJ: Oxford University Press, 2000, pp. 700–18.
78   Cowper, W., 'The garden', in *The Works of William Cowper*, J.S. Memes (ed.), vol. 3, Edinburgh: Fraser & Co, 1835.
79   Ibid., p. 276.
80   Marshall, 'The picturesque', p. 701.
81   Brown, *The Forester*, p. 45.
82   Ibid., p. 154.
83   Price, *An Essay on the Picturesque*, p. 263.
84   http://www.ramsar.org/cda/en/ramsar-documents-official-docs/main/ramsar/1-31%5E7761_4000_0__ (accessed 11 March 2013).
85   Brown, *The Forester*, p. 404.
86   Grusin, R.A., *Culture, Technology, and the Creation of America's National Parks*, Cambridge: Cambridge University Press, 2004, p. 21.
87   Olmsted, F.L., *Yosemite and the Mariposa Grove: A Preliminary Report*, 1865, available at: http://www.yosemite.ca.us/library/olmsted/ (accessed 11 March 2013).
88   Ibid.
89   *The National Parks: America's Best Idea* was the title of a documentary film for television (2009) and a book by Burns, K., *The National Parks: America's Best Idea*, New York: Knopf Publishing Group, 2009.
90   Downing, A.J., *A Treatise on the Theory and Practice of Landscape Gardening, Adapted to North America*, New York: Putnam, 1849.
91   Meason, *On the Landscape Architecture of the Great Painters of Italy*, p. 74.
92   Ibid., p. 118.
93   Antonetti, N., 'William Andrews Nesfield and the origins of the landscape architect', *Landscape History*, 33(1), 2012, pp. 69–86.

8   Arts and Crafts gardens, 1880–1970

1   Ruskin, J., *The Seven Lamps of Architecture*, London: n.p., 1866.
2   Dixon, L.S. and Chu, P.t-D. (eds), *Twenty-First-Century Perspectives on Nineteenth-Century Art: Essays in Honor of Gabriel P. Weisberg*, Newark: University of Delaware Press, 2008, p. 104.
3   Gilpin, W., *Three Essays: On Picturesque Beauty; On Picturesque Travel; And On Sketching Landscape*, 3rd edn, London: n.p., 1808, p. 61.
4   Hunt, J.D., *Gardens and the Picturesque: Studies in the History of Landscape Architecture*, Cambridge, MA: MIT Press, 1992, p. 193.
5   Hunt, J.D., *The Wider Sea: A Life of John Ruskin*, London: J.M. Dent, 1982, p. 432.
6   Beeching, P.Q., 'The eighteenth-century background of Ruskin's *The Poetry of Architecture*', thesis, Graduate School of Saint Louis, 1956, p. 122.
7   Morris, W., *News from Nowhere: Or, an Epoch of Rest, Being Some Chapters from a Utopian Romance*, London: Kelmscott Press, 1893.
8   Hamilton, J., *The Gardens of William Morris*, London: Frances Lincoln, 1998, p. 54.
9   Cook, E.T. (ed.), *The Life of John Ruskin*, vol. 2, *Volumes 1860–1900*, London: George Allen & Co., 1911, p. 50.
10   Cook, E.T. and Wedderburn, A. (eds), *The Works of John Ruskin*, vol. 1, London: George Allen & Co., 1903–12, p. xxxvii.
11   Ibid., pp. 36–7.
12   Cook, *The Life of John Ruskin*, p. 38.
13   Beeching, 'The eighteenth-century background of Ruskin's *The Poetry of Architecture*', p. 44.
14   Illingworth, J., 'Ruskin and gardening', *Garden History*, 22(2), Winter 1994, 218–33.
15   Ruskin, J., in *The Architectural Magazine*, vol. 5, 1838, p. 249.
16   Hardman, M., *Six Victorian Thinkers*, Manchester: Manchester University Press, 1991, p. 42.
17   Ibid., p. 42.
18   Ruskin, J., in *The Architectural Magazine*, vol. 4, 1837, p. 555.
19   Gilpin, W., *Observations, Relative Chiefly to Picturesque Beauty, made in the Year 1772, on Several Parts of England; particularly the Mountains, and Lakes of Cumberland, and Westmorland*, London: R. Blamire, 1792, p. 209.
20   Price, U., *An Essay on the Picturesque, as Compared with the Sublime and the Beautiful*, London: J. Robson, p. 162.
21   Knight, R.P., *An Analytical Inquiry into the Principles of Taste*, London: n.p., 1805, p. 224.
22   Ibid., p. 219. The same point is made by Meason, G.L., *On the Landscape Architecture of the Great Painters of Italy*, London: n.p., 1828, p. 71.
23   Wheeler, M. and Whiteley, N., *The Lamp of Memory: Ruskin, Tradition, and Architecture*, Manchester: Manchester University Press, 1992, p. 108.
24   Wordsworth, W., *The Excursion: Being a Portion of The Recluse, A Poem*, London: n.p., 1814.
25   Wordsworth, W., *A Farewell*, London: n.p., 1802.
26   Wright, J. (ed.), *The Letters of Horace Walpole, Earl of Orford*, vol. 5, London: n.p., 1840, p. 58.
27   Long, G. (ed.), *The Penny Cyclopaedia*, London: Society for the Diffusion of Useful Knowledge, 1845, p. 505.
28   Austen, J., *Sense and Sensibility: A Novel*, London: R. Bentley, 1833, Chapter XIV, p. 216.
29   Engels, F., *The Condition of the Working Class in England*, W.O. Henderson and W.H. Chaloner (trans.), Oxford: Blackwell, 1958, p. 48.
30   Loudon, J.C., *An Encyclopaedia of Gardening*, London: n.p., 1835, p. 1226.
31   Ibid., p. 1227.
32   Ibid., p. 1227.
33   Pfister, M., *The Fatal Gift of Beauty: The Italies of British Travellers*, Amsterdam: Editions Rodopi, 1996, p. 277.

Notes

34 Ruskin, J. and Tuthill, L.C., *The True and the Beautiful in Nature, Art, Morals and Religion*, 3rd edn, New York: Wiley & Halstead, 1859, p. 131.

35 Robinson, W. *The English Flower Garden*, 4th edn, London: John Murray, 1895, p. 9.

36 Ruskin, J., in *The Architectural Magazine*, vol. 5, 1839, p. 249.

37 Ibid., p. 249.

38 Robinson, W., *The Parks, Promenades & Gardens of Paris*, London: John Murray, 1869, p. 241.

39 Ibid., p. 242.

40 *The Gardener's Chronicle and Agricultural Gazette*, 10 August 1867.

41 Ibid., 29 June 1867.

42 Robinson, W., *Gleanings from French Gardens*, London: n.p., 1868, p. 4.

43 Ruskin and Tuthill, *The True and the Beautiful in Nature, Art, Morals and Religion*, p. 336.

44 Ruskin, J., *Stones of Venice*, New York: John Wiley, 1860, p. 299.

45 Robinson, W., *The Wild Garden*, London: John Murray, 1870, p. 8.

46 Ibid.

47 Hussey, C., *The Life of Sir Edwin Lutyens*, London: Country Life, 1950, p. 83.

48 Kemp, E., *How to Lay Out a Small Garden*, London: Bradbury & Evans, 1858, p. 130.

49 M'Intosh, C., *The Book of the Garden*, Edinburgh and London: William Blackwood & Sons, 1853, p. 663.

50 Walter Scott wrote of 'the hereditary gardeners of the Earls of Monteith'. See Lockhart, J.G., *Memoirs of the Life of Sir Walter Scott, bart.*, Paris: A. & W. Galignani & Co., 1838, p. 145.

51 Milward, R., *The Table-Talk of John Selden*, London: n.p., 1786, p. 3.

52 Barrett, C., *Diary and Letters of Madame D'Arblay, 1788 to 1796*, London: n.p., 1842, p. 579.

53 *Gardener and Practical Florist*, vol. 2, 1843, p. 217.

54 Beresford, J., *The Miseries of Human Life, or, the Last Groans of Timothy Testy and Samuel Sensitive: With a Few Supplementary Sighs from Mrs. Testy, with which Are Now for the First Time Interspersed, Varieties, Incidental to the Principal Matter, in Prose and Verse, in Nine Additional Dialogues as Overheard*, vol. 2, London: printed for W. Miller, 1807, p. 280.

55 Ruskin, J., *On the Nature of Gothic Architecture*, London: n.p., 1854, p. 12.

56 Morris, W., *Hopes and Fears for Art*, London: Ellis & White, 1882, p. 128.

57 Mackail, J.W. *The Life of William Morris*, New York: Haskell House Publishers, 1899, p. 73.

58 Sedding, J.D., *Garden-Craft Old and New*, London: Kegan Paul & Co., 1895, Preface.

59 James, T., *The Flower Garden: With an Essay on the Poetry of Gardening*, London: n.p., 1852, p. 85.

60 Ibid., p. 23.

61 Sedding, *Garden-Craft Old and New*, p. 113.

62 Blomfield, R., *The Formal Garden in England*, 3rd edn, London: Macmillan & Co., 1901, p. 236.

63 Jekyll, G., *A Gardener's Testament*, London: Country Life, 1937, p. 33.

64 Blomfield, *The Formal Garden in England*, Preface.

65 Jekyll, G., 'Gardens and garden craft', *Edinburgh Review*, vol. 184, July 1896, p. 180.

66 Sedding, *Garden-Craft Old and New*, p. 118.

67 Jekyll, G., *Wall and Water Gardens*, London: George Newnes Ltd, 1901, p. 150.

68 Brown, J., *Gardens of a Golden Afternoon – Story of a Partnership: Edwin Lutyens and Gertrude Jekyll*, London: Allen Lane, 1982, p. 150.

69 Hussey, *The Life of Sir Edwin Lutyens*, p. 78.

70 Hussey, quoted in Massingham, B., *Gertrude Jekyll*, Aylesbury: Shire Publications, 1975, p. 74.

71 Jones, N.R., *Architecture of England, Scotland, and Wales*, Westport, CT: Greenwood, 2005, p. 178.

72 Cowley, A., *The Works in Prose and Verse of Mr A. Cowley with Notes by Dr Hurd*, vol. 3, London: n.p., 1809, p. 173.

73 Mawson, T.H., *The Art and Craft of Garden Making*, London: B.T. Batsford and G. Newnes, 1900.

74 Brown, *Gardens of a Golden Afternoon – Story of a Partnership*.

75 Mawson, *The Art and Craft of Garden Making*.

76 Ibid., p. 3.

77 http://www.manderston.co.uk/history1.asp (accessed 11 March 2013).

78 Triggs, H.I., *Formal Gardens in England and Scotland*, London: B.T. Batsford, 1902.

79 Elgood, G.S. and Jekyll, G., *Some English Gardens*, London: Longmans, 1904, p. 48.

80 Ottewill, D., *The Edwardian Garden*, New Haven, CT: Yale University Press, 1989, p. 136.

81 Ibid., p. 137.

82 Hussey, *The Life of Sir Edwin Lutyens*, p. 23.

83 Jekyll, G., *Colour Schemes for the Flower Garden*, London: Country Life, 1925, p. 36.

84 Ibid., p. 218.

85 Ibid., p. 294.

86 Jekyll, G., *Colour Schemes for the Flower Garden*, Woodbridge: Antique Collectors' Club, 1982, preface by Tom Turner.

87 Hayward, A., *Norah Lindsay: The Life and Art of a Garden Designer*, London: Frances Lincoln, 2007, p. 79.

9   Abstract Modern gardens, 1925–80

1 The year 1863, when Édouard Manet exhibited *Le déjeuner sur l'herbe* in the Salon des Refusés, is often used as a starting point.

2 Ruhrberg, K. *et al.* (eds), *Art of the 20th Century*, London: Taschen, 1998, p. 410ff.

3 Robinson, J.B., *Nineteenth-Century Music*, London: University of California Press, 1989, p. 334.

4 Ibid., p. 334.

5 Jencks wrote that 'Modern Architecture died in St. Louis, Missouri, on July 15, 1972, at 3:32 p.m. (or thereabouts) when the infamous Pruitt–Igoe scheme, or rather several of its slab blocks, were given the final coup de grâce by dynamite.' Jencks, C., *The New Paradigm in Architecture: The Language of Post-Modernism*, 7th edn, New Haven, CT: Yale University Press, [1977] 2002, p. 9.

6 Descartes, R., *Discourse on the Method and Meditations on First Philosophy*, L.J. Lafleur (trans.), New York: The Liberal Arts Press, 1960.

7 Nelson, R.S. and Shiff, R., *Critical Terms for Art History*, Chicago: University of Chicago Press, 1996, p. 188.

8 Lewis, P., *The Cambridge Introduction to Modernism*, Cambridge: Cambridge University Press, 2007, p. 1.

9 Elkins, J., *Stories of Art*, London: Routledge, 2002, p. 13.

10 Read, H., *A Concise History of Modern Painting*, London: Thames & Hudson, 1974, p. 87.

11 Kleiner, F.S., *Gardner's Art through the Ages: The Western Perspective*, vol. 2, Florence, KY: Wadsworth Publishing, 2009, p. 724.

12 *The Suprematist Manifesto*, 1926, cited in Malevich, K., *The Non-Objective World: The Manifesto of Suprematism*, Mineola, NY: Dover Publications, 2003.

13 Harrison, C. and Wood, P., *Art in Theory, 1900–2000*, Oxford: Blackwell, 2003, p. 300.

14 Behr, S. *et al.* (eds), *Expressionism Reassessed*, Manchester: Manchester University Press, 1993, p. 1.

15 Donahue, N.H., *A Companion to the Literature of German Expressionism*, Woodbridge: Camden House, 2005, p. 39.

16 Jaffé, H.L.C., *De Stijl 1917–1931: The Dutch Contribution to Modern Art*, Nijmegen: Alec Tiranti, 1956, p. 61.

17 Strickland, E., *Minimalism: Origins*, Bloomington: IN: Indiana University Press, 2000, p. 4.

18 Page, R., *The Education of a Gardener*, London: Collins, 1962, p. 54.

19 Tunnard, C., 'The influence of Japan on the English garden', *Landscape and Garden*, Summer 1935, 2(2): 49.

20 Tunnard, C., *Gardens in the Modern Landscape*, 2nd edn, London: Architectural Press, 1948, p. 9.

21 Ibid., p. 6.

22 Ibid., p. 72.

23 Ibid., p. 65.

24 Ibid., p. 62.

25 http://www.hughpearman.com/2006/08.html (accessed 23 November 2010).

26 Richardson, T., *The Arcadian Friends: Inventing the English Landscape Garden*, London: Bantham Press, 2007, p. 125.

27 Ibid., p. 125.

28 *The Journal of Horticulture, Cottage Gardener, and Country Gentleman*, 1867, p. 585.

29 Jones, O., *On the True and False in the Decorative Arts: Lectures Delivered at Marlborough House*, June 1852, 1863, p. 110.

30 Saletnik, J., *Bauhaus Construct: Fashioning Identity, Discourse and Modernism*, London: Routledge, 2009, p. 20.

31 Mawson, T., *Bolton As It Might Be*, Bolton: Tillotson & Son/London: B. T. Batsford, 1916, p. 15.

32 Jellicoe, G.A., *The Guelph Lectures on Landscape Design*, Guelph: University of Guelph, 1983, p. 111.

33 Blomfield, R., *Modernismus*, London: Macmillan, 1934, p. vi.

34 Shepherd, J.C. and Jellicoe, G.A, *Italian Gardens of the Renaissance*, London: Benn, 1925, p. 18.

35 Jellicoe, G.A. and Shepherd, J.C., *Gardens and Design*, London: Benn, 1927, p. 85.

36 Jellicoe, G.A., 'Ronald Tree and the gardens of Ditchley Park', *Garden History*, 10(1): 80–91.

37 Shepheard, P., *Modern Gardens*, London: Architectural Press, 1953.

38 Jacques, D. and Woudstra, J., *Landscape Modernism Renounced: The Career of Christopher Tunnard (1910–1979)*, London: Routledge, 2009, p. 1.

39 Tunnard, *Gardens in the Modern Landscape*, p. 93.

40 Ibid., p. 9.

41 Naylor, G., *The Bauhaus*, London: Studio Vista, 1968, p. 9.

42 *Landscape and Garden*, 5(2): 101.

43 Hitchcock, H.R., *Modern Architecture in England*, New York: Museum of Modern Art, 1937, p. 25.

44 Aldous, T. and Clouston, B., *Landscape by Design*, London: Heinemann, 1979.

45 Allen of Hurtwood, Lady and Jellicoe, S., *Gardens*, Harmondsworth: Penguin, 1953.

46 Crowe, S., *Garden Design*, London: Country Life, 1958, p. 12.

47 Ibid., p. 138.

48 Alison, A., *Essays on the Nature and Principles of Taste*, 4th edn, London: n.p., 1810, p. 48.

49 Loudon, J.C., *An Encyclopaedia of Cottage, Farm, and Villa Architecture*, London: Longman, Orme, Brown, Green, & Longmans, 1839, p. 994.

50 Kemp, E., *How to Lay Out a Small Garden*, London: Bradbury & Evans, 1858, p. 306.

51 Brookes, J., *Room Outside*, London: Thames & Hudson, 1979, p. 81.

52 Crowe, S., *Garden Design, Garden Art*, Woodbridge: Suffolk Press, 1994, p. 73.

53 Ibid., p. 119.

54 Ibid., p. 166.

55 Ibid., p 135.

56 Ibid., p. 140.

57 Ibid., p. 144.

58 Doescher, R.L. *et al.*, 'When the sky ran red: the story behind *The Scream*', *Sky & Telescope*, February 2004, 107(2): 28.

59 Hobhouse, P., *Colour in Your Garden*, London: Collins, 1985.

60 Pope, N. and Pope, S., *Colour by Design: Planting the Contemporary Garden*, London: Conran Octopus, 1998.

61 Richardson, T., *English Gardens in the Twentieth Century: From the Archives of 'Country Life'*, London: Aurum, 2005, p. 190.

62 'Design' can be distinguished from 'art' by the presence of a function. Art can be regarded as the 'process of originating systems and predicting their fulfilment of given objectives', while art is 'unspecified experimental modelling' (Banathy, B.H., *Designing Social Systems in a Changing World*, New York: Plenum Press, 1996, p. 17). Arnheim wrote: 'A building is a work of art, but at the same time it fulfills a specific function as a practical object in our life space. For this reason it is different in form from a piece of abstract sculpture. It expresses a Weltanschauung.' (Arnheim, R., *Art and Visual Perception: A Psychology of the Creative Eye*, Berkeley, CA: University of California Press, 1974, p. 112).

10 Post-Abstract and sustainable gardens, post-1980

1 Donne, J., *The Poetical Works of John Donne*, Edinburgh: Apollo Press, 1779, p. 10.

2 Repton, H. and Loudon, J.C., *The Landscape Gardening and Landscape Architecture of the Late Humphry Repton*, Edinburgh: Longman, 1840, p. 500.

3 Belloc, H., 'Jim', in *Cautionary Tales for Children*, London: Duckworth, 1907.

4 Jencks, C., *The Language of Post-Modern Architecture*, London: Academy Editions, 1984, p. 6.

5 Murphie, A. and Potts, J., *Culture and Technology*, Basingstoke: Palgrave, 2002, p. 56.

6 *RHS Chelsea Flower Show Catalogue*, p. 40.

7 The search was conducted on Google on 25 November 2010. The results for an image search were dominated by images from interior design, with other images from the Gardenvisit.com website. The search was repeated on 14 September 2011 and the search engine research page can be seen at: http://www.gardenvisit.com/history_theory/garden_landscape_design_articles/garden_design_ideas/postmodern_garden_design_14_september_2011.

8 Richardson, T. and Jones, A., *Great Gardens of America*, London: Frances Lincoln, 2009, p. 244.

9 http://www.nationaltrust.org.uk/west-green-house-garden (accessed 11 March 2013).

10 http://www.ehow.com/how_4501499_create-modernist-garden.html (accessed 11 March 2013).

11 Turner, T., *City as Landscape: A Post-Postmodern View of Design and Planning*, London: E. & F.N. Spon, 1996.

12 Farrell, T., *Maximalism and the Postmodern Legacy: Terry Farrell Interiors*, London: Laurence King, 2011.

13 Rivers, C., *Maximalism: The Graphic Design of Decadence & Excess*, Hove: Rotovision, 2007, p. 8.

14 Jarman, D., *Derek Jarman's Garden*, London: Thames & Hudson, 1995, p. 47.

15 Bell, B.I., *Postmodernism and Other Essays*, Milwaukee, WI: Morehouse Publishing Company, 1926.

16 Shepherd, J.C. and Jellicoe, G.A., *Italian Gardens of the Renaissance*, London: Benn, 1925, p. 1. This section of the chapter is an edited extract from an essay on Jellicoe and the subconscious.

17 Johnson, S., *A Dictionary of the English Language, in Which Words are Deduced from Their Originals*, London: n.p., 1775.

18 Shepherd and Jellicoe, *Italian Gardens of the Renaissance*, p. 23.

19 Ibid., p. 18.

20 Jellicoe, G.A. and Jellicoe, S., *The Landscape of Man*, London: Thames & Hudson, 1975, p. 374.

Notes

21 Jencks, C., *The Architecture of the Jumping Universe: A Polemic: How Complexity Science Is Changing Architecture and Culture*, London: Academy Editions, 1995, p. 156.

22 Spens, M., *Gardens of the Mind: The Genius of Geoffrey Jellicoe*, Woodbridge: Antique Collectors' Club, 1992.

23 Jellicoe, G.A. and Jellicoe, S., *Modern Private Gardens*, London: Abelard-Schuman, 1968, p. 10.

24 Jellicoe, G.A., 'Sutton Place: allegory and analogy in the garden', *Landscape Design*, October 1983: 9.

25 Hunt, J.D., *Nature Over Again: The Garden Art of Ian Hamilton Finlay*, London: Reaktion Books, 2008, p. 161.

26 Higgins, H., 'Concrete poetry', in A. Preminger and T.V.F. Brogan (eds), *Encyclopedia of Poetry and Poetics*, Princeton, NJ: Princeton University Press, 1993, p. 233.

27 Ibid., p. 171.

28 LeWitt, S., 'Paragraphs on conceptual art', *Artforum*, June 1967, 5(10): 79.

29 *Flash Art*, 216–218: 223.

30 Scottish National Gallery of Modern Art, available at: http://www.nationalgalleries.org/visit/history-architecture/ (accessed 11 March 2013).

31 Lee, D. (ed.), *Plato: The Republic*, Harmondsworth: Penguin, 1974.

32 Scottish National Gallery of Modern Art, available at: http://www.nationalgalleries.org/visit/history-architecture/ (accessed 11 March 2013).

33 Jencks, C., *The Universe in the Landscape: Landforms by Charles Jencks*, London: Frances Lincoln, 2011, p. 257.

34 Deleuze, G., *Fold: Leibniz and the Baroque*, London: Athlone Press, 1993.

35 Deleuze, G., *Expressionism in Philosophy: Spinoza*, New York: Zone Books, 1992, p. 175.

36 http://www.vogt-la.com/en/project/laban-dance-center (accessed 11 March 2013).

37 Turner, T., *English Garden Design: History and Styles Since 1650*, Woodbridge: Antique Collectors' Club, 1986, p. 226.

38 Hampton Court Palace Flower Show, Tuesday 3 to Sunday 8 July, Summary of Regulations: Conceptual Gardens, Royal Horticultural Society HC/CG/002.12.

39 http://www.london2012.com/about-us/the-people-delivering-the-games/the-olympic-delivery-authority/oda-priority-themes/legacy.php (accessed 18 September 2011).

40 http://www.london2012.com/olympic-park (accessed 18 September 2011).

41 http://www.hughpearman.com/2008/14.html (accessed 16 September 2011).

42 Ibid.

43 The Report of the Brundtland Commission, *Our Common Future*, was published by Oxford University Press in 1987. One of the first published uses of the term 'sustainable garden' is in the *Proceedings*, vol. 13, parts 1–2, Third World Conference Foundation, 1987, p. 319: 'Local seed production is advisable for creating a sustainable garden program.'

44 Hessayon, D.G., *The Green Garden Expert*, London: Transworld Publishers, 2009, p. 3.

45 McHarg, I.L., *Design with Nature*, Garden City, NY: Doubleday/Natural History Press, 1971, p. 26.

46 http://www.uvm.edu/~gflomenh/ENV-NGO-PA395/articles/Lynn-White.pdf.

47 Miller, N., *Environmental Politics: Stakeholders, Interests, and Policymaking*, London: Routledge, 2009, p. 123.

48 http://en.wikipedia.org/wiki/Green_politics (accessed 12 September 2011).

49 Agar, M., *Garden Design in Theory and Practice*, London: Sidgwick & Jackson, 1911, p. 253.

50 Darwin, C., *The Annotated Origin: A Facsimile of the First Edition of On the Origin of Species by Charles Darwin*, J.T. Costa (ed.), p. 441: 'It is absurd to talk of one animal being higher than another.'

51 I invite a future author to write the book and put me right.

52 Turner, T., *Landscape Planning and Environmental Impact Design*, London: UCL Press, 1998, p. 399.

53 http://www.guardian.co.uk/money/2009/jun/02/allotments-shortage-waiting-lists (accessed 11 March 2013).

54 http://www.telegraph.co.uk/gardening/7471941/Vegetable-seed-sales-jump-as-grow-your-own-takes-root.html (accessed 14 September 2011).

55 Davies, A.P. and McCuen, R.H., *Stormwater Management for Smart Growth*, New York: Springer, 2005, p. 241.

56 Charles, Prince of Wales and Lycett Green, C., *The Garden at Highgrove*, London: Weidenfeld & Nicolson, 2000, p. 6.

57 Holden, H. and Liversedge, J., *Construction for Landscape Architecture*, London: Laurence King, 2011, p. 9.

58 Pearson, D., 'Splendour in the grass', *Daily Telegraph*, 24 September 2005, available at: http://www.telegraph.co.uk/gardening/3336260/Splendour-in-the-grass.html (accessed 11 March 2013).

59 Lovejoy, A.O., *The Great Chain of Being: A Study of the History of an Idea*, Cambridge, MA: Harvard University Press, 1936.

60 Bowler, P.J., *The Eclipse of Darwinism*, Baltimore, MD: Johns Hopkins University Press, 1992, p. 22.

61 Lloyd, C., *The Year at Great Dixter*, Harmondsworth: Viking, 1987, p. 13.

62 Lloyd, C., *Meadows*, London: Cassell Illustrated, 2004, p. 16.

63 King, M. and Oudolf, P., *Gardening with Grasses*, London: Frances Lincoln, 1998, p. 14.

64 Pearson, in *Daily Telegraph*.

65 Baines, C., *How to Make a Wildlife Garden*, London: Elm Tree, 1985.

66 Baines, C., in *Daily Telegraph*, 28 October 2000, available at: http://www.telegraph.co.uk/gardening/4792215/Just-wild-about-suburbia.html (accessed 11 March 2013).

67 Turner, T., *City as Landscape*, Chapter 8.

68 Turner, T., *European Gardens: History, Philosophy and Design*, London: Routledge, 2011, pp. 5–8.

Appendix I

1 The style diagrams can be thought of 'Page 26 Diagrams', since this is the page on which they appear in both *Asian Gardens: History, Beliefs and Design* (2010) and *European Gardens: History, Philosophy and Design* (2011) (both by T. Turner for Routledge).

2 Turner, T., *City as Landscape: A Post-Postmodern View of Design and Planning*, London: E. & F.N. Spon, 1996, p. 144.

3 Ibid., p. 144.

4 Frost, R., *Fire and Ice*, 1920.

5 Jencks, C. *The Universe in the Landscape: Landforms by Charles Jencks*, London: Frances Lincoln, 2011.

Appendix II

1 Carlyle, T., *Critical and Miscellaneous Essays*, London: n.p., 1845.

2 Turner, T., *English Garden Design: History and Styles Since 1650*, Woodbridge: Antique Collectors' Club, 1986.

3 Davey, P., *Arts and Crafts Architecture: The Search for Earthly Paradise*, London: Architectural Press, 1980, pp. 74, 188.

4 Crowe, S., *Garden Design*, London: Country Life, 1958.

5 Hunt, J.D., *The Picturesque Garden in Europe*, London: Thames & Hudson, 2002.

6 Kemp, E., *How to Lay Out a Small Garden*, London: Bradbury & Evans, 1858, p. 126.

Appendix III

1 Simonsen, M., *The Designed Landscape at Wollaton* (2011), available at: http://www.simonsen.de/blog/work/wollaton-hall (accessed 11 March 2013).

2   http://www.nottinghamcity.gov.uk/index.aspx?articleid=1037   (accessed   11
     March 2013).
3   Taylor, H.A., *Restoration and Management Plan*, Wollaton Park, Nottingham,
     2002. Post-medieval phases considered in this study: (1) Renaissance; (2)
     Mannerist; (3) Early Baroque; (4) Late Baroque; (5) Brownian; (6) Reptonian and
     Victorian; (7) Functionalist-Modernist; (8) post-2012.
4   du Cerceau, J.A., *Les plus excellents bastiments de France*, Paris: n.p., 1576–9.
5   http://www.wollatonparkgolfclub.com (accessed 11 March 2013).
6   Jellicoe, G.A., *The Guelph Lectures on Landscape Design*, Guelph: University of
     Guelph, 1983, p. xi.

Illustration credits

The author and publisher with to thank these individuals and organisations for permission to reproduce material. Other photographs, scans and drawings are by the author. Every effort has been made to contact and acknowledge copyright holders for those images not in the public domain, but if any errors or omissions have been made we will be happy to correct them at a later printing and on the companion website: http://www.gardenvisit.com/history_theory/british_gardens_companion.

Frontispiece Margaret Turner

P.0 Blue Marble image, NASA
P.1 Renaissance Dyeing

1.0 Eleanor Atkinson
1.2 Alaster Rae
1.3 Mr Patterson
1.8 Brholden/Wikipedia
1.15 Andrew Emptage/Dreamstime
1.18 Joseph Gough/Dreamstime
1.23 a Joseph Gough/Dreamstime
1.24 a Marcel Meier
1.26 a Dave Price
1.36 Dieser Benutzer/Wikipedia

2.0 Charlotte Leaper/Dreamstime
2.1 Heidemarie Niemann, Mainz, Germany
2.11 d Public domain
2.30 David Morrison/Dreamstime
2.33 a, b Rwendland/Wikipedia

3.3 a Gail Johnson
3.11 Colin J. Campbell
3.19 Jessica P. Opfer
3.22 Jon Buckingham
3.33 Gernot Keller/Wikipedia
3.39 Arian Zwegers

4.0 Ljupco Smokovski
4.2 Pierre Marcel, artist and photographer
4.13 a Public domain
4.16 a Public domain
4.34 Michael Simonsen
4.38 Brian Mossemenear
4.39 Michael Simonsen
4.40 a John Speed/Wikipedia
4.44 Metropolitan Museum of Art
4.48 b Public domain
4.56 Public domain
4.60 a Public domain

5.5 a Davide Romanini/Dreamstime
5.5 b Vladislav Gurfinkel/Dreamstime
5.11 b George Carter
5.27 Public domain
5.30 a Michael Simonsen

6.0 Public domain
6.5 b Jeff Arris
6.7 Davidmartyn/Dreamstime
6.14 Public domain
6.15 a Thomas Perkins/Dreamstime
6.35 a Ollirg/Dreamstime
6.35 b Valeria Cantone/Dreamstime
6.38 b Tom and Louisa
6.47 b David J.Coombes
6.50 a, b Public domain
6.59 Ava Babili
6.62 Lydiard House/Wikipedia
6.63 b Brian Clift
6.64 a Public domain
6.76 Public domain
6.79 Harry Lawford
6.82 Public domain
6.89 Gail Johnson/Dreamstime
6.93 Rixie/Dreamstime
6.96 Keith Moseley

7.0 Public domain
7.3 University of Bristol
7.5 Dulwich Picture Gallery
7.6 Public domain
7.7 Public domain
7.31 a AlexTimaios/Dreamstime
7.57 b Margaret Turner
7.60 Ian Cunliffe
7.77 a LeonWP
7.77 b Alaskan Dude

8.0 Kevin Eaves/Dreamstime
8.4 Public domain
8.7 Ally McGurk

8.14 Stephen Colebourne
8.31 a, b Sarah Turner

9.5 a Public domain
9.7a Public domain
9.10 James Durie (design)
9.15 b Rev Stan
9.16 a Armin/Flickr
9.16 b Arboresce
9.27 a Philip Nixon (design)
9.27 b David Cubreo and James Wong (design)
9.28 a Public domain

10.9 Elliott Brown
10.14 a, b, c Margaret Turner
10.15 a, b Margaret Turner
10.17 b, c Alsu Galimova
10.20 a Rebecca Butterworth, Victoria Pustygina, Ludovica Ginanneschi (design)
10.20 b Ivan Tucker (design)
10.25 Rkaphotography/Dreamstime
10.26 a Eden Project (design)
10.26 b Laurie Chetwood, Patrick Collins (design)
10.27 a Sarah Eberle (design)
10.27 b Mandy Buckland (design)
10.29 b Tommaso del Buono and Paul Gazerwitz (design)
10.31 c Paul Hensey (design)
10.23 a, b Tommaso del Buono and Paul Gazerwitz (design)
10.34 a Sarah Eberle (design)
10.34 b Darren Saines (design)
10.35 Sarah Eberle (design)
10.39 a,b Andrew Butler
10.40 b Ivan Hicks (design)
10.41 b Nigel Fenwick (design)
10.42 Eden Project (design)
10.43 b Jo Thompson (design)

AIII Drawings by Michael Simonsen

Index

Index